The Effects of Taxation on Multinational Corporations

A National Bureau
of Economic Research
Project Report

The Effects of Taxation on Multinational Corporations

Edited by Martin Feldstein,
James R. Hines, Jr., and
R. Glenn Hubbard

The University of Chicago Press

Chicago and London

MARTIN FELDSTEIN is the George F. Baker Professor of Economics at Harvard University and president of the National Bureau of Economic Research. JAMES R. HINES, JR., is associate professor of public policy at the John F. Kennedy School of Government of Harvard University and a faculty research fellow of the National Bureau of Economic Research. R. GLENN HUBBARD is the Russell L. Carson Professor of Economics and Finance at the Graduate School of Business of Columbia University and a research associate of the National Bureau of Economic Research.

The University of Chicago Press, Chicago 60637
The University of Chicago Press, Ltd., London
© 1995 by the National Bureau of Economic Research
All rights reserved. Published 1995
Printed in the United States of America
04 03 02 01 00 99 98 97 96 95   1 2 3 4 5
ISBN: 0-226-24095-9 (cloth)

Library of Congress Cataloging-in-Publication Data

The Effects of taxation on multinational corporations / edited by Martin
    Feldstein, James R. Hines, Jr., and R. Glenn Hubbard.
        p.   cm.—(National Bureau of Economic Research project report)
    Papers presented at a conference held in January 1994.
    Includes bibliographical references and index.
    1. International business enterprises—Taxation—Congresses. 2. International business enterprises—Finance—Congresses. 3. Investments, Foreign—Taxation—Congresses. 4. Capital market—Congresses.
I. Feldstein, Martin S. II. Hines, James R. III. Hubbard, R. Glenn.
IV. Series
HD2753.A3E33 1995
336.24'3—dc20   95–6344
                                                                                      CIP

Relation of the Directors to the
Work and Publications of the
National Bureau of Economic Research

1. The object of the National Bureau of Economic Research is to ascertain and to present to the public important economic facts and their interpretation in a scientific and impartial manner. The board of Directors is charged with the responsibility of ensuring that the work of the National Bureau is carried on in strict conformity with this object.

2. The President of the National Bureau shall submit to the Board of Directors, or to its Executive Committee, for their formal adoption all specific proposals for research to be instituted.

3. No research report shall be published by the National Bureau until the President has sent each member of the Board a notice that a manuscript is recommended for publication and that in the President's opinion it is suitable for publication in accordance with the principles of the National Bureau. Such notification will include an abstract or summary of the manuscript's content and a response form for use by those Directors who desire a copy of the manuscript for review. Each manuscript shall contain a summary drawing attention to the nature and treatment of the problem studied, the character of the data and their utilization in the report, and the main conclusions reached.

4. For each manuscript so submitted, a special committee of the Directors (including Directors Emeriti) shall be appointed by majority agreement of the President and Vice Presidents (or by the Executive Committee in case of inability to decide on the part of the President and Vice Presidents), consisting of three Directors selected as nearly as may be one from each general division of the Board. The names of the special manuscript committee shall be stated to each Director when notice of the proposed publication is submitted to him. It shall be the duty of each member of the special manuscript committee to read the manuscript. If each member of the manuscript committee signifies his approval within thirty days of the transmittal of the manuscript, the report may be published. If at the end of that period any member of the manuscript committee withholds his approval, the President shall then notify each member of the Board, requesting approval or disapproval of publication, and thirty days additional shall be granted for this purpose. The manuscript shall then not be published unless at least a majority of the entire Board who shall have voted on the proposal within the time fixed for the receipt of votes shall have approved.

5. No manuscript may be published, though approved by each member of the special manuscript committee, until forty-five days have elapsed from the transmittal of the report in manuscript form. The interval is allowed for the receipt of any memorandum of dissent or reservation, together with a brief statement of his reasons, that any member may wish to express; and such memorandum of dissent or reservation shall be published with the manuscript if he so desires. Publication does not, however, imply that each member of the Board has read the manuscript, or that either members of the Board in general or the special committee have passed on its validity in every detail.

6. Publications of the National Bureau issued for informational purposes concerning the work of the Bureau and its staff, or issued to inform the public of activities of Bureau staff, and volumes issued as a result of various conferences involving the National Bureau shall contain a specific disclaimer noting that such publication has not passed through the normal review procedures required in this resolution. The Executive Committee of the Board is charged with review of all such publications from time to time to ensure that they do not take on the character of formal research reports of the National Bureau, requiring formal Board approval.

7. Unless otherwise determined by the Board or exempted by the terms of paragraph 6, a copy of this resolution shall be printed in each National Bureau publication.

(Resolution adopted October 25, 1926, as revised through September 30, 1974)

Contents

Preface

The tax rules of the United States and of foreign countries affect multinational corporations in a variety of ways. Researchers at the National Bureau of Economic Research have been studying the impact of taxation on multinational corporations for several years. From time to time, the results of this research have been presented at NBER conferences and subsequently published in NBER volumes. The papers in the current volume, which were presented at such a conference in January 1994, were the result of studies during the previous two years.

During this period, the researchers met several times to present research plans and to discuss preliminary results. All of those who participated in the project also benefited from discussions during the NBER Summer Institute with a wider group of economists interested in these international tax issues as well as from meetings with tax lawyers from leading international corporations and from discussions at the regular meetings of the NBER Public Economics program.

We are grateful to the U.S. Treasury Department for making unpublished data available to the research group and for the opportunity to collaborate with members of the Treasury staff. Funding that made this project possible was provided by the Ford Foundation, the Bradley Foundation, the Starr Foundation, and several multinational corporations.

In order to make the results of this work more widely available, a less technical conference was held in Washington, D.C., in April 1994. The papers prepared for that meeting appear in a separate volume, *Taxing Multinational Corporations* (University of Chicago Press, 1995), which we edited.

We are grateful to the members of the NBER staff for their assistance with all of the details involved in the planning and execution of this research and of the many meetings that took place along the way. In addition to the researchers and research assistants named in the individual papers, we are grateful to Kirsten Foss Davis, Mark Fitz-Patrick, and Deb Kiernan for providing logistical support.

Introduction

Martin Feldstein, James R. Hines, Jr.,
and R. Glenn Hubbard

The growing worldwide importance of international business activities has in recent years lead to serious reexaminations of the ways that governments tax multinational corporations. In the United States, much of the debate concerns the competitive positions of U.S. firms in international product and capital markets. In addition, there are those who agree that U.S. international tax rules have become more complex and more distorting in recent years, particularly since the passage of the Tax Reform Act of 1986. Discussions in the U.S. Congress and the administration since 1992 reveal a willingness to consider significant reforms. In Europe, increased liberalization of capital markets prompted discussions by the European Commission of harmonization of corporate taxation. These policy developments around the world not only suggest dissatisfaction with certain features of modern tax practice, but also raise deeper questions of whether current systems of taxing international income are viable in a world of significant capital-market integration and global commercial competition.

Academic researchers have expressed renewed interest in studying the effects of taxation on capital formation and allocation, patterns of finance in multinational companies, international competition, and opportunities for income shifting and tax avoidance. This research program brings together approaches used by specialists in public finance and international economics. The studies presented in this volume analyze the interaction of international tax rules and the investment decisions of multinational enterprises. The 10 pa-

Martin Feldstein is the George F. Baker Professor of Economics at Harvard University and president of the National Bureau of Economic Research. James R. Hines, Jr., is associate professor of public policy at the John F. Kennedy School of Government of Harvard University and a faculty research fellow of the National Bureau of Economic Research. R. Glenn Hubbard is the Russell L. Carson Professor of Economics and Finance at the Graduate School of Business of Columbia University and a research associate of the National Bureau of Economic Research.

1

pers fall into three groups: (1) assessing the role played by multinational firms and their foreign direct investment (FDI) in the U.S. economy and the design of international tax rules for multinational investment, (2) analyzing channels through which international tax rules affect the costs of international business activities such as FDI, and (3) examining ways in which international tax rules affect financing decisions of multinational firms. The results suggest that there are likely to be significant effects of international tax rules on firms' investment decisions and provide analytical input for future discussions of tax reform.

The Context: Multinational Firms, FDI, and International Tax Rules

Robert Lipsey's paper provides a review of evidence concerning the impact of outbound FDI on employment and economic activity in the United States. Lipsey notes that most "industrial organization" explanations for the rise of multinational firms are based on the notion that multinational enterprises possess specific assets or marketing skills that can be exploited most profitably by producing in many markets. Lipsey argues that the use of foreign production locations helped U.S. multinationals retain global market shares in spite of the decline in the U.S. share of world trade. In addition, the extensive empirical evidence analyzed by Lipsey offers no empirical support for the proposition that overseas production by U.S. multinationals reduces employment in the United States. Instead, the evidence supports the idea that firms experiencing an increase in their multinational activity increase their managerial and technical employment at home.

In the volume's second background paper on FDI, Martin Feldstein addresses the longstanding question of whether outbound FDI by U.S. multinationals reduces domestic investment in the United States. Feldstein's research uses aggregate evidence on investment flows in the OECD countries during the 1970s and 1980s in order to provide information on the general equilibrium effects of FDI. Extending the analytical approach he developed with Charles Horioka to study cross-country correlations of domestic saving and investment (Feldstein and Horioka 1980), Feldstein finds that, holding constant domestic saving, outbound FDI reduces domestic investment by significantly less than one for one. Indeed, his results suggest that each dollar of assets in foreign affiliates reduces the domestic capital stock by between 20 and 40 cents. This finding can be explained by the use of local debt to finance firms' overseas investment. Feldstein argues that local debt finance is available in foreign countries primarily to firms that invest in capital in those countries, due to transaction and information costs associated with financing direct investment. Feldstein's paper makes clear that domestic policymakers might consider the advantages associated with the local financing that accompanies FDI when evaluating the effect of outbound FDI on the domestic economy.

Standard models of optimal taxation predict that small open economies will not impose source-based taxes on capital income. This theoretical prediction is inconsistent with observed tax rules in most developed countries, in which corporate tax rates are high—indeed, comparable to maximum tax rates on individuals. Roger Gordon and Jeffrey MacKie-Mason argue that this apparent inconsistency is not surprising if the principal task of the corporate tax were not so much to raise revenue, but instead to discourage income shifting between the individual and corporate tax bases (and between domestic and foreign subsidiaries). In an international taxation setting, a country needs to tax the overseas incomes of domestically owned subsidiaries in order to prevent firms from facing tax incentives to exploit technologies abroad rather than domestically. Moreover, if the tax rates imposed by foreign governments were lower than the domestic corporate tax rate, multinationals would face incentives to circumvent domestic taxes by shifting their profits abroad through aggressive transfer pricing even if the firms that own the profitable technologies remain at home. Gordon and MacKie-Mason extend their research on the consequences of income shifting for the design of domestic capital taxes to show that avoidance of income shifting can explain a number of features of actual international tax rules, including transfer-pricing regulations and enforcement penalties, allocation rules for interest and R&D expenses, and the foreign tax credit. Their research suggests the potential importance of considering income shifting in any normative analysis of international tax rules, as well as the importance of studying empirically the extent to which income shifting occurs in response to tax rate differences.

International Tax Rules and the Cost of Capital for FDI

Tax policy influences investment decisions through its effects on cost of capital and the returns to different activities. Tax systems influence the investment decisions of multinational firms through a complicated interaction of home- and host-country taxation and differences across countries in the tax treatments of debt and equity finance. Joosung Jun's paper estimates the extent to which international tax rules affect the cost of capital for transnational investment, focusing on a comparison of the costs of capital incurred by U.S. firms and their competitors in major markets. Jun's calculations suggest that foreign subsidiaries of U.S. firms that are financed by parent equity generally face higher costs of capital than do local firms in major foreign markets. These U.S.-owned subsidiaries generally are disadvantaged vis-à-vis competing firms from countries in which some form of corporate tax integration is in place. The increasing internationalization of capital markets implies that differences in tax rules play an important role in explaining differences in the cost of capital faced by firms investing overseas.

Many policy discussions focus on the sensitivity of FDI to changes in the cost of capital for FDI. That cost of capital is affected not only by pretax financial costs of capital, but also by tax parameters in "home" (residence) and "host" (source) countries. Jason Cummins and R. Glenn Hubbard use previously unexplored (for this purpose) panel data on outbound FDI by several hundred subsidiaries of U.S. multinational firms during 1980–91 to measure more precisely the effect of taxation on FDI, and to analyze subsidiaries' investment decisions. The authors consider tax incentives created by host-country tax rates, investment incentives, and depreciation rules, and by variation (over time and across firms) in the tax cost of repatriating dividends from foreign subsidiaries. The authors fit a neoclassical model with tax considerations to the data on U.S. subsidiaries' investments in Canada, the United Kingdom, Germany, France, Australia, and Japan. The results reject a simple specification in which taxes do not influence investment. The estimated tax effects are economically important: Each percentage-point increase in the cost of capital reduces by 1–2 percentage points a subsidiary's annual rate of investment (investment during the year divided by the beginning-of-period capital stock).

As it does in the domestic corporate tax system, the alternative minimum tax (AMT) complicates the foreign investment incentives of U.S. corporations. The presence of the AMT is not merely a wrinkle: in 1990, 53 percent of all assets, and 56 percent of the foreign-source income of U.S. multinational corporations, was accounted for by firms subject to the AMT. The AMT's restrictions on deductions, inclusion of certain income excluded under the regular tax, lower tax rate than that in the regular tax system, and limitation on foreign tax credits modify the incentives for subsidiaries to invest and to repatriate dividends. In their paper, Andrew Lyon and Gerald Silverstein analyze these incentives. The authors show that the AMT may strengthen the incentive for AMT firms to invest abroad rather than in the United States. In addition, the AMT may create a temporary timing opportunity in which firms may repatriate overseas income at lower cost than if the firms were subject to the rules of the regular system. Using Treasury tax return data for 1990, Lyon and Silverstein analyze the prevalence of AMT status among U.S. multinationals, their receipt of foreign-source income, and the tax prices faced by these firms on additional foreign-source income. The results suggest that repatriation decisions respond to AMT incentives. Future research using tax return data over many years is, of course, necessary to determine whether these patterns persist over time.

Most empirical analyses of business fixed investment assume that firms exploit fully incentives for investment offered by the tax code, whether or not tax rules differ from those used to measure income for financial accounting purposes. Jason Cummins, Trevor Harris, and Kevin Hassett investigate the reasonableness of this assumption by comparing the responsiveness of investment to tax incentives in countries with different tax accounting and financial accounting reporting requirements ("two-book" countries) with the responsiveness in countries in which tax accounting and financial accounting reporting are identical ("one-book" countries). The United States is an example of the first type of country, while Germany is an example of the second. Cummins, Harris, and Hassett formulate a neoclassical model of domestic investment using firm-level panel data from 13 countries to test whether, all else equal, firms in one-book countries are less responsive to tax incentives than are firms in two-book countries. The empirical results suggest that differences in accounting regimes generate significant differences in the responsiveness of investment to tax policy; in particular, firms operating in "pure" one-book systems behave as though they face additional costs when taking advantage of investment incentives. The research program begun in this paper suggests fruitful extensions to studies of the impact on investment of interactions of accounting and tax regimes.

Economists and policymakers often argue that the presence of technologically advanced industries enhances national prosperity, in part due to the spillover effects of research and development (R&D) activities. Because externality-generating R&D activities may be underprovided by private markets, many governments subsidize R&D in some form. Whether these subsidies in fact stimulate additional R&D activity is the subject of a vigorous debate. James Hines analyzes the impact of withholding taxes on cross-border royalty payments on the R&D activities of multinational firms. High withholding tax rates make it costly for foreign subsidiaries to import technology from their U.S. parents. The high cost of technology should stimulate local R&D if local R&D is a substitute for imported technology, or dampen local R&D if it is a complement for imported technology. Hines tests a model of subsidiary R&D activity using country-level data on tax rates and R&D expenditures by U.S. subsidiaries. He examines the effect of royalty taxes on the local R&D intensities of foreign affiliates of multinational corporations, looking both at foreign-owned affiliates in the United States and at U.S.-owned affiliates in other countries. He finds that higher royalty taxes are associated with greater R&D intensity on the part of affiliates, suggesting that local R&D is a substitute for imported technology.

International Tax Rules and Financing Decisions

A longstanding question in the analysis of taxation of multinational corporations is whether home-country taxes due on repatriation of foreign-source income affect subsidiaries' repatriation decisions. In principle, as long as the home-country tax does not change, and parent firms derive no value from a particular pattern of repatriations, taxes due upon repatriation are unavoidable costs. Hence, neither the investment decisions nor the repatriation decisions of mature foreign subsidiaries should be affected by home-country taxation of repatriated earnings. Studies using cross-sectional data on firms indicate, however, that U.S. subsidiaries' dividend remittances are sensitive to the U.S. repatriation taxes. Panel data are needed to proceed further in this line of inquiry because such data allow an investigator to distinguish between effects of transitory and permanent variation in U.S. tax rates on repatriations. This is precisely the agenda pursued by Rosanne Altshuler, Scott Newlon, and William Randolph. These authors analyze a data set consisting of U.S. tax return information for a large sample of foreign subsidiaries and their U.S. parent firms for the years 1980, 1982, 1984, and 1986. The empirical tests exploit information about cross-country differences in tax rates to estimate separate effects on remittances attributable to the permanent and transitory components of tax prices of dividend repatriations. The intuition is that, while cross-country differences in average repatriation tax prices or statutory tax rates are correlated with permanent components of tax price variation, they are uncorrelated with transitory variations. Hence, these measures can be used to construct instrumental variables for tax prices that permit separate identification of permanent and transitory tax price effects. Altshuler, Newlon, and Randolph find that the transitory tax price effect is larger than the permanent effect, suggesting that subsidiaries concentrate repatriations to U.S. parents in periods in which the tax prices of repatriations are transitorily low.

Kenneth Froot and James Hines argue that the investment and financing of multinational firms may be affected by the changes in interest allocation rules introduced by the Tax Reform Act of 1986. The rules reduce the tax deductibility of interest expenses for firms in excess foreign tax credit positions. The resulting increase in the cost of debt finance gives firms incentives to use forms of financing other than debt. Furthermore, to the extent that perfect substitutes for debt are not available, the overall cost of capital rises. Froot and Hines test this proposition by comparing investment before and after 1986 by firms in deficit credit and excess credit positions, holding constant other determinants of investment. The study analyzes data on 416 firms with international business operations. The authors find that, over the 1986–91 period, firms that could not fully deduct their U.S. interest expenses both borrowed less (on average, 4.2 percent less debt measured as a fraction of firm assets) and invested less in property, plant, and equipment (on average, 3.5 percent less) than firms whose deductions were not affected by the interest allocation rules. These results suggest that firms substitute away from debt as it becomes more expensive, and that firms reduce their capital investments in response to higher borrowing costs produced by the change in interest allocation rules.

Reference

Feldstein, Martin, and Charles Horioka. 1980. Domestic saving and international capital flows. *Economic Journal* 90: 314–29.

1 Outward Direct Investment and the U.S. Economy

Robert E. Lipsey

Any judgment about the wisdom of tax changes that raise or lower the profitability of American firms' foreign operations must involve some judgment as to the desirability of increasing or decreasing the extent of these operations. The purpose of this paper is to review past research on the effects of U.S. firms' overseas activities on the U.S. economy and to report some further analysis with more recent data.

The first question to be answered is what we mean by the U.S. economy. The ambiguity of the term troubles appraisals of many policies. One way of looking at it is to ask whether the object is to maximize gross national product or gross domestic product. The former is an ownership-based concept that includes the profits from overseas operations of U.S. firms and other income earned overseas by U.S. residents, but excludes profits earned in the United States by foreign residents. The latter is a geographically based concept that covers production that takes place in the United States, regardless of ownership. It thus excludes profits and other income earned overseas (from overseas production), but includes all income earned in the United States (from production in the United States) by both U.S. and foreign residents. One way in which the distinction surfaces in policy discussions is over whether various types of assistance or preferences are to be applied to U.S.-controlled firms, regardless of where they operate, or to firms producing in the United States, whether domestically or foreign owned.

I will try to construe the issue broadly. That means I will consider effects of outward foreign direct investment on the labor employed in the United States by the investing companies and also those on the companies themselves, in-

Robert E. Lipsey is professor of economics at Queens College and the Graduate Center, City University of New York, and a research associate of the National Bureau of Economic Research.

cluding their stockholders, and more generally on the trade and other aspects of the U.S. economy.

Various studies of the behavior of multinational firms, including some of my own, view the firms as facing fixed, or relatively fixed, worldwide markets for their products and making decisions mainly about how to supply that demand most profitably. The firm is pictured as choosing whether to supply the demand by exporting from the United States, by producing abroad, or by licensing technology, patents, or other assets owned by the firm to foreign licensees who would produce outside the United States.

The assumption of a fixed market for a firm tends to bias conclusions toward finding that foreign production by U.S. firms substitutes for production in the United States. An alternative view is that production abroad is often mainly a way of enlarging a firm's share of foreign markets, or of preventing or slowing a decline in that share. The inadequacy of the fixed-market assumption is obvious in any attempt to examine the impact of direct investment in service industries since the nature of most of these industries precludes substantial exporting from one country to another and market share is almost completely contingent on production at the site of consumption. While this is most obvious for service industries, it applies equally to the service component of manufacturing industries, a major part of the final value of sales of manufactured products.

1.1 The Growth of Internationalized Production

The establishment of foreign operations by American firms—and the establishment by any country's firms of production, including sales and service activities, outside the home country—is often referred to as the internationalization of production. In order to understand the process, and the reasons behind it, it is useful to ask whether it is uniquely or mainly an American phenomenon or is, under some circumstances, common to foreign firms as well.

The studies of Cleona Lewis (1938) and Mira Wilkins (1989) on foreign investment in the United States make it clear that direct investment and internationalized production were not an American invention. When the United States lagged technologically in many fields, foreign firms found it profitable to develop marketing and production facilities in the United States to exploit their superior sophistication. The industrial distributions of these operations from different countries clearly reflected some specific technological advantages, such as those of Great Britain in various aspects of the textile industry and of Germany in chemicals.

What has been unique about the United States is that direct investment has been the characteristic form of U.S. foreign investment as far back as data exist, even when the United States was still, on balance, importing capital (Lipsey 1988). That fact, and the lists of early U.S. investors (Lewis 1938; Southard 1931; Wilkins 1970) concentrated among the leading firms in various U.S. industries, emphasize the association of direct foreign investment not with large aggregate supplies of financial or physical capital but with the possession of firm-specific assets, knowledge, and techniques, sometimes reflected in patents or brand names, that are mobile within firms, even across national borders, but not among firms.

Not only was direct investment the dominant form of U.S. outward investment, but the United States was the dominant source of the world's direct investment for a long period. The U.S. share of the world's stock of outward direct investment was over half around 1970, with the United Kingdom, the next most important investor, far behind at about 15–17 percent and no other single country the source of more than 6 percent. The share of the developed countries' outward direct investment flows originating in the United States was well over half in the 1960s and still over 40 percent in the 1970s. In the late 1980s, however, less than 20 percent of the world's outward flows originated in the United States, and in a reversal of roles, the United States absorbed over 40 percent of the flows from other countries (Lipsey 1993). In the early 1990s, Japan's role as a source of direct investment flows and the U.S. role as a recipient both declined sharply. In 1992, the United States was again the largest supplier, at about a quarter of the OECD total, and was not a significant net recipient, withdrawals and losses equaling or exceeding gross inflows (OECD 1993, table I).

The heyday of outward U.S. direct investment outflows, in the 1960s and at least part of the 1970s, involved a considerable internationalization of U.S. firms' production, in the sense that higher and higher proportions of the production they controlled took place abroad, larger proportions of their employees were outside the United States, and larger shares of their assets came to be located abroad. Since then, however, the degree of internationalization of U.S. companies has stabilized or declined, as if the firms had overshot some desirable level and found it desirable to retreat somewhat.

The peak in the extent of internationalization in this sense for the U.S. economy as a whole was reached some time in the late 1970s (we cannot date it more closely because comprehensive data exist only for occasional foreign investment census years). For example, employment in all overseas affiliates of U.S. firms was almost 11 percent of total U.S. nonagricultural employment in 1977, but only 7.5 percent in 1989. Plant and equipment expenditures by majority-owned foreign affiliates were over 15 percent of domestic U.S. plant and equipment expenditures in U.S. dollars in 1974–76 but fell below 10 percent from 1984 to 1988 and have not recovered their earlier levels. Since the exchange value of the U.S. dollar was low in the late 1980s, the decline in real terms was even larger.

U.S. manufacturing firms have long been much more internationalized than firms in other industries, with their overseas employment reaching about a quarter of domestic manufacturing employment in 1977 (from only 10 percent in 1957) and then declining only slightly to about 22 percent in the late 1980s. Overseas plant and equipment expenditures in manufacturing reached over 20 percent of domestic expenditure in dollar terms for a few years in the 1970s. It fell almost to 10 percent when the exchange value of the dollar was near its peak, and then recovered, but so far not to earlier peak levels.

Within those U.S. firms that are multinational, the changes have not been so sharp, partly because of the importance of manufacturing firms in the universe of multinationals. However, the time pattern has been similar since 1977 (there is little parent firm information available before that).

Within manufacturing multinationals, foreign affiliate net sales, a crude measure of production, were larger in the late 1980s relative to parent sales than in 1977, and affiliate employment was close to the earlier levels relative to parent employment. Thus, this group of firms has not exhibited the shift away from internationalized production that has characterized U.S. multinationals in general or the U.S. manufacturing sector as a whole. The affiliate share of production may even have increased (though it is too volatile to provide a quick judgment that there is an upward trend), and the affiliate share of employment has not changed much since 1977.

The strongest case for increased internationalization in U.S. manufacturing is in exports. Affiliates accounted for less than a third of U.S. multinationals' worldwide exports in 1966, but for more than half in the second half of the 1980s and the early 1990s. Their importance relative to total manufactured exports from the United States also more than doubled over this period.

The contrast between the changes in internationalization within U.S. parents and those for the U.S. economy as a whole reflects the declining role of multinational parents within the U.S. economy. Parent employment in the United States fell from 28 percent of U.S. nonagricultural employment in 1977 to barely over 20 percent in the late 1980s, not because employment was moved overseas, where affiliate employment was also declining, but because these multinationals were declining in importance as part of the U.S. economy. This decline was not simply a reflection of the decline of manufacturing's share of U.S. employment, but took place within manufacturing as well, where manufacturing parent firms' share of total domestic manufacturing employment fell from over 60 percent in 1977 to a little over 50 percent in 1988–90. Thus, the shrinking of many large, established U.S. manufacturing firms affected both their domestic and their foreign employment. The many anecdotes about the shifting of domestic employment abroad do not seem to add up to much in the aggregate, especially for the U.S. economy as a whole.

There is one reason why it is as yet difficult to judge whether the apparent retreat of U.S. firms from foreign operations during the 1980s is a long-term trend. The enormous shift in direct investment toward the United States by foreign firms, to the point where the United States absorbed an unprecedented share of the rest of the world's outflow of direct investment, suggests that the United States was an exceptionally attractive location for investment during this period. If that was the case, it might have been particularly attractive, relative to locations in other countries, to American firms as well as to foreign firms, and that attractiveness would show up as a retreat from internationalization for U.S. firms while it tended to increase the degree of internationalization of foreign firms.

One reason for this apparent retreat of American firms from overseas activity may have been the growth of efficient and aggressive foreign competitors. The levels of internationalization of the German and Japanese economies were much lower than that of the United States in the 1970s. Since then, the internationalization pioneered on a large scale by American firms has been copied by European and Japanese firms, and now even by firms from developing countries.

How widespread is internationalized production in the sense of firms producing outside their home countries? And is it expanding in the world economy as a whole? Two opposite influences are at work. Internationalization is most prevalent in manufacturing and least common in services. The rising powers in manufacturing, such as Japan and some of the developing countries of Southeast Asia, are increasing the degree to which their companies carry out their manufacturing outside the home countries. At the same time, the share of manufacturing in most of the world's economies is declining, and that of services is increasing. The net result of these two forces, and of the opposite directions of changes in the United States and in other countries, is that the share of internationalized production in world output, after increasing greatly in the 20 years after 1957, perhaps tripling, has grown little since then. The share of Japanese, German, and Swedish firms' internationalized production has been rising, but that rise has been offset by the fall in the much larger U.S. share. Internationalized production by firms from other countries has almost certainly been rising, but it is starting from too low a level to have much impact on the total. The share of such production in worldwide GDP may have been in the range of 10–15 percent in 1990. The U.S. companies accounted for half or more of this total, and if the rise from the recent low point in 1988 continues, internationalized production will again be of growing importance.

A less equivocal story can be told about the share of production outside home countries in world trade in manufactured goods. That share is clearly over 10 percent and seems to have risen even since 1977, mainly because of the growth of Japanese affiliate exports, but also because U.S. affiliates have held on to or even increased their shares since 1977. Thus, world trade in manufactures, if not necessarily aggregate world production or employment, is increasingly made up of exports from internationalized production.

What can we conclude from these trends in the extent of internationalized production? The practice of producing outside the home country is well entrenched, especially in manufacturing, not only for U.S.-based companies but, increasingly, for firms based in other countries. It is increasingly common for firms in at least the more successful developing countries, such as Korea and Taiwan. Presumably, it is an avenue for increasing profitability, probably through increasing market shares that provide economies of scale in the exploitation of the firm's assets, such as patents, other technological assets, reputation, and more generally, skills in production and marketing.

1.2 Overseas Production and Export Market Shares in Manufacturing

The share of the United States, as a country, in world export markets for manufactured goods has been declining over most of the last quarter century. In the early 1990s, after some recovery from the low point in 1987 that resulted partly from the earlier period of high exchange values for the dollar, the share was about 12 percent, 25–30 percent below the level in 1966 (table 1.1). U.S. multinational firms, exporting from the United States and from their overseas production, held on much more successfully. By 1985, when the United States had already lost more than 20 percent of its share of 20 years earlier, U.S. multinationals had increased their share of world exports (table 1.2). They then lost some of that in the next two years, but in the early 1990s retained a share a little above that of 1966. How was this relative stability achieved? Performance was very different for the parent firms, exporting from the United States, and the affiliates, exporting from other countries.

Until at least 1985, the parent firms lost less of their world export shares than did nonmultinational U.S. firms (table 1.3). Then the parent share fell sharply, more rapidly than that of other U.S. firms. In the meantime, more and more of multinational exports were supplied by their overseas affiliates, more than half since 1986, and a record high proportion in 1990–92. Thus, one way the U.S. multinationals kept their export markets, as the United States lost

Table 1.1   **U.S. Share of World[a] Exports of Manufactured[b] Exports (%)**

Year	Share
1966	17.1
1977	13.2
1982	14.6
1985	13.4
1986	11.9
1987	11.3
1988	12.1
1989	12.8
1990	12.1
1991	12.6
1992	12.4

Source: United Nations trade tapes, extended to 1991 and 1992 by estimates derived from data in United Nations (1993, 1994).

[a]Market economy.

[b]As defined in Bureau of Economic Analysis (BEA) investment data, including manufactured foods, but excluding petroleum and coal products.

Table 1.2   **Exports by U.S. Manufacturing Multinationals[a] as a Share of World Manufactured Exports (%)**

Year	Share
1966	15.8
1977	15.5
1982	17.4
1985	18.1
1986	16.6
1987	15.6
1988	16.1
1989	16.4
1990	16.1
1991	16.4
1992	16.0

Source: United Nations trade tapes and Lipsey (1995).
Note: For other definitions, see table 1.1.
[a]Parents and majority-owned affiliates.

Table 1.3   **Parent and Affiliate Export Shares (%)**

	Share of World Manufactured Exports		
Year	U.S. Parents	Majority-Owned Affiliates	Affiliate Share of Multinational Exports
1966	11.0	4.8	30.4
1977	9.1	6.4	41.2
1982	9.3	8.1	46.4
1985	9.4	8.7	48.2
1986	8.2	8.4	50.9
1987	7.5	8.2	52.2
1988	7.7	8.3	52.0
1989	8.0	8.4	51.4
1990	7.3	8.8	54.4
1991	7.6	8.8	53.8
1992	7.2	8.8	54.8

Source: United Nations trade tapes and Lipsey (1995).
Note: For definitions, see tables 1.1 and 1.2.

competitiveness in their industries, was by supplying these markets increasingly from overseas operations, a strategy obviously not available to nonmultinational U.S. firms. (The affiliate shares included in this calculation are only shares of export trade and exclude the much more important affiliate sales in their host-country markets.)

This rise in the importance of exporting from foreign affiliates was not unique to the United States. Even in Japan, an extremely successful exporter from home-country production, exports by overseas affiliates rose from 8 percent of exports from Japan in 1974 to 14 percent or more in 1986–89. Japan's share of world manufactured exports reached a peak in 1986, shortly after the high point in the exchange value of the dollar, and the declined from 1986 to 1990 before recovering slightly (table 1.4). As the country's export share declined, the share of overseas manufacturing affiliates in their firms' total exports grew from 1986 to 1989, and almost certainly after that as well. Thus, in Japan, as in the United States, foreign operations seemed to play a defensive role in retaining export markets for firms under adverse conditions for parent exporting (table 1.5).

Sweden underwent large losses in trade shares similar to those of the United

Table 1.4 **Japanese Share of World Manufactured Exports (%)**

Year	Share
1965	6.8
1970	8.7
1974	10.5
1977	11.1
1982	12.1
1986	13.7
1987	12.5
1988	12.4
1989	12.0
1990	10.9
1991	11.5
1992	11.4

Source: United Nations trade tapes.
Note: For definitions, see tables 1.1 and 1.2.

Table 1.5 **Affiliate Share of Japanese Multinational Worldwide Exports (%)**

Year	Share
1974	7.2
1977	7.1
1980	8.0
1983	13.4
1986	10.7
1988	12.2
1989	12.3

Source: Lipsey (1995).
Note: For definitions, see tables 1.1 and 1.2.

States, although not quite as large. Swedish multinational firms, over the same period, retained or increased their shares, though the increase was concentrated in 1965–70 (table 1.6). This stability in the share of Swedish multinationals was accompanied by, or possibly accomplished by, a large shift in the sources of export production, with the portion of exports sold by foreign affiliates rising from a tenth of total multinational exports in 1965 to over a third in 1990 (table 1.7).

These three countries are the only ones that collect fairly comprehensive information on the trade of their multinationals' overseas affiliates. The data suggest that one major role for overseas production has been that of retaining market shares when home-country economic conditions and exchange rate changes made the home countries less suitable locations for export production.

An alternative interpretation of the data, discussed below, might be that it was the growth of affiliate production and exports that caused the reduction in home-country exports. However, home-country shares can be explained to a large extent by home-country price and exchange rate movements, not a likely path for influences stemming from decisions to produce abroad.

Table 1.6   **Swedish Share of World Manufactured Exports and Exports by Swedish Multinationals as a Share of World Manufactured Exports (%)**

Year	Sweden	Swedish Multinationals
1965	3.0	1.6
1970	2.9	2.0
1974	2.9	2.0
1978	2.4	1.8
1986	2.3	1.8
1990	2.1	1.7

Source: United Nations trade tapes; Swedenborg et al. (1988); data from the Industriens Utredningsinstitut of Stockholm.

Table 1.7   **Affiliate Share of Swedish Multinational Worldwide Exports (%)**

Year	Share
1965	10.4
1970	12.5
1974	15.9
1978	19.3
1986	24.3
1990	34.6

Source: Swedenborg et al. (1988); data from the Industriens Utredningsinstitut of Stockholm.

1.3   Does Foreign Production Substitute for Home-Country Exports?

Most antagonism against foreign direct investment has historically been toward inward investment, on the ground that it displaced home-country firms in home markets. However, there has also been opposition to outward investment, often led by labor organizations, on the ground that outward investment "exports jobs," partly by producing products to be imported to the home-country market but mostly by replacing home-country exports by overseas production. In the United States, the campaign against outward direct investment reached a peak with the effort to pass the Burke-Hartke bill in the 1960s, the Voluntary Program of Capital Restraints from 1965 through 1967, and then with the compulsory Office of Foreign Direct Investment (OFDI) regulations. These came into effect in 1968 as an effort to "improve" the U.S. balance of payments and were specifically directed against the outflow of capital for foreign direct investment. The government restrictions were ceilings on the export of funds for foreign direct investment, particularly to Western Europe, but were not aimed at the expansion of U.S. firms' foreign operations if the expansion was financed from foreign sources (Fiero 1969). With the defeat of Burke-Hartke and the demise of the OFDI in 1974, the campaign has faded, although the AFL-CIO continues to take a dim view of outward investment in its annual statements on economic policy.

Attempts to measure the effects of overseas production on home-country exports face the problem of defining substitution and of defining a believable counterfactual case. Exports from Japan's recently established or recently enlarged operations in Southeast Asia may "replace" exports that formerly came from Japan, but few would claim, after the rise in the exchange value of the yen, that they are replacing exports that could now be made from Japan. A cross-sectional analysis does not necessarily escape the problem; it may be precisely those more labor-intensive industries that can no longer export from the home country that establish production abroad.

A long line of studies has attempted to find evidence of a relationship between overseas production and home-country exports. One of the earliest U.S. studies, by Gary Hufbauer and F. M. Adler (1968), identified the crucial importance of the assumptions used to the interpretation of any relationships found, and a similar wide range of possible effects was reported in a major U.S. Tariff Commission (1973) study a few years later. The Reddaway reports (1967, 1968) explicitly assumed that in the absence of British foreign affiliates, their markets would have been supplied not by British exports but by local or other foreign suppliers.

The preponderance of evidence from empirical studies points to either no effect or a positive effect of overseas production in a host-country market on home-country exports to that market. Lipsey and Weiss (1981), in a cross-sectional analysis examining exports in 14 manufacturing industries by the United States and by 13 other developed countries, to many destinations, found that the level of production by U.S.-owned affiliates in a country was positively related to U.S. exports in that industry to that country and, in some markets, negatively related to exports by other developed countries. On the other hand, the presence of affiliates from countries other than the United States was positively related to those countries' exports to that host country and, where there was any significant relationship, negatively related to U.S. exports to the country. In other words, the presence of, and production by, a home country's affiliates in a host country tended to attract exports from that home country and to discourage exports to that host country from other countries. Thus, the main substitution that seemed to take place was of country A's host-country production in country C for country B's exports to country C, and of country B's host-country production in country C for country A's exports to country C. In these calculations, the variables for U.S.-owned and foreign-owned affiliate activity were superimposed on a set of standard gravity equations including host-country income or aggregate imports, distance from home to host country, and trade bloc membership. The estimated trade position in the absence of direct investment is represented by the value of exports when the home-country affiliate activity variable is set at zero while the other variables, including foreign country affiliate variables, are at their actual levels. Since the dependent variables in these equations are total U.S. and other country exports, rather than the exports by parents, they take account of any displacements of one firm's exports to a country by the production in that country by affiliates of another firm from the same home country.

Each dollar of overseas production by U.S. affiliates in these cross-sectional equations added, on average across the statistically significant coefficients, about $0.16 to U.S. exports. Most of the coefficients were below $0.20. The coefficients for displacements of other countries' exports were not so consistently significant and varied widely, but whenever coefficients for both U.S. and other countries' exports were significant, the displacement of other countries' exports was larger than the addition to U.S. exports. That is a reasonable result since the addition to U.S. exports to a host country is the net balance of positive and negative effects of U.S.-owned production there, while the effect on other countries' exports to that host country are generally only negative, with no offsetting gains. One exception to this negative relation to foreign countries' exports would be the case in which the U.S. parent has affiliates in the other countries that are potential suppliers to the host country. Thus a U.S.-owned auto assembly plant in, say, the Netherlands might give rise to exports of auto components from the same company's German affiliate rather than, or in addition to, exports from the parent in the United States.

If a U.S.-owned affiliate in one country exported to other countries, it could displace U.S. exports to those countries without the offsetting effect of exports of components and other inputs to the manufacturing process. That displacement would be missed in the equations just described, and Lipsey and Weiss (1984) therefore examined the effects of aggregate affiliate production abroad on the total exports to all destinations of the cross section of parent firms. The results were that the displacement of U.S. exports to third countries, if it existed, was not large enough to offset the positive effects on parent exports to host countries; that is, in each industry, firms that produced more abroad also exported more in the aggregate.

It is natural to think that exports by affiliates to third countries would necessarily displace parent exports to them, but that is not necessarily the case. A plane, truck, or car assembled or even produced completely by a U.S. affiliate in country A and exported to country B could later give rise to the export of parts, accessories, and related products from the United States to country B.

An examination of the same question for a later period (Blomström, Lipsey, and Kulchycky 1988), using the direct investment census for 1982 (U.S. Department of Commerce 1985), produced more ambiguous results. The later study lacked the information on affiliates of non-U.S. firms that had been part of the earlier study, but did distinguish between affiliate production for export and affiliate production for local sale in the host country, and also included some equations for production by minority-owned U.S. affiliates not available earlier.

When there was any statistically significant relation at all (a minority of industries), affiliate export sales, or production for export from the affiliate's host country, were consistently associated with higher U.S. exports to that host country. That is to be expected, since substitution of affiliate production for U.S. exports, if there was any, would take place outside the host country, in the third country, and would be unobserved. For sales within the host country, most coefficients were positive, but there were more negative (5 out of 30 industries) than positive coefficients among those that were statistically significant at the 5 percent level.

When data for minority-owned affiliates in the host countries, including those 50 percent owned, were added to the U.S. export equations, these affiliate operations were found to be associated with higher levels of U.S. exports to the host countries. In addition, the inclusion of these affiliate operations had a strong effect on the coefficients for production by majority-owned affiliates, moving many from showing negative effects on U.S. exports to positive effects.

The role of minority-owned affiliates is puzzling, and we can only speculate on the explanation. One factor is their very uneven distribution across countries. They are, for example, almost the only form of direct investment in Japan and quite important there. We have speculated that minority ownership has this strong positive relationship to U.S. exports because it may be a last resort in countries or industries where the U.S. parent would otherwise be barred from a market. These may be markets with more stringent barriers to imports, or where barriers to imports are associated with barriers to majority ownership of affiliates. Minority-owned affiliates may, in such cases, be a price for market entry more often than in the case of majority ownership.

Sweden is the only country outside the United States for which individual firm data are available that permit an analysis similar to those carried out for the United States. A series of Swedish outward direct investment surveys was carried out by the Industriens Utredningsinstitut (IUI), of Stockholm, and analyzed in Swedenborg (1973, 1979, 1982, 1985) and, for the 1986 survey, in Swedenborg, Johansson-Grahn, and Kinnwall (1988). They examined the effects of overseas production by Swedish firms on Swedish parent exports. Because of the small number of Swedish parent firms, it was not possible to run separate equations for individual industries, particularly industries as narrowly defined as in the U.S. studies. However, the Swedish calculations included many firm characteristics that, in effect, incorporated industry characteristics, and also separated companies based on Swedish resource industries.

The Swedish studies included an effort to solve the problem of the possible simultaneity of direct investment production decisions and home-country export decisions by a 2SLS approach in which the first stage estimated the level of production by Swedish affiliates in each host country. The second-stage equation used the estimated production levels from the first stage, among other variables, in the explanation of parent exports to each host country. These equations were applied to each of the survey years and in a pooled time-series–cross-sectional analysis. Swedenborg concluded (1985, 235) that OLS estimations, such as those reported above for the United States, overstated the positive effects of affiliate production on parent exports. Her own estimate, from the 2SLS equations, was that each dollar of Swedish affiliate production added about $0.10 to Swedish parent exports, not very far from the U.S. results mentioned above. From a breakdown of parent exports by type she concluded that only 2 percent of the sales provided by foreign production would be replaced by parent exports if foreign production were abandoned.

A somewhat different analysis was performed by Blomström et al. (1988) for 1978, using the same data source as for Swedenborg's studies but in more aggregated form and with each industry's total manufactured exports from Sweden, rather than only parent exports, as the dependent variable. All the coefficients on affiliate sales were positive and, in fact, larger in a 2SLS analysis than in the OLS equations. There was no evidence in the comparison with Swedenborg's estimates for parent exports that the positive effect on Swedish parent exports came at the expense of exports by other Swedish firms. It seems more likely, although the equations are too different from Swedenborg's to produce a definitive conclusion, that affiliate production encouraged not only parent exports to the affiliates' host countries, but also exports to the same countries by other Swedish firms.

An examination of changes over 1970–78, from the same source of data, showed similar results: the greater the increase in Swedish affiliate production in a country, the greater the growth of exports of manufactures from Sweden to that host country. A single exception was metal manufacturing, where both a high 1970 level of Swedish-controlled production and high growth in that production in 1970–78 were associated with reductions in Swedish exports.

A recent IUI report (Svensson 1993) challenges the earlier findings for Sweden using some of the same data along with the latest, still unpublished, survey for 1990. The report concludes that an increase of $1 in affiliate production for local host-country sale reduces parent exports by $0.14 and that affiliate production for export to third countries reduces parent exports by over $0.40 for each dollar of such affiliate production.

The apparent contradiction of earlier results is attributed by the author to his accounting for the effect of affiliate production for export on parent sales to third countries. However, such effects were included in the analysis of total parent exports by U.S. firms in Lipsey and Weiss (1984) without producing any similar negative effects. The major source of the difference from earlier results seems to be the formulation of the equations, which normalizes across firms by the total worldwide sales of the multinational firm rather than by parent sales, as in Swedenborg's earlier studies. The difference is never pointed out and this normalization is described as a way of eliminating heteroskedasticity. In fact, the result is that what is being tested is the relationship between the share of worldwide sales provided by production carried out in a host country and the share of home-country (parent) exports to that country in the firm's worldwide sales. It is virtually a certainty that these coefficients for host-country production shares will be negative, but those negative coefficients can be interpreted as a negative influence on the absolute value of home-country exports only under an odd implied assumption that is never discussed. The assumption is that in the absence of foreign production the total size of the multinational firm's worldwide sales or production would be the same as with foreign production—if Electrolux did not produce in many countries, it would have the same worldwide sales as it has with foreign production. That assumption would seem to guarantee a negative coefficient for foreign production on home-country exports, but it is not a plausible assumption on which to rest a study.

On the whole, then, it would seem reasonable to conclude that production outside the United States by U.S.-based firms has little effect on exports from the United States by parent firms or by U.S. firms as a whole, and that to the extent there is an effect, it is more likely to be positive than negative. This relationship is probably a characteristic of other countries' multinationals as well. One reason this is true is that foreign production is undertaken to expand or retain a parent firm's foreign markets and parent exports are incidental to these decisions. As foreign affiliates mature, their imports from their parents become marginal to their total activity and fluctuate with exchange rate changes and other developments, but there is no indication that the absolute level of imports from the home country declines over long periods.

1.4   Foreign Production and Home-Country Labor

Aside from the relation of overseas production to exports from the United States, such production could affect the overall demand for labor within the

United States by parent firms, and the demand for labor of different types, even if total production in the United States were not affected. For example, the demand for labor by parent firms might be reduced if more labor-intensive products were allocated to multinationals' foreign operations, while more capital-intensive operations were allocated to U.S. operations. Similarly, the demand for unskilled labor by parents might decline if parts of the production process or products requiring highly skilled labor were allocated to the United States, while processes or products requiring relatively low skills were allocated to overseas affiliates.

The opportunity for multinational firms to engage in such geographical allocation of their production presumably requires that the product be tradable. If a firm's output must be consumed where it is produced, as in many service industries, production will take place where the goods and services are sold and will respond to host-country demand and to host-country costs. There could still be differences among production locations in capital intensity and skill intensity. These might reflect the elasticity of substitution between capital and labor or between labor of different skills if there are significant differences in factor prices, but these should affect the affiliate operations rather than those of the parents. More important, there could still be effects of affiliate operations on parent capital or skill intensity if the needs for certain typically central functions, such as coordination, management, and research and development, were affected by affiliate operations.

In this analysis, the level of home-country (parent) production is taken as given, and the question is whether, within this fixed level of home-country production, the composition of parent production is affected by the parent firm's foreign production activity in such a way as to alter the parent firm's demand for labor and for more-skilled, as compared with less-skilled, labor.

One sign that more labor-intensive activities were being allocated to foreign affiliates or that production methods were being changed in response to differences in factor prices would be a lower capital intensity in affiliate production than in parent production and a lower capital intensity in low-income countries than in high-income countries. The data on net property, plant, and equipment per worker from the latest U.S. outward investment census indicate that in manufacturing as a whole, the physical capital intensity of production in developed countries by all affiliates of manufacturing parents was about 80 percent of that of parents in the United States. The capital intensity of manufacturing affiliates in developing countries was only 42 percent of that in developed countries. In contrast, in a broadly defined services group—including all industries except manufacturing, petroleum, agriculture, mining, and transportation, communication, and public utilities—the physical capital intensity of affiliates was higher than that of their parents in the United States. And for affiliates in developing countries outside of those in manufacturing and petroleum, physical capital intensity was higher than for affiliates in the developed countries (U.S. Department of Commerce 1993, tables II.B8, II.B13, II.G4, II.G11, II.L1, and II.P1). Of course, some of the difference in these aggregate comparisons may rest on differences in industry composition not related to responses to factor price differences at all. However, it is hard to avoid the impression that manufacturing firms adapt affiliate production to differences in factor prices to a much larger extent than service industry firms do.

A much more thorough investigation of whether multinational firms adapted their factor proportions to relative factor prices (Lipsey, Kravis, and Roldan 1982) concluded that these firms did use more labor-intensive methods of production, as measured by property, plant, and equipment per worker, in low-wage countries. The form that the adaptation took could have been selecting labor-intensive subindustries for production in low-wage countries, selecting labor-intensive production processes for such production, selecting small-scale operations for which only labor-intensive methods of production were available, or operating in a labor-intensive way, whatever technologies were selected. These relationships were visible not only within industries but also within individual firms, and for Swedish as well as American multinationals.

Judging from these aggregate data, manufacturing firms were more responsive to factor price differences in allocating their direct investment activity than were service industry firms. The reason could be simply a higher elasticity of substitution between capital and labor in manufacturing than in services, or it could be that the tradability of manufactured products makes them more suitable for the allocation of, for example, labor-intensive activities to labor-abundant, cheap-labor countries. In the former case, of higher elasticity of substitution in manufacturing, there should not be any effect of overseas production on parent labor intensity. In the latter case, of allocation of activities in response to factor prices, larger overseas operations should produce less employment in the United States relative to sales (lower labor intensity of production).

The predominance of evidence for individual manufacturing firms and their affiliates in six industry groups in the 1982 investment census was that higher overseas production was associated with lower employment at home, given the level of parent production (Kravis and Lipsey 1988). That was the case for all manufacturing firms as a group and within most of the six major industry groups. The only exceptions were that sales by majority-owned affiliates in electrical machinery and by minority-owned affiliates in nonelectrical machinery were positively related to parent employment, for any level of parent production.

Some calculations from the latest outward investment census, for 1989, suggest a similar relationship, as in equation (1):

(1) $\text{PEMP} = 1{,}234 \quad + 6.14 \text{ PNS} - .77 \text{ ANS}, \quad \bar{R}^2 = .867,$
$\qquad\qquad\quad (5.0) \quad (58.1) \qquad (5.9)$

where

PEMP =   parent employment;
PNS =   parent net sales (sales less imports from affiliates), in million
dollars; and
ANS =   affiliate net sales (sales less imports from the United States), in
million dollars.

Each million dollars of affiliate production (as proxied by affiliate net sales) gave rise to a loss of almost one parent employee, given the level of parent firm production.

If we separate net sales of affiliates into those of manufacturing and of non-manufacturing affiliates, we find that the negative relationship comes from the manufacturing production; each million dollars of manufacturing affiliate production subtracts about 1.4 workers from parent employment, while each million dollars of nonmanufacturing affiliate production adds 1.2 parent employees:

$$(2) \qquad \text{PEMP} = 1{,}160 \quad + 6.16 \text{ PNS} - 1.38 \text{ MANS}$$
$$\qquad\qquad\quad (4.7) \;\; (58.7) \qquad\quad (7.6)$$
$$\qquad\qquad + \; 1.21 \text{ NMANS}, \qquad \bar{R}^2 = .870;$$
$$\qquad\qquad\quad (2.8)$$

where

MANS =   manufacturing affiliate net sales; and
NMANS =   nonmanufacturing affiliate net sales.

These equations assume that the impact on parent employment is related to the absolute value of affiliate production: an addition of a million dollars of affiliate production has the same impact on parent employment whether the affiliates are one-tenth the parent's size, in the aggregate, or twice the parent's size.

The same calculations can be performed within the major manufacturing industry groups, reducing the influence of interindustry differences. Across industries, any relation between parent labor intensity and foreign operations is more likely to represent an effect of labor intensity on the tendency to produce abroad than of foreign production on domestic labor intensity.

The parent employment level equations for major industry groups are summarized in table 1.8. Within the major industry groups, the relationships are mixed. In transportation equipment, the group with the largest affiliate sales, the relation is negative; each million dollars of affiliate net sales is associated with parent firms' having five fewer employees.[1] In the next largest industry in

1. There may be an interindustry effect here; the group includes two very different industries, motor vehicles and equipment and other transportation equipment, mainly aircraft. The motor vehicle industry accounts for almost all the foreign affiliate sales, while the other transportation equipment industry accounts for more than half the parent employment.

Table 1.8   **Equations for Parent Employment as a Function of Parent and Foreign Affiliate Production, 1989 (six major industry groups)**

Industry	Constant Term	Parent Net Sales	Coefficients for Affiliate Net Sales — Total	Manufacturing	Non-manufacturing	$\bar{R}^2$
Food and kindred products	4,125	4.87 (5.7)	−.58 (.4)			.453
	4,125	4.86 (5.7)		−.28 (.8)	−.18 (.9)	.443
Chemicals	840	4.93 (18.0)	−.20 (.6)			.864
	1,033 (2.5)	4.82 (17.5)		−.67 (1.6)	.81 (1.3)	.867
Metals	611 (2.5)	6.04 (26.8)	−.90 (1.9)			.866
	629 (2.6)	5.98 (26.1)		−.40 (.7)	−1.82 (2.1)	.867
Machinery, except electrical	480 (2.4)	6.47 (28.2)	.77 (5.8)			.968
	475 (2.4)	6.54 (26.9)		.83 (5.7)	.52 (1.6)	.968
Electrical and electronic machinery	1,642 (5.1)	4.87 (30.6)	3.34 (4.9)			.967
	1,618 (5.4)			4.03 (6.1)	−5.33 (2.6)	.970
Transportation equipment	−257 (.3)	9.10 (47.2)	−4.73 (20.2)			.986
	−250 (.4)	9.18 (77.5)		−7.53 (26.5)	7.89 (7.1)	.995

Notes: Parent employment in number of employees. Parent and affiliate sales in million dollars. Numbers in parentheses are *t*-statistics.

terms of affiliate sales, machinery, except electrical, each million dollars of affiliate sales adds one employee to the parent rolls (the story is similar in the other, much smaller, electrical and electronic machinery group). And in the other major investing industry group, chemicals, there is no relation to parent employment.

If we separate the affiliates into manufacturing and sales, we see that the total affiliate sales coefficients are dominated by those for manufacturing affiliates, again positive in the two machinery groups and negative in transportation equipment.

On the whole, these equations for absolute levels of parent employment are inconclusive, with a mixture of positive and negative relations. We would not conclude from these results that there is any clear effect of affiliate production on aggregate parent employment, given the level of parent production.

A different view of the effect of overseas production on parent labor intensity is provided by relating employment per dollar of net parent sales—a measure of labor intensity—to the ratio of overseas (affiliate) to domestic (parent) production, as in equation (3). Virtually none of the variation in parent employment per dollar of output is explained by the following:

$$(3) \qquad \frac{PEMP}{PNS} = \underset{(6.3)}{9.45} + \underset{(1.1)}{1.53} \frac{ANS}{PNS}, \qquad \bar{R}^2 = .000.$$

The statistically insignificant coefficient suggests a positive relationship, with a 1 percentage point increase in the ratio of overseas production to home production associated with a 1.5 percentage point increase in the ratio of parent employment to sales. Such a positive relation might occur if affiliate production gave rise to needs for supervisory, research, or other types of auxiliary employment in headquarters operations. The addition of parent net sales as a variable, on the theory that larger parent firms might be either more efficient or more bureaucratic than smaller ones, did not reveal any effect of parent size.

A distinction between manufacturing and nonmanufacturing affiliates pointed to the former as having no impact on parent labor intensity and the latter as being close to statistical significance at the 5 percent level but still a negligible degree of explanation of the variance in parent employment per dollar of production:

$$(4) \qquad \frac{PEMP}{PNS} = \underset{(8.1)}{9.53} - \underset{(1.0)}{.0003} \, PNS + \underset{(.4)}{.66} \, MANS$$
$$+ \underset{(1.8)}{6.48} \, NMANS, \qquad \bar{R}^2 = .001.$$

Within the six major industry groups, the evidence points to a positive impact of foreign affiliate production, and particularly foreign manufacturing affiliate production, on parent employment per dollar of production (table 1.9). The only statistically significant coefficients are in the two machinery groups, and also for manufacturing production in the food industry. Thus, from these calculations, we see no evidence of more capital-intensive activities at home from an allocation of labor-intensive activities to affiliates. More foreign affiliate production, particularly more manufacturing production, seems to lead to more parent employment in the United States relative to U.S. production. Most likely this is supervisory or other headquarters employment, but we have no evidence for this conjecture.

The corresponding equation for parent employment in all service industries combined, from the 1982 data, showed much larger coefficients than for manufacturing, negative for majority-owned affiliate sales and positive for minority-owned affiliate sales. However, the equations for individual service industries

Table 1.9   **Equations for Parent Employment per Dollar of Production as a Function of Parent Size and Ratio of Foreign Affiliate to Parent Production, 1989** (six major industry groups)

			Coefficients for			
			Ratio between Parent Net Sales and Net Sales of			
Industry	Constant Term	All Affiliates	Manufacturing Affiliates	Nonmanufacturing Affiliates	Parent Net Sales	$\bar{R}^2$
Food and kindred	6.50	2.04				.024
products	(5.6)	(1.6)				
	7.01	2.01			−.165	.018
	(5.2)	(1.6)			(.8)	
	7.29		2.61	−7.87	−.124	.038
	(5.5)		(2.0)	(1.2)	(.6)	
Chemicals	5.92	.37				−.002
	(17.7)	(.9)				
	6.11	.41			−.153	.006
	(17.1)	(.9)			(1.5)	
	6.13		.29	.68	−.155	.000
	(16.9)		(.5)	(.6)	(1.5)	
Metals	8.49	−.059				−.006
	(28.4)	(.2)				
	8.96	−.065			−.745	.048
	(27.5)	(.3)			(3.2)	
	8.98		−.046	−.63	−.739	.043
	(27.0)		(.2)	(.4)	(3.2)	
Machinery, except	8.22	1.84				.093
electrical	(26.8)	(5.2)				
	8.33	1.97			−.285	.109
	(27.1)	(5.5)			(2.4)	
	8.48		2.46	−.09	−.241	.135
	(27.6)		(6.3)	(.1)	(2.0)	
Electrical and electronic machinery	9.11	6.34				.284
	(13.7)	(6.0)				
	9.32	6.28			−.206	.288
	(13.7)	(8.0)			(1.4)	
	10.15		8.06	−9.02	−.207	.421
	(16.1)		(10.5)	(3.5)	(1.5)	
Transportation	9.74	−1.88				−.001
equipment	(16.3)	(1.0)				
	9.71	−.09			−.080	.027
	(16.4)	(.0)			(1.8)	
	9.81		.637	−12.66	−.061	.032
	(16.5)		(.3)	(1.2)	(1.3)	

Notes: Parent employment in number of employees. Parent sales in billion dollars. Affiliate sales in million dollars. Numbers in parentheses are *t*-statistics.

produced mixed results: half the significant coefficients for majority-owned affiliate sales were positive and half negative. For most industries, no effect was visible, and only one coefficient for minority-owned affiliates was statistically significant. Durable goods wholesale trade and insurance were the two service industries in which foreign affiliate sales were positively related to parent employment per dollar of parent sales, and nondurable goods wholesaling and engineering were the two with negative relationships (Kravis and Lipsey 1988).

One problem with interpreting the data for some service industries, particularly those in finance, is that the location of production is hard to define. Part of the sales attributed to a foreign affiliate on the books of the company for tax or related reasons may involve activity actually carried out in the United States. However, banking and insurance activities for host-country customers, in contrast to those for international customers such as U.S. multinationals, are likely to require both host-country employment, without any substitution for domestic U.S. employment, and also some supervisory or service employment in the U.S. parent firm. It is this likely effect, and the impact on multinational firm profits, that is the motivation behind the insistence of the United States on including service industry entry rules in the Uruguay round of GATT negotiations.

A rough estimate can be made of the effect of changes in rules for entry into the insurance industry in various countries. Cross-country regressions of U.S. insurance affiliate sales (premium values) in various countries against income and various country characteristics, including the severity of restrictions on entry by foreign firms, suggested that a shift by all host countries to the most liberal regulation regimes would double the sales (premium values) of life insurance by U.S.-owned affiliates and increase the sales of nonlife insurance by as much as a third. From the equation for the relation of insurance parent employment to affiliate sales in Kravis and Lipsey (1988), it can then be estimated that parent employment in the United States would increase by something in the neighborhood of 10 percent.

Aside from effects on the parent firms' level of employment, the extent of foreign operations might also affect the composition of parent employment in the United States and the demand and wages for different skills. To the extent that parent firms in manufacturing can allocate activities at different skill levels to different locations to serve worldwide markets, we might expect that operations intensive in low-skilled labor would be allocated to foreign affiliates, especially those in countries where low-skilled labor is cheap, and that high-skill functions would tend to be concentrated in the United States or, possibly, in other highly developed countries.

Two types of evidence might shed light on this possibility. One is simply the allocation of activities within U.S. multinationals. Another is the degree to which a larger share of production carried out abroad is associated with a higher level of skill in a firm's U.S. labor force.

The data collected on employment include very little on the characteristics of the parent or affiliate labor forces. One of the few bits of information is the proportion of employees engaged in R&D activities, and another is the average compensation of employees, as a rough indicator of skill levels.

The data on R&D employment emphasize the concentration of R&D activity in parent companies (table 1.10).

The share of parent employment in R&D is more than twice that in affiliates in almost every major industry group. It would be more appropriate to compare parents with their own affiliates, but those data are not published. Thus, many of the affiliates in wholesale trade are subsidiaries of manufacturing parents, and including them in the manufacturing sector would heighten the contrast between parents and affiliates in both manufacturing and wholesale trade. Judging by the data on R&D expenditures, there is a further allocation of R&D activities between affiliates in developed and developing countries, with much higher R&D intensity in the former group (Lipsey, Blomström, and Kravis 1990).

An indication of responses to the price of skilled relative to unskilled labor was provided by data for a cross section of Swedish firms and their affiliates. Although the definition of skilled and unskilled labor was a crude one (salaried vs. wage workers) and only a small portion of the variation in skill composition was explained, there did seem to be a consistent relationship in which more skill-intensive activities were allocated to countries where the price of skilled labor was lower relative to that of unskilled labor.

Within U.S. multinational firms, the average level of compensation per worker, as a crude indicator of average skill levels, can be related to the extent of production in majority-owned affiliates (Kravis and Lipsey 1988). In manufacturing, the association is weak. The $\bar{R}^2$s are low and are significant at the 5 percent level only for total manufacturing and for the food industry. In both cases, the share of assets overseas explained more of parent compensation levels than the share of production. The only coefficients that are statistically significant at the 5 percent level are positive ones for affiliate production shares in the same industries (Kravis and Lipsey 1988, appendix table 5). If parent

Table 1.10   Employment in R&D as a Share of Total Employment, 1989 (%)

Industry	Parents[a]	Affiliates[b]
Manufacturing	5.46	2.42
Petroleum and coal products	3.74	.66
Wholesale trade	1.82	1.15
Computer and data processing services	8.94	1.05
Communication and public utilities	2.52	1.01

Source: U.S. Department of Commerce (1993, tables II.P1 and III.G2).

[a]All nonbank parents of nonbank affiliates.

[b]Majority-owned affiliates, by industry of affiliate.

output and sales by minority-owned and majority-owned affiliates in absolute terms are used to explain parent compensation, a little better explanation is reached, but only parent output and minority affiliate output are ever statistically significant, and the coefficients are always positive (Kravis and Lipsey 1988, table 1). Thus the general impression is that if there is any influence of foreign operations it is a tendency toward high skill levels at home.

Among service industries, the share of majority-owned affiliates in production produced significant $\bar{R}^2$s only for wholesale trade in nondurable goods, for all services, and for business services (Kravis and Lipsey 1988, appendix table 5). Adding the other variables produced little improvement in the degree of explanation, but the few significant coefficients for affiliate production were positive.

On the whole, we can say that in both manufacturing and service industries the effect of foreign operations on the average skill levels in parent companies, if any, was to raise them, but the effect was not strong and not universal across industries.

1.5   Foreign and Domestic Investment as Competitors for Funds

One channel by which a decision by a firm to invest in foreign production could affect investment in domestic production is the financial one. The mechanism that would explain such an interdependence or interaction would presumably imply an upward-sloping supply function for the firm's external finance, so that investments in different locations compete for investment funds. It is a channel that would escape the notice of most analyses that take the level of production in each location as given, or as determined only by demand and costs of production in each location.

Studies of this question by Herring and Willett (1973)—and, to some extent, by Severn (1972) and Noorzoy (1980)—found mostly positive relationships over time between domestic and foreign investment. Such relationships, derived mainly from aggregate data, could reflect common fluctuations or trends in demand rather than any interdependence.

A study by Stevens and Lipsey (1992), based on individual firm plant and equipment expenditure data running for 15–20-year periods between the 1950s and the 1970s, attempted to disentangle these effects. Although only seven firms had data complete enough to be analyzed, the results were fairly consistent in suggesting that there was such interdependence. A 1 percent exogenous rise in foreign demand or in a firm's overseas output was estimated to reduce the parent firm's U.S. fixed investment by amounts ranging from 0.3 to 0.8 percent in most of the firms.

This is a tentative finding based on a small number of firms in a period of expanding foreign production by U.S. firms. It would be interesting to test the same model over the period of contracting or stagnant overseas production by U.S. firms and also on larger numbers of firms or on industry aggregates.

In any case, the possibility of this type of competition between foreign and domestic fixed investment is worth further investigation.

1.6 Conclusions

Many of the analyses of the effects of outward direct investment reviewed here implicitly assume that differences among firms and industries in various characteristics can be at least partly explained by differences in the degree to which they operate abroad. These same characteristics are also used to explain the propensity of firms and industries to operate abroad. The explanation of the existence of direct investment and foreign production is centered on the idea that firms possess individual firm-specific assets, such as technologies, or patents, or skills in advertising or marketing, that can be exploited most profitably by producing in many markets. These assets are mobile across international borders but not among firms, and firms cannot realize their value by selling them to other firms or by licensing them to other firms.

The opportunity to exploit these firm-specific assets via direct investment adds to the incentive to acquire them. If R&D intensity and human capital intensity are the strongest explanations of the worldwide trade shares of U.S. multinationals (Kravis and Lipsey 1992), and possibly of their shares in world production as well, a restriction on direct investment would reduce the value of investment in such assets and therefore reduce firms' investment in them. If much of foreign direct investment is defensive, as suggested earlier, it may make investment in firm-specific assets more profitable by extending the length of time over which they can be exploited, a suggestion made many years ago by Vernon (1966).

While firms from different countries tend to possess different comparative advantages, the leading firms in each country tend to internationalize their production. With the long-term decline in costs of international travel and communication, the costs of controlling widespread production must be declining, and firms from most of the countries in the world are increasing the extent to which they produce outside their home countries. With that fact as background, it seems unlikely that the decline in internationalization of American firms' production will go much further and seems more likely that it will be reversed.

The availability of foreign production locations appears to have contributed a great deal to the ability of American multinational firms to retain their market shares in the face of declines in the market share of the United States as a country. The same seems to be true for the trade shares of firms from other countries, and this flexibility applies to softening not only the effects of long-term national declines in export shares and in comparative advantage in individual industries, but also those of short-term events such as large changes in exchange rates.

The frequently expressed fear that American multinationals have been, in some sense, "exporting jobs" by substituting foreign production for American production has very little empirical support. For one thing, overseas employment and fixed investment have been, for the most part, declining relative to domestic employment and fixed investment for 10 or 15 years. And U.S. firms that produce more abroad than others tend also to export more in general and to the countries where the foreign production takes place. The same relationship is evident for firms based in Sweden, the only other country collecting similar data on multinational parents and affiliates. Overseas production has much more to do with contesting market shares than with finding low-cost production locations, although the latter is also a motivation.

Within multinational firms, the higher the share of overseas operations in the total production of the multinational, the higher the ratio of home employment to home production, more often than not. A possible explanation is that a larger share of foreign production requires a larger number of headquarters employees, such as R&D staff and supervisory personnel, whose contribution to output is not confined to the firm's domestic production. The relationship is not unambiguous, since higher absolute (rather than relative) production abroad is more often associated with lower home employment, given the level of home production, a finding we at one time interpreted as implying an allocation of more capital-intensive parts of total production to the United States and of more labor-intensive parts to affiliates, especially those in developing countries. The interpretation that it is technical activities and management that are allocated to home operations is reinforced by the fact that higher proportions of foreign activity are associated with higher average compensation at home.

On the whole, the evidence suggests that the effect of overseas production on the home-country labor market involves the composition of a firm's home employment rather than the total amount. That change in composition is mainly a shift toward more managerial and technical employment, much like the effects of increasing trade and other aspects of the evolution of the American economy.

References

Blomström, Magnus, Robert E. Lipsey, and Ksenia Kulchycky. 1988. U.S. and Swedish direct investment and exports. In *Trade policy issues and empirical analysis,* ed. Robert E. Baldwin, 259–97. Chicago: University of Chicago Press.

Fiero, Charles E. 1969. Statement by Charles E. Fiero, Director, Office of Foreign Direct Investments, U.S. Department of Commerce, before the Subcommittee on International Exchange and Payments of the Joint Economic Committee, January 15.

Herring, Richard, and Thomas D. Willett. 1973. The relationship between U.S. investment at home and abroad. *Rivista Internazionale di Scienze Economiche e Commerciali* 20:72–80.

Hufbauer, Gary C., and F. M. Adler. 1968. *Overseas manufacturing investment and the balance of payments.* Tax Policy Research Study no. 1. Washington, D.C.: Department of the Treasury.

Kravis, Irving B., and Robert E. Lipsey. 1988. The effect of multinational firms' foreign operations on their domestic employment. NBER Working Paper no. 2760. Cambridge, Mass.: National Bureau of Economic Research, November.

———. 1992. Sources of competitiveness of the United States and of its multinational firms. *Review of Economics and Statistics* 74, no. 2 (May): 193–201.

Lewis, Cleona. 1938. *America's stake in international investments.* Washington, D.C.: Brookings Institution.

Lipsey, Robert E. 1988. Changing patterns of international investment in and by the United States. In *The United States in the world economy,* ed. Martin Feldstein, 475–545. Chicago: University of Chicago Press.

———. 1993. Foreign direct investment in the United States: Changes over three decades. In *Foreign direct investment,* ed. Kenneth M. Froot, 113–70. Chicago: University of Chicago Press.

———. 1995. The transnationalization of economic activity. Report to the Division on Transnational Corporations and Investment. Geneva: UNCTAD.

Lipsey, Robert E., Magnus Blomström, and Irving B. Kravis. 1990. R&D by multinational firms and host country exports. In *Science and technology: Lessons for development policy,* ed. Robert E. Evenson and Gustav Ranis, 271–300. Boulder and San Francisco: Westview.

Lipsey, Robert E., Irving B. Kravis, and Romualdo A. Roldan. 1982. Do multinational firms adapt factor proportions to relative factor prices? In *Trade and employment in developing countries: Factor supply and substitution,* ed. Anne O. Krueger, 215–55. Chicago: University of Chicago Press.

Lipsey, Robert E., and Merle Yahr Weiss. 1981. Foreign production and exports in manufacturing industries. *Review of Economics and Statistics* 63, no. 4 (November): 488–94.

———. 1984. Foreign production and exports of individual firms. *Review of Economics and Statistics* 66, no. 2 (May): 304–8.

Noorzoy, M. S. 1980. Flows of direct investment and their effects on U.S. domestic investment. *Economic Letters* 5:311–17.

OECD (Organisation for Economic Co-operation and Development). 1993. *International direct investment statistics yearbook: 1993.* Paris: OECD.

Reddaway, W. B., in collaboration with J. O. N. Perkins, S. J. Potter, and C. T. Taylor. 1967. *Effects of U.K. direct investment overseas: An interim report.* Occasional Paper 12, Department of Applied Economics, Cambridge University.

Reddaway, W. B., in collaboration with S. J. Potter and C. T. Taylor. 1968. *Effects of U.K. direct investment overseas: Final report.* Occasional Paper 15, Department of Applied Economics, Cambridge University.

Severn, Alan. 1972. Investment and financial behavior of American direct investors in manufacturing. In *The international mobility and movement of capital,* ed. Fritz Machlup, Walter Salant, and Lorie Tarshis, 367–96. New York: National Bureau of Economic Research.

Southard, Frank A., Jr. 1931. *American industry in Europe.* Boston and New York: Houghton Mifflin.

Stevens, Guy V. G., and Robert E. Lipsey. 1992. Interactions between domestic and foreign investment. *Journal of International Money and Finance* 11, no. 1 (March): 40–62.

Svensson, Roger. 1993. *Production in foreign affiliates: Effects on home country exports and modes of entry.* Stockholm: Industriens Utredningsinstitut.

Swedenborg, Birgitta. 1973. *Den svenska industrins investeringar i utlandet.* Stockholm: Industriens Utredningsinstitut.

———. 1979. *The multinational operations of Swedish firms: An Analysis of determinants and effects.* Stockholm: Industriens Utredningsinstitut.

———. 1982. *Svensk Industri i Utlandet: En Analys av Drivkrafter och Effekter.* Stockholm: Industriens Utredningsinstitut.

———. 1985. Sweden. In *Multinational enterprises, economic structure, and international competitiveness,* ed. John Dunning, 217–48. London: Wiley.

Swedenborg, Birgitta, Goran Johansson-Grahn, and Mats Kinnwall. 1988. *Den Svenska Industrins Utlandsinvesteringar, 1960–1986.* Stockholm: Industriens Utredningsinstitut.

United Nations. 1993. *Yearbook of international trade statistics, 1992.* New York: United Nations.

United Nations. 1994. *Monthly Bulletin of Statistics.* May. New York: United Nations.

U.S. Department of Commerce. Bureau of Economic Analysis. 1985. *U.S. direct investment abroad: 1982 Benchmark Survey data.* Washington, D.C.: Government Printing Office.

———. 1993. *U.S. direct investment abroad: 1989 Benchmark Survey, final results.* Washington, D.C.: Government Printing Office.

U.S. Tariff Commission. 1973. *Implications of multinational firms for world trade and investment and for U.S. trade and labor,* Report to the Senate Committee on Finance (93-1). Washington, D.C., February.

Vernon, Raymond. 1966. International investment and international trade in the product cycle. *Quarterly Journal of Economics* 80 (May): 190–207.

Wilkins, Mira. 1970. *The emergence of multinational enterprise.* Cambridge: Harvard University Press.

———. 1989. *The history of foreign investment in the United States to 1914.* Cambridge: Harvard University Press.

Comment   S. Lael Brainard

Introduction

Bob Lipsey is certainly the person best qualified to synthesize what we know about the relationship between overseas affiliate activity and U.S. domestic activity, since most of what we know comes from his careful analyses of BEA data over the years. In this paper he draws on findings from a multitude of his own papers along with work by a variety of other authors and data from the most recent Bureau of Economic Analysis (BEA) Benchmark Survey of U.S. Direct Investment Abroad to characterize this relationship along a variety of dimensions. His careful perusal leads him to draw several conclusions:

1. The internationalization of production by U.S. firms on aggregate has declined relative to its peak in the 1970s, but this is less true for the manufacturing sector, and untrue for U.S. multinationals. At the same time, the internationalization of production by foreign firms has increased substantially.

S. Lael Brainard is the Mitsubishi Career Development Assistant Professor of Applied Economics at the Sloan School of the Massachusetts Institute of Technology and a faculty research fellow of the National Bureau of Economic Research.

2. Overseas affiliate sales do not appear to substitute for U.S. exports. Indeed, the two are positively correlated in aggregate. On the other hand, they do compete with exports from other countries.

3. Domestic employment by U.S. parents is negatively correlated with sales by overseas manufacturing affiliates and positively with sales by overseas sales affiliates. Further, the R&D intensity of parent employment is positively correlated with overseas affiliate sales. In addition, labor/capital ratios in overseas affiliate production are negatively correlated with wages in the destination market, and are on average higher than that of U.S. parents.

4. There is some evidence of a negative relationship between increases in foreign affiliate sales and fixed investment by the parent at home. I will not say much about this since it will be addressed further in Martin Feldstein's paper (chap. 2 in this volume).

These conclusions come from a careful reading of the data and empirical research over the past 10 years and are carefully and conservatively stated.

Lipsey's research has touched on most of the interesting issues involving outward direct investment and its effect at home. Luckily for researchers such as myself, there is enough ambiguity in some of the results to leave scope for alternative ways of addressing these questions, so we are not compelled simply to wait for additional years of survey data. I will go into greater depth in some of the areas to amplify certain findings and highlight ambiguities, and then suggest areas that warrant additional research.

Exports and Affiliate Sales

The relationship between exports and affiliate sales is interesting and important because it goes to the heart of the question whether increased overseas activity by U.S. firms stimulates or substitutes for activity in the United States.

Most of the research in this area has focused on interesting questions but has estimated them in equations that are tenuously related to economic theory. For instance, many of the regressions use exports as the dependent variable and include affiliate sales as an independent variable (Swedenborg 1979; Blomström, Lipsey, & Kulchycky 1988; Lipsey and Weiss 1981). Yet I have not seen any models which generate this type of reduced-form equation. For instance, neither of the two broad frameworks that have been developed in recent years by trade theorists to analyze multinationals' location decisions would be consistent with such a specification.

Factor proportions models of vertical expansion across borders—the dominant view of multinational enterprises (MNEs) in trade theory—make a complicated set of predictions regarding the relationship between exports and affiliate sales (Helpman 1984; Markusen 1984; Ethier and Horn 1990). When cross-border investment is motivated solely by factor price differentials, multinational activities arise only in a single direction within an industry between economies with strong factor proportions differences. The creation of multinationals may give rise to increased exports of intermediates in the same direction and of final goods in the reverse direction, in both cases diminishing the share of intraindustry trade. However, the model's implications for the effect of multinational activity on the total volume of trade are ambiguous.

Proximity-concentration models explain horizontal expansion across borders motivated by advantages of proximity to consumers or specialized suppliers at the expense of concentration advantages such as scale economies (Krugman 1983; Horstmann and Markusen 1992; Brainard 1992). These models predict that multinationals arise in industries characterized by high transport costs and trade barriers and low investment barriers and plant scale economies, even between countries with similar factor proportions. Such circumstances give rise to two-way penetration by multinationals. These models predict that affiliate sales substitute for exports of final goods but may generate intraindustry exports of intermediate goods, so again the predictions for the total volume of trade are ambiguous.

Indeed, I know of only one model that posits a causal linkage between affiliate sales and exports, as is implied by the specification. In markets where the local presence of U.S. multinationals enhances the quality reputation of all U.S. firms due to reputational spillovers, increased multinational activity expands demand for both locally produced and imported varieties of U.S. products (Raff 1992).

Of course, it is also possible that both the exports of U.S. parents to their affiliates and the affiliates' sales are counted in the same industry category due to the high level of industry aggregation at which BEA data are available (between 2- and 3-digit SIC) or to the misclassification of manufacturing affiliates as sales affiliates. Some evidence for this is suggested simply by netting out exports to affiliates, which significantly reduces the positive correlation, as shown in table 1C.1.

In any case, both the factor proportions and proximity-concentration models suggest that the positive correlation between affiliate sales and exports is likely to be attributable to determinants that affect both similarly rather than to a causal relationship. And indeed, there is evidence to support this. Grubert and Mutti (1991) find that an instrumental variables approach to estimating exports

Table 1C.1   Correlations

	Trade	Affiliate Sales	Net Affiliate Sales
Inward			
Imports		.20	–
Net imports		–	.10
Outward			
Exports		.64	–
Net exports		–	.20

Source: Estimates from Brainard (1993b) using data from U.S. Department of Commerce (1990a, 1990b).

yields negative insignificant coefficients on affiliate sales, controlling for policy variables and income. Unfortunately, however, there are very few if any instruments that are truly independent.

Alternatively, instead of using either affiliate sales or exports as an independent variable and the other as a dependent variable, the proximity-concentration model suggests estimating the extent to which exogenous variables such as trade and investment policies and transport cost differences affect the share of total sales accounted for by affiliate sales as opposed to exports. In research along these lines, I find quite different results, which are shown in table 1C.2 and summarized below (Brainard 1993b):

Factors that raise both exports and affiliate sales:
　Destination market income
　Home market income
Factors that raise affiliate sales relative to exports:
　Transport costs
　Trade barriers and nontariff barriers
　Per capita income similarities
　Sustained depreciation of destination market currency
Factors that reduce affiliate sales relative to exports:
　Plant scale economies
　FDI barriers
Ambiguous factors:
　Average corporate tax rate

An alternative approach is to estimate the levels of affiliate sales and exports netting out exports mediated by affiliates; as is shown in table 1C.2, this yields surprisingly similar results with the exception of transport costs.

Despite disagreement about the specification, this evidence has in common with the papers cited by Lipsey that it provides little support for the factor proportions hypothesis. Indeed, related work (Brainard 1993a) suggests that the same empirical relationships that cast doubt on the importance of factor proportions differences for explaining trade flows hold equally strongly for affiliate sales. The evidence shows that intraindustry affiliate sales (the share of two-way flows within an industry relative to total flows) are increasing in factor proportion similarities, and the total volume of affiliate sales is increasing in relative income similarities. Of course, in some industries and in some countries, factor substitution seems to be the key driver. This is particularly evident in markets where foreign affiliates export a large share of production back to the United States (e.g., the share exceeds 30 percent for Singapore, Taiwan, Hong Kong, and Canada). However, on aggregate it is only 13 percent.

Foreign Affiliate Employment and Domestic Employment

The obvious implication of casting doubt on the factor proportions hypothesis is to cast doubt on the degree to which multinationals substitute between

Table 1C.2   **Determinants of Affiliate Sales**

	Outward Affiliate Sales		Inward Affiliate Sales	
Variable	SUR: Share (1)	OLS: Net Level (2)	SUR: Share (3)	OLS: Net Level (4)
Transport cost	0.2123**	−0.4024**	0.4440**	−0.0856
	(4.81)	(−5.42)	(6.24)	(−0.81)
Tariffs	0.1629**	0.4490**	0.0271	0.4757**
	(3.10)	(5.34)	(0.27)	(3.84)
GDP		0.6710**		0.4898**
		(9.13)		(5.49)
Per capita GDP	0.7602**	0.9343**	0.6335**	0.3949†
	(5.81)	(3.94)	(4.02)	(1.56)
$ Depreciation	−0.2685**	−0.2699*	−0.0548	0.4135**
	(−3.98)	(−2.15)	(−0.50)	(2.75)
Tax rate	0.8868**	0.7913	1.2941**	0.7887
	(2.86)	(1.39)	(3.67)	(1.38)
Trade openness	−0.2735	−0.2552		
	(−0.73)	(−0.35)		
FDI openness	2.0570**	3.2336**		
	(6.64)	(5.61)		
Plant scale	−0.1510**		−0.1862	
	(−4.37)		(−3.13)	
Constant	−6.0239**	−27.1645**	−0.6366	−8.1360**
	(−3.67)	(−7.62)	(−0.33)	(−3.24)
Observations	771	815	513	584
Adjusted R^2	0.2018	0.2226	0.1843	0.1539

Source: Estimates from Brainard (1993b) using data from the 1989 Bureau of Economic Analysis survey.

Note: Col. (1) reports estimates (using seemingly unrelated regression [SUR]) of the log of the share of sales by U.S. affiliates overseas in total U.S. sales to foreign markets (outward affiliate sales plus exports) and col. (2) reports estimates (using OLS) of the log of the level of U.S. affiliate sales in foreign markets net of U.S. exports to the affiliates, where the independent variables are in logs. Similarly, col. (3) reports estimates of the log of the share of sales by foreign affiliates in the U.S. over total foreign sales in the U.S. market, and col. (4) reports estimates of the log of the level of foreign affiliate sales into the U.S. market net of U.S. imports by foreign affiliates. *T*-statistics are in parentheses.

**1 percent significance level.
*5 percent significance level.
†10 percent significance level.

foreign and domestic factors of production. I think the question of how employment overseas affects parent employment at home is a very interesting one.

In Lipsey, Kravis, and Roldan (1982) using data from 1966 and 1970, Lipsey et al. show that the labor intensity of affiliate production exceeds that of parent production and is greatest for affiliates in developing countries. They also show that the labor intensity of production is negatively correlated with the destination market wage. In both cases, they provide evidence that these factor intensity differentials are attributable to within-industry and possibly within-firm differences rather than to industry selection, suggesting that firms vary their choice of production techniques to exploit factor price differences, or that different activities are undertaken in different locations. This would be consistent with a factor proportions account.

In the current paper, Lipsey examines regressions of parent employment on parent sales and sales by overseas affiliates, using 1989 data. He finds that the relationship between parent employment and affiliate employment is generally negative, and more so for manufacturing affiliates. Here again, however, the regression is a bit problematic since there is likely to be correlation of the errors associated with parent employment and parent sales. Indeed, in similar equations normalizing by the level of parent sales, Lipsey finds that a greater ratio of parent employees to sales is associated with increases in affiliate sales of both manufacturing and nonmanufacturing affiliates, which is inconsistent with a factor proportions account.

There is also substantial interest in determining whether increases in overseas affiliate employment abroad affects industry employment or wages in the United States. Obviously, this is only an interesting issue if there are rigidities in interindustry labor adjustment or industry wage premia apart from compensating differentials. Substantial empirical evidence suggests there are.[1]

In recent research, Slaughter (1993) provides some evidence that suggests that domestic employment and foreign affiliate employment are weakly complementary at a highly aggregated level. Table 1C.3 shows that total U.S. manufacturing employment shrank 10 percent between 1979 and 1989, and that total overseas affiliate employment shrank 14 percent between 1977 and 1989. Southeast Asia is the only region to have experienced substantial growth.

Lipsey's paper also distinguishes the employment effect for R&D employees, and I agree that the heart of the matter may lie in shifts between different types of labor. Unfortunately, the BEA distinguishes production from nonproduction employees only in the benchmark surveys for the affiliates and does not distinguish at all in the parent data. Even so, it is interesting to note that foreign affiliates expanded their nonproduction labor abroad relative to their production labor between 1977 and 1989, a period in which demand for production labor in the manufacturing sector in the United States was stagnant and the relative demand for nonproduction labor grew. Table 1C.3 shows that while employment of production workers shrank 15 percent between 1979 and 1989 in the United States, overseas affiliate production employment shrank 21 percent between 1977 and 1989; it even contracted in Southeast Asia. During the same periods, employment of nonproduction workers grew by 5 percent in the United States while falling slightly overseas overall; in Southeast Asia it grew by 50 percent. These numbers yield little to no support to the claim that

1. See Katz and Summers (1989) for a survey of the literature.

Table 1C.3   **Manufacturing Employment in U.S. and Overseas Affiliates, 1977–89 (thousands)**

Region	Production 1989	Non-production 1989	Total 1989	Production Change 1977–89	Non-production Change 1977–89	Total Change 1977–89	Nonproduction/ Production Ratio 1989
World	1,875	1,369	3,244	−0.21	−0.02	−0.14	0.73
Europe	831	673	1,504	−0.31	−0.10	−0.23	0.81
Canada	271	179	450	−0.24	−0.12	−0.20	0.66
Latin America	453	289	742	0.01	0.09	0.04	0.64
Southeast Asia	197	106	303	−0.03	0.54	0.11	0.54
United States[a]	12,356	5,437	17,793	−0.15	0.04	−0.10	0.44
World/U.S.	0.15	0.25	0.18	0.23	−0.14	0.27	1.66

Sources: 1977 and 1987 BEA benchmark surveys; U.S. Bureau of the Census (1979, 1989).
[a]U.S. data is from 1979 rather than 1977.

expansion by U.S. multinationals overseas was an important cause of reduced demand for production workers at home over the 1980s. Obviously, these numbers are only rough indicators, and more systematic analysis is called for.

Tax

Lipsey's paper focuses on the real effects of overseas production. Most of the other papers in this volume focus on taxation. There is an interesting set of issues at the intersection of the two that are not generally addressed because of the separation between research in international trade theory and public finance: namely, how do tax factors distort the location of real economic activity? Of course, there has been a fair amount of research investigating the effects of taxes on FDI using both state and international data; here I am referring to overseas production rather than investment.

The results in Grubert and Mutti (1991) suggest that U.S. exports and overseas affiliate sales are both decreasing in destination market tax rates. The analysis in Brainard (1993b) of the factors influencing location decisions also included a tax variable, with puzzling results. The ratio of foreign affiliate sales in the United States to imports is increasing in the source market tax rate, as expected. However, it appears that the ratio of U.S. affiliate sales to exports is also increasing in the tax rate in the destination market. This may be due to correlation with other macro-variables, or perhaps to the use of the wrong tax rate. In any case, it warrants further investigation.

Conclusion

The issues that Lipsey raises are important because of the central role of multinationals in cross-border competition. Overseas affiliate sales by U.S.

multinationals are more than double the level of U.S. exports in manufactures, and the ratio exceeds one on the inward side. Moreover, multinationals are major conduits for international trade, mediating as much as half of U.S. manufacturing trade.

These issues are also important because multinationals are a lightning rod for domestic politics. Organized labor has long resisted outward FDI on the grounds that it reduces demand for labor at home. On the inward side, some critics are equally vehement in resisting control of U.S. assets by foreigners.

For both of these reasons, it is important that we develop a better understanding of the actual effects on the U.S. economy of overseas production by U.S. multinationals as well as inward penetration by foreign multinationals. Lipsey's synthesis of the existing empirical literature addresses important questions and interprets the findings in an appropriately cautious and relevant way.

The additional findings I have cited above are consistent with his in suggesting that the majority of overseas activity is not motivated primarily by access to lower factor costs, but rather by market access considerations. This in turn suggests that labor employed by U.S. firms abroad may not substitute for domestic employment in the same industry.

There are many areas with potential for future research. Given the nature of this audience, I will emphasize one. I would encourage more integration of public finance models with trade and investment models so that real and financial factors can be considered simultaneously. Such integration has occurred in the investigation of FDI, but not of overseas production and sales.

References

Blomström, Magnus, Robert Lipsey, and Ksenia Kulchycky. 1988. U.S. and Swedish direct investment and exports. In *Trade policy issues and empirical analysis,* ed. Robert Baldwin, 259–97. Chicago: University of Chicago Press.

Brainard, S. Lael. 1992. A simple theory of multinational corporations and trade with a tradeoff between proximity and concentration. MIT Sloan Working Paper no. 3492-92-EFA, Massachusetts Institute of Technology.

———. 1993a. An empirical assessment of the factor proportions explanation of multinational sales. MIT Sloan Working Paper no. 3624-93-EFA, Massachusetts Institute of Technology.

———. 1993b. An empirical assessment of the proximity-concentration tradeoff between multinational sales and trade. MIT Sloan Working Paper no. 3625-93-EFA, Massachusetts Institute of Technology.

Ethier, Wilfred, and Henrik Horn. 1990. Managerial control of international firms and patterns of direct investment. *Journal of International Economics* 28 (1–2): 25–45.

Grubert, Harry, and John Mutti. 1991. Taxes, tariffs, and transfer pricing in multinational corporate decision making. *Review of Economics and Statistics* 73:285–93.

Helpman, Elhanan. 1984. A simple theory of international trade with multinational corporations. *Journal of Political Economy* 92, no. 3 (June):451–71.

Horstmann, Ignatius, and James Markusen. 1987. Licensing vs. direct investment: A model of internalisation by the multinational enterprise. *Canadian Journal of Economics* 20:464–81.

————. 1992. Endogenous market structures in international trade. *Journal of International Economy* 32:109–29.

Katz, Lawrence F., and Lawrence H. Summers. 1989. Industry rents: Evidence and implications. *Brookings Papers on Economic Activity: Microeconomics* 209–75.

Krugman, Paul. 1983. The "new theories" of international trade and the multinational enterprise. In *The multinational corporation in the 1980s*, ed. D. B. Audretsch and Charles Kindleberger, 57–73. Cambridge: MIT Press.

Lipsey, Robert, Irving Kravis, and Romualdo Roldan. 1982. Do multinational firms adapt factor proportions to relative factor prices? In *Trade and employment in developing countries: Factor supply and substitution*, ed. Anne Krueger, 215–55. Chicago: University of Chicago Press.

Lipsey, Robert, and Merle Yahr Weiss. 1981. Foreign production and exports in manufacturing industries. *Review of Economics and Statistics* 63:488–94.

Markusen, James. 1984. Multinationals, multi-plant economies, and the gains from trade. *Journal of International Economics* 16:205–26.

Raff, Horst. 1992. Foreign direct investment versus exporting when product quality is unknown. Mimeograph, Université Laval.

Slaughter, Matt. 1993. International Trade, multinationals, and American wages. Mimeograph, Massachusetts Institute of Technology.

Swedenborg, Birgitta. 1979. *The multinational operations of Swedish firms*. Stockholm: Industriens Utredningsinstitut.

U.S. Bureau of the Census. 1979, 1989. *Annual survey of manufactures: Statistics for industry groups and industries*. Washington, D.C.: Government Printing Office.

U.S. Department of Commerce. Bureau of Economic Analysis. 1990a. *Foreign direct investment in the United States: Operations of U.S. affiliates, revised 1989 estimates*. Washington, D.C.: Government Printing Office.

————. 1990b. *U.S. direct investment abroad, revised 1989 estimates*. Washington, D.C.: Government Printing Office.

2 The Effects of Outbound Foreign Direct Investment on the Domestic Capital Stock

Martin Feldstein

Foreign direct investment (FDI) plays an important role in the international transfer of both capital and technology and has a significant impact on the pattern of international trade. The most recent detailed government survey of U.S. direct investment abroad found that in 1989 the foreign affiliates of U.S. multinational corporations had assets of more than $1.2 trillion, approximately 25 percent of U.S. gross domestic product in that year.

Companies make direct investments abroad by acquiring existing business assets of foreign companies, by starting new businesses with "green field" investments in plant and equipment, and by increasing their investments in foreign businesses that they already own. These foreign investments can be either wholly owned by the parent company or owned jointly with foreign partners.[1] The heterogeneity of FDI reflects the diversity of motives for making such investments.[2] At one extreme, some FDI (like the purchase of commercial real estate) is not fundamentally different from portfolio investment and the motivation is the standard desire to diversify portfolio assets. A more traditional motivation for FDI is to take advantage of low-cost labor or proximity to raw materials. The primary reason is probably to maintain or increase foreign sales

Martin Feldstein is the George F. Baker Professor of Economics at Harvard University and president of the National Bureau of Economic Research.

The author is grateful to Joosung Jun for detailed discussions about measurement issues and data sources and to Todd Sinai for help with the regression analysis presented in sections 2.3 and 2.4. The author benefited also from comments on an earlier draft by Ken Froot, Jim Hines, Glenn Hubbard, Robert Lipsey, and Joel Slemrod.

1. The minimum extent of the parent company's ownership share required to make an investment qualify as "direct" rather than portfolio investment depends on the particular definition of FDI. The common balance-of-payments definition of FDI is based on ownership of at least 10 percent of the equity in the foreign business. For some purposes, it is more sensible to concentrate on businesses where the parent has a majority ownership interest.

2. See Froot (1993) and Graham and Krugman (1991), and the references cited in those books, for a general discussion of FDI with particular reference to the United States.

and market share. Thus, manufacturing companies that make products for industrial customers invest abroad in order to have closer working relations with customers, especially when their products must be specifically designed or modified for their customers. Many service companies must invest abroad if they want to provide services to those local markets. And some manufacturers acquire foreign firms in order to gain entry into local markets.

Government policies significantly influence the pattern of FDI, sometimes intentionally and sometimes inadvertently. Some governments require local investment (to create industrial jobs or achieve technology transfers) as a condition of access to government procurement or licensing. Other governments use favorable tax and credit policies to attract foreign investment. In contrast, some governments (e.g., Japan) are notorious for the regulatory barriers that deter inbound FDI.

The effects of government policies on FDI are not always intended, but may be the inadvertent byproducts of policies designed to serve other purposes. Tariffs and other trade barriers intended to protect domestic producers induce inbound FDI. The taxation of multinational companies can encourage or impede both inbound and outbound FDI.

There has been a substantial public policy debate about the effects of inbound and outbound FDI on the domestic economy.[3] Much of the public concern is stated in terms of the effect of FDI on employment, with opponents of outbound FDI arguing that such FDI "takes production abroad" and reduces employment at home, while proponents of outbound FDI counter that such FDI creates markets for U.S. exports to affiliates and through affiliates to foreign buyers. Economists recognize that this is a misplaced concern because the American labor market works well in assuring that all who want jobs at wages that reflect their skills can find work within a relatively short period of time. As Graham and Krugman emphasize: *"The net impact of FDI on U.S. employment is approximately zero,* and the truth of this assertion has nothing to do with job gains and losses at the industry level" (Graham and Krugman 1991, 49). Studies that calculate the numbers of jobs "lost" because particular firms shift activity abroad (e.g., Bergsten et al. 1978; Hufbauer and Adler 1968) do not take into account the absorption of those American workers by other firms and industries.

A related and more plausible concern is often expressed in terms of the impact of FDI on the "quality" of jobs. The worry is that although the forces of supply and demand maintain total employment, the shift of investment to foreign countries causes a substitution in the United States of low-wage jobs for the higher-wage manufacturing jobs that have gone abroad. As a general proposition, this is again incorrect. In a well-functioning labor market like ours, wages reflect the skills of the workers and are therefore not affected by

---

3. See, e.g., the discussions in Bergsten, Horst, and Moran (1978), Graham and Krugman (1991), and Hufbauer and Adler (1968).

the entry or exit of individual firms. There are some ways, however, in which foreign investment could affect wages. Market imperfections that permit workers in some industries to be paid substantially more than individuals with similar skills in other industries (e.g., union power or the monopoly power of firms that share their monopoly profits with employees) do provide a mechanism by which the mix of firms can affect the distribution of wages. In addition, even without such market imperfections, FDI can affect the quality of jobs if it alters the marginal product of labor. This can happen if FDI changes the domestic capital stock. It can also happen if FDI increases or decreases the kinds of jobs that are more likely to involve substantial on-the-job training. Training reflects the mix of industries and may be more important in capital-intensive industries than in other industries.[4]

This leads naturally to two questions about the effect of FDI on the capital stocks of both the parent and host countries. First, what impact does an increase in the assets of foreign affiliates have on the parent country's capital stock? Second, what impact does an inflow of FDI have on the host country's capital stock? The answers to these questions may well depend on the form of the FDI and on the reason for the particular inflow or outflow of such investment.[5] Although the available data do not permit such a disaggregated analysis, it is possible to assess the extent to which countries that experience sustained high rates of inbound or outbound FDI have higher or lower levels of domestic investment than would otherwise be expected. The current study focuses on estimating the extent to which outbound FDI reduces domestic investment in the parent country.

Previous studies of this question have been microeconomic partial equilibrium analyses that have asked whether *firms* that invest more abroad reduce their investment at home.[6] Although these studies can shed interesting light on the behavior of multinational companies, they do not indicate the net effect on the economy as a whole when individual firms increase their outbound FDI. When firms increase their overseas investment, the funds that they might otherwise have used in the United States might instead finance greater domestic investment by others, leaving both the aggregate capital outflow and the level of domestic investment unchanged. Alternatively, the process of outbound FDI might increase the aggregate net capital outflow and therefore reduce total do-

---

4. For an extensive discussion of the impact of outbound FDI on employment in the United States, see Lipsey (chap. 1, this volume). Lipsey concludes that the effect of increased outbound FDI on the domestic employment by multinational companies is probably slightly positive (as outbound FDI increases exports) and that the mix of domestic jobs shifts toward more higher-paying technical and managerial positions.

5. Since FDI is an endogenous variable in the complex system of trade and capital flows, it would in principle be desirable to estimate a more fully articulated structural model in which one can assess the extent to which changes in exogenous variables that alter FDI influence domestic investment through this route. I return to this issue in section 2.4 below.

6. These studies include Blomström, Lipsey, and Kulchycky (1988), Lipsey and Weiss (1984), Severn (1972), and Stevens (1969).

mestic investment. Resolving the policy debate about the effect of FDI on domestic investment requires resolving this macroeconomic general equilibrium issue.

This paper presents information on the general equilibrium effect of FDI based on aggregate evidence about investment flows in the OECD countries. The analysis focuses on the effect of outbound FDI and implies that such investment does reduce domestic investment but that each dollar of assets in foreign affiliates reduces the domestic capital stock by substantially less than a dollar. The best summary of the evidence is that each dollar of assets in foreign affiliates reduces the domestic capital stock by between 20 and 40 cents.

Before looking at the basis for these conclusions, it is useful to begin by considering several alternative concepts of FDI and the relevant magnitude of each for the United States. This is the subject of section 2.1. Section 2.2 discusses alternative theories of how outbound FDI could affect the domestic capital stock. Sections 2.3 and 2.4 present investment equations that are estimated using the OECD data. The implications of this for the displacement question are discussed in the final section. The appendix presents the basic data used in sections 2.3 and 2.4.

2.1   Three Concepts of FDI

Several alternative concepts of the stock of FDI are possible. A very narrow definition measures the stock of FDI as the accumulated cross-border flow of equity and debt from the parent company to its foreign subsidiary. The parent company may, however, have control over a much larger volume of foreign assets, including those financed by retained earnings and by borrowing from foreign and other domestic creditors.

This section starts with the narrowest definition of outbound FDI and then presents a series of building blocks that can be used to construct broader measures of FDI. For each building block, there is an estimate of the value from the point of view of U.S. parents as of the end of 1989.

To avoid the special problems of comparing bank assets and liabilities with those of other types of businesses, this analysis is limited to nonbank affiliates of nonbank U.S. corporate parents. Similarly, in order to focus on foreign investments in which the U.S. parent has an unambiguous controlling interest, the analysis is limited to majority-owned nonbank affiliates of U.S. nonbank parents.[7]

These calculations are based on data from the 1989 benchmark survey of

7. The restrictions to nonbank firms and to those with majority ownership by the U.S. parent together reduce the measured stock of U.S.-owned FDI (according to the balance-of-payments measure) by approximately 18 percent. All U.S. FDI had a value (according to the balance-of-payments measure) in 1989 of $553 billion, while the corresponding figure for majority-owned nonbank affiliates was $452 billion. Both figures are estimates of current (1989 dollar) cost values.

U.S. investment abroad reported in the *Survey of Current Business* (U.S. Department of Commerce 1991). Although the benchmark survey data report the current dollar values of the debts of foreign affiliates,[8] the value of assets and therefore the value of equity is stated only as historic cost values. The value of original equity investments and of retained earnings must therefore be adjusted for past price changes to calculate the corresponding current cost values.

In the absence of the necessary detail on annual investment flows, I have done so by using the historic cost and current cost values for the total equity of all U.S. FDI (not just majority-owned nonbank affiliates of nonbank parents) that are published by the Department of Commerce. At year-end 1989, the total value of all U.S. FDI abroad[9] was $553 billion at current cost (1989 dollars) and $370 billion at historic cost (U.S. Department of Commerce 1992). Since the debt component of this balance-of-payments measure of the stock of FDI was $24 billion, the corresponding equity amounts were $529 billion at current cost and $346 billion at historic cost, a ratio of 1.53. Despite the obvious limitations of using a single ratio for both initial equity investments and subsequent retained earnings, this ratio will be used to adjust all historic cost equity values in the 1989 benchmark survey to the corresponding current cost estimates.

I turn now to an analysis of the different concepts of the FDI in the nonbank affiliates of nonbank U.S. parents. The narrowest definition of FDI is the *net external finance from the U.S. parent to the foreign affiliate*. This external finance at year-end 1989 consisted of $202 billion of initial equity investments of U.S. parents (at current cost)[10] and $25 billion of net debt provided by those same parents.[11]

1. Net External finance from U.S. parents $227 billion
1a. Equity from U.S. parents   ($202 billion)
1b. Net debt from U.S. parents   ($25 billion)

A small amount of additional equity investment and credit is extended to these overseas affiliates by other U.S. investors and creditors. The equity invested in majority-owned businesses by American companies other than the parent company is very small, only a cumulative $1 billion. American creditors other than the parent firm provided credit of $22 billion.[12]

---

8. The foreign debt is translated into U.S. dollars at current exchange rates but is not adjusted for changes in value due to changes in interest rates since the debt was issued.

9. This is the "balance-of-payments" measure of FDI. It is the sum of the initial equity investments of U.S. parents, the subsequent retained earnings, and any net debt from U.S. parents to their foreign affiliates.

10. The historic cost number reported in the 1989 benchmark survey (U.S. Department of Commerce 1991, table III.C.1) is $132 billion. Multiplying this by the factor 1.53 produces the current cost estimate of $202 billion.

11. The gross debt from U.S. parents to their foreign affiliates was $84 billion. This was offset in large part by $59 billion of credit from affiliates to parents, leaving a net debt of affiliates to parents of $25 billion. The balance-of-payments measure of FDI includes only the net debt, and I follow that procedure in the current analysis.

12. The credit from the U.S. parent as well as from other U.S. sources includes trade credit as well as other forms of credit.

2. External finance from other U.S. sources $23 billion
   2a. Equity from other U.S. investors   ($1 billion)
   2b. Debt from other U.S. sources   ($22 billion)

The external finance from U.S. sources is substantially augmented by equity and debt from foreign sources. Even among those affiliates that are majority owned by their U.S. parents, foreign sources invested equity of $92 billion at current cost[13] and foreign creditors provided $567 billion.[14]

3. External finance from foreign sources $659 billion
   3a. Equity from foreign sources   ($92 billion)
   3b. Debt from foreign sources   ($567 billion)

The final source of capital in the foreign affiliates is the retained earnings that were reinvested after paying dividends to parents and others. The 1989 current cost estimate for the accumulated value of these retained earnings was $328 billion. Dividing this aggregate among the three classes of investors in proportion to their historic cost values of retained earnings implies:

4. Retained earnings $328 billion
   4a. Share of U.S. parents   ($225 billion)
   4b. Share of other U.S. investors   ($1 billion)
   4c. Share of foreign equity investors   ($102 billion)

With these building blocks, it is possible to define three progressively broader concepts of outbound FDI. The first is the *net external finance from U.S. sources.* This is the sum of amounts 1 and 2 above, or $250 billion.

The second measure of U.S. FDI adds the value of the retained earnings of foreign affiliates attributable to U.S. investors (the sum of amounts 4a and 4b, or $226 billion) to the net external finance from U.S. parents and other U.S. sources. This *net finance from U.S. sources*[15] had a value of $476 billion.

The third natural definition is the value of the assets in the foreign affiliate, regardless of who finances those assets and of whether the finance is by debt or equity. This definition, the *value of assets of U.S. foreign affiliates,* is the sum of the four building blocks, or $1,237 billion.

The three concepts and the associated magnitudes are shown in table 2.1.

13. This current dollar figure is based on the historic cost value of $60 billion.

14. The 1989 benchmark survey reports that the total liabilities of the majority-owned nonbank affiliates of nonbank U.S. parents was $673 billion. This included current liability and long-term debt of $562 billion and "other liabilities" (including deferred taxes of the subsidiary) of $111 billion. Subtracting the $106 billion of gross debt provided by U.S. parents and other U.S. sources (i.e., the sum of $25 billion of net debt from parents, $59 billion of offsetting debt from affiliates to parents that is counted as part of the gross debt of the affiliates, and $22 billion of debt from other U.S. sources) leaves a balance of $567 billion of debt supplied by foreign sources.

15. This exceeds the official balance-of-payments definition of the stock of U.S. foreign investment by including the value of the equity and debt of U.S. investors and creditors who are not parents of the foreign affiliates.

Table 2.1   **Alternative Measures of FDI**

Concept of FDI	Value at Year-End 1989
1. Net external finance from U.S. sources (1 + 2)	$ 250 billion
2. Net finance from U.S. sources (1 + 2 + 4a + 4b)	$ 476 billion
3. Value of assets of U.S. foreign affiliates (1 + 2 + 3 + 4)	$1,237 billion

Note: All values are adjusted to current cost in 1989 dollars.

2.2   Displacement Effect of Outbound Direct Investment: Partial Equilibrium versus General Equilibrium Analysis

How does the decision of an American firm to invest abroad in a foreign subsidiary affect the total amount of investment in the United States? Despite the widespread interest in this question, there has been no formal analysis or empirical investigation of the general equilibrium effect of outbound FDI on domestic investment.

2.2.1   Behavior of Individual Firms

The common popular discussion of this issue treats it as a partial equilibrium question of where corporate production will occur. As noted above, opponents of outbound FDI argue that such investment reduces domestic production by substituting for exports, while defenders of outbound FDI argue that overseas subsidiaries increase the market for U.S. exports and therefore increase production in the United States. There are undoubtedly examples of both possibilities in actual practice. These countervailing effects may explain why the very careful study of individual multinational firms by Stevens and Lipsey (1992) failed to find any significant effects of overseas production on domestic exports and investment.[16]

An alternative partial equilibrium analysis would start with the corporate financial decisions and ask whether a firm that invests more abroad will invest less at home. In the simplest textbook version of the investment decision, the firm can borrow as much as it wants at a fixed interest rate and therefore invests until the marginal product of capital equals that rate of interest. In such an economy, borrowing to finance overseas investment does not alter the firm's funds available for domestic investment.

Actual corporate experience is very far from these textbook models. The following simplified version of corporate capital budgeting shows how a firm's decision to invest abroad could reduce its domestic investment. In this view,

16. Similar evidence that outbound FDI is not associated with export displacement is reported in Blomström et al. (1988) and in Lipsey and Weiss (1981, 1984).

the company starts with a fixed amount of after-tax profits and a dividend payout that its shareholders expect. There is some but very little room to vary dividends from the expected amount. The combination of the retained earnings (after this dividend payout) and the company's desired debt-to-capital ratio determines the amount that the company can borrow and therefore the firm's total funds available for capital investments.[17] Since this capital budget calculation is done for the multinational corporation as a whole rather than for individual subsidiaries, the result is a capital budget for the entire corporation. Any use of that capital abroad reduces the amount of capital available for domestic investment within the firm.[18]

However, as the analysis of section 2.1 indicated, much of the capital invested in U.S. affiliates overseas is raised abroad. It is clear that the share of foreign-source debt and equity in the U.S. foreign affiliates is far greater than the share of such foreign-source debt and equity in the financing of the domestic U.S. industry. This reflects the fact that most American firms are more likely to borrow abroad to finance overseas assets than to finance domestic assets. The reason for this is unclear. It may reflect a desire to hedge foreign currency profits with foreign currency debt, an ability to borrow more cheaply when collateral is available, or other aspects of the risk and return of financing behavior. This segmentation of borrowing may be a form of suboptimal behavior similar to the widely observed failure of portfolio managers to diversify investment.

Similarly, American firms are more likely to seek foreign joint-venture partners for overseas subsidiaries (in order to get market access or other benefits of having a local partner) than they are to seek such equity investors here in the United States. The foreign equity investor is also likely to regard such direct investment as a joint-venture partner within its own country as less risky than investing in the United States.

In short, even if outbound FDI substitutes for other investments within the firm's capital budget, more of the funds to finance that outbound FDI are likely to come from foreign sources than would be the case for domestic investment.

2.2.2 Macroeconomic General Equilibrium Effects

To assess the net impact of outbound FDI on total investment in the United States it is important to look beyond the partial equilibrium analysis of individual firms. The net impact of outbound FDI depends on the extent to which that

---

17. The company could of course modify this by new equity issues, share repurchases, and divestitures, but these should be seen as unusual events rather than as part of the annual capital budgeting process.

18. Stevens and Lipsey (1992) investigate the financial interdependence between foreign investment and domestic investment over time in a sample of U.S. multinational firms and find that overseas investment does reduce domestic investment through this channel. Their formal model lies between the two extremes described in the current text: firms do not have a fixed debt-to-capital ratio, but the cost of funds is a function of that ratio.

outbound FDI changes the aggregate net outflow of capital from the United States, including net portfolio investment as well as net direct investment.

In a world of perfect capital mobility in which the total pool of world savings moves to finance those investments with the highest risk-adjusted rates of return, an increase in U.S. direct investment abroad need not have any effect on the U.S. capital stock. Funds would automatically flow in to finance domestic U.S. investments that earn the required rate of return.

But although the integration of global capital markets appears to be increasing, we are still a long way from the textbook model of perfect capital-market integration. Gross international capital flows are large, but sustained net flows are relatively small. As Charles Horioka and I showed nearly 15 years ago (Feldstein and Horioka 1980), a nation's savings tend to be invested in the country where they originate.[19] The "saving retention coefficient" (the fraction of a marginal dollar of saving that is invested domestically) is estimated to be between 0.8 and 0.9 on average for the OECD countries. This is dramatically different from the world of perfect capital mobility in which a nation's rate of investment would not depend on its saving rate and therefore in which the saving retention coefficient would be zero.

Paradoxically, the extreme no-net-capital-flow case (a saving retention coefficient of 1.0 that is uninfluenced by the volume of outbound or inbound FDI) has the same implication in the current context as the perfect capital mobility case: an outflow of direct investment does not change the amount of net domestic investment. Any net outflow of FDI in this case would be offset by a reduction in outbound portfolio investment or an increase in inbound portfolio investment. The previous estimates of the Feldstein-Horioka–type investment-saving equations did not explicitly test whether the amount of domestic investment is influenced by the outbound or inbound FDI. That is the subject of the next two sections.

A more likely possibility is that the Feldstein-Horioka relation applies to portfolio investment rather than to direct investment. In the extreme case, an extra dollar of national saving would remain in domestic portfolio assets unless it is used by a multinational corporation to finance a cross-border direct investment. Such an outbound FDI would reduce the funds available for domestic investment by an equal amount, as the above corporate budget example suggests. If the portfolio investments were completely segmented into national markets in this way, the effect of the outbound FDI on domestically available funds would not be offset by any international flow of portfolio capital and the aggregate domestic investment would be reduced by the full amount of the direct investment outflow.

---

19. This fact has since been replicated many times. See Frankel (1991) and Mussa and Goldstein (1993) for discussions of this literature and comments on the reasons why savings remain at home even in a world capital market that appears to be quite closely linked and very active. See also Baxter and Crucini (1993) and Feldstein and Bacchetta (1991).

The evidence in the next two sections supports the idea that FDI transfers capital across borders with very little offsetting net portfolio investment. More specifically, the evidence indicates that each dollar of outbound FDI reduces domestic investment by approximately one dollar.

2.3   Estimates of the Effects of FDI on Domestic Investment

The estimates presented in this section are an extension of earlier work reported in a number of papers beginning with Feldstein and Horioka (1980).[20] The basic Feldstein-Horioka specification relates the ratio of gross domestic investment to GDP to the ratio of gross national saving to GDP. Since these ratios are calculated as decade averages, the analysis relates to sustained differences among countries rather than year-to-year changes. The specification assumes that the national differences in saving determine national differences in investment rather than the reverse. Since these specification issues have been discussed extensively in previous articles,[21] I will not comment on them here.

The innovation in the current study is to add data on inbound and outbound FDI to the previous bivariate specification. The simplest form of the resulting equation is

$$\text{GDI/GDP} = a + b \, (\text{GNS/GDP}) + c \, [(\text{FDI-out})/\text{GDP}] + d \, [(\text{FDI-in})/\text{GDP}] + u,$$

where GDI is gross domestic investment, GNS is gross national saving, GDP is gross domestic product, the two types of FDI are denoted FDI-out and FDI-in, and u is a stochastic disturbance. The individual variables in the numerator and denominator of each ratio are flows at annual rates denominated in current dollars in national currencies. The ratios are decade averages of annual ratios for each country. More general specifications with additional variables are discussed in section 2.4.

By definition, GDI includes only the investment done within the geographic boundaries of the home country. Investment by foreign affiliates of the home country's multinationals are excluded. Investment within the geographic boundaries of the home country that is done by the local affiliates of foreign multinationals is included in GDI. The GNS figures include the saving in the form of retained earnings of foreign affiliates of the home country's multinationals. The FDI values are based on the balance-of-payments definition and refer to all foreign affiliates, not just majority-owned or nonbank affiliates. These data are not ideal, but they are the best data available for this study.

---

20. See Frankel (1991) and Mussa and Goldstein (1993) for summaries of this literature.
21. See Feldstein (1983) and Feldstein and Bacchetta (1991) as well as the references cited in n. 20.

Table 2.2   **Effects of National Saving and FDI on Domestic Investment**

Equation	Period	RE[a]	N	Constant	GNS	FDI-Out	FDI-In	Adjusted R^2
(1)	1970s	–	15	0.04	0.87			0.85
				(0.02)	(0.10)			
(2)	1980s	–	18	0.07	0.74			0.67
				(0.03)	(0.12)			
(3)	Pooled	–	33	0.05	0.80			0.79
				(0.02)	(0.07)			
(4)	1970s	No	15	0.05	0.84	−1.73	0.80	0.87
				(0.03)	(0.10)	(0.90)	(1.11)	
(5)	1980s	No	18	0.08	0.74	−1.65	0.47	0.74
				(0.03)	(0.12)	(0.69)	(0.86)	
(6)	Pooled	No	33	0.07	0.77	−1.58	0.59	0.84
				(0.02)	(0.07)	(0.47)	(0.62)	
(7)	1970s	Yes	9	0.06	0.76	−1.42	2.18	0.90
				(0.03)	(0.12)	(0.46)	(0.63)	
(8)	1980s	Yes	10	0.10	0.59	−1.87	2.51	0.67
				(0.05)	(0.23)	(0.63)	(1.09)	
(9)	Pooled	Yes	19	0.08	0.66	−1.71	2.38	0.82
				(0.03)	(0.11)	(0.37)	(0.59)	

[a]Indicates whether the FDI variables include or exclude the retained earnings of the foreign affiliates.

Although the OECD produces consistent data on GDI, GNS, and GDP, there are no official OECD data on FDI. The data on FDI come from the International Monetary Fund.[22] The limited availability of data on FDI restricts the sample to 18 of the 24 OECD countries for the decade of the 1980s and 15 of those countries for the decade of the 1970s. This section presents separate results for both samples as well as for a pooled sample of 33 observations. For all of these countries it is possible to obtain estimates of FDI excluding retained earnings (RE). It is also possible to obtain the amount of retained earnings of these foreign affiliates for 9 of the countries during the decade of the 1970s and 10 of the countries during the decade of the 1980s. Estimates are also presented for these smaller samples.

The first three equations presented in table 2.2 are the standard investment-savings relation without FDI. The estimated savings retention coefficients for this sample of OECD countries are 0.87 (s.e. = 0.10) for the 1970s and 0.74 (s.e. = 0.12) for the 1980s, very similar to the estimates obtained with the larger samples of OECD countries in past research. The savings retention coefficient for the pooled data is 0.80 (s.e. = 0.07) and lies between the two individual decade estimates.

In equation (4) of table 2.2, the coefficient of the FDI-out variable is −1.73

---

22. These data are published in the Balance of Payments Yearbook. The current study uses updated unpublished data. The actual data are presented in the appendix to this paper.

(s.e. = 0.90) and the coefficient of the FDI-in variable is 0.80 (s.e. = 1.11). Adding these two FDI variables to the traditional saving-investment equation leaves the estimated savings retention coefficient virtually unchanged at 0.84 (s.e. = 0.10).

The coefficient of the FDI-out variable, which is of primary interest in the current analysis, is quite stable in the different time periods and specifications. It is always negative, implying that the aggregate level of domestic investment in a country declines when outbound FDI increases. Since this effect is conditional on given levels of national saving and inbound FDI, it implies that other international capital flows (inbound and outbound portfolio investment and borrowing) do not adjust to offset the direct effect of outbound FDI on domestic investment. The coefficient of outbound FDI is −1.73 (s.e. = 0.62) in the 1970s and −1.65 (s.e. = 0.69) in the 1980s when FDI is defined as a cross-border capital transfer (i.e., excluding retained earnings of the foreign affiliates). Adding the retained earnings of foreign affiliates (eq. [7]) leaves the coefficient for 1970 essentially unchanged (−1.42 with s.e. = 0.40) and increases the absolute size of the 1980 coefficient only slightly (−1.87 with s.e. = 0.63).

It would of course be desirable to distinguish the response of domestic investment to outbound cross-border FDI flows from the response of domestic investment to the retained earnings of the foreign affiliates. Unfortunately, there are too few observations to make such an estimate. Attempts to use the samples corresponding to equations (7)–(9) to look at the RE variable separately (in addition to the other variables already in those equations) results in almost no residual degrees of freedom and therefore leads to very unstable coefficient estimates with very large standard errors. It is not possible to determine statistically whether a one-dollar increase in GNS due to an increase in the RE of foreign affiliates has the same impact on GDI as a one-dollar rise in GNS due to domestic savings.[23] Similarly, when outbound FDI is defined to include the retained earnings of foreign affiliates (eqs. [7]–[9]), it is not clear whether the reaction to the cross-border FDI flow is the same as the reaction to FDI-out that is achieved without a cross-border flow by an increase in the retained earnings of the affiliate.

The reaction of domestic home-country investment to a dollar of dividends that is repatriated by the subsidiary to the parent company is ambiguous a priori as well. Although the direct effect of the dividend repatriation would be to add to the domestic capital stock, this could be offset to the extent that the dividend induces a reduction in inbound portfolio investment or an increase in outbound direct or portfolio investment. Since the econometric evidence cannot resolve this ambiguity, section 2.5 examines the implications of the two alternative extreme assumptions that subsidiary retained earnings reduce do-

---

23. Recall that gross national saving includes the retained earnings of foreign affiliates.

mestic (home-country) investment dollar for dollar and, alternatively, that they do not affect domestic investment at all.

2.4   Additional Variables and Simultaneity Problems

The interpretation of the coefficients in table 2.2 is clouded by the fact that the saving rate and the two FDI ratios are endogenous variables in the overall economic system. In particular, the levels of inbound and outbound FDI are likely to be correlated with variables that favor higher domestic rates of investment. A country that offers a "good environment" for domestic investment is also likely to attract more inbound FDI and may also experience less outbound FDI. This section shows that this problem of missing variables does indeed bias the coefficients shown in section 2.3, increasing the absolute size of both the FDI-out and FDI-in coefficients.

The results in this section are thus quite different from the earlier studies of potential bias in the estimated savings retention coefficient in the simpler Feldstein-Horioka specification. Since it is certainly possible that some of the same factors that cause a country to have a higher saving rate might also cause it to have a higher investment rate, Feldstein and Bacchetta (1991) also estimated the basic specification by an instrumental variable (IV) estimation procedure using demographic characteristics and social security variables as instruments for the national saving rate. Although the relatively small sample of fewer than two dozen countries limits the relevance of the consistency property of IV estimation, the similarity of the OLS and IV estimates provides some reassurance that the potential endogeneity of the savings rate is not a source of significant bias. Further support for the assumption that long-term intercountry differences in saving cause long-term differences in investment (rather than the reverse or a simultaneous equations relation) is obtained by dividing national saving into private saving and government saving and noting that both components of national saving have essentially the same effect on domestic investment in a generalized Feldstein-Horioka specification (Feldstein and Bacchetta 1991).

Although it would be desirable to reestimate the equations in table 2.2 using an IV approach, I have been unable to find any variables that would be satisfactory instruments. I decided therefore to pursue a different approach to reducing the possible bias in the estimated FDI coefficients by expanding the specification of the investment equation to include additional determinants of investment that might also be correlated with either or both of the FDI variables. Although some bias might remain even in this specification because not all possible variables are included, this method is preferable to using an IV estimation procedure with a very small sample and very inadequate instruments.

Table 2.3 summarizes the results of these more general specifications. The evidence confirms that outbound FDI does reduce domestic investment, but the

Table 2.3   **Impact of Additional Variables on the Estimated Effect of FDI on Domestic Investment**

Equation	Period	RE	N	GNS	FDI-Out	FDI-In	Other Variables	Adjusted R^2
(1)	Pooled	No	33	0.76	−1.17	0.16	E**, SIZE**, INF**, GRO	0.90
				(0.07)	(0.47)	(0.50)		
(2)	Pooled	No	33	0.79	−1.10	−0.04	E**, SIZE**, INF*, INT**	0.92
				(0.05)	(0.40)	(.44)		
(3)	1970s	No	15	0.85	−0.92	−0.03	E, SIZE*, INF*, GRO	0.89
				(0.17)	(0.91)	(1.21)		
(4)	1970s	No	15	0.87	−0.83	0.00	E, SIZE*, INF, INT	0.89
				(0.11)	(1.04)	(1.16)		
(5)	1980s	No	18	0.65	−0.80	−0.19	E**, SIZE**, INF**, GRO	0.91
				(0.09)	(0.55)	(0.57)		
(6)	1980s	No	18	0.65	−0.81	−0.20	E**, SIZE**, INF*, INT	0.91
				(0.10)	(0.54)	(0.54)		
(7)	Pooled	Yes	19	0.49	−1.59	1.41	E, SIZE**, INF, GRO	0.89
				(0.14)	(0.42)	(0.58)		
(8)	Pooled	Yes	19	0.62	−1.36	0.94	E*, SIZE**, INF, INT*	0.92
				(0.11)	(0.38)	(0.54)		
(9)	Pooled	Yes	19	0.55	−1.37	0.92	E*, SIZE**, INT**	0.93
				(0.11)	(0.31)	(0.49)		

Note: Each equation also contains a constant term. The FDI-in and FDI-out variables exclude retained earnings in eqs. (1)–(6) and include retained earnings in eqs. (7)–(9). See text for definitions of "other variables."

coefficients are now absolutely smaller, indicating that the previously omitted variables were common factors that affected FDI-out and GDI in similar ways.[24]

For example, equation (1) of table 2.3 (which is estimated for the pooled sample of 33 country-decade observations) includes four variables in addition to the saving rate and FDI variables: (1) a dummy variable indicating whether the country is in Europe (E), (2) the size of the country as measured by its average population during the decade (SIZE), (3) the average inflation rate during the decade (INF), and (4) the average growth rate of GDP during the decade (GRO). These variables are listed as "other variables" in the description of equation (1). Those other variables with a *t*-statistic between 1 and 2 are marked with an asterisk, while those with a *t*-statistic in excess of 2 are marked with two asterisks. Thus E, SIZE, and INF have *t*-statistics greater than 2, while GRO is not statistically significant. In this specification, the coefficient of FDI-out is −1.17 with a standard error of 0.47.

24. The coefficients of FDI-in change even more substantially and are now insignificant in every case, indicating that the inflow of FDI does not appear to alter the domestic investment rate. Presumably the capital inflow in the form of inbound FDI substitutes for inbound portfolio investment or induces other balancing transactions.

Equation (2) adds the average short-term interest rate (INT) and deletes the insignificant growth variable. This specification, which has the highest adjusted R^2 of all the variable combinations that I have examined, also suggests that the coefficient of FDI-out is approximately -1, i.e., that each dollar of FDI-out reduces GDI by about one dollar.

The next four equations in table 2.3 are for the individual decades. The absolute values of the coefficient of FDI-out are slightly smaller than 1 in each of these specifications. The large standard errors in these equations should be interpreted in the context of the smaller samples for individual decades (only 15 observations for the 1970s and 18 observations for the 1980s) which, together with the additional variables, leave as few as seven residual degrees of freedom. But taken together with the pooled data of equations (1) and (2) and the separate decade estimates for the simpler specifications in table 2.2, it seems most appropriate to conclude that each dollar of cross-border FDI-out reduces domestic investment by approximately one dollar.

The FDI variables reported in equations (1)–(6) of table 2.3 all measure FDI excluding retained earnings. Although eliminating the eight countries that do not provide information on retained earnings would leave too small a sample of observations for either decade alone, it is possible to use the pooled sample for 19 observations for the two decades. The results are shown in equations (7), (8), and (9). The first two of these repeat the two specifications of equations (1)–(6), while equation (9) is the specification with the highest adjusted R^2 when the FDI variables are defined to include retained earnings.

The coefficients are similar in all three specifications. The estimated effect of FDI-out is slightly larger in absolute size than in the pooled estimates of equations (1) and (2) but, given the small sample and large standard errors, is not significantly different from -1.0. The major difference from the other equations in table 2.3 is that the coefficient of the FDI-in variable rises to approximately 1.0 and becomes nearly twice its standard error. This implies that the retained earnings of foreign affiliates in a given host country, like other forms of domestic saving in that country, increase domestic investment in that host country.

More generally, the evidence in this section implies that outflows of FDI reduce domestic investment on a dollar-for-dollar basis and that this reduction is not offset by an international shift in portfolio investment. This is consistent with a view that the Feldstein-Horioka segmentation of capital markets applies to portfolio investment and that direct investment circumvents this barrier to capital mobility. Similarly, FDI induces U.S. firms to use much more foreign debt and equity finance in their majority-owned foreign affiliates than they would use for domestic investments. In that way, the financing of FDI also makes available the advantages of foreign portfolio financing in a way that would not occur without the direct investment.

2.5 Effect of Outbound FDI on Foreign Assets and the Domestic Capital Stock

By combining the parameter estimates of sections 2.3 and 2.4 with the evidence on the sources of capital of foreign affiliates of U.S. multinationals in section 2.2 it is possible to answer the fundamental question of how much the U.S. domestic capital stock declines per dollar of additional capital in the foreign affiliates of U.S. multinationals.

The answer to this question depends on how that foreign affiliate capital is financed. The parameter estimates of sections 2.3 and 2.4 imply that on average within the OECD each dollar of cross-border external finance reduces domestic investment by one dollar. The data analyzed in section 2.2 show that approximately 20 cents of each dollar of the existing U.S. foreign affiliate capital is financed by such a cross-border flow of capital from the United States. Of the remainder, 18 cents comes from the U.S. share of retained earnings of the foreign affiliate and 62 cents comes from foreign debt and equity sources.

Before considering the implication of this average financing mix, I will consider two simpler cases.

2.5.1 Pure Parent Finance

Consider first the simplest case in which the incremental foreign affiliate capital is financed exclusively by the U.S. parent with no foreign equity or debt. If the U.S. general equilibrium response to cross-border capital outflows is similar to the average OECD response, each dollar of parent-to-affiliate finance reduces the U.S. domestic capital stock by one dollar. In this extreme case, each dollar of increased capital in the foreign affiliate reduces the U.S. domestic capital stock by one dollar.

2.5.2 Leveraged Retained Earnings Finance

As a second and much more common case, consider the foreign affiliate that uses retained earnings to finance an incremental investment and that combines those foreign retained earnings with local debt. The sources of financing per unit of incremental capital in the subsidiary can be defined as:

$s =$ the retained earnings of the subsidiary attributable to the U.S. parent and other U.S. equity investors;

$s^* =$ the retained earnings of the subsidiary attributable to non-U.S. sources; and

$b^* =$ the debt supplied by non-U.S. creditors.

By assumption, in this case $s + s^* + b^* = 1$.

The alternative to investing the retained earnings of the subsidiary would be to distribute them as dividends to the U.S. and foreign equity owners. The econometric analysis of sections 2.3 and 2.4 was not able to measure the average OECD response to changes in retained earnings or dividend repatriations. The effect on domestic capital formation in the home country of the subsidiary's choice between retaining earnings and repatriating those earnings as dividends cannot be settled by a priori analysis either. Consider therefore the alternative possibilities. If a dollar of repatriated dividends would add one dollar to the U.S. gross domestic investment, an additional dollar of foreign affiliate capital financed with leveraged retained earnings reduces the U.S. capital stock by $s < 1$ dollars. To the extent that the repatriation of retained earnings displaces other financial capital inflows or increases financial capital outflows, the depressing effect on the U.S. capital stock would be smaller than s.

The analysis of section 2.1 shows that the retained earnings attributable to U.S. investors (corresponding to s in the current calculation) were $226 billion in 1989, that the retained earnings attributable to foreign investors was $102 billion, and that the debt from foreign sources was $567 billion. If the relative magnitudes of these three financing sources are used to approximate the financing of the leveraged retained earnings investment, we obtain $s = 226/895 = 0.25$. With these assumptions, an additional dollar of foreign affiliate capital financed with leveraged retained earnings reduces the U.S. capital stock by 25 cents. This is an upper limit of the plausible range because it is based on the assumption that any retained earnings that are not invested by the foreign subsidiary would otherwise add dollar for dollar to the U.S. capital stock.

2.5.3   Average Financing

The observed aggregate financing mix described in section 2.1 reflects both new equity and debt transfers from parents to affiliates and the subsequent reinvestment of retained earnings. Both types of investments are leveraged with foreign debt. While individual investments will use different financing mixes, the overall financing mix may remain relatively unchanged if the mix of new investment and reinvestment continues to be about the same.[25]

To analyze this overall average financing case, the three sources of financing identified in the "leveraged retained earnings case" must be expanded to include:

$e =$ the external equity capital provided by the U.S. parent and other U.S. investors;

$e^* =$ the external equity capital provided by non-U.S. sources; and

$b =$ the debt supplied by the U.S. parent and other U.S. creditors.

Now $e + e^* + b + b^* + s + s^* = 1$.

---

25. It would be desirable to compare the composition of financing of U.S. foreign affiliates in the 1989 benchmark survey with the financing composition in earlier studies.

The econometric results of section 2.3 and 2.4 imply that each dollar of cross-border equity and debt (*e* and *b* in the current notation) reduces domestic investment by one dollar. If we assume also that each dollar of foreign affiliate retained earnings that is not invested in the affiliate would otherwise be repatriated and would add dollar for dollar to domestic investment in the United States, an additional dollar of foreign affiliate capital financed with the observed average mix of financing sources would reduce the U.S. capital stock by $e + b + s < 1$ dollars. Once again this is an upper limit because the repatriation of subsidiary retained earnings may not increase domestic investment dollar for dollar.

The analysis of section 2.1 showed that, of the $1,237 billion of total assets, the external equity finance from U.S. sources was $203 billion, the debt from U.S. parents and other U.S. creditors was $47 billion, and the share of retained earnings attributable to U.S. parents and other investors was $226 billion. In this case, $e + b = 0.20$ and $e + b + s = 0.38$. If each dollar of retained earnings would otherwise be repatriated and add one dollar to domestic investment, each dollar of foreign affiliate investment financed by this average mix of sources reduces the U.S. capital stock by 0.38 dollars. At the other extreme, if the inflow of repatriated earnings would only displace some other portfolio inflow or induce a portfolio outflow, each dollar of foreign affiliate investment financed by this average mix of sources reduces the U.S. capital stock by only 0.20 dollars.

Although individual investments will use different financing mixes, this overall financing case is probably the best indication of how the financing of the foreign affiliate capital stock evolves. If so, it implies that each dollar of displaced domestic capital in the United States adds between $2.60 and $5.00 to the capital stock of U.S. foreign affiliates.

This relation between forgone domestic investment and the increase in the capital stock of U.S. foreign affiliates is important for assessing the impact of outbound FDI on the national income of the United States. The effect of outbound U.S. FDI on U.S. national income depends on the rate of return earned on such investments, the cost of the foreign capital, and the amount of taxes paid to the foreign government. Although U.S. firms that invest abroad presumably select the allocation of capital that maximizes the present value of the firms' after-tax profits, the existence of foreign taxes implies that their decisions will not in general maximize U.S. national income. The firm may be indifferent between paying taxes to the U.S. government and a foreign government, but only the former remains a part of U.S. national income. An evaluation of whether the outbound U.S. FDI increases or decreases U.S. national income requires balancing the tax losses to foreign governments against the advantage of the increased use of foreign-source capital that accompanies FDI. That analysis is the subject of a separate study (Feldstein 1994).

Appendix

Table 2A.1   **Decade Averages of Investment, Saving, and FDI Ratios: 1970–79**

			Ratios to GDP			
Country	GDI	GNS	Outbound FDI[a]	Inbound FDI[a]	Outbound RE	Inbound RE
Australia	0.250	0.238	0.001	0.007	0.001	0.006
Austria	0.286	0.278	0.001	0.005	n.a.	n.a.
Belgium/Luxembourg	0.227	0.232	0.007	0.015	n.a.	n.a.
Canada	0.240	0.224	0.008	0.007	n.a.	n.a.
Finland	0.285	0.265	0.002	0.002	n.a.	n.a.
France	0.255	0.259	0.003	0.004	0.000	0.000
Germany	0.234	0.244	0.005	0.003	0.001	0.001
Italy	0.258	0.260	0.002	0.003	n.a.	n.a.
Japan	0.345	0.353	0.003	0.000	n.a.	n.a.
Netherlands	0.234	0.246	0.018	0.010	0.006	0.002
New Zealand	0.260	0.217	0.001	0.008	0.001	0.008
Spain	0.266	0.251	0.001	0.006	n.a.	n.a
Sweden	0.216	0.209	0.006	0.001	0.000	0.000
United Kingdom	0.199	0.180	0.010	0.009	0.009	0.005
United States	0.194	0.197	0.003	0.001	0.005	0.001

Note: n.a. = not available.
[a]Excludes retained earnings (RE).

Table 2A.2   **Decade Averages of Investment, Saving, and FDI Ratios: 1980–90**

			Ratios to GDP			
Country	GDI	GNS	Outbound FDI[a]	Inbound FDI[a]	Outbound RE	Inbound RE
Australia	0.244	0.198	0.007	0.013	0.003	0.004
Austria	0.245	0.242	0.003	0.003	n.a.	n.a.
Belgium/Luxembourg	0.176	0.171	0.014	0.020	n.a.	n.a.
Canada	0.215	0.198	0.012	0.003	n.a.	n.a.
Denmark	0.181	0.152	0.006	0.003	n.a.	n.a.
Finland	0.258	0.237	0.012	0.002	0.000	0.001
France	0.209	0.204	0.010	0.006	0.000	0.000
Germany	0.206	0.227	0.009	0.003	0.001	0.000
Italy	0.225	0.216	0.004	0.003	n.a.	n.a.
Japan	0.300	0.321	0.007	0.000	n.a.	n.a.
Netherlands	0.197	0.225	0.027	0.013	0.009	0.005
New Zealand	0.242	0.182	0.005	0.010	0.005	0.006
Norway	0.259	0.267	0.011	0.006	n.a.	n.a.
Portugal	0.282	0.237	0.001	0.015	0.000	0.001
Spain	0.221	0.208	0.003	0.015	n.a.	n.a

(*continued*)

Table 2A.2   (continued)

			Ratios to GDP			
Country	GDI	GNS	Outbound FDI[a]	Inbound FDI[a]	Outbound RE	Inbound RE
Sweden	0.188	0.169	0.020	0.004	0.005	0.001
United Kingdom	0.176	0.166	0.015	0.012	0.012	0.006
United States	0.179	0.163	0.000	0.008	0.003	0.000

Note: n.a. = not available.

[a]Excludes retained earnings.

References

Baxter, Marianne, and Mario Crucini. 1993. Explaining saving-investment correlations. *American Economic Review* 83(3): 416–36.

Bergsten, C. Fred, Thomas Horst, and Theodore H. Moran. 1978. *American multinationals and American interests.* Washington, D.C.: Brookings Institution.

Blomström, Magnus, Robert E. Lipsey, and Ksenia Kulchycky. 1988. U.S. and Swedish direct investment and exports. In *Trade policy issues and empirical analysis,* ed. Robert E. Baldwin, 259–97. Chicago: University of Chicago Press.

Feldstein, Martin. 1983. Domestic saving and international capital movements in the long run and the short run. *European Economic Review* March–April: 129–51.

———. 1994. Taxes, leverage and the national return on foreign direct investment. NBER Working Paper no. 4689. Cambridge, MA: National Bureau of Economic Research, March.

Feldstein, Martin, and Phillipe Bacchetta. 1991. National saving and international investment. In *The economics of savings,* ed. John Shoven and Douglas Bernheim. Chicago: University of Chicago Press.

Feldstein, Martin, and Charles Horioka. 1980. Domestic savings and international capital flows: The 1970 W. A. Mackintosh Lecture at Queen's University. *Economic Journal* 90:314–29.

Frankel, Jeffrey. 1991. Quantifying international capital mobility in the 1980s. In *National saving and economic performance,* ed. D. Bernheim and J. Shoven. Chicago: University of Chicago Press.

Froot, Kenneth. 1993. *Foreign direct investment.* Chicago: University of Chicago Press.

Graham, Edward M., and Paul Krugman. 1991. *Foreign direct investment in the United States.* Washington, D.C.: Institute for International Economics.

Hufbauer, Gary C., and F. M. Adler. 1968. *Overseas manufacturing investment and the balance of payments.* Tax Policy Research Study no. 1. Washington, D.C.: Department of the Treasury.

Lipsey, Robert, and Merle Yahr Weiss. 1981. Foreign production and exports in manufacturing industries. *Review of Economics and Statistics* 63, no. 4 (November): 488–94.

———. 1984. Foreign production and exports of individual firms. *Review of Economics and Statistics* 66, no. 2 (May): 304–8.

Lowe, Jeffrey H., and Raymond J. Mataloni, Jr. 1991. U.S. direct investment abroad: 1989 benchmark survey results. *Survey of Current Business* 71(10): 29–55.

Mussa, Michael, and Morris Goldstein. 1993. The integration of world capital markets.

In *Changing capital markets: Implications for monetary policy,* 245–314. Kansas City: Kansas City Federal Reserve Bank.

Severn, Alan. 1972. Investment and financial behavior of American direct investors in manufacturing. In *The international mobility and movement of capital,* ed. Fritz Machlup, Walter Salant, and Loria Tarshis. New York: National Bureau of Economic Research.

Stevens, Guy. 1969. Fixed investment expenditures of foreign manufacturing affiliates of U.S. firms: Theoretical models and empirical evidence. *Yale Economic Essays* 9(1): 137–98.

Stevens, Guy, and Robert Lipsey. 1992. Interactions between domestic and foreign investment. *Journal of International Money and Finance* 11:40–62.

U.S. Department of Commerce. Bureau of Economic Analysis. 1991. U.S. direct investment abroad: 1989 Benchmark Survey results. *Survey of Current Business* 71(10): 29–55.

———. 1992. *Survey of Current Business.*

Comment   Kenneth A. Froot

Over a decade ago, Feldstein posed a substantial puzzle to international economists. In his paper with Charles Horioka (Feldstein and Horioka 1980), he argued that an increase in the national savings rate resulted in a one-for-one increase in investment. Notwithstanding economists' views about the ease with which capital flows across borders, savings and investment behave as though there is no international capital mobility. This conclusion has been subjected to much further research, but with little change—by the measure of net asset flows, international capital mobility seems surprisingly low.

In the paper in this volume, Feldstein applies this line of research to foreign direct investment (FDI). If the Feldstein-Horioka view of the world is correct, then there is little room for net international capital flows—current accounts are effectively fixed. Thus, an increase in FDI outflows from (in this case) the United States should result in an increase in capital inflows, and result in no overall effect on domestic investment. Furthermore, domestic investment is insensitive to FDI flows under complete international capital mobility. As long as domestic opportunities are not correlated with FDI, then FDI flows should have no influence on the current account or level of domestic investment.

In contrast to the predictions of these theories, Feldstein finds that each dollar of FDI outflow (holding fixed gross national savings) results in a one-dollar reduction in domestic investment. This is a striking finding, as it seems to contradict both the Feldstein-Horioka and perfect-capital-markets views of the world. A similar, although considerably weaker, result seems to hold for U.S. inflows of FDI.

Kenneth A. Froot is professor of business administration at Harvard Business School and a research associate of the National Bureau of Economic Research.

In this comment, I want to do two things. First, I will argue that some, although probably not all, of the effect in the paper may be due to measurement issues in the data. This implies that a truly exogenous one-dollar increase in FDI results in a less-than-one-dollar decrease in domestic investment, but a decrease nonetheless. Second, I want to try to interpret this result in terms of the literature that links investment to corporate cash flow.

To see the measurement error issue, it is important to note that many capital transactions between a foreign affiliate and its U.S. parent can affect both FDI and domestic savings. For example, when an affiliate has retained earnings, those earnings are counted as domestic saving and as FDI outflows. Similarly, if for tax reasons a firm wants to repatriate a dividend from its foreign affiliate in a specific year, yet does not want to reduce the affiliate's cash resources, it would be recorded as both an increase in domestic savings and an FDI outflow. One might guess that these transactions have little influence on domestic savings, yet they will tend to bias the regression coefficient on FDI outflows toward that of domestic savings.

To see this, let us partition observed domestic savings into a component unrelated to these intracorporate transactions and the transactions themselves:

(1) $$S_0 = S + \varepsilon,$$

where S_0 is observed gross national savings, ε is a measure of intracorporate transactions which is unrelated to domestic investment, and S is all other domestic savings. FDI outflows can be decomposed in the same way:

(2) $$\text{FDI}_0 = \text{FDI} + \varepsilon.$$

Next, suppose that the *true* Feldstein-Horioka relationship between savings and investment is given by

(3) $$I = \beta S + \mu,$$

where μ is a random error term. If we run the regression of investment on observed savings and FDI, we will find the coefficient on FDI_0 is biased toward $-\beta$, even if FDI flows have no effect on domestic investment. The larger the portion of FDI volatility contributed by ε, the closer to $-\beta$ will the estimated coefficient on FDI_0 be. A further implication of this setup is that when FDI_0 is omitted from the regression, the measurement error affects the estimated coefficient on S_0 more severely, causing it to be more severely biased below β.

The results in tables 2.2 and 2.3 provide some evidence to support this story. The coefficients on saving tend to be higher when FDI_0 is not included and lower when it is included. Furthermore, the coefficients on FDI_0 (for inflows as well as outflows) are larger (especially in table 2.3) when retained earnings are included in FDI flows. Since retained earnings are an important source of the ε-measurement error, this is what we would expect. This quick analysis suggests that it might be worth taking the time to clean the FDI data of intracorporate transactions. One could, for example, focus on FDI flows from mergers and acquisitions only to eliminate the potential for this type of bias.

Having said this, let us take seriously the hypothesis that FDI outflows do indeed negatively affect domestic investment. Thus, my second question becomes, How might we rationalize the Feldstein result? That is, why would FDI be expected to affect domestic investment, *given* domestic savings?

One explanation would rely on models of capital-market imperfections which arise from informational asymmetries or agency problems. Specifically, these models generate deadweight costs which make it more expensive for firms to tap external funds than to use internal funds. One prediction of these models is that investment spending by corporations is liquidity constrained, so that an increase in corporate liquidity—for example, corporate savings—results in an increase in investment even when holding investment opportunities fixed. This follows because the increase in internal funds lowers a firm's effective cost of capital, and therefore raises investment.[1]

In such a world, we might think of domestic saving as proxying for corporate and household liquidity. This would then help us understand the original Feldstein-Horioka results, which imply that increases in saving themselves generate increases in investment. Of course, to test this theory more precisely, one would want to include an additional variable in the original regression of investment on savings: a control for investment opportunities. For public corporations, such a control is available in the form of the companies' stock prices (relative to book values). However, for countries it is harder to think of an observable indicator of future investment opportunities.

In spite of the omission of a control for investment opportunities, this model can help us understand the results of Feldstein's paper as well. If the availability of internal funds to U.S. firms largely drives their total investment spending, then the sum of FDI outflows and domestic investment should be roughly constant. (This ignores the impacts on domestic investment of foreign firms' FDI inflows, but these can be thought of as exogenous and separate forces which are also driven by the availability of internal funds, i.e., foreign corporate savings.) This would imply that increases in FDI decrease one-for-one domestic investment.

Of course, this is an extreme version of the "cash-flow" hypothesis. In practice, companies do have access to external funds, even if they are somewhat more expensive. Thus, when an FDI opportunity comes along, it may not crowd out domestic investment one for one, because the firm borrows additional funds for the domestic investment from some combination of foreign and domestic households. Nevertheless, this suggests that a model of costly external funds can indeed generate results similar to those in the paper.

---

1. General references on this literature include Fazarri, Hubbard, and Petersen (1988), Froot and Stein (1991), and Hoshi, Kashyap, and Scharfstein (1991).

References

Fazzari, S., G. Hubbard, and B. Petersen. 1988. Financing constraints and corporate investments. *Brookings Papers on Economic Activity,* 141–206.

Feldstein, M., and C. Horioka. 1980. Domestic savings and international capital flows: The 1970 W. A. Mackintosh Lecture at Queen's University. *Economic Journal* 90:314–29.

Froot, K., and J. Stein. 1991. Exchange rates and foreign direct investment: An imperfect markets approach. *Quarterly Journal of Economics* 56:1191–1219.

Hoshi, T., A. Kashyap, and D. Scharfstein. 1991. Corporate structure, liquidity, and investment: Evidence from Japanese industrial groups. *Quarterly Journal of Economics* 56:33–60.

3   Why Is There Corporate Taxation in a Small Open Economy? The Role of Transfer Pricing and Income Shifting

Roger H. Gordon and Jeffrey K. MacKie-Mason

The role of the corporate income tax in distorting capital investment and savings decisions has been investigated at length in the academic literature.[1] While much progress has been made in understanding the behavioral implications of the tax, the recent literature has increasingly raised questions regarding why such taxes continue to exist. For example, Gordon (1986) and Razin and Sadka (1991) argued that a small open economy should not impose a source-based tax such as a corporate income tax on capital income. If capital is mobile and the country is a price-taker in the world capital market, capital cannot bear the incidence of the tax. Firms would continue to locate in the country only if other factor prices (primarily for land and labor) drop by enough to compensate firms for the higher amount they have to generate before tax so as to be able to provide capital owners the going rate of return after tax. But if these other factors bear the tax anyway, it would be better to tax them directly, thereby eliminating a distortion that discourages capital investment in the country.

While the theory forecasts that small open economies should not impose source-based taxes on capital income, in fact essentially all developed economies do impose corporate income taxes. Not only are corporate tax rates nonzero, but in recent years they tend to be roughly comparable with the top per-

Roger H. Gordon is professor of economics at the University of Michigan and a research associate of the National Bureau of Economic Research. Jeffrey K. MacKie-Mason is associate professor of economics and public policy at the University of Michigan and a research associate of the National Bureau of Economic Research.

The authors thank Scott Newlon for comments on an earlier draft and Yong Yang for most able research assistance. The views expressed in this paper are those of the authors and not necessarily those of the National Bureau of Economic Research. MacKie-Mason was a visitor at the Department of Economics, University of Oslo, while this paper was written. Financial support for this paper was in part provided through National Science Foundation grant SES 9122240.

1. See Auerbach (1983), e.g., for a recent survey of the effects of the tax on corporate investment.

sonal tax rate in each country. Are countries systematically using a tax that is dominated by other available instruments? Or has something important been omitted from the existing theories?[2]

The problem with the existing theories cannot be simply that they assume economies are small and open. If economies are large, then they certainly have an incentive to take advantage of their market power in world capital markets. Capital importers would want to reduce their capital imports to drive down the interest rate they pay on these imports, and so would want to tax domestic investment and encourage domestic savings. Conversely, capital exporters would want to reduce their capital exports by taxing domestic savings and subsidizing domestic investment. But we do not see opposite patterns of taxation in capital-importing and capital-exporting countries, nor do we see sign changes when countries change from exporting to importing capital (as the United States did in the 1980s).

What if countries are not that open? Feldstein and Horioka (1980) provided striking empirical evidence suggesting that capital is quite immobile internationally. If economies are relatively closed, it might appear that pressures due to capital mobility would be much abated, allowing capital income taxes to survive. But any conclusions here will depend critically on what factors limit capital mobility. Gordon and Bovenberg (1993) explore the policy implications of various possible explanations for the observed capital immobility and find little prospect for rationalizing existing corporate taxes through this route.

The puzzles are not confined to government behavior. Firm behavior is also puzzling. Existing theories forecast, for example, that multinationals based in high-tax-rate countries are at a distinct tax disadvantage when investing in low-tax-rate countries. As do all firms located there, they pay corporate income taxes to the local government. However, they pay additional taxes to their home government when profits are repatriated. This surtax should put the multinational at a tax disadvantage. Yet U.S. multinationals invest heavily even in the lowest-tax-rate countries; see, for example, Hines and Rice (1994).

Reported rates of return also contradict the theoretical predictions. Domestic surtaxes on foreign earnings are postponed until repatriation, so multinationals face lower effective tax rates in countries with lower statutory rates. This implies that the pretax competitive rate of return should be lower in low-tax countries. But Hines and Hubbard (1990) and Grubert and Mutti (1987) find that pretax profit rates are *higher* in low-tax countries.

Observed investment and profit rates in low-tax countries are almost certainly explained by the ease with which a multinational can shift its accounting profits from high-tax to low-tax jurisdictions. For example, a subsidiary in a high-tax country can charge artificially low prices for outputs and pay artifi-

---

2. A more extended discussion of alternative explanations for corporate taxation, and their limitations, can be found in Gordon (1992).

cially high prices for inputs that it exchanges with a subsidiary in a low-tax country. This lowers higher-taxed income and raises lower-taxed income, reducing the firm's global tax liabilities. Locating subsidiaries in tax havens facilitates this process, and it is not surprising that these subsidiaries as a result report a high pretax rate of return. Evidence confirming the prevalence of income shifting is provided by Harris et al. (1993). They find that firms with subsidiaries in low-tax countries pay lower U.S. taxes and firms with subsidiaries in high-tax countries pay higher U.S. taxes, suggesting income shifting from high- to low-tax locations.

Cross-border income shifting alone cannot explain the puzzling aspects of government behavior, however. If we take account of not only the mobility of real capital but also the mobility of accounting profits, the pressures to reduce corporate tax rates are only increased. The forecast is still that corporate tax rates should equal zero.

Transfer pricing is not, however, the only important type of income shifting that is likely to occur. Musgrave (1959), for example, argued that a primary role for the corporate income tax is to close off opportunities for individuals to shift labor income to an otherwise untaxed corporate tax base. Without a corporate tax, for example, owner/managers of closely held firms could incorporate, retain earnings rather than pay them out as wages, then sell some of their shares, making their earnings subject to capital gains tax rates rather than labor income tax rates. A corporate tax would offset this tax incentive and reduce the efficiency costs that such income shifting might induce.

In this paper, we model explicitly the effects of both forms of income shifting on behavior and on optimal tax policy. In section 3.1, we introduce only domestic income shifting (between personal and corporate income) and explore its effects on optimal tax design. We find that optimal source-based taxation on corporations is positive, with a tax rate equal to the labor income tax rate. The optimal tax is a pure profits or cash-flow tax.

In section 3.2, we add cross-border income shifting (transfer pricing) to the model. In response to transfer pricing, countries face incentives to tax elements of reported income that are most subject to transfer pricing at a reduced rate, or to make them only partially deductible. The optimal corporate tax rate is now somewhat less than the rate on labor, which is consistent with most tax systems in developed countries (at least for the top tax rates on labor, which presumably apply to those people best able to shift income to the corporate sector).

We explore a variety of other seemingly puzzling aspects of existing corporate tax codes in section 3.3. Why, for example, do many countries allow multinationals to receive credits rather than deductions for taxes they paid abroad? Why are they taxed only when profits are repatriated? Why do host countries tax the income of foreign subsidiaries? We argue that these aspects of the law also make sense if the primary pressure affecting the design of the law is the need to prevent income shifting.

3.1   Tax Policy with Domestic Income Shifting

We first explore two approaches to modeling tax policy in the face of domestic income shifting. In the first, the model we will ultimately use for the host countries, individuals can shift the form of payment of their labor income from cash wages to nonwage forms, taxed in practice at the corporate tax rate. For example, a closely held firm in which the shares are owned by the manager and employees can retain what would otherwise have been wage payments, generating capital gains for the shareholder/employees.[3] Eliminating wage deductions generates income subject to corporate taxes, while we assume for simplicity that the capital gains received by employees on their shares are free of personal taxes.[4] Such income shifting presumably imposes real costs on the firm, however, since these alternative forms of compensation affect employees' liquidity and risk bearing and may create complications due to asymmetric information about the value of these shares.

The second model, which we apply to home countries, assumes that only corporate entrepreneurs are in a position to shift their form of pay at a reasonable cost. When individuals make a career choice between becoming an entrepreneur or an employee, and between incorporating or not, they take into account that income earned as an employee (or noncorporate entrepreneur) would be taxed under the personal income tax, whereas income earned as a corporate entrepreneur could in practice be taxed under the corporate tax but exempt from personal taxes. The choices to become an entrepreneur and to incorporate both involve a variety of nontax considerations, however, that must be traded off with any tax factors.[5]

In each model, a corporate income tax can be used to reduce the tax incentives that would otherwise exist to shift one's form of pay or one's career path. This role for the corporate income tax was mentioned at least as far back as Musgrave (1959). To focus on this role for the corporate tax, we will not introduce capital into the model. Our objective is not to rationalize the existence of *capital* income taxes, but of *corporate* income taxes. While existing corporate taxes do distort capital investment decisions, much of the revenue seems to be collected from the taxation of pure profits, which we interpret to represent the return to entrepreneurial ideas and effort.[6] We are able to introduce a distor-

---

3. Alternatively, the firm can pay employees in the form of stock transfers or qualified stock options rather than wages, generating extra taxable income for the firm due to the lost wage deductions and normally generating only capital gains income for the employees.

4. In most countries, personal capital income in at least some forms is taxed more lightly than labor income. Examples include a zero tax on capital gains that are passed to heirs at death, a lower tax rate on dividends, and favorable treatment of pension savings.

5. See Gravelle and Kotlikoff (1989), MacKie-Mason and Gordon (1991), and Gordon and MacKie-Mason (1994) for more detailed analyses of the decision whether to incorporate.

6. Gordon and Slemrod (1988) and Shoven (1991) have calculated that although the U.S. corporate income tax generates substantial revenues, capital income taxes in the United States in total have generated *negative* revenues in recent years.

tionary tax that captures the essential features of a corporate income tax without modeling capital explicitly.

3.1.1 Optimal Tax Policy in Home Countries

Consider first a situation in which corporate entrepreneurs but not other individuals can shift their income from the personal to the corporate tax base. In particular, assume that the population consists of a composite individual. This individual spends some fraction $1 - h$ of his work effort as an employee, earning a wage w that is taxed at the personal tax rate t. The remaining work effort is spent running corporations. Here, the net return per unit of effort before tax equals π; this income is taxable at rate τ leaving $\pi_n \equiv (1 - \tau)\pi$ net of tax.[7] Setting up a new corporation requires an outlay of resources, however, and we assume that there are diminishing returns to these expenditures. These start-up costs are assumed to be deductible against the profits tax. On net, we therefore describe the individual's net wage rate, w_n, by

$$w_n = (1 - h)w(1 - t) + h(1 - \tau)\pi - (1 - \tau)c(h),$$

where $c(h)$ measures the cost of setting up a new corporation of sufficient size to absorb the fraction h of one's work time. The individual's resulting utility can be expressed by the indirect utility function $V(w_n)$.

Individuals decide how much to work, and how to split this time between being an employee versus being an entrepreneur. The first-order condition for h simply implies that $w(1- t) = (1 - \tau)(\pi - c')$, so that the net returns from the two career paths are equalized at the margin, after taking into account the costs of becoming an entrepreneur.

Consider the optimal tax policy in this country. The government's objective is to choose the tax rates t and τ so as to maximize the objective

$$W = V(w_n) + \lambda L[(1 - h)tw + h\tau\pi - \tau c(h)],$$

where L represents total hours of work and where λ measures the marginal utility received from extra government expenditures. Consider the effect of increasing τ and cutting t simultaneously so as to leave w_n unaffected. To keep w_n unaffected, we need that $\partial t/\partial \tau = -[h\pi - c(h)]/[(1 - h)w]$. With w_n fixed, L also remains unchanged. Since $\partial W/\partial t = \partial W/\partial \tau = 0$ under the optimal policies, this combined tax change should leave welfare unaffected at the margin. The resulting first-order condition for this proposed tax change, after some simplification, equals

$$\text{(1)} \qquad \frac{\partial W}{\partial h}\left(\frac{\partial h}{\partial \tau} + \frac{\partial h}{\partial t}\frac{\partial t}{\partial \tau}\right) = 0.$$

---

7. In general, τ includes both corporate and personal taxes due on corporate income. For simplicity of discussion, we will refer to τ as the corporate tax rate, as if no personal taxes are due on this income, whether it is paid out as dividends or realized as capital gains. Since the entrepreneur

Raising corporate taxes (τ) and lowering labor taxes *(t)* leads to an unambiguous decrease in *h*, lowering the time spent as an entrepreneur and increasing time spent as an employee. Therefore, this first-order condition implies that $\partial W/\partial h = 0$, implying that $\tau(\pi - c') = tw$ under the optimal tax policy—the same taxes are paid regardless of career choice, so as not to distort the individual's choice of *h*. Substituting for $\pi - c'$ from the individual's first-order condition, we find that $\tau = t$ under the optimal policy.

In addition, we can show that the government would not want to introduce a distorting tax on corporate activity. Consider, for example, some distorting tax σ on the firm, leaving it with net profits $(1 - \tau)[\pi - S(\sigma,X)]$, where *X* represents the real decisions made by the firm which are distorted by σ. The government's policy objective would now equal

$$W = V(w_n) + \lambda L\{(1 - h)tw + h[\tau\pi + (1 - \tau)S] - \tau c(h)\}.$$

In order to show that the optimal value of σ is zero, consider the effects of raising σ and simultaneously lowering τ so as to leave w_n and thus *L* unchanged. This requires that $\partial\tau/\partial\sigma = -\{(1 - \tau)h/[h(\pi - S) - c]\}\partial S/\partial\sigma$. The resulting first-order condition for *W* is[8]

$$(2) \qquad \frac{\partial W}{\partial h}\left(\frac{\partial h}{\partial\sigma} + \frac{\partial h}{\partial\tau}\frac{\partial\tau}{\partial\sigma}\right) + \lambda Lh\left[\tau\frac{\partial\pi}{\partial X} + (1 - \tau)\frac{\partial S}{\partial X}\right]\frac{\partial X}{\partial\sigma}.$$

By equation (1), $\partial W/\partial h = 0$ under the optimal tax policy, so that the first term in equation (2) is zero. Since the firm's first-order condition for *X* implies that $\partial\pi/\partial X = \partial S/\partial X$, equation (2) implies that $\partial S/\partial X = 0$ under the optimal policy. Since, by assumption, σ distorts the firm's choice of *X*, $\partial S/\partial X$ can equal zero only when $\sigma = 0$. The optimal tax policy therefore consists of a wage tax plus a nondistortionary cash-flow corporate tax at equal rates.

3.1.2   Optimal Tax Policy in Host Countries

Consider next a slightly different model, in which all employees are in a position to shift the tax treatment of their labor income. In particular, assume that there is only one source of employment, working to produce some good *X*. This good is produced using a constant returns technology subject to free entry, so that there are no pure profits in equilibrium. Normally, we would assume that all earnings are paid out as wages, taxed at the personal rate t^*. Now add the complication that if the tax rate on a firm's income, denoted by τ^*, is lower than that on labor income, then the firm can pay individuals in a form that is taxed at the firm's rate rather than at the individual's rate. This income shifting is not costless, however. If the individual receives the fraction

---

has the option to pay all income out as wages, the maximum effective tax rate on corporate income is *t*.

8. Since a pure profits tax rate is nondistorting, changing τ cannot change the firm's choice of *X*.

s of her labor income $w*$ in a form taxable at the firm's tax rate, we assume that the labor costs to the firm equal $w*[1 + b(s)]$. Here, $b(s)$ represents the real costs of shifting the tax treatment of labor income, where by assumption $b(s)$ is convex, $b' > 0$, and $b(0) = 0$. In equilibrium, firms continue to break even, so that $p = w*(1 + b)$.

The net wage rate, w_n^*, of the representative individual therefore equals

$$w_n^* = w*[(1 - s)(1 - t*) + s(1 - \tau*)].$$

The individual chooses s so as to maximize her after-tax wage, holding fixed the wage costs of the firms, giving as a first-order condition for s

(3)
$$\frac{b'}{1+b} = \frac{t* - \tau*}{(1 - t*) + s(t* - \tau*)}$$

It is straightforward to show that s is increasing in $t* - \tau*$. This individual's utility equals $V*(w_n^*)$. Denote the individual's labor supply by $L*$.

Consider next the optimal policy of a host-country government. The objective function of this government is

$$W* = V*(w_n^*) + \lambda*L*\{\tau*p - \tau*w*[1 + b(s)] + t*w*(1 - s) + \tau* sw*\},$$

where again $\lambda*$ represents the marginal utility received from extra government expenditures. What happened if the government raises $\tau*$ and simultaneously lowers $t*$ by an amount chosen so as to leave w_n^* and therefore $L*$ unchanged? Note that, given the lack of pure profits, changes in $\tau*$ leave firms unaffected as well. However, these changes make income shifting less attractive, so s falls, causing $w*$ to rise. The resulting change in social welfare equals

$$\left[\frac{\tau* - t*}{(1 - t*) + s(t* - \tau*)}\right]\left(\frac{\partial s}{\partial \tau*} + \frac{\partial t*}{\partial \tau*}\frac{\partial s}{\partial t*}\right) = 0.$$

Given that this policy change leads to a drop in income shifting, the term in brackets should equal zero, implying that $\tau* = t*$. Again, the optimal tax system consists of a wage tax plus a cash-flow corporate tax at equal rates.

An alternative to this wage tax, combined with a cash-flow tax on firms to prevent income shifting, would have been simply to tax output of firms at some rate $\sigma*$. Given our assumptions, raising $\sigma*$ is equivalent to raising $\tau*$ and $t*$ simultaneously—both simply tax labor income and distort only the labor supply decision. This is simply the equivalence of a uniform value-added tax and a labor income tax.

3.2 Tax Policy with Cross-Border Income Shifting

With domestic income shifting alone, we find that countries face an incentive to supplement a labor income tax with a cash-flow tax on corporate income at the same rate. How does this optimal tax structure change if we now take into account that each economy is open, that multinationals can set up subsidiaries abroad, and that transfer pricing allows these firms to shift accounting income easily between the parent firm and the subsidiary? Many types of situations could be examined. We focus on the effects of possible transfer pricing between the parent firm and its subsidiaries and ignore other forms of mobility across borders.

To capture these ideas formally, we develop a model with two types of countries, home countries and host countries. We allow for multiple countries of each type and assume that each is a price-taker in international markets. We will examine policies for some representative home country j or representative host country i.

Multinationals are based in countries of type j and use an imported good X to produce a good Q. If the representative individual in a country j allocates time h to producing Q, we assume that the resulting output equals $hf(X) - c(h)$, produced using inputs hX, where $f(0) = 0, f' > 0$, and $f'' < 0$.[9] The firm takes as given the price for Q in the output market, and this price is the numeraire. The input X can be purchased on the international market at price p, or alternatively the firm can acquire a subsidiary in some country i, produce X there, then sell this good to the parent firm for some accounting price p^*. We assume that the same accounting price, p^*, must be used for tax purposes in the host country.

In any country i, X can be produced by either domestic firms or foreign subsidiaries. Labor is the only input used to produce X, and the production function is simply $X = L^*$. For simplicity, we assume that multinationals have no technological advantage in producing X—the only reason for a multinational to open up a foreign subsidiary is to take advantage of transfer pricing. The going net-of-tax wage rate is w_n^*. As described above, the firm can either pay workers cash wages or, at a cost, pay them in a form taxed at the corporate rate rather than the personal rate. If the fraction s of labor income is paid in a form taxed at the corporate rate, then the pretax wage rate faced by the firm equals $w^*[1 + b(s)]$, where w^* adjusts so as to leave workers with the going net-of-tax wage, w_n^*.

Each country is assumed to tax pure profits, with a rate τ in country j and a rate τ^* in country i. In addition, we assume that country j (country i) imposes a surtax on sales revenue at rate σ (σ^*). Surtax payments are assumed to be deductible under the pure profits part of the tax. For example, a firm in country i buying inputs on the open market would pay in taxes $[\tau(1 - \sigma) + \sigma]f(X) - \tau pX$.[10,11]

9. The rest of his time is still spent as an employee earning a wage w taxable at rate t.

10. We capture the difference in existing corporate taxes from a pure profits tax by this surtax on output. For example, if X represents capital equipment, then this rate difference can capture the fact that revenues are taxable immediately whereas the amount spent buying capital is deductible

For convenience of notation, we let $T = \tau(1 - \sigma) + \sigma$ represent the effective tax rate on gross sales revenue for operations in country j, so that a firm in country j pays $Tf(X) - \tau p X$ in taxes. We define T^* analogously.

Consider the incentive faced by firms in country j to acquire subsidiaries in country i. If a multinational acquires a subsidiary in country i, it must pay taxes to the host country on its operations there, and it may also owe some surtax to home country j on the income generated in i.[12] Denote the resulting effective gross tax rate on subsidiary revenues by T_r. Due to the home-country surtax, $T_r \geq T^*$, but because the tax is deferred until the income is repatriated, $T_r \leq T$.[13] Similarly, denote the effective tax rate on subsidiary wage deductions by τ_r, where $\tau^* \leq \tau_r \leq \tau$. Given T_r and τ_r, we define σ_r implicitly by the relation $(1 - \tau_r)(1 - \sigma_r) = (1 - T_r)$. In order to parameterize the degree to which surtaxes are due on foreign-source income, we assume that $T_r = \rho T + (1 - \rho)T^*$ and that $\tau_r = \rho\tau + (1 - \rho)\tau^*$ for some ρ, where $0 \leq \rho \leq 1$.[14]

We focus on tax systems that give multinationals an incentive to shift profits out of the home country. With a subsidiary that provides an input, profits can be shifted by paying a higher price for the input. The increased factor cost in the home country is deducted at the rate τ, while the increased revenue for the subsidiary is taxed at an effective rate of T_r. Therefore, to make transfer pricing attractive, we assume for purposes of discussion that $\tau > T_r$.

If the firm can set its own factor transfer price by choosing some arbitrary accounting price p^* for the input X, and if $\tau > T_r$, then we would forecast without other additions to the model that *all* taxable profits would be shifted to the subsidiary. That rarely seems to be the case.[15] To rationalize this, we assume that the tax authorities expend resources trying to prevent use of transfer pricing, and that the threat of being caught and fined limits a firm's use of transfer pricing.[16]

---

only gradually over time. If instead X represents materials, then inventory accounting rules can also lead to a postponed deduction.

11. In country j, the entrepreneur's start-up costs are also deductible at the corporate tax rate, so total corporate taxes are reduced by $\tau c(h)$. However, this deduction affects only the individual's time allocation, not the firm's optimal choices of p^* and X, and so we suppress this tax term when studying firm behavior.

12. Many countries, including the United States, tax foreign-source income when it is repatriated, with a credit given for foreign taxes paid on this income. Firms may or may not have sufficient foreign tax credits to eliminate all home-country tax on the subsidiary's income.

13. Deferral is a gain only to the extent to which funds kept abroad can be invested there earning a higher after-local-tax rate of return than the individual's after-home-tax discount rate. If there were no taxation of capital income and full capital mobility, then $T_r = T$ in spite of deferral.

14. If the firm repatriates profits every year and does not have excess credits, then $\rho = 1$; if the firm systematically has excess credits, then $\rho = 0$. In general, the value of ρ depends on the length of time repatriation is deferred, the gain from deferral given the rate of return abroad relative to the discount rate, and the likelihood that the firm has excess credits. It is worth noting that σ_r, which is defined implicitly by $(1 - \sigma_r) = (1 - T_r)/(1 - \tau_r)$, does *not* satisfy $\sigma_r = \rho\sigma + (1 - \rho)\sigma^*$.

15. U.S. firms taking advantage of the "possessions tax credit" by manufacturing in Puerto Rico apparently come close to total income shifting; see Grubert and Slemrod (1993).

16. In an earlier version of this paper we also constructed a model in which the accounting

In particular, in order to limit use of transfer pricing, the government is assumed to expend resources trying to detect use of transfer pricing. Due to these enforcement efforts, the government would have some probability θ of documenting the use of transfer prices, where θ should be an increasing function of p^*. If the firm is caught using transfer prices, it would need to pay in additional taxes an amount $\tau(p^* - p)FX$ on domestic earnings, where F reflects any fines that are imposed (and perhaps any systematic deviation of the corrected price from p). If the corrected price is then used in assessing the tax at repatriation on foreign-source income, then the firm also receives back an amount $\rho T(p^* - p)FX$ on the taxes paid on repatriated foreign earnings if caught using transfer pricing,[17] implying an expected net penalty of $(\tau - \rho T)(p^* - p)FX\theta$. We explore the concrete example where $\theta = a[(p^* - p)/p]^\beta$, with $\beta > 0$, and for simplicity assume risk neutrality.

3.2.1   Behavior of Multinationals with Cross-Border Shifting

For any given h, a multinational chooses X and p^* to maximize its net profits of

$$(4) \quad \pi_n = (1 - T)f(X) - (1-\tau)p^*X + (1 - T_r)p^*X - (1 - \tau_r)w^*(1 + b)X \\ - (\tau - \rho T)(p^* - p)FX\theta.$$

Given this objective function, the first-order condition for p^* can easily be solved to show that

$$p^* = p\left\{1 + \left[\frac{\tau - T_r}{(\beta + 1)aF(\tau - \rho T)}\right]^{1/\beta}\right\}.$$

The optimal value of p^* is decreasing in the severity of enforcement, as measured here by aF.[18] In addition, p^* is increasing in τ, but decreasing in T^* and T. Increasing τ raises the value of deducting a high input cost, p^*. Increasing T^* or T (and thus T_r) reduces the value of reporting a high foreign unit revenue, p^*. Also, $p^* > p$ as long as $\tau > T_r$.

It will prove convenient to note that at this optimal value of p^*, the value of $F\theta$ equals[19]

---

price, p^*, is used by the parent firm's manager in deciding how much X to purchase, creating an inefficiency since the transfer price is artificially high. Such inefficiencies might arise within a firm due to principal agent problems, or due to the high transactions costs of keeping one set of books for tax reporting and another set for management operations. (Transfer price accounting is at a much finer level of detail and complexity than the separate tax and financial reporting income statements and balance sheets that firms in many countries are required to maintain.) The results of this model were qualitatively similar to the results we present, so we do not report the details here.

17. We assume here that the fine is assessed on the net change in overall tax liability, and that foreign tax payments are unaffected by these recalculations of domestic tax liabilities.

18. In general, the direction of effect of β on p^* is ambiguous.

19. Note that the equilibrium probability of being caught is independent of a and a decreasing function of β.

$$F\theta = \frac{\tau - T_r}{(\beta + 1)(\tau - \rho T)}.$$

If we substitute this expression for $F\theta$ into the profit measure, we find that net profits equal[20]

$$\pi_n = (1 - T)f(X) - (1 - \tau)pX + \frac{\beta}{\beta + 1}(\tau - T_r)(p^* - p)X$$
$$- \rho(1 - \tau_r)(\sigma - \sigma^*)pX.$$

Here, the first two terms measure what profits would have been, had the firm simply purchased X on the open market. The third term measures the net gain from use of transfer pricing, after taking into account the effects of tax enforcement—tax enforcement not only lowers p^* but also recaptures the fraction $1/(1 + \beta)$ of the tax savings from transfer pricing. This term in itself raises profits. The last term reflects the fact that, without use of transfer pricing, the subsidiary operates at a competitive disadvantage because of the surtaxes due when profits are repatriated.

The first-order condition for X can be written, after substituting for the value of $F\theta$, as

(5) $$(1 - T)f' = (1 - \tau)p - \frac{\beta}{\beta+1}(\tau - T_r)(p^* - p)$$
$$+ \rho(1 - \tau_r)(\sigma - \sigma^*)p.$$

Here, the left-hand side equals the value of the extra output whereas the right-hand side equals the net-of-tax cost of the extra input. Only the first term on the right-hand side appears if the firm does not set up a subsidiary. Since the second term on the right-hand side is negative whereas the third term is positive, it would appear that the change in X due to the use of transfer pricing is ambiguous. However, we show next that X must increase whenever the subsidiary is worth acquiring.

When is the subsidiary worth acquiring? The answer depends on the extent of enforcement in the home country. Comparing profits with and without the subsidiary, and simplifying using a second-order approximation to output around the output level without the subsidiary, the change in profits from opening the subsidiary equals

(6) $$\Delta\pi_n \approx 0.5(1 - T)f''(X_s - X)^2 + X_s\left[\frac{\beta}{\beta+1}(\tau - T_r)(p^* - p)\right.$$
$$\left. - \rho(1 - \tau_r)(\sigma - \sigma^*)p\right],$$

where X_s is the chosen output level with the subsidiary and X is the chosen output level without it. For the subsidiary to be worth opening, the sum of the

20. In simplifying this expression, we have assumed that competitive firms survive in the host country, so that $(1 - \sigma^*)p = w^*(1 + b)$.

terms inside the brackets must be positive, since the first term is necessarily negative. Equation (5) then implies that $X_s > X$. Therefore, a necessary but not sufficient condition for the subsidiary to be worth opening is that desired output increase with the subsidiary. As tax enforcement (measured by aF) increases, the first term inside the brackets becomes smaller, due to the fall in p^*, and is eventually dominated by the second term.[21] Therefore, subsidiaries and transfer pricing would no longer be attractive if there is sufficient tax enforcement. Similarly, as ρ rises, increasing the importance of the surtax at repatriation, then T_r increases and p^* falls. Both these changes cause the first term inside the brackets to fall. In addition, the rise in ρ causes the second term to become more negative, again making the subsidiary less attractive.

If X is produced in various countries, each with its own tax structure, where will the multinational prefer to invest? Assume that w^* has been set so that competitive firms break even in all countries where X is produced, implying that $p(1 - \sigma^*) = w^*(1 + b)$. To judge the locational preferences of a multinational we examine how the firm's aggregate profits, as measured in equation (4), change as we vary the tax rates faced in country i. The derivative of the firm's profits with respect to τ^*, taking into account the forecast that wages will not vary, equals $-(1 - \rho)X[(1 - \sigma^*)p^* - w^*(1 + b)]$. Since this expression equals zero when $p^* = p$, it is necessarily negative given that $p^* > p$, yielding the expected conclusion that multinationals prefer to invest in countries with lower τ^*.[22] Put differently, they would be willing to pay somewhat higher wage rates in countries with lower τ^*, potentially leading to production where real resource costs are not minimized.

Similarly, if we differentiate equation (4) with respect to σ^*, taking into account the forecasted change in w^*, we get

$$(7) \qquad \frac{\partial \pi_n}{\partial \sigma^*} = X[(1 - \tau_r)p - (1 - \rho)(1 - \tau^*)p^*].$$

The first term on the right-hand side reflects the fact that countries with a higher σ^* have lower wage rates, making them more attractive locations, everything else equal. However, the higher σ^* also means higher local tax payments, which are only partly offset by the credit received against home-country taxes when profits are repatriated. If repatriation of profits can be deferred for a long time, so that $\rho \approx 0$, then the second term dominates and the firm would prefer to invest in countries with a low value of σ^*. But this is not generally true.

3.2.2   Optimal Tax Policy in the Host Country

Consider next the optimal tax policy in the host country, now allowing for the possible setup of subsidiaries and the resulting use of transfer pricing. The objective of the government now equals

---

21. In general, however, increasing β has ambiguous effects on the net gain from transfer pricing.

22. As expected, introducing transfer pricing enables us to rationalize the substantial activity by multinationals in tax havens.

$$W^* = V(w_n^*) + \lambda^* L^* \{ T^* p^* - \tau^* w^* [1 + b(s)] + t^* w^* (1 - s) + \tau^* sw^* \}.$$

In analyzing this case, we assume that multinationals own all production facilities, and that the wage is set so that they are indifferent to locating in this country rather than in some other country. If the country is small, then at the margin the domestic wage must adjust in response to any given tax change so as to leave net profits of multinationals unaffected. (If the wage falls far enough, domestic ownership will replace foreign ownership.)

Consider then what happens if the government raises σ^* while simultaneously lowering τ^* so as to leave profits of multinationals unaffected at the existing wage rate. Under these simultaneous tax changes, T^* falls to compensate for the fall in the rate that applies to tax deductions, leading to a rise in p^*. In addition, assume that the government simultaneously raises t^* to compensate for the fall in τ^* so as to leave w_n^* and therefore L^* unaffected. These tax changes cause s to rise, leading to a compensating fall in w^* so as to leave $w^*(1 + b)$ unchanged. The resulting change in social welfare must equal zero, implying that

$$(8) \quad T^* \left(\frac{\partial p^*}{\partial \sigma^*} + \frac{\partial p^*}{\partial \tau^*} \frac{\partial \tau^*}{\partial \sigma^*} \right) = \frac{w^*(t^* - \tau^*)}{(1 - t^*) + s(t^* - \tau^*)} \left(\frac{\partial s}{\partial t^*} \frac{\partial t^*}{\partial \sigma^*} + \frac{\partial s}{\partial \tau^*} \frac{\partial \tau^*}{\partial \sigma^*} \right).$$

We conclude from equation (8) that $\text{sign}(T^*) = \text{sign}(t^* - \tau^*)$. Given the need for government revenue, the sign of each must be positive, implying that $T^* > 0$ and $t^* > \tau^*$. Not only is there a positive corporate tax, but in general this tax will be distorting—there is nothing in equation (8) causing T^* to equal τ^*.

Simply taxing labor income directly leads to efficiency losses due to income shifting, whereas the alternative of taxing output creates an efficiency loss by making the country a less attractive location for multinationals. These two sources of efficiency loss are traded off under the optimal tax system.

Note that if domestic income shifting is not a problem, so that s is not responsive to tax policy, then the right-hand side of equation (8) equals zero. We then infer that $T^* = 0$ under the optimal policy, making the country a very attractive location for multinationals, in effect a tax haven. Given the lack of domestic income shifting, taxes are simply collected on labor income. If all labor income is paid out as wages, this can be done either through a personal tax on labor income, a payroll tax at the firm level, or a refundable value-added tax (VAT).[23]

If, instead, domestic income shifting is responsive enough to tax policy, so that the optimal value of T^* is high, then multinationals would be outbid for workers by domestic firms. But with only domestic operations surviving, output prices would no longer be responsive to tax policy, implying as in the origi-

---

23. Note that if the VAT is not refundable, and adjustment occurs instead through changes in the exchange rate, then the tax still distorts the transfer pricing decisions of foreign subsidiaries.

nal model that the tax system simply consists of a tax on labor income, taking the form either of a personal wage tax supplemented by a cash-flow corporate tax at an equal rate, or instead a VAT.

In general, there are two local optima for tax policy. One has a low T^* satisfying equation (8), leading foreign multinationals to set up local subsidiaries. The second has a high T^*, no activity by multinationals, but no domestic income shifting. Which local optima dominates would depend on the country's circumstances. In choosing between the two local optima, a country would make a conscious decision whether to be a tax haven and thereby attract foreign multinationals at the expense of undermining its domestic tax system.

One other result worth noting is that the host country does not attempt to take advantage of the credits offered to multinationals when they repatriate profits—as seen in equation (8), the size of any credit, which is captured by ρ, does not affect the host country's optimal tax policy. This result holds as long as $\rho < 1$ and stands in contrast to the results in Gordon (1992), derived assuming $\rho = 1$. Even though the net cost of a host-country tax may be small to a multinational, competition among host countries drives this tax to zero.

3.2.3 Optimal Tax Policy in the Home Country

What can be said about optimal tax policy in the home country, once we take into account the ability of multinationals to shift their profits abroad? The government's objective function now becomes

$$(9) W = V(w_n) + \lambda L\{(1 - h)tw - e(a) - \tau c(h) + h[Tf(X) - \tau p^* X \\ + \rho(T - T^*)p^*X - \rho(\tau - \tau^*)w^*(1 + b)X + (\tau - \rho T)(p^* - p)XF\theta]\}.$$

Here, $e(a)$ measures the real costs of monitoring the use of transfer pricing at an intensity level a.

We first consider the optimal revenue surtax, σ. We showed above that with no cross-border shifting $\sigma = 0$, and the optimal corporate tax was a nondistortionary cash-flow tax. That result no longer holds when firms can use transfer pricing to shift income across borders.

In the appendix we show that $\partial W/\partial X > 0$ when tax rates are optimized. To use this result, first differentiate W with respect to X to find that

$$(10) \qquad Tf' - \tau p^* + \rho(T - T^*)p^* - \rho(\tau - \tau^*)w^* (1 + b) \\ + (\tau - \rho T)(p^* - p)F\theta > 0.$$

We can rewrite equation (5), the first-order condition for X, as

$$(11) \qquad (1 - T)f' - (1 - \tau)p + (\tau - T^*)(p^* - p) - \rho(T - T^*)p^* \\ + \rho(\tau - \tau^*)w^* - (\tau - \rho T)(p^* - p)F\theta = 0.$$

Since we have shown that $(1-T)f' < (1-\tau)p$ (i.e., X is greater with a subsidiary than without), the sum of the last four terms of equation (11) must be positive when opening a subsidiary is profitable. Multiplying equation (11) by $\tau/(1-\tau)$ and subtracting from equation (10) yields

(12) $\sigma f' - T^* (p^* - p) - \dfrac{1}{1-\tau}[(\tau - T^*)(p^* - p) - \rho(T - T^*)p^*$

$+ \rho(\tau - \tau^*)w^* - (\tau - \rho T)(p^* - p) F\theta] > 0.$

We showed in equation (11) that the sum of the terms in the brackets is positive. Therefore, $\sigma > 0$ under the optimal policy, which means that a distortionary corporate tax is used. Taxing entrepreneurs using τ is now more costly because it induces transfer pricing. As a result, entrepreneurs are taxed instead, at least in part, by a distorting tax, σ, on gross revenue. This tax also prevents an excessive shift into entrepreneurial activity and *lessens* the firm's use of transfer pricing, but at the cost of distorting the firm's internal decisions.

We now characterize the relationship between the optimal t, τ, and T. To do so, we make use of another result proved in the appendix: that $\partial W / \partial h < 0$ (holding w_n constant) when policies are at their optimal values. Since, by utility maximization, $\partial w_n / \partial h = 0$, this result implies that, at the optimal policy, tax revenue—the other component of social welfare—falls at the margin as h increases. As a result, the labor income tax must exceed the effective tax rate on time spent as an entrepreneur, another distortion not present without transfer pricing. The opportunity for transfer pricing makes it more difficult to tax entrepreneurial activity. Under optimal policy, there is a tradeoff between cutting the distortion favoring entrepreneurial activity and increasing the distortion encouraging transfer pricing.

To show this more formally, take the derivative of W with respect to h, holding w_n constant, to get

(13) $Tf - X[\tau p^* - \rho(T - T^*)p^* + \rho(\tau - \tau^*)w^* (1+b) -$
$(\tau - \rho T)(p^* - p)F\theta] - tw - \tau c' < 0.$

Multiplying equation (10), $\partial W / \partial X$, by X and subtracting from equation (13) yields

(14) $T(f - Xf') - tw - \tau c' < 0.$

Multiply the individual's first-order condition for h by $\tau/(1-\tau)$ and subtract to find that

(15) $T(f - f'X) - \dfrac{(t - \tau)}{1 - \tau}w - \dfrac{\tau}{1 - \tau}\pi_n < 0.$

Now multiply the firm's first-order condition for X by X and rearrange to find

(16) $\dfrac{\pi_n}{1 - \tau} = (1 - \sigma)(f - f'X).$

Substituting and rearranging terms yields

(17) $\sigma(f - f'X) - \dfrac{(t - \tau)}{1 - \tau}w < 0.$

Since the concavity of $f(X)$ ensures that the first term is positive, we learn that $t > \tau$ under the optimal policy.

Finally, we can also show that $T < t$ under the optimal policy. To see this, first combine the first-order conditions for X and for h to get $(1 - T)(f-Xf')$ $-(1-\tau)c'=w(1-t)$. Similarly, combine the inequalities characterizing $\partial W/\partial h$ and $\partial W/\partial X$ to get $T(f-Xf')-\tau c' < tw$. If we multiply the first equation by t and the second equation by $1-t$, then substract the first equation from the second, we find that

$$(18) \qquad (t - T)(f - Xf') > (t - \tau)c'.$$

Since $\tau < t$, we therefore learn in addition that $T < t$. Since $\sigma > 0$, we find that $t > T > \tau$ under the optimal policies. In contrast, without transfer pricing, $t = T = \tau$ under the optimal policies.

3.2.4   Discussion

To some degree U.S. tax policy appears to have responded to these pressures. Except for the period 1986–93, corporate tax rates have been below the top personal tax rate, the rate probably most applicable when considering the behavior of potential entrepreneurs. In addition, the United States has introduced some special provisions to lower the incentives to make use of transfer pricing. For example, in 1986 the United States introduced new rules for allocating interest expenses among the various countries in which a multinational operates. Previously a firm could shift income by locating its interest expense where it was most advantageous. The new rules require U.S. multinationals to allocate a fixed fraction of the parent's interest expense to foreign-source income,[24] reducing the deductibility of the parent's interest payments and thereby reducing the incentive for intracorporate borrowing.[25] A similar allocation procedure is used for R&D expenses.

A change in enforcement policy now under discussion is to judge the plausibility of a multinational's domestic profits as a whole, rather than the plausibility of each of the prices used in calculating profits. This would be done presumably by comparing a ratio of the firm's profits to sales or capital, to an equivalent ratio for purely domestic firms operating in the same industry. In the limit, the firm would simply be assigned profits for tax purposes equal to the profits-to-sales ratio observed for domestic firms times the subsidiary's reported sales. As a result, the tax becomes a tax on sales rather than a tax on income, with the rate varying by industry. Transfer pricing would no longer affect a firm's tax liabilities, except to the degree to which it affected reported

---

24. Usually the allocation fraction is equal to the ratio of foreign to worldwide assets. This allocation rule is itself vulnerable to shifting; for example, firms could reduce the allocation by leasing foreign assets and buying assets used in domestic operations.

25. Gordon and MacKie-Mason (1991) examine the theoretical implications of the new U.S. interest allocation rule for borrowing location, while Froot and Hines (chap. 10, this volume) and Collins and Shackelford (1992) provide empirical evidence regarding its impact on firm behavior.

sales revenue, or reported capital values. In the notation of our model, this policy has a positive σ but a zero value of τ, a policy not directly consistent with the results from the model but arguably not a distant approximation.

Note that we have assumed in this model that only inputs are subject to transfer pricing, so that a tax tied to sales revenue is not vulnerable to transfer pricing. It could equally well be the case, however, that outputs are subject to transfer pricing; for example, intermediate goods could be sent abroad for assembly. Some of our specific results certainly change if we allow for the export of outputs. But the main conclusion should be robust: countries face pressure to keep corporate rates low to discourage transfer pricing, at the expense of distorting individual career choices.[26]

So far, we have taken the value of ρ as given. What happens as ρ is changed? If ρ is raised, use of transfer pricing drops. For high enough values of ρ, multinationals will choose not to set up subsidiaries abroad, eliminating any problems from transfer pricing. The tax system would then revert to a wage tax supplemented by an equal-rate cash-flow corporate tax, given the assumptions of the model. Within the model, there is no efficiency loss from taxing more heavily the pure profits earned by foreign subsidiaries, since transfer pricing aside they earn no pure profits, so this would be the optimal policy.

One way to raise the value of ρ is to force more rapid repatriation of profits from abroad, and in the limit to tax foreign-source income at accrual. Such a policy may be costly to enforce. Another way would be to decrease the tax on domestic-source capital income, thereby reducing the gain from having funds accumulate abroad free of this domestic tax. In the limit, if there were no domestic tax on capital income, there would be no gain from the deferral until repatriation of the tax due on foreign-source income.[27] We can also solve for the optimal values of a versus F. Here, the result is immediate and clear. Holding aF fixed, and thereby holding p^* fixed, the government would want to lower a in order to save on resource costs, and increase fines to compensate. Fines can equally well discourage transfer pricing, but involve a redistribution from the firm to the government rather than a loss of real resources. This is simply a replication of the results in Becker (1968).

Imposing large fines on those caught using transfer pricing results in firms facing sizable risks, however, since it is uncertain whether use of transfer prices will be detected by the government. Polinsky and Shavell (1979) have argued against such aggressive use of fines because of the risk-bearing costs this policy imposes. But idiosyncratic risk faced by publicly traded firms should impose little or no risk-bearing costs on diversified shareholders. Large fines can well lead to heavy litigation costs, however, and these litigation costs must be traded off with the real costs of greater enforcement efforts. Another problem

26. The policy proposal to base taxes on sales is obviously very vulnerable to transfer pricing on exported outputs.

27. This is equivalent to arguing that the current tax treatment of pensions would not affect the return to labor in a setting with a proportional wage tax and no capital income taxes.

with high fines is that the government's assessment of the market price may be systematically in error, so that the high potential fines force the firm to make use of distorted prices for tax purposes, thereby distorting its real decisions. Since the government may be in a poor position to guess the appropriate market price for each of the thousands of specific items transferred within a firm, large fines could well lead to substantial distortions to internal allocation decisions within firms.

Rather than the government expending resources on enforcement, it could instead require firms to expend resources, for example, to document more carefully the criteria used in setting their transfer prices, to aid the government in its enforcement efforts. Simply shifting resource costs to the firm, however, does not eliminate the loss of real resources.[28] Note in addition that this approach may be more effective at raising β than at raising a, yet increases in β have ambiguous effects on the firm's net gain from using transfer pricing.

3.3   Other Tax Implications of Income Shifting

The above model helps explain the existence of at least cash-flow corporate taxes in small open economies and justifies some deviations from a cash-flow tax in order to lessen the amount of transfer pricing that occurs. The mere existence of corporate income taxes is not the only puzzle raised in the recent theoretical analyses of optimal tax policy in an open economy, however. Many detailed aspects of existing taxes have also seemed puzzling. In particular, the past literature argues that residence-based taxes on the return to savings can be appropriate for a small open economy, but that source-based taxers would not be. Yet existing corporate taxes deviate in a variety of ways from a residence-based tax. To begin with, existing taxes apply equally to all firms operating in a country, whereas a residence-based tax would not tax the return earned by foreign-owned firms operating in the country—doing so prevents the country from taking full advantage of the gains from trade in the world capital market. Second, when domestic-owned subsidiaries operating abroad face local taxes, a number of authors (e.g., Hamada 1966) have argued that these taxes should be treated as a deductible expense, rather than credited against domestic taxes as under U.S. law. The idea is that a tax system should be designed so that the return to the country on domestic versus foreign investments is equated, and the return to the country on foreign investments would be measured net of any taxes paid abroad. Third, under a pure residence-based tax domestic-owned subsidiaries operating abroad would be taxed on their income at accrual (so that income from domestic and foreign sources is taxed at the same rate), rather than at repatriation as under existing taxes.

---

28. It is certainly possible that resources expended by firms gathering internal information may improve enforcement more than equivalent resources expended by the government attempting to acquire the same information from a distance.

Each of these aspects of existing corporate taxes seems puzzling if the corporate tax were in fact being designed to tax the return to savings by domestic residents. As argued above, however, another important use of a corporate tax is as a backstop to the tax on the labor income of domestic residents. If this is the sole role for the corporate tax, that is, if there is no attempt to tax the return to savings by domestic residents, then the above features of the corporate tax can be rationalized easily.

Consider the first puzzle: Why do countries impose a source-based tax on foreign firms at the same rate as the residence-based tax on domestic firms? We will treat the case of a host country. We showed above that host countries would have an incentive to impose at least some taxes on foreign subsidiaries located in the country if domestic income shifting is a problem. However, in that model domestic firms are not competitive with multinationals, so all ownership is foreign and we cannot determine the optimal tax rules for domestic firms. If we alter our assumptions to allow some domestic firms to survive in equilibrium (perhaps in a different industry), what would be the appropriate policy? If these firms were not multinationals, they would not be able to shift income across borders. Then by our arguments in section 3.1, the optimal policy would be a cash-flow tax at rate t^*, so as to avoid domestic income shifting. This suggests that domestic-owned and foreign-owned firms would face different tax rates, and only employees of foreign-owned firms would engage in domestic income shifting. But if tax rates differed by ownership, then a new form of income shifting becomes possible: domestic owners can give away their firms to foreign owners, who receive nothing in return since the firms continue to break even. However, the domestic employees of these firms gain because they can now shift part of their labor income into corporate form, making it subject to the lower corporate tax rate faced by foreign-owned firms. If this nominal transfer of ownership to foreigners is easy enough, then no rate differential between domestic-owned and foreign-owned firms can survive. A similar argument would also achieve this result for foreign and domestic firms that both operate in a home country.

Next consider the second puzzle: Why do countries give credits for foreign taxes paid? To begin with, we have already shown that a government would want to tax income earned abroad, and that the tax on foreign-source income should be designed to limit the incentives for cross-border income shifting. In the model above, this is most directly accomplished by setting $\rho = 1$, so that foreign income is taxed at the same rate as domestic income. In fact, international income shifting can take a variety of forms in addition to transfer pricing, increasing the pressure to keep ρ high. For example, if the tax rate on foreign earnings is less than the domestic tax rate on labor income, then domestic entrepreneurs have the incentive to set up subsidiaries abroad that make use of their ideas, rather than at home. (In this case, the subsidiary embodies the ideas of the home-country entrepreneur; in the previous case, it embodied the ideas of the host-country entrepreneur.) Following the logic of section

3.1, the optimal tax treatment would again involve taxing this foreign source income at the same rate as domestic-source income.

Together these pressures would lead us to expect a subsidiary to be taxed at the maximum of the corporate tax rates prevailing in the host and the home countries, to prevent tax avoidance by either domestic or foreign residents. This is precisely what happens under existing crediting schemes (assuming deferral has no effect on the net tax rate). Does crediting introduce other distortions due to the differential tax treatment of foreign and domestic firms operating in the same country? Suppose a domestic entrepreneur considers selling his firm to foreigners. If he keeps the firm himself, he faces the domestic tax rate, but if he sells it to foreigners the firm would face the maximum of the domestic and the foreign rates, which would seem to discourage such a sale even though there might be good economic grounds for it. The foreign firm can avoid this surtax, however, simply by making royalty or wage payments to the original entrepreneur equal to the profits earned from his ideas. The return to the entrepreneur's ideas would still be taxed at the labor income tax rate. Net of these royalty/wage payments, the firm would break even, so that any cash-flow surtax on the firm would collect no revenue and would be nondistorting.[29] Therefore, existing crediting schemes can readily be rationalized.[30]

The third puzzle we discuss is: Why do countries tax foreign-source income upon repatriation rather than when it accrues? In fact, the deferral of tax on foreign-source income creates no problems as long as the after-local-tax rate of return earned abroad equals the firm's discount rate.[31] If the return earned abroad were lower, then the domestic owner could simply repatriate earnings as they accrue. Deferral is only a problem if the rate of return earned on funds kept abroad exceeds that available at home. If the domestic government does not tax the return to savings, then capital mobility implies this cannot occur. Deferral remains a puzzle, however, to the extent that there is a domestic tax on the return to savings, unless the costs of enforcing a tax at accrual are too high.

While we have provided a rationale for a variety of aspects of existing corporate income taxes, some other puzzles remain. For one, we have not addressed the question raised in the prior literature concerning why existing corporate taxes include the return to capital in the tax base.[32] In addition, while we have

---

29. If the foreign corporate tax is distorting, then the sale can increase tax payments. However, if the foreign tax applies uniformly to firms owned by foreign residents, regardless of where these firms are located, then it simply reduces the return to labor in the foreign countries rather than affecting the attractiveness of acquiring such a firm, leaving the above results unchanged.

30. This theory rationalizes the use of credits, but does not preclude the use of deductions. If taxes paid abroad were allowed as a deduction rather than credited against domestic tax liabilities, as recommended in Hamada (1966), the tax rate on foreign-source income would be yet higher. It would certainly be high enough to prevent income shifting, yet without income shifting it would still apply to a zero tax base and so impose no distortions.

31. See n. 13, above.

32. While the above model could rationalize limiting the deductions for capital purchases if physical capital inputs were particularly subject to transfer pricing, this explanation does not seem very plausible.

argued that countries have an incentive to tax foreign-source income at the same effective rate as domestic-source income, some countries (e.g., France and the Netherlands) exempt foreign-source income from tax. This also seems puzzling, unless their domestic tax rates are low enough that residents would not gain by shifting income abroad. An intermediate position is taken by Norway, which exempts foreign-source income earned in countries with tax rates at least two-thirds as high as Norway's rate, while taxing income from low-tax countries.

Several further complications could be added to the model, changing the results. For example, given the setup of the model, the optimal tax scheme ignoring transfer pricing would impose equal tax rates on employees and entrepreneurs, in order to avoid distorting career choices. But a major activity of entrepreneurs is to develop new ideas for profitable business activities. The return earned by entrepreneurs on these new ideas can differ from the social return to the ideas for a variety of reasons, justifying a differential tax treatment to correct for these distorted incentives. For example, others can learn an entrepreneur's ideas from observation and set up competing firms using the same ideas, diluting the profits of the original entrepreneur.[33] In addition, the original entrepreneur can use his new information to profit from trading on the securities market. As argued by Hirshleifer (1971), the resulting profits from trade can well exceed the social return to the idea. If returns to the entrepreneur's ideas result from acquired monopoly rents, for example, from successful rent-seeking behavior, then the social return to the effort will again be less than the private return. Therefore, a variety of questions can be raised about the appropriate relative tax rates on employees versus entrepreneurs.

One response to transfer pricing by U.S. states is to shift from separate accounting to formula apportionment. Under separate accounting, transfer prices are needed for all goods and services traded across state lines, raising severe enforcement problems. In contrast, under formula apportionment, national rather than state profits are calculated. These national profits are then apportioned among the various states based on the fraction of the firm's capital, payroll, and sales located in each state. This approach effectively eliminates pressures from transfer pricing among domestic operations of firms, at least as long as the factors in the formula are not themselves subject to transfer pricing. Would this approach also make sense for taxation at a world level? Not if income shifting is the primary consideration justifying the presence of a corporate income tax. To prevent income shifting, a country would want an entrepreneur to face the same tax rate on his corporate income as he would have faced instead on his personal income. But under formula apportionment, the effective tax rate faced by an entrepreneur would be a weighted average of the tax rates prevailing in all the jurisdictions in which he does business. The entrepre-

---

33. Patents provide some limited protection for certain types of ideas, but many profitable ideas are not patentable.

neur therefore has the incentive to invest in low-tax jurisdictions, thereby raising the return to being an entrepreneur.

3.4 Conclusions

Several papers, such as Gordon (1986) and Razin and Sadka (1991), show that standard theoretical models forecast that a small open economy will not impose source-based taxes on capital income. Unless residence-based capital income taxes can include foreign-source as well as domestic-source income, which in practice is unlikely given the difficulties a government faces in monitoring foreign-source income, then as argued by Razin and Sadka (1991) residence-based taxes would not be feasible. Optimal taxes simply consist of taxes on immobile domestic factors, presumably labor and land. But this theoretical forecast stands in stark contrast to the observed tax law in essentially all developed countries, where corporate taxes not only exist but are roughly comparable to the top personal tax rates.

In this paper, we argue that many aspects of the existing corporate tax law would seem quite sensible if the primary role of the corporate tax is to discourage income shifting between the personal and the corporate tax bases, or between domestic and foreign subsidiaries. Unless corporate tax rates are roughly comparable to personal tax rates, business owners would be able to avoid taxes by retaining earnings within their firm, and later selling shares in the firm, so that the earnings are taxed at capital gains rates rather than at personal rates. Unless foreign-owned firms operating in the country are subject to domestic taxes at the same rate, a domestic business owner would be able to avoid taxes on the returns to his ideas by selling his firm to foreign owners. Similarly, a country would need to tax the income of domestic-owned subsidiaries operating abroad to prevent entrepreneurs from facing a tax incentive to make use of their ideas abroad rather than in the home country.

If the tax rate on domestic-owned subsidiaries abroad were less than the domestic corporate tax rate, then an additional distortion would be created because multinationals can avoid domestic taxes by shifting their profits abroad through transfer prices even if the firms embodying their profitable ideas remain at home. While taxing foreign-source income at the same rate as domestic-source income eliminates this pressure, a second-best response is to lower the domestic tax on elements of the income statement that are most subject to transfer pricing. For example, the United States has reduced the effective tax rate applying to interest deductions of multinationals through its §482 rules.

Viewing the corporate tax as primarily a backstop to the personal tax on labor income, rather than as primarily a tax on capital income, requires an important change in focus from that of the recent academic literature. Given the ease with which existing tax policy can be rationalized based on this role for the corporate tax, such a change in focus appears warranted. How great are the pressures from income shifting between the personal and the corporate tax bases? We have presented some evidence in Gordon and MacKie-Mason (1994) and MacKie-Mason and Gordon (1991) on the degree to which firms change between corporate and noncorporate status in response to tax incentives. There has been virtually no attempt to date in the tax literature, however, to measure the degree to which individuals shift their form of pay in response to tax differences. Since our model suggests that this form of income shifting appears to be a major consideration in the design of existing tax structures, measuring the degree to which such income shifting occurs in response to tax differences is an important topic for future research.

Appendix

Proof That $\partial W/\partial h < 0$ When w_n Is Held Constant

In the model with both domestic and cross-border income shifting, consider the effects in the home country of raising τ and in addition raising T by enough to keep firms' choices for X unchanged, given p^*. Assume in addition that t is simultaneously cut by enough so as to keep w_n unchanged.[34] Under the optimal tax policy, the resulting marginal change in welfare should be zero. The resulting change in welfare equals

$$(A1) \qquad \frac{\partial W}{\partial p^*}\left(\frac{\partial p^*}{\partial \tau} + \frac{\partial p^*}{\partial T}\frac{\partial T}{\partial \tau}\right) + \frac{\partial W}{\partial h}\left(\frac{\partial h}{\partial \tau} + \frac{\partial h}{\partial T}\frac{\partial T}{\partial \tau} + \frac{\partial h}{\partial t}\frac{\partial t}{\partial \tau}\right) = 0.$$

It is straightforward to demonstrate that the combined increases in τ and T cause p^* to rise, and that this rise in p^* lowers welfare. Therefore, the second term in equation (A1) must be positive. But the increase in business taxes and the drop in labor taxes will cause h to fall, implying that $\partial W/\partial h$ must be negative, when evaluated at the optimal policies.

Proof That $\partial W/\partial X > 0$ When w_n Is Held Constant

In the model with both domestic and cross-border income shifting, consider the effects of raising σ, while cutting t so as to leave w_n unchanged. The first-order condition is

$$(A2) \qquad \frac{\partial W}{\partial h}\left(\frac{\partial h}{\partial \sigma} + \frac{\partial h}{\partial t}\frac{\partial t}{\partial \sigma}\right) + \frac{\partial W}{\partial p^*}\frac{\partial p^*}{\partial \sigma} + \frac{\partial W}{\partial X}\frac{\partial X}{\partial \sigma} = 0.$$

This tax policy raises corporate taxes and cuts personal taxes. As a result, h will fall, implying that the first term in equation (A2) is positive. In addition, raising the surtax on repatriated profits by raising σ makes transfer pricing

---

34. That the required change in t is negative is straightforward but tedious to demonstrate.

relatively less attractive. Thus p^* decreases, implying that the second term is also positive. Therefore, the third term must be negative. But the increase in the surtax on revenues leads to a reduction in X, implying that $\partial W/\partial X > 0$ under the optimal policies.

References

Auerbach, Alan. 1983. Taxation, corporate financial policy, and the cost of capital. *Journal of Economic Literature* 21:905–40.

Becker, Gary S. 1968. Crime and punishment: An economic approach. *Journal of Political Economy* 76:169–217.

Collins, Julie H., and Douglas A. Shackelford. 1992. Foreign tax credit limitations and preferred stock issuances. Working paper, University of North Carolina Business School.

Feldstein, Martin S., and Charles Horioka. 1980. Domestic savings and international capital flows. *Economic Journal* 90:314–29.

Gordon, Roger H. 1986. Taxation of investment and savings in a world economy. *American Economic Review* 76:1086–1102.

———. 1992. Can capital income taxes survive in open economies? *Journal of Finance* 47:1159–80.

Gordon, Roger H., and A. Lans Bovenberg. 1993. Why is capital so immobile internationally? Possible explanations and implications for capital income taxation. Manuscript, University of Michigan.

Gordon, Roger H., and Jeffrey K. MacKie-Mason. 1991. Effects of the tax reform act of 1986 on corporate financial policy and organizational form. In *Do taxes matter? The impact of the Tax Reform Act of 1986,* ed. Joel Slemrod. Cambridge: MIT Press.

———. 1994. Tax distortions to the choice of organizational form. *Journal of Public Economics* 55:279–306.

Gordon, Roger H., and Joel Slemrod. 1988. Do we collect any revenue from taxing capital income? *Tax Policy and the Economy* 2:89–130.

Gravelle, J. G., and L. J. Kotlikoff. 1989. The incidence and efficiency costs of corporate taxation when corporate and noncorporate firms produce the same good. *Journal of Political Economy* 97:749–81.

Grubert, Harry, and John Mutti. 1987. The impact of the Tax Reform Act of 1986 on trade and capital flows. In *Compendium of tax research 1987.* Washington, D.C.: Department of Treasury.

Grubert, Harry, and Joel Slemrod. 1993. The effects of taxes on investment and income shifting to Puerto Rico. Mimeograph, University of Michigan.

Hamada, Koichi. 1966. Strategic aspects of taxation on foreign investment income. *Quarterly Journal of Economics* 80:361–75.

Harris, David, Randall Morck, Joel Slemrod, and Bernard Yeung. 1993. Income shifting in U.S. multinational corporations. In *Studies in international taxation,* ed. Alberto Giovannini, R. Glenn Hubbard, and Joel Slemrod. Chicago: University of Chicago Press.

Hines, James, Jr., and R. Glenn Hubbard. 1990. Coming home to America: Dividend repatriations by U.S. multinationals. In *Taxation in a global economy,* ed. Assaf Razin and Joel Slemrod. Chicago: University of Chicago Press.

Hines, James R., Jr., and Eric M. Rice. 1994. Fiscal paradise: Foreign tax havens and American business. *Quarterly Journal of Economics* 109:149–82.

Hirshleifer, Jack, 1971. The private and social value of information and the reward to inventive activity. *American Economic Review* 61:561–74.

MacKie-Mason, Jeffrey K., and Roger H. Gordon. 1991. Taxes and the choice of organizational form. NBER Working Paper no. 3781. Cambridge, Mass.: National Bureau of Economic Research.

Musgrave, Richard. 1959. *The theory of public finance.* New York: McGraw-Hill.

Polinsky, A. Mitchell, and Steven Shavell. 1979. The optimal tradeoff between the probability and magnitude of fines. *American Economic Review* 69:880–91.

Razin, Assaf, and Efraim Sadka. 1991. International tax competition and gains from tax harmonization. *Economics Letters* 37:69–76.

Shoven, John. 1991. Using the corporate cash flow tax to integrate corporate and personal taxes. *Proceedings of the 83rd Annual Conference of the National Tax Association* 83:19–26.

Comment   T. Scott Newlon

With this paper, Roger Gordon and Jeffrey MacKie-Mason have made an interesting and useful contribution to the body of work on tax policy in open economies. The paper takes the first steps in introducing income-shifting possibilities, both domestic and cross border, into a model with international investment to analyze the effects of such possibilities on individual and firm behavior and on optimal tax policies.

The authors start by posing the question of why there should be a corporate income tax in a small open economy. To the extent that the corporate income tax is a source-based tax on capital income, it would, at first blush, make no sense for a country in this situation to impose such a tax. Where a country is a price-taker in the global capital market, the tax would be shifted entirely onto immobile factors of production such as land and labor. Hence, it would be more efficient simply to tax the immobile factors directly. And yet most countries do impose corporate income taxes, and generally at substantial rates.

The authors turn to a justification for this behavior that, as they recognize, is not new. The corporate income tax may act as a backstop for the personal income tax. In particular, in the absence of a tax on corporate income, individuals may have an incentive to shift income into the corporate sector. This shifting may occur, for example, through career choices, distortions to the organizational form of economic activity, tax-sheltering activities, and so forth. The authors then go on to examine some of the effects under these conditions of the potential for cross-border income shifting, between parent firms and their foreign subsidiaries, on firm behavior and optimal tax policy.

To carry out the analysis, a relatively simple model is formulated that allows

T. Scott Newlon is an economist in the Office of Tax Analysis of the U.S. Department of the Treasury.

The views expressed in this Comment are those of the author and do not necessarily represent the views of the U.S. Treasury Department.

some specific kinds of domestic income shifting, either career choice or purely unproductive tax-sheltering activities, and cross-border income shifting by multinational corporations through their transfer prices. In this model the only reason for cross-border investment is to take advantage of cross-border income-shifting possibilities.

The problem is approached in two stages. In the first stage, only domestic income shifting is permitted. The results here are not surprising. The optimal tax policy is to set uniform tax rates on wage and corporate income. This policy does not distort individuals' career choices and makes unproductive tax-sheltering activities unattractive.

Although these results are unsurprising, it was a clever idea to introduce domestic income shifting into this model. It provides a good reason for having a corporate income tax in the first place and thus allows the authors to model various policy tradeoffs when cross-border income shifting is introduced into the analysis. Moreover, domestic income shifting is an empirically important phenomenon. For example, the desire to limit this sort of income-shifting activity was one of the reasons for bringing the top personal and corporate tax rates closer together under the Tax Reform Act of 1986. And concerns regarding increased incentives for such income shifting were raised with respect to the increases in top personal tax rates enacted in 1993. So perhaps it should not be a puzzle that corporate income is taxed at all; the real puzzle may instead by why it is taxed so heavily in many countries.

In the second stage of the analysis, the possibility of international investment and cross-border income shifting are introduced. In the model, the only type of international investment is acquisition of firms in countries that produce the production input (host countries) by the firms in countries that use that input (home countries). Since there is nothing special about the home-country firms in this model, the only reason for them to become multinational is to take advantage of income-shifting opportunities. The tax rate is assumed to be lower in the host countries than in the home countries to provide an incentive for income shifting. Where home-country firms do acquire a host-country subsidiary, the total tax rate on the subsidiary's profit is lower than the home-country tax rate but higher than the host-country tax rate, thereby implicitly assuming that the home country taxes its firms on a residence basis with deferral for foreign income.

The authors have chosen to model the cost to a firm of cross-border income shifting as the possibility that it will be caught and fined. Another type of income-shifting cost could result from distortions to management incentives caused by setting transfer prices that are different from market prices; however, this seems likely to be much less important in determining the level of income shifting than the expected costs associated with tax enforcement. Firms have many different ways to decouple managers' incentives from the accounting transfer prices they face. Furthermore, survey evidence presented in Wilson

(1993) suggests that firms that use transfer prices aggressively do not consider distortions to productive efficiency to be a serious problem.

Under these assumptions, the paper derives a series of results for optimal tax policy in the host and home countries. For both host and home countries the optimal tax policy should include a positive tax on corporate income, but at a lower rate than the tax on labor income. This trades off losses from domestic income shifting against losses, in the case of host countries, from making the country a less attractive location for multinational investment, and, in the case of home countries, from cross-border income shifting. The greater the scope for cross-border income shifting, the lower should be the corporate tax rate relative to the wage tax. Thus, even though domestic income shifting provides a justification for having a corporate income tax in an open economy, cross-border income shifting provides another reason for keeping the rate of that tax relatively low.

One of the important results is a confirmation of something already known by tax-policy-makers: by eliminating deferral the home country eliminates the incentive for cross-border income shifting by its multinational corporations. One of the reasons for the various antideferral measures contained in the U.S. tax code is that they serve to relieve pressure on the transfer-pricing rules. Of course, this only works in the case of a country's own corporations and not where income may be shifted out of the country by corporations resident in other countries. Given that the focus in policy circles in the United States is currently largely on transfer-pricing issues associated with foreign-controlled companies, eliminating deferral is not likely to be viewed as the answer to transfer-pricing abuses.

The results also imply that transfer-pricing enforcement should rely heavily on penalties for noncomplicance and only lightly on monitoring of taxpayers. This is a well-known result for models such as this, since fines have no resource cost while monitoring does. To some extent tax policy in the United States has followed the first part of this policy prescription, if not the second. Congress passed a stiff set of transfer-pricing penalties in 1990 and then toughened those penalties even more in 1993.

Given the simplicity of the model, however, compliance and enforcement issues cannot be given their full due. There is general agreement among tax practitioners that tough penalties are not likely to be enough. Firms are likely to pay little heed to the most severe penalties that are likely to be imposed if the tax authorities are unable to catch transfer-pricing abuses or make tax adjustments stick in the courts. The IRS has had a poor record in prosecuting transfer-pricing cases.

What is missing from the analysis, and could be a topic for fruitful future research, are the informational aspects of transfer-pricing enforcement. One of the most important aspects of transfer-pricing enforcement may be the informational asymmetry between taxpayers and the government. Firms generally start with a much better knowledge of their business and the markets they operate in than the tax authorities have. The tax authorities must often incur heavy initial costs to acquire information that taxpayers already possess. Taking into account this informational asymmetry, the optimal enforcement policy is likely to include mechanisms that induce taxpayers to reveal information about themselves and their transfer-pricing practices. U.S. transfer-pricing policy has recently been headed down exactly this track. Recently imposed rules link the avoidance of large transfer-pricing penalties in the event of an assessment to the taxpayer having set its transfer prices reasonably in the first place, documented how the transfer prices were arrived at, and provided IRS examiners with their documentation on request.

In summary, this paper represents an important contribution to the analysis of optimal tax policies in open economics. By integrating domestic and cross-border income shifting into the same model, useful insights are gained about the effects of both on tax policy.

Reference

Wilson, G. Peter. 1993. The role of taxes in location and sourcing decisions. In *Studies in international taxation,* ed. Alberto Giovannini, R. Glenn Hubbard, and Joel Slemrod. Chicago: University of Chicago Press.

4 The Impact of International Tax Rules on the Cost of Capital

Joosung Jun

A sharp rise in cross-border investments in recent years has raised new questions about the competitiveness of U.S. firms in world markets and the role of tax rules in determining the cost of capital for these firms. Tax rules affect the ability of U.S. foreign subsidiaries to compete in foreign markets with local companies and with local subsidiaries of companies based in other countries. The primary channel through which taxes exert this influence is by changing the cost of capital.

The competitive ability of firms that face different costs of capital depends on how capital intensive they are and how sensitive the demand for their product is to the price. This paper does not attempt to look at specific products, but does estimate how tax rules alter the cost of capital for U.S. firms and competing firms in a variety of foreign markets.

Past comparative studies of the cost of capital have been concerned mainly with a comparison between countries of the cost of capital for domestic investment.[1] This cost differs from country to country basically for two reasons. First, the domestic cost of funds may differ across countries. Second, capital income is taxed differently, at both the personal and the corporate levels, in each country. Although previous studies did not always reach identical conclusions because of methodological differences, a typical finding of these studies is that during the past decade, the cost-of-capital gap has been largely attributable to differences in the domestic cost of funds, leaving little room for the role of tax systems.

Joosung Jun is assistant professor of economics at Ewha University.

The author thanks Martin Feldstein, James Hines, Glenn Hubbard, John Wilkins, Pete Wilson, and conference participants for comments and suggestions, and Tom Meyer for outstanding research assistance.

1. See, e.g., King and Fullerton (1984), Bernheim and Shoven (1987), McCauley and Zimmer (1989), OECD (1991), and Jorgenson (1993). For a survey of the U.S.-Japan comparison, see Poterba (1991).

In the case of multinational investment, however, an international comparison of the cost of capital is complicated by the possibility of overlapping tax jurisdictions and the possibility of raising investment funds in different countries and transferring those funds between the parent and the subsidiary. Thus, comparing the cost of capital for domestic investments between countries may lead to very misleading implications for the competitiveness of multinationals.

The objective of this paper is to estimate the degree to which international tax rules affect the cost of capital, with particular attention to U.S. firms competing with firms from other countries in major markets. The analysis involves dealing not only with multiple tax systems but also with the potential interaction of these systems. The paper first attempts to modify the conventional cost-of-capital formula in a way that incorporates the impact of international tax rules; then it estimates the cost of capital for inbound and outbound direct investment in 11 major investing countries.[2]

The evidence presented in this paper suggests that, other things being equal, corporate tax rules related to foreign investment make U.S. firms operating in major foreign markets, on average, face about a 20 percent higher cost of capital than domestic firms in the United States when U.S. source equity capital is used as the marginal source of investment funds. These U.S. firms may very likely face a higher cost of equity capital than do local firms in foreign markets. U.S. firms may also face a cost-of-capital disadvantage vis-à-vis firms from other countries in a given foreign market partly because the United States has no dividend imputation scheme and partly because the United States has relatively strict rules about the exemption or deferral of home-country tax on foreign-source income and foreign tax credit utilization.

The paper begins, in section 4.1, with a discussion of basic tax rules related to international investment. Section 4.2 presents a framework for deriving the cost of capital for foreign investment. Section 4.3 discusses the results based on the basic corporate tax systems. The implications of personal taxes and the dividend imputation scheme for the cost of equity transfers are presented in section 4.4, and the implications of international tax rules for financing foreign subsidiaries are presented in section 4.5, which is followed by a concluding section.

---

2. The first attempt to estimate empirically the cost of capital for international investment was made by the OECD (1991), which presented an extensive set of international comparisons of the cost of capital for both domestic and international investment in 24 member countries. Since the OECD study takes the broad perspective of evaluating the neutrality of the tax systems in the member countries and suggesting ways to coordinate national tax policies, typically the results are reported in an averaged format. This study also provides an excellent data source on tax rules related to domestic and international investment in OECD countries.

The present paper, on the other hand, focuses on several specific tax propositions that arise in a very specific setting, namely, competition among firms of different nationalities in a given location.

4.1   Tax Rules Related to International Investment

Income from international investment is subject to several layers of taxation. Host governments typically impose corporate taxes on income earned within their jurisdictions regardless of the ownership of capital. Many countries subject foreign-source income to home-country personal income taxation. In certain cases, corporate surtaxes are imposed by the home government. Countries also impose withholding taxes on income repatriated from abroad.

Such overlapping tax jurisdictions subject certain foreign-source income to both home-country and host-country taxation. Such double taxation of international income should be a deterrent to international investment because of the implied high effective tax rates. In order to avoid double taxation of international investment income and encourage free flows of capital, countries typically provide some kind of tax relief on foreign-source income. The exact nature and extent of double-taxation relief differs across countries and types of income.[3]

The most extreme, simplistic, and generous way to provide double-taxation relief is to exempt foreign-source income from home-country taxation. In this case, the only taxes charged for foreign-source income are the income and withholding taxes imposed by the host government. Only a few countries (e.g., the Netherlands) adopt this "territorial" system under which there is no residence-based taxation of foreign-source income.[4] As a result of bilateral tax treaties, however, this exemption method is, in practice, more prevalent than implied by the tax statutes of each country. A pair of countries can agree to exempt from domestic taxation their residents' income earned in the other country.

Most countries assert the right to tax the income of their residents regardless of where the income is earned. Under this more conventional "residence" system, foreign-source income is subject to home-country taxation, but a credit or deduction is allowed for taxes paid to the host government.[5]

In practice, no country allows unlimited foreign tax credits. Foreign tax credits are typically limited to home-country tax liability on foreign-source income. Investors whose potentially creditable foreign taxes exceed the actual credit limit are said to be in an "excess credit" position.[6] Thus, foreign tax credit limitations are likely to be binding when the firm invests in a high-tax

---

3. The approaches used to avoid double taxation of foreign-source income have been well documented in the literature (e.g., Ault and Bradford 1990; OECD 1991). This section highlights some basic aspects of double-taxation conventions that will be referred to in later sections.

4. France exempts 95 percent of foreign-source dividends from home-country taxation.

5. Countries using the territorial system tend to tax passive foreign-source income (e.g, most portfolio income) on a residence basis.

6. In some countries, these excess credits may be carried backward or forward (two or five years, respectively, in the United States).

country. If the foreign taxes paid are less than the limitation on credits, the firm is said to be in a "deficit credit" or "full credit" position.

When a multinational invests in several foreign countries, it is normally allowed to pool the income repatriated from all of these countries and credit against the domestic taxes due on this income any corporate and withholding taxes paid abroad on this income. In doing so, it can use excess credits from operations in one country to reduce any domestic taxes due on operations in another country. If, in total, its credits are sufficient to wipe out its domestic tax liabilities on its worldwide foreign operations, then no domestic corporate taxes are due. In this case, its final net income is the same as in the territorial case.

In addition to providing foreign tax credits, residence-system countries typically allow their firms to defer home-country tax on certain types of foreign-source income until the income is repatriated. In general, active business income belongs to this category. Income from passive investment (dividends and interest, e.g.) is typically taxed on an accrual basis; however. And most countries do not allow tax deferral for foreign-branch income. Tax deferral can be an important source of tax benefits since under certain circumstances it may lower the effective tax rate on foreign investment.

The asymmetric treatment of a given economic activity across different jurisdictions may significantly influence the way multinationals allocate capital between domestic and foreign operations.[7] Local investment incentives and financing sources in the host country will further complicate the investment and financing decisions of this firm.

The common notion of tax-induced location choice is based on the comparison of after-tax rates of return in different places. Thus, the argument goes, given the pretax rates of return, the statutory tax rates and investment incentives in each country will determine its attractiveness as an investment location for international investors. The main flaw with such conventional wisdom is its failure to recognize the additional layers of taxation that may be imposed on international investment, as discussed earlier. When choosing between the home country and a foreign country as a location for investment, a multinational may compare the effective tax rate on domestic investment in the home country, not with that on domestic investment in the host country, but with the total effective tax burden on international investment, which is determined by the home-country tax treatment of foreign-source income as well as host-country taxes. Even under the exemption system, in which the home country does not tax foreign-source income, the effective tax rate on international investment can differ from that for host-country competitors due to the withholding tax on repatriated income.

---

7. There have been a growing number of studies analyzing tax effects on multinational incentives. See Giovannini, Hubbard, and Slemrod (1993), e.g.

4.2   Cost of Capital for Foreign Investment

This section sets out a framework within which the cost of capital for foreign investment is estimated. The focus is on the way in which tax rules related to international investment influence the cost of capital.

4.2.1   Basic Model

All shareholders are assumed to live and be taxed in the home country. The foreign subsidiary is wholly owned by the domestic parent, which maximizes shareholder wealth. While the subsidiary can finance its investment through a variety of sources, the model focuses on the case where the subsidiary uses equity transfers from the parent as the basic source of funds for its investment, in order to highlight the differential tax effects on domestic and foreign investment given the same cost of funds. There are two sources of equity funds for the parent to finance its domestic investment or transfers to the subsidiary: retained earnings and new share issues. The subsidiary can also retain earnings to finance its investment.[8]

There is no uncertainty in the model, and all tax rates are perceived to be constant over time. As a notational convention, an asterisk superscript will denote host-country or subsidiary variables.

Capital-market equilibrium for the parent is attained when the shareholder earns his required rate of return ρ:

$$(1) \qquad \rho V_t = (1 - m)D_t + (1 - z)(V_{t+1} - V_t - N_t),$$

where V_t is the market value of the firm's equity at the beginning of period t, D_t is dividend payments in period t, N_t is the value of new equity issued in period t, and m and z are the effective tax rates on dividends and capital gains, respectively.

Solving equation (1) subject to an appropriate transversality condition, we can express the value of the parent V_t as the present discounted value of after-tax dividends, net of the present value of new share issues:

$$(2) \qquad V_t = \sum_{j=0}^{\infty} \left(1 + \frac{\rho}{1 - z}\right)^{-j} \left(\frac{1 - m}{1 - z}D_{t+j} - N_{t+j}\right).$$

The parent maximizes its value subject to various constraints.

The budget constraints for the parent and the subsidiary are

$$(3) \qquad D_t + N_t^* + T_t + I_t = D_t^* + F(K_t) + N_t$$

and

$$(4) \qquad D_t^* + T_t^* + I_t^* = F^*(K_t^*) + N_t^*,$$

8. Alternative financing sources are discussed in detail in section 4.5.

where T_t is the total tax due in the home country, including taxes on repatriated subsidiary earnings, T_t^* is the host-country tax liability, and I_t, I_t^*, $F(K_t)$, and $F^*(K_t^*)$ denote investments and profits for domestic and foreign operations.

The global budget constraint for the parent can be derived by adding equations (3) and (4):

(5) $$T_t + T_t^* + I_t + I_t^* + D_t = F(K_t) + F^*(K_t^*) + N_t.$$

Other constraints include:

(6) $$D_t \geq 0,$$

(7) $$N_t \geq \bar{N}, \text{ where } \bar{N} \leq 0,$$

(8) $$D_t^* \geq 0,$$

(9) $$N_t^* \geq \bar{N}^*, \text{ where } \bar{N}^* \leq 0,$$

(10) $$K_{t+1} = (1 - \delta)K_t + I_t,$$

(11) $$K_{t+1} = (1 - \delta^*)K_t^* + I_t^*.$$

Equations (6) and (8) are nonnegativity conditions for dividends. Equation (7) represents restrictions on the parent's ability to repurchase shares. Similarly, equation (9) reflects restrictions on the subsidiary's ability to repatriate tax-exempt funds to the parent.[9] Equations (10) and (11) denote the evolution of the capital stock for the parent and the subsidiary, respectively, where δ and δ^* are the rates of economic depreciation.

Tax Parameters

Taxable profits of the parent and the subsidiary are

(12) $$\pi_t^T = F(K_t) - \delta^T K_{t+1}^T,$$

(13) $$\pi_t^{T*} = F^*(K_t^*) - \delta^{T*} K_{t+1}^{T*},$$

where K_{t+1}^T is net value of the parent firm's capital stock for tax purposes at the start of period $t+1$. Note that K_{t+1}^T will evolve along different paths depending on the depreciation method (e.g., straight line or declining balance) used and, in any case, will evolve differently than the actual capital stock, K_{t+1}. The quantity δ^T is the rate of tax depreciation allowed in the home country. For foreign investment, the same variables are used with the asterisk superscript.

The tax liability of the parent company in the home country is the sum of the taxes due on its own operations and the taxes due upon repatriation of subsidiary profits:

9. The subsidiary can repatriate its equity capital ($N^* < 0$) as well as its earnings. In principle, the redemption of equity capital is tax exempt, while the repatriated earnings are taxable in the home country. In order to prevent a firm from treating all repatriated funds as equity capital, as a general rule all remissions are treated as taxable earnings as long as accumulated repayments are less than accumulated earnings.

$$(14) \qquad\qquad T_t = T_t^P + T_t^S.$$

Taxes due by the parent on domestic operations are

$$(15) \qquad\qquad T_t^P = \tau\pi_t^T + (w - c)D_t^C,$$

where τ is the home-country statutory corporate tax rate, w is the home-country withholding rate on dividends, and c is the rate of dividend imputation credit available in the home country. The variable D_t^C is parent dividend payments gross of any imputation credits:

$$(16) \qquad\qquad D_t^C = \frac{D_t}{1 - c}.$$

It is also convenient to define the dividends, grossed up at the corporate tax rate:

$$(17) \qquad\qquad D_t^G = \frac{D_t}{1 - \tau}.$$

If the home government provides the full dividend credit ($c = \tau$), D_t^C equals D_t^G. If the country adopts a classical system ($c = 0$), D_t^C equals D_t, the net dividend.

The tax liability of the subsidiary in the host country is

$$(18) \qquad\qquad T_t^* = \tau^*\pi_t^{T*} + (w^* - c^*)D_t^{C*},$$

where grossed-up subsidiary dividends are defined as

$$(19) \qquad\qquad D_t^{C*} = \frac{D_t^*}{1 - c^*},$$

$$(20) \qquad\qquad D_t^{G*} = \frac{D_t^*}{1 - \tau^*}.$$

The parent firm may also owe taxes on repatriated subsidiary profits (T_t^S).[10] Depending on the treatment of foreign-source income in the home country, T_t^S will take on different values:

1. Under a territorial system or a treaty that exempts foreign-source income from home-country taxation, there is no home-country tax on foreign-source dividends:

$$(21) \qquad\qquad T_t^S = 0.$$

2. Under a tax credit system, foreign-source dividends may face home-country corporate surtaxes (deficit credit position). Assuming that the home country uses the same tax base as the host country, which is D_t^{G*},

10. Deferral of home-country taxes on unrepatriated foreign-source dividends is implicitly assumed in the model.

(22) $$T_t^S = \max\left\{\left[\frac{(\tau - \tau^*)(1 - c^*)}{1 - \tau^*} - (w^* - c^*)\right]D_t^{C^*}, 0\right\}.$$

3. Under a deduction system,

(23) $$T_t^S = \tau[1 - (w^* - c^*)]D_t^{C^*}.$$

Before proceeding to the expression for the cost of capital, it will prove convenient to define two further parameters. First, let u be the total tax rate on repatriated foreign-source dividends. Depending on which of the three regimes for the treatment of foreign-source income is in force in the home country, u will take on different values, as shown in table 4.1.

Column (1) denotes the second term of equation (18), which reflects host-country taxes on repatriated dividends. Column (2) reproduces equations (21)–(23). The total tax burdens on foreign-source dividends are summarized in column (3). Notice that the value of u essentially determines the degree to which international tax rules affect the cost of capital in the model.

The other parameter, γ, is the tax discrimination variable. It indicates discrimination between retained earnings and new equity finance in the parent company and is given by

(24) $$\gamma = \frac{1 - m}{(1 - z)(1 + w - c)}.$$

The Cost of Capital

The cost of capital is the pretax rate of return that a corporation must earn in order to pay the rate of return required by the providers of capital. The cost of capital, p and p^*, depends on the discount rate as well as several other considerations such as the tax treatment of capital income and the depreciation of the investment asset:

(25) $$p = \frac{(\rho' + \delta)(1 - z)}{1 - \tau},$$

(26) $$p^* = \frac{(\rho' + \delta^*)(1 - z^*)}{1 - \tau^*},$$

where ρ' is the appropriate discount rate and z and z^* are tax savings from depreciation allowances in the home and host countries, respectively.

The cost of capital critically depends on the discount rate, which is in turn determined by the source of finance and relevant tax parameters. Table 4.2 presents discount rates under alternative regimes of financing domestic and foreign investment.

If the parent uses retained earnings as the source of financing domestic investment, shareholders can accumulate wealth at a rate of return that is taxed by a capital gains tax rather than a dividend tax. If the after-corporate-tax, before-personal-tax yield of a project is ρ', then the shareholder would require

Table 4.1   Effective Tax Rate on Foreign-Source Dividends $D^{C*}(u)$

Home-Country Tax System	Host-Country Taxes (1)	Home-Country Taxes (2)	Total Tax on Foreign-Source Dividends (3)=(1)+(2)
Exemption system	$w^* - c^*$	0	$w^* - c^*$
Credit system	$w^* - c^*$	$\max\left\{\dfrac{(\tau - \tau^*)(1 - c^*)}{1 - \tau^*} - (w^* - c^*), 0\right\}$	$\max\left\{\dfrac{(\tau - \tau^*)(1 - c^*)}{1 - \tau^*}, w^* - c^*\right\}$
Deduction system	$w^* - c^*$	$\tau[1 - (w^* - c^*)]$	$(w^* - c^*) + \tau[1 - (w^* - c^*)]$

Table 4.2   **Discount Rate under Alternative Financing Regimes**

Regime	Discount Rate
Domestic investment	
1. Financed by parent retained earnings	$\rho/(1-z)$
2. Financed by parent new equity	$\dfrac{\rho/(1-z)}{\gamma}$
Foreign investment	
3. Financed by subsidiary retained earnings	$\rho^*/(1-z^*)$
4. Financed by transfer of parent retained earnings	$\dfrac{\rho/(1-z)}{1-u}$
5. Financed by transfer of parent new equity	$\dfrac{\rho/(1-z)}{\gamma(1-u)}$

Note: See table 4.1 for the values of u. See eq. (24) for value of γ.

that $\rho'(1-z) = \rho$. The discount rate for the retained earnings is given by $\rho' = \rho/(1-z)$, as shown on line 1 of table 4.2.[11]

When the parent finances investment by new share issues, the shareholder receives $(1-m)\rho'/(1+w-c)$ as the after-tax dividend yield.[12] In equilibrium, this yield must be equated with ρ, the required rate of return. The parent's discount rate for new equity is, therefore, given by $\rho' = (1+w-c)\rho/(1-m)$, which is the same expression as the one shown on line 2.[13]

Consider now the appropriate discount rates for the finance of foreign investment. When the subsidiary uses its retained earnings to finance the investment, the cost of capital is defined to be the same as that for domestic investment financed through retained earnings in the host country.[14]

If the subsidiary draws funds from the parent, the discount rate should reflect the additional taxes associated with repatriated dividends. As indicated on lines 4 and 5 of table 4.2, this international tax effect can be summarized by the term $1/(1-u)$, where u is the effective tax rate on foreign-source dividends as described in table 4.1. From the perspective of the parent, whose objective is to maximize the wealth of its domestic shareholders, the net receipts from a dollar of repatriation equal $1-u$ dollars. Since the opportunity cost of transfering a dollar to the subsidiary is the dollar equivalent of forgone domestic

---

11. If the required rate of return ρ is set to be $(1-m)i$, the opportunity cost of investing in the firm, where i is the interest rate, then ρ' equals $i/[(1-m)/(1-z)]$ as in King and Fullerton (1984, 23).

12. Note that net dividend payments are grossed up at the net imputation $(c-w)$ rate.

13. Again, if ρ is set to be $(1-m)i$, $\rho' = (1+w-c)i$.

14. This assumption will make the empirical results of this study comparable to those in OECD (1991). Jun (1989) defines the discount rate for subsidiary earnings in an alternative way that links the yield on foreign investment and the opportunity cost of domestic investment.

Table 4.3   **Impact of International Tax Rules on Discount Rate: An Example**

	Host-Country System					
Home-Country System	Classical, or No Dividend Credit to Foreign Firms $(c^* = 0)$ (1)		Full Dividend Credit to Foreign Firms $(c^* = \tau^*)$ (2)		Limited Dividend Credit to Foreign Firms $(c^* = w^*)$ (3)	
	u	$1/(1-u)$	u	$1/(1-u)$	u	$1/(1-u)$
Exemption	0.05	1.05	−0.35	0.74	0	1.00
Credit	0.17	1.20	0.10	1.11	0.16	1.19
Deduction	0.53	2.13	0.33	1.49	0.50	2.00

Note: $\tau = 0.5$, $\tau^* = 0.4$, $w^* = 0.05$.

investment, the parent should require that foreign investment earn a yield at the rate of $1/(1 - u)$ times the rate of return required on domestic investment.

The magnitude of u depends on the tax treatment of foreign-source dividends both in the home and host countries as shown in table 4.1. Table 4.3 shows an example in which the impact of international tax rules on the discount rate $(1/(1 - u))$ is calculated using realistic parameter values under different tax systems in both the home and the host countries. Each column reflects a different extent to which a multinational receives dividend imputation credits for corporate taxes paid to the host government.

In order to focus on the impact of the home-country tax system on the discount rate, consider first the most common case, where there are no dividend imputation credits available for foreign firms (col. [1]).[15] Under the exemption system in the home country, $u = w^*$ and the discount rate for foreign investment will be 5 percent larger than that for domestic investment using the same source of funds. Under the credit system, however, there arises a home-country surtax at the rate of 17 cents per dollar of dividends paid by the subsidiary. This surtax translates into a 20 percent higher discount rate. The impact of the deduction method on the discount rate is more than twice that of the exemption method.

The tax treatment of repatriated dividends in the host country may also significantly influence the discount rate. Withholding taxes on dividend payments to foreign parent companies are typically reduced by a tax treaty (typically by 5–15 percent) and do not show much variation among countries. A potentially more important and more uncertain aspect of host-country taxation of subsidiary dividends is the extent to which a country extends dividend imputation credits to foreign shareholders. Few countries provide unlimited dividend

---

15. This is either because the host country does not have any imputation scheme (the classical system) or because the host country denies foreign shareholders such credits.

credits to foreign shareholders. Among the major imputation countries, the United Kingdom has the statutory rules that are the most generous toward foreign parents receiving dividends from their subsidiaries but still only a half-credit is allowed for the residents of a limited number of countries.

Multinationals may, however, have substantial flexibility in avoiding such statutory restrictions. A subsidiary may pay dividends to another subsidiary located either in a country that receives more favorable treatment or even in the same host country. If a multinational succeeds in receiving the full imputation credits available, this firm can substantially lower the discount rate for foreign investment as shown in column (2).

Column (3) depicts an example of partial credits. In any case, the impact of dividend imputation credits available in the host country on the cost of capital for foreign investment is likely to be unpredictable and variable across countries.[16]

4.2.2 Measuring the Cost of Capital

In the remainder of the paper, various cost-of-capital measures for U.S. firms and their major competitors in foreign markets are presented. The methodology used to calculate the cost of capital in this paper closely follows the approach developed by King and Fullerton (1984) and OECD (1991).

There are three rates of return on an investment, p, r, and s: the pretax rate of return, the after-corporate-tax rate of return, and the after-corporate-and-personal-tax rate of return, respectively. This study adopts the "fixed-r" approach in which for a given real interest rate (r), the pretax rate of return (p) is calculated using the tax code. A common real interest rate of 5 percent is assumed for the purpose of focusing on the tax effects on the cost of capital and maintaining comparability between countries. Thus, the cost-of-capital measures reported in the following sections are the pretax rates of return necessary to earn a given after-corporate-tax rate of return (real interest rate) of 5 percent.

In the base case estimation, personal taxes are ignored. In practice, the role of personal taxes in determining the cost of capital may be less clear in the case of the parent-subsidiary relationship than the shareholder-parent relationship. The parent, as a single shareholder, may be subject to different rules and incentives than individual shareholders. The most important aspect of the parent's being a shareholder of the foreign subsidiary is the role of the dividend imputation scheme in the home and host countries in determining the cost of capital for foreign investment, which is fully discussed in section 4.4.

While the base case focuses on all-equity financing regimes, debt financing, often ignored in the literature, has been an important source of foreign investment. Especially significant is the presence of local borrowing by foreign sub-

---

16. See section 4.4 for more discussion of this issue.

Table 4.4   **Cost of Capital for U.S. and Competing Firms in Foreign Markets**

Host Country	Local Firms (1)	U.S. Firms (2)	Japanese Firms (3)	U.K. Firms (4)	German Firms (5)
United States	7.6	7.6	10.7	8.5	10.9
Japan	9.0	10.6	9.0	11.3	12.8
Canada	8.1	9.5	11.8	10.1	13.7
France	7.3	9.7	11.2	10.8	11.2
Germany	9.5	8.3	11.7	7.8	9.5
Netherlands	7.1	7.8	10.9	8.0	10.3
United Kingdom	7.7	8.6	11.8	7.7	7.7
Italy	9.1	9.9	10.8	6.8	13.0
Sweden	7.2	8.8	12.0	8.2	8.5
Switzerland	6.6	8.2	11.4	7.6	9.6
Australia	9.0	11.5	12.1	12.5	15.1
Average (foreign investment)	8.0	9.3	11.5	9.2	11.3

sidiaries. Section 4.5 discusses the implications of international taxation for the financing policy of subsidiaries.

A common inflation rate of 4.5 percent is used everywhere. Thus, all the variations in the cost of capital for foreign investment across countries are due purely to differences in their corporate tax systems. For comparability, the values for tax parameters are drawn from the OECD and relate to the systems in force as of January 1, 1991.[17] A 11 × 11 matrix of the cost of capital for 11 countries investing in each other is calculated under each financing regime. These 11 countries are Australia, Canada, France, Germany, Italy, Japan, the Netherlands, Sweden, Switzerland, the United Kingdom, and the United States. While the OECD reports various average measures across its member countries, the main focus of this study is on U.S. firms competing with firms from other countries in foreign markets. The major findings are described in the following sections. The appendix reports the full cost-of-capital matrices for the base case.

4.3   Effects of the Basic Corporate Tax Systems

This section focuses on the effects on the cost of capital of the basic corporate statutes in the sample countries. Results based on possible behavioral responses by multinationals are reported in the following sections.

4.3.1   Domestic Investment versus Foreign Investment

Compare first the costs of capital for domestic investment and foreign investment. Table 4.4 presents the cost of capital for U.S., Japanese, U.K., and Ger-

17. For a complete list of data parameters, see OECD (1991, 220–33).

man firms as well as local firms operating in the 11 sample countries. In this base case, parent retained earnings are assumed to be the marginal source of funds for both domestic and foreign investment.

Column (1) reports the cost of capital for domestic investment. This result can be comparable to traditional international comparisons of the cost of capital except that this study isolates the impact of corporate taxes from other influences. The effects of corporate tax rules on the cost of capital differentials for domestic investment between countries do not appear to be large, which is in line with the findings of most previous studies. Across countries, the required pretax rates of return on domestic investment are higher in Japan, Germany, Italy, and Australia than in other countries, reflecting their relatively high corporate tax rates. U.S. domestic firms face a lower cost of capital (7.6 percent) than Japanese domestic firms (9.0 percent) because of relatively high corporate tax rates in Japan. Note that several studies have found that U.S. firms are at a competitive disadvantage relative to firms in Japan. In McCauley and Zimmer (1989) and Bernheim and Shoven (1987), for example, the cost-of-capital gap in 1988 was 4.0 and 7.0 percent, respectively. The cost-of-capital advantage of U.S. firms in this study (1.4 percent), therefore, reiterates the significance of the difference in the cost of funds between the two countries in the 1980s.

Now consider the cost of capital for firms from major investing countries. As shown in column (2), U.S. firms face a significantly higher cost of equity capital for foreign investment than for domestic investment. In the sample host countries, U.S. firms face about a 20 percent higher cost of capital on average than in the case of U.S. domestic investment (9.3 vs. 7.6 percent). In Japan, the cost of capital for foreign investment is about 40 percent higher than that for domestic investment in the U.S. (10.6 vs. 7.6 percent).

Firms from other countries also face similar tax costs when they invest abroad. Columns (3)–(5) indicate that the average costs of capital for Japanese, U.K., and German firms investing in the sample countries are about 20–30 percent higher than for domestic investment in their home countries. Corporate taxes seem to play an important role in affecting the competitiveness of firms in foreign markets, contrary to the case when the costs of capital for domestic investment are compared.

4.3.2   Competition with Local Firms

The results in table 4.4 also indicate that because of the tax costs associated with foreign investment, firms investing abroad may very likely face a higher cost of capital than local competitors. For example, a 20 percent higher cost of capital for foreign investment would put U.S. multinationals in a disadvantageous position in most foreign markets. Comparing columns (1) and (2) indicates, in fact, that U.S. firms face a higher cost of capital than their local counterparts in every sample country. Similar results are obtained for firms from other countries.

Table 4.5   **Cost of Capital for Foreign Firms Operating in Japan, the United Kingdom, and Germany**

Home Country	In Japan (1)	In the United Kingdom (2)	In Germany (3)
United States	10.6	8.6	7.4
Japan	9.0	11.8	8.2
Canada	11.1	6.0	7.9
France	11.7	8.0	5.4
Germany	12.8	7.7	9.5
Netherlands	10.6	6.3	8.2
United Kingdom	11.3	7.7	7.8
Italy	11.8	14.0	6.4
Sweden	10.6	6.3	8.2
Switzerland	10.6	6.3	8.2
Australia	13.9	7.7	7.4
Average (foreign investment)	11.5	8.3	7.5

Because of the tax costs associated with international investment, U.S. firms face a higher cost of equity capital than do local firms in Japan (10.6 vs. 9.0 percent), according to the calculations that underlie the figures reported in table 4.4. As noted above, Japanese firms have enjoyed a cost-of-capital advantage over U.S. firms due mainly to the difference in the cost of funds between the two countries. Since the results reported here are based on the assumption that there are no cost-of-funds differentials between countries, the negative impact of international tax rules on the cost of capital can be interpreted as an additional source of disadvantage for U.S. firms operating in Japan when these firms draw transfers from their domestic parents.

4.3.3 Competition among Foreign Firms

In a foreign market, U.S. firms compete not only with local firms but also with firms from other investing countries. Table 4.5 shows the cost-of-capital measures for firms from different countries operating in Japan, the United Kingdom, and Germany.

In Japan, the variation of the cost of capital across investing countries is not large. This is mainly because the high Japanese corporate tax rate dominates the tax rates in investor countries in determining the overall effective tax rate on foreign investment in Japan. The cost of capital for U.S. firms (10.6 percent) is not greater than for firms from other countries, though the difference is not large. One interesting observation is that those firms whose cost of capital is higher than that for U.S. firms are from countries with a dividend credit scheme (Canada, France, Germany, the Netherlands, the United Kingdom, Italy, and Australia).[18]

18. A related discussion is presented in the next section.

In other countries, the cost of capital for U.S. firms is close to the sample average. Note that the cost of capital for foreign firms in the United Kingdom shows relatively greater variation across investor countries. This is because low U.K. corporate taxes are often dominated by home-country taxation of U.K.-source income in determining the cost of capital.

4.4   Personal Taxes and the Dividend Imputation Scheme

The costs of two sources of parent equity funds—new equity and retained earnings—are different mainly for two tax reasons, as discussed in section 4.2. First, a personal tax advantage for capital gains relative to dividends will lower the cost of retained earnings for the parent. On the other hand, a dividend imputation scheme will make the cost of parent new equity lower than that for parent retained earnings for financing domestic investment.

4.4.1   Effects of the Dividend Imputation Scheme in the Home Country

Some countries try to restrict investors' ability to use the dividend imputation scheme on dividends from domestic corporations financed by earnings from abroad. Typically, countries require that dividends eligible for the dividend imputation scheme be less than the firm's after-tax profits from domestic operations. Unless a firm desires an abnormally high dividend payout rate, however, this restriction is unlikely to be binding.

If shareholders in the countries with the dividend imputation scheme are allowed to take such dividend imputation credits for foreign-source dividends, firms from some of these countries can possibly lower the cost of capital for foreign investment by using parent new equity instead of parent retained earnings as the source of transfers. Table 4.6 presents the cost-of-capital measures that reflect personal taxes and dividend credits for firms investing in Japan.

Columns (1) and (2) show the impact of the home-country imputation scheme on the relative costs of capital for the two sources of equity transfers. Personal taxes are ignored to highlight the influence of the dividend imputation scheme. For firms from countries with the classical system, therefore, the cost of capital is the same for the two cases. Firms from countries with a dividend imputation scheme have a clear advantage over U.S. firms. Without dividend credit benefits, the cost of capital for U.S. firms is at the low end of the spectrum (col. [1]). With credits available, however, the average cost of capital over firms from imputation countries is 5.4 percent, about half of the cost of capital for U.S. firms (col. [2]). This result suggests the potential importance of integrating personal and corporate taxation in enhancing U.S. competitiveness.

Columns (3) and (4) report the results that combine the effects of personal taxes and dividend credits. Overall, the cost of capital is lower here than in the base case since the nominal required rate of return is defined to be $(1 - m)i$ in the calculations. The effects of relatively lower effective tax rates on capital gains are dominant in most of the sample countries, though the impact of the

Table 4.6   **Personal Taxes and Dividend Imputation Credits in the Home
                        Country: Firms Operating in Japan**

Home Country	No Personal Taxes		Personal Taxes	
	Parent Retained Earnings[a] (1)	Parent New Equity[b] (2)	Parent Retained Earnings[a] (3)	Parent New Equity[b] (4)
Japanese domestic	9.0	9.0	6.6	11.2
United States	10.6	10.6	5.3	7.8
Canada	11.1	7.3	2.6	4.2
France	11.7	6.8	7.9	17.7
Germany	12.8	2.4	1.8	2.4
Netherlands	10.6	10.6	0.4	10.6
United Kingdom	11.3	6.4	4.9	3.9
Italy	11.8	4.6	6.3	7.3
Sweden	10.6	10.6	6.4	8.5
Switzerland	10.6	10.6	3.0	10.6
Australia	13.9	4.7	4.1	1.6
Average (foreign investment)	11.5	7.5	4.3	7.5

[a]Transfer of parent retained earnings.
[b]Transfer of parent new equity with dividend credits for foreign-source dividends.

imputation scheme has a significantly offsetting impact in those countries with such a scheme. In Australia and the United Kingdom, parent new equity is still the cheaper of the two sources.

In the presence of widespread foreign financing sources (see the next section) and international portfolio investment with the possibility of tax evasion,[19] the role of personal taxes in determining the required rate of return on foreign investment in not as clear as in the model presented earlier. In principle, there must be no dividend credits when there is no dividend taxation. However, the corporate veil between domestic shareholders and foreign investment may be thick and complex enough for multinationals to somehow manage to get some dividend credits even when personal taxation on the level of domestic shareholders does not affect their cost of capital. If this is the case, the first two columns of table 4.6 will represent a more realistic picture of the cost-of-capital gap across financing sources and investor countries.

4.4.2   Effects of the Dividend Imputation Scheme in the Host Country

The presence of the dividend imputation scheme provides incentives to reduce the cost of capital, not only for the subsidiaries of the domestic parent,

---

19. For a discussion of tax effects on international portfolio investment, see Gordon and Jun (1993).

Table 4.7   Dividend Imputation Credits to U.S. Firms in the Host Country

Host Country	Limited Credits (1)	Full Credits (2)
United States	7.6	7.6
Japan	10.6	10.6
Canada	9.5	8.6
France	9.7	7.6
Germany	8.3	6.3
Netherlands	7.8	7.8
United Kingdom	8.6	8.6
Italy	9.9	6.7
Sweden	8.8	8.8
Switzerland	8.2	8.2
Australia	11.5	8.9
Average (foreign investment)	9.3	8.2

but also for the local subsidiaries of firms in other countries. As discussed in section 4.2, most countries deny dividend credits to foreign shareholders. However, some firms may have enough flexibility to avoid such statutory restrictions. Table 4.7 presents results based on the assumption that U.S. firms can get the full credits available in foreign countries. Column (1) produces column (2) of table 4.4, the base case result based on the notion that restrictions in the tax statutes are strictly binding.[20]

In most sample countries with the imputation scheme, U.S. firms can lower the cost of capital.[21] In the United Kingdom, there is no change in the cost of capital, which is not surprising. The United Kingdom taxes corporate income rather lightly, and benefits from the full credit ($c = 0.250$) are not a large addition because U.S. firms are already allowed to take a half-credit (0.125). U.S. firms, therefore, must still face a U.S. surtax, and the total effective tax rate is determined mostly by the U.S. taxes. On average, U.S. firms can lower their cost of capital about 12 percent (from 9.3 to 8.2 percent) in the sample countries.

4.5   Implications for Local Financing Sources

In the face of a high cost of capital for foreign investment financed through equity transfers by the parent, the subsidiary may seek alternative sources of funds. First, parent transfers can be made in debt instead of equity. These two types of transfer differ in terms of the rate of withholding tax in the host country and the tax treatment of repatriated income in the home country. While

20. Note that personal taxes in the home country are ignored for the results in this table.
21. These countries are Canada, France, Germany, Italy, and Australia.

many countries in the sample adopt the exemption method for foreign-source dividends,[22] all sample countries adopt the credit method for foreign-source interest. In the host countries, on the other hand, interest payments face lower withholding taxes than dividend payments in many cases. The cost-of-capital difference between these two types of transfers in the actual calculation is small and not separately reported.[23]

4.5.1 Local Debt Financing

It is likely that more important alternative sources of funds lie in the host country. Local borrowing, which is ignored by most previous studies of foreign investment, has been an important source of funds for foreign investment. At the end of 1989, the share of local and other foreign borrowing in total external finance for U.S. firms operating abroad was 60.3 percent. The corresponding figure for foreign firms operating in the United States was 71.2 percent.

In general, because interest payments are tax deductible, debt financing should be preferred to equity financing as far as taxes are concerned. Column (3) of table 4.8 shows that the cost of capital for foreign investment financed by local borrowing is much lower than that for equity financing regimes. The deduction benefits are proportional to the marginal corporate tax rate in a country, and debt financing is particularly attractive in Japan and Germany because of their relatively high corporate tax rates.

Local debt may be an especially attractive way of financing foreign investment for the following reasons. First, the tax cost of not using debt is much higher for foreign investment than for domestic investment, as shown in column (5) of table 4.8. For domestic investment in the United States, the tax cost of using equity financing is 5.0 percent. For U.S. firms operating in Japan, for example, the cost can be as large as 9.0 percent. This result reflects the tax costs associated with international investment.

Firms usually do not raise the leverage ratio as much as tax benefits would suggest because of various nontax costs associated with leverage, such as perceived bankruptcy or agency costs. In the case of multinational investment, however, the nontax cost of using debt may not be as significant as for domestic investment. A multinational may face less risk of default, since it can pool relatively independent risks from its operations in several different countries and so be able to borrow more. In addition, if it can use its combined assets as collateral for loans, regardless of which affiliate does the borrowing, then it can concentrate its borrowing in the country where the deductions are most valuable.

Thus, the tax benefits of an interest deduction may be a much more important determinant of corporate leverage for a foreign subsidiary than for a

22. These countries are Canada, France, Germany, the Netherlands, Sweden, Switzerland, and Australia, assuming a tax treaty for residence-system countries.
23. In most sample countries, debt transfer has a slight edge over equity transfer.

Table 4.8   Advantage of Local Financing for U.S. Multinationals

Host Country	Transfer of Parent Equity (1)	SRE[a] with Tax Deferral (2)	Local Debt Financing (3)	Tax Cost of Not Using SRE[a] ((1)–(2)) (4)	Tax Cost of Not Using Local Debt ((1)–(3)) (5)
U.S. domestic	7.6	7.6	2.6	0.0	5.0
Japan	10.6	9.0	1.6	1.6	9.0
Canada	9.5	8.1	3.5	1.4	6.0
France	9.7	7.3	3.2	2.4	6.5
Germany	8.3	9.5	0.6	−1.2	7.7
Netherlands	7.8	7.1	2.8	0.7	5.0
United Kingdom	8.6	7.7	3.5	0.9	5.1
Italy	9.9	9.1	1.9	0.8	8.0
Sweden	8.8	7.2	3.6	1.6	5.2
Switzerland	8.2	6.6	3.1	1.6	5.1
Australia	11.5	9.0	3.6	2.5	7.9
Average (foreign investment)	9.3	8.1	2.7	1.2	6.6

[a]SRE = subsidiary retained earnings.

purely domestic firm. In addition, foreign borrowing is an important way to hedge against exchange risks associated with foreign-source income.

When borrowing abroad, a U.S. multinational may have an incentive to concentrate its borrowing where tax benefits are large. Japan, Germany, Italy, and Australia are more attractive places for foreign borrowing than Canada, France, the Netherlands, the United Kingdom, Sweden, and Switzerland as far as taxes are concerned. This observation might become more relevant as integrated world capital markets narrow differences in interest rates between countries.

4.5.2 Tax Deferral and Subsidiary Retained Earnings

If, for some nontax reasons, a U.S. firm has to finance foreign investment using an equity source, subsidiary retained earnings are typically cheaper than parent equity transfers, except in Germany where split corporate tax rates discriminate against retained earnings (table 4.8, col. [4]). Note, however, that the cost of capital for subsidiary retained earnings as reported in this study implicitly assumes that home-country taxes on unrepatriated earnings can be deferred. If such deferrals are not allowed in the United States, then the cost of capital for foreign investment financed through subsidiary retained earnings will be higher for firms that are in a deficit credit position than those reported in column (2).[24]

Unlike the foreign tax credit, the main objective of which is to avoid double taxation of foreign-source income, tax deferrals have been a source of controversy in the United States because this provision gives home-based multinationals a tax incentive to keep placing their earnings in foreign countries. Further, the deferral of the home tax on foreign-source income is often regarded as a violation of the principle of tax neutrality between domestic and outward foreign investment (capital export neutrality) since taxation of domestic-source income generally cannot be deferred.

4.6 Conclusions

Tax rules related to international investment significantly raise the cost of capital for foreign investment. The tax costs associated with foreign investment will easily put foreign subsidiaries in a disadvantageous position relative to local companies. The extent to which tax rules raise the cost of capital for foreign investment varies across investor countries. Firms from countries with a dividend imputation scheme may face a lower cost of equity transfers than those from countries with no such benefits, such as the United States.

The evidence presented in this paper suggests that, as an effect of tax rules, U.S. foreign subsidiaries that draw equity transfers from their parent firms

---

24. Technically, in such a case, the cost of capital for subsidiary retained earnings becomes equivalent to that for transfer of parent equity (col. [1]), in the setting of this paper.

likely face a higher cost of capital than local firms in major foreign markets. This is an addition to the much heralded cost-of-funds disadvantage in the United States. U.S. firms may also face a cost-of-capital disadvantage in foreign markets vis-à-vis competing firms that face low-cost equity transfers due to dividend imputation schemes in their home countries.

There are several additional factors that may add to the competitive burden of U.S. firms operating abroad. Among major investor countries, the United States has the tightest rules regarding the exemption or deferral of home-country tax on foreign-source income and regarding the limitation of foreign tax credits. For example, the Tax Reform Act of 1986 has made pooling of worldwide income more difficult for U.S. firms by confining the eligibility to earnings from majority-owned subsidiaries, while many other countries tried to adopt the exemption method by statutes or by treaties; unlike its major competitors, the United States considers a loan that a subsidiary makes to its parent to be the equivalent of a dividend, to which a U.S. surtax may be applied; a recent U.S. tax bill (H.R. 5270: *Foreign Income Tax Rationalization and Simplification Act of 1992*) includes a provision that repeals tax deferral; the United States is the only major developed country that does not grant tax-sparing credits to developing countries, possibly making U.S. multinationals face a much higher effective tax rate in developing countries than firms from other countries with a treaty including tax-sparing credits.

As the increasing international integration of financial markets narrows the cost-of-funds differentials between countries, tax rules will play a more important role in determining the cost of capital for firms investing in foreign markets.

Appendix

Table 4A.1   Cost of Capital Financed through Equity Transfer of Parent Retained Earnings

Host	Home											Average	Standard Deviation
	Japan	Canada	France	Germany	Netherlands	United Kingdom	Italy	Sweden	Switzerland	Australia	United States		
Japan	9.0	11.1	11.7	12.8	10.6	11.3	11.8	10.6	10.6	13.9	10.6	11.3	1.2
Canada	11.8	8.1	10.4	13.7	9.5	10.1	13.5	10.4	10.4	12.3	9.5	10.9	1.7
France	11.2	11.6	7.3	11.2	9.7	10.8	15.4	9.0	9.7	16.1	9.7	11.1	2.5
Germany	11.7	7.9	5.4	9.5	8.2	7.8	6.4	8.2	8.2	7.4	8.3	8.1	1.5
Netherlands	10.9	8.9	8.3	10.3	7.1	8.0	12.8	7.1	7.1	11.3	7.8	9.1	1.9
United Kingdom	11.8	4.7	8.0	7.7	6.3	7.7	14.0	6.3	6.3	7.7	8.6	8.1	2.5
Italy	10.8	8.3	13.4	13.0	9.1	6.8	9.1	10.8	11.8	14.2	9.9	10.7	2.2
Sweden	12.0	10.0	7.2	8.5	7.2	8.2	15.2	7.2	7.8	11.1	8.8	9.4	2.4
Switzerland	11.4	9.4	7.8	9.6	6.6	7.6	14.4	7.3	6.6	10.5	8.2	9.0	2.3
Australia	12.1	5.8	12.9	15.1	11.5	12.5	13.3	11.5	11.5	9.0	11.5	11.5	2.3
United States	10.7	9.5	8.8	10.9	8.3	8.5	11.8	8.3	8.3	11.9	7.6	9.5	1.5
Average	11.2	8.7	9.2	11.1	8.6	9.0	12.5	8.8	8.9	11.4	9.1	9.9	2.0
Standard deviation	0.8	2.0	2.4	2.2	1.6	1.8	2.6	1.7	1.9	2.6	1.2	1.9	

Table 4A.2   Cost of Capital Financed through Equity Transfer of Parent New Equity

	Home												
Host	Japan	Canada	France	Germany	Netherlands	United Kingdom	Italy	Sweden	Switzerland	Australia	United States	Average	Standard Deviation
Japan	9.0	7.3	6.8	2.4	10.6	6.4	4.6	10.6	10.6	4.7	10.6	7.6	2.8
Canada	11.8	5.5	6.2	2.8	9.5	5.9	5.3	10.4	10.4	4.4	9.5	7.4	2.8
France	11.2	7.4	4.4	2.1	9.7	6.1	5.5	9.0	9.7	5.1	9.7	7.3	2.7
Germany	11.7	5.2	3.1	1.6	8.2	4.5	2.4	8.2	8.2	2.5	8.3	5.8	3.1
Netherlands	10.9	5.7	4.8	1.6	7.1	4.5	4.6	7.1	7.1	3.6	7.8	5.9	2.4
United Kingdom	11.8	4.1	4.9	1.5	6.3	4.6	5.3	6.3	6.3	2.8	8.6	5.7	2.7
Italy	10.8	8.2	7.7	8.4	9.1	4.0	3.7	10.8	11.8	4.8	9.9	8.1	2.7
Sweden	12.0	6.5	4.3	1.6	7.2	4.7	5.5	7.2	7.8	3.8	8.8	6.3	2.7
Switzerland	11.4	6.0	4.4	1.5	6.6	4.2	4.9	7.3	6.6	3.3	8.2	5.9	2.5
Australia	12.1	8.2	7.7	3.3	11.5	7.4	5.6	11.5	11.5	3.6	11.5	8.5	3.2
United States	10.7	6.1	5.1	1.8	8.3	4.8	4.4	8.3	8.3	3.9	7.6	6.3	2.5
Average	11.2	6.4	5.4	2.6	8.6	5.2	4.7	8.8	8.9	3.9	9.1	6.8	2.7
Standard deviation	0.8	1.2	1.4	1.9	1.6	1.0	0.9	1.7	1.9	0.8	1.2	1.3	

References

Ando, Albert, and Alan J. Auerbach. 1988. The cost of capital in the United States and Japan: A comparison. *Journal of the Japanese and International Economies* 2:134–58.

Ault, Hugh J., and David F. Bradford. 1990. Taxing international income: An analysis of the U.S. system and its economic premises. In *Taxation in the global economy,* ed. Assaf Razin and Joel Slemrod, 11–46. Chicago: University of Chicago Press.

Bernheim, B. Douglas, and John B. Shoven. 1987. Taxation and the cost of capital: An international comparison. In *The consumption tax: A better alternative?* ed. Charls E. Walker and Mark A. Bloomfield, 61–86. Cambridge, Mass.: Ballinger.

Boskin, Michael J., and Charles E. McLure, Jr., eds. 1990. *World tax reform.* San Francisco: ICS.

Giovannini, Alberto, R. Glenn Hubbard, and Joel Slemrod, eds. 1993. *Studies in international taxation.* Chicago: University of Chicago Press.

Gordon, Roger, and Joosung Jun. 1993. Taxes and the form of ownership of foreign corporate equity. In *Studies in international taxation,* ed. Alberto Giovannini, R. Glenn Hubbard, and Joel Slemrod. Chicago: University of Chicago Press.

Hartman, David. 1985. Tax policy and foreign direct investment. *Journal of Public Economics* 26:107–21.

Hatsopoulos, George N., and Stephen H. Brooks. 1986. The gap in the cost of capital: Causes, effects, and remedies. In *Technology and economic policy,* ed. R. Landau and D. Jorgenson. Cambridge, Mass.: Ballinger.

Jorgenson, Dale W. 1993. Tax reform and the cost of capital: An international comparison. *Tax Notes International* 6 (April 19): 981–1008.

Jun, Joosung. 1989. Tax policy and international direct investment. NBER Working Paper no. 3048. Cambridge, Mass.: National Bureau of Economic Research.

King, Mervyn A., and Don Fullerton. 1984. *The taxation of income from capital.* Chicago: University of Chicago Press.

McCauley, Robert N., and Stephen Zimmer. 1989. Explaining international differences in the cost of capital. *Quarterly Review* (Federal Reserve Bank of New York) 14(2): 7–28.

OECD (Organisation for Economic Co-operation and Development). 1991. *Taxing profits in a global economy: Domestic and international issues.* Paris: Organisation for Economic Co-operation and Development.

Poterba, James. 1991. Comparing the cost of capital in the United States and Japan: A survey of methods. *Quarterly Review* (Federal Reserve Bank of New York) 16 (Winter): 20–32.

Comment Joel Slemrod

In 1991 the Organisation for Economic Co-operation and Development (OECD) published a massive 469-page volume entitled *Taxing Profits in a Global Economy;* its goal was to examine how the OECD member countries taxed corporate profits and the potential implication of these apparent differ-

Joel Slemrod is professor of business economics and of economics at the University of Michigan and a research associate of the National Bureau of Economic Research.

ences in taxation for domestic and international investment flows. Included in the study was the most careful calculation up to that time, of the cost of capital for domestic, and more specifically, cross-border direct investments. This volume contains scores of charts and thousands of numbers about the cost of capital for a company resident in country X investing in country Y, so many that the report itself despairs that "it is difficult to draw any general conclusions from such a large quantity of data." It then proceeds to venture some conclusions, including that "all countries appear to discourage outward investment compared to domestic investment by their resident companies. They also place a high effective tax rate on inward investment by foreign companies compared to domestic companies and compared to domestic investment by resident companies. Further, this result holds irrespective of the means of financing the subsidiary chosen by the parent, unless the subsidiary merely retains its earnings" (OECD 1991, 158). The OECD report also concludes that, on average, the required return of Japanese multinationals is significantly higher than that of U.S. multinationals, except for investments located in Japan itself.

In this paper Joosung Jun uses the OECD data and apparently uses something very similar to the OECD methodology to arrive at more or less these same conclusions as in the OECD report. In spite of the apparent similarity in methodology and conclusions, this paper contains several noteworthy incremental contributions. Let me try to summarize them.

1. The cost-of-capital measures are derived in a more straightforward way, and the results are presented in a tighter, and to my mind, clearer way than in the OECD report.

2. The cost-of-capital calculations highlight the role of the assumptions made about the parent company's source of financing. Although column (1) of Jun's table 4.6 is, except for one entry, exactly the same as the information in the OECD report's table 5.1, the others are new, but very similar to the OECD calculations, particularly in the ordering. The differences arise because the OECD report presents cost-of-capital calculations only under the assumption that the parent companies finance their subsidiaries using a weighted average of retentions, new equity, and debt, the same weighted average for all countries. Jun presents the cost of calculation separately for each kind of financing.

3. It highlights the role in the cost of capital of corporate and personal tax integration, and particularly how foreign owners are treated under these regimes (see also Devereux and Freeman 1994). In most cases integration benefits are not passed on to foreign owners, and the benefits of integration to domestic shareholders are not available on foreign direct investment. With regard to the former restriction, Jun devotes his table 4.7 to cost-of-capital calculations assuming that foreign firms "have enough flexibility" to avoid such statutory restrictions, suggesting that this may be closer to the truth than assuming the restrictions are binding. This is an important assertion that cries out for some supporting evidence. Can it really be as easy as setting up two tiers of

affiliate corporations so that the dividends paid from the first to the second-tier affiliate receive the imputation credit?

4. It highlights the empirical and conceptual importance of local debt financing and makes the interesting point that, considering tax advantages, local debt financing looks even more attractive than in a domestic context, because it can potentially avoid three, rather than two, layers of tax on equity-financed capital.

Although this paper raises insightful new issues within the now-standard framework introduced by King-Fullerton and used by the OECD, it does not extend this framework in some directions that I believe are critical to understanding the impact of taxation on foreign direct investment.

For example, the standard model ignores differences in how domestic-source and foreign-source income are calculated by a given country. For example, the United States uses an earnings and profits concept to measure the foreign-source income for the purpose of calculating the limitation on the foreign tax credit: this is different from both the U.S. concept of taxable income and any host country's definition of income; accelerated depreciation does not apply, nor are there research and development or investment tax credits.

The definition of what is domestic-source and what is foreign-source income also differs across countries. This raises the possibility of double or zero taxation, even when tax rates are the same across countries. Thus, it is crucial to examine the effect on the cost of capital of such provisions as interest allocation rules, R&D allocation rules, and the U.S. export-source rule, under which half of the income earned on U.S.-produced exports is denoted foreign source. This is of no importance to a purely domestic company, but to a multinational in an excess credit position, it expands the foreign tax credit limit and can thereby increase the amount of foreign income taxes that can be credited against U.S. tax liability.

The most glaring omission in the standard model is income shifting. Implicitly, it assumes that income is costlessly observable by the tax enforcement agency. That is an untenable assumption in a closed domestic economy. It is completely unrealistic in an open economy, where the very concept of where income is earned is slippery, and there is substantial empirical evidence of nontrivial income shifting done by multinational enterprises. An important question is to what extent the ability to shift taxable income from high-tax to low-tax countries offsets the tax disadvantage to multinationals due to overlapping jurisdictions that is documented in Jun's paper and others. The potential for income shifting also affects the allocation of real investment. Ireland is more attractive than otherwise as a site for multinational investment because it has a low statutory corporation income tax that makes it a magnet for income shifting. The same marginal effective tax rate on investment could be achieved with a higher statutory tax rate and more nonrate incentives such as accelerated depreciation, but this would not be as attractive for real investment, as multinationals look ahead to the possibility that once real operations are located in Ireland, income shifting can occur. What is required is an "income shifting adjusted" cost of capital, as calculated in Hines and Rice (1994) and Grubert and Slemrod (1993).

Finally, I suggest that there is a large payoff for more disaggregated studies of the taxation of cross-border investment. For example, the residual tax imposed upon repatriation is likely to place a large penalty on a U.S. company which operates predominantly in low-tax countries, but not on companies which operate largely in high-tax countries. In this sense, the issue is not country specific as much as it is sector specific or firm specific. A firm-specific approach would allow one to take advantage of information concerning whether a firm is in an excess or deficit foreign tax credit position.

I would like to close my remarks with a few random thoughts about the thriving cost-of-capital "industry," of which this paper is a part. First, an easy point. It is well documented that cost-of-capital calculations such as those in this paper are very sensitive to essentially arbitrary assumptions about such things as rate of inflation, real rate of return, and the sources of marginal financing. On a more constructive note, I encourage the participants in this industry to do more to justify its existence. In particular, it remains to be seen whether the marginal effective tax rates that are generated by these procedures are more successful in explaining phenomena such as the pattern of foreign direct investment than less conceptually appealing, but also less arbitrary, alternatives based on average tax rates.

To sum up, this paper by Joosung Jun is a careful and thoughtful addition to the literature that uses the King-Fullerton framework to address the tax disincentives to foreign direct investment. This framework needs to be extended to properly address some of the critical issues in the taxation of multinational corporations.

References

Devereux, Michael P., and Harold Freeman. 1994. The implications of alternative tax integration schemes for foreign direct investment. International Tax Policy Forum Working Paper. Washington, D.C.: International Tax Policy Forum, March.

Grubert, Harry, and Joel Slemrod. 1993. Tax effects on investment and income shifting in Puerto Rico. Manuscript, University of Michigan.

Hines, James R., Jr., and Eric M. Rice. 1994. Fiscal paradise: Foreign tax havens and American business. *Quarterly Journal of Economics* 109:149–82.

OECD (Organisation for Economic Co-operation and Development). 1991. *Taxing profits in a global economy: Domestic and international issues.* Paris: OECD.

5   The Tax Sensitivity of Foreign Direct Investment: Evidence from Firm-Level Panel Data

Jason G. Cummins and R. Glenn Hubbard

5.1   Introduction

Understanding the determinants of foreign direct investment is important for analyzing capital flows and the industrial organization of multinational firms. Most empirical studies of foreign direct investment, however, have focused on case studies of nontax factors in overseas investment decisions or on discerning reduced-form relationships between some measure of direct investment and variables relating to nontax and tax aspects of the investment decision. These studies (which we review in section 5.2) have helped to assess the qualitative effects of changes in underlying determinants on firms' overseas investment activities. It is more difficult, we argue below, to infer structural links between tax parameters and foreign direct investment in existing studies. Our interest in investigating those structural links stems both from a desire to extend models of foreign direct investment and from a concern that policymakers' consideration of using tax instruments to influence foreign direct investment requires a more formal empirical analysis.

At one level, this task is straightforward. A number of authors have related tax parameters in "home" (residence) and "host" (source) countries to financial variables such as the cost of capital or Tobin's q. Given such relationships, one could extend and exploit conventional neoclassical investment models devel-

Jason G. Cummins is assistant professor of economics at New York University and John M. Olin Fellow at Columbia University. R. Glenn Hubbard is the Russell L. Carson professor of economics and finance at the Graduate School of Business of Columbia University and a research associate of the National Bureau of Economic Research. Cummins acknowledges the financial support of the Center for International Business Education and the Chazen Institute at Columbia University.

The authors are grateful to Rosanne Altshuler, Debbie Compton, Martin Feldstein, Trevor Harris, David Hartman, Kevin Hassett, James Hines, Donald Kirk, James Poterba, and the conference participants for helpful comments and suggestions.

oped to explain firms' domestic investment decisions to estimate effects of tax parameters on outbound or inbound foreign direct investment.

In practice, this exercise is not so easy. Studies of effects of tax parameters on (generally inbound) U.S. foreign direct investment have relied on aggregated (by country) data on investment flows calculated by the Bureau of Economic Analysis. Because these data do not distinguish between new capital investment and acquisitions of existing assets, it is difficult to use them in tests of formal models of investment decisions. Given our interest in the effects of tax policy on foreign direct investment, this definitional problem is a significant one. In particular, Auerbach and Hassett (1993) have noted that the consequences of neglecting the different tax treatments of the two forms of U.S. inbound foreign direct investment are substantial.

In this paper, we examine the effects of taxation on foreign direct investment using previously unexplored (for this purpose) panel data on outbound foreign direct investment by subsidiaries of U.S. multinational firms collected by Compustat's Geographic Segment file project. These firm-level data contain information on new capital investment overseas, which enable us to measure tax influences on foreign direct investment more precisely and allow us to focus on structural models of subsidiaries' new investment decisions. The paper is organized as follows. Section 5.2 reviews the existing empirical literature on the determinants of foreign direct investment. Our model of the effect of tax and nontax factors on firms' foreign direct investment decisions is presented in section 5.3. Section 5.4 describes the panel data on multinational parent firms and their foreign subsidiaries that we use to estimate the model. We analyze empirical results for U.S. outbound foreign direct investment in section 5.5 and discuss in section 5.6 implications of those results for analyzing the role of tax policy in firms' overseas investment decisions. Section 5.7 concludes.

5.2 Empirical Literature on FDI

Existing empirical studies of foreign direct investment (FDI) reflect researchers' interest in industrial organization or taxation.[1] Industrial organization inquiries have generally ignored tax considerations and analyzed FDI as being governed by firms' desire to exploit the value of ownership-specific assets (such as valuable intangibles) or location-specific advantages (related to sourcing or marketing). Empirical research has centered on reduced-form, cross-sectional tests of FDI in a particular sector as a product of proxies for ownership-specific and location-specific variables (see, e.g., the studies in Dunning 1985).[2] Public finance inquiries have focused on the role of differen-

---

1. An exception is the survey in Caves (1982), which discusses both considerations.

2. Two other "industrial organization" approaches have also appeared in the literature. Wilson (1993) has used case studies to examine the roles played by nontax and tax considerations in

tial tax treatment as determining the source and location of FDI, holding constant nontax determinants.[3]

A significant body of empirical research by public finance economists has emphasized effects of taxation on FDI into the United States. This literature has generally examined reduced-form relationships between capital flows and measures of after-tax rates of return or effective tax rates on capital income.

Several studies have used annual aggregate data for FDI financed by subsidiary earnings and parent company transfers of funds, following Hartman's (1981, 1984, 1985) contributions.[4] Hartman used as a theoretical benchmark the "tax capitalization" approach to analyzing firms' dividend and investment decisions (see the derivation in King 1977; Auerbach 1979; Bradford 1981).[5] In that approach, dividend payouts are a residual in firm decisions. Payout ratios do not affect firms' required rate of return on equity, and permanent changes in individual tax rates do not affect dividend payouts or the cost of capital. In the context of FDI, these implications permit Hartman to ignore effects of (at least permanent changes in) home-country tax parameters on FDI in "mature" subsidiaries—that is, those paying dividends to their parent firms.[6] We return to this issue in section 5.3.

Hartman (1984) estimated the effects of U.S. inbound FDI of changes in the after-tax rates of return received by foreign investors in U.S. inbound FDI and by investors in U.S. capital generally, with the intent of measuring impacts of shifts in returns to new FDI. He also includes as an explanatory variable the tax rate on U.S. capital owned by foreign investors relative to that owned by U.S. investors.[7] His estimated models do not incorporate measures of U.S. withholding taxes, foreign income taxes, or rates of return on non-U.S. investments.

---

location decisions. In a different vein, Froot and Stein (1991) study the influence of capital-market imperfections on the source of FDI.

3. Theoretical analyses in this vein include Gersovitz (1987) and Alworth (1988). We review empirical studies below. For overviews of systems for taxing income from FDI, see Ault and Bradford (1990), Frisch (1990), Hines and Hubbard (1990), U.S. Joint Committee on Taxation (1990, 1991), and U.S. Department of the Treasury (1993).

4. Hartman used data on FDI for 1965–79, provided by the Bureau of Economic Analysis (BEA); the data are separated according to whether investment was financed by subsidiary retained earnings or transfers from foreign parent companies.

5. Sinn (1984) also demonstrated that retention-financed investments by subsidiaries are independent of home-country tax parameters. The work of Hartman and Sinn built on the earlier work by Horst (1977), who maintained that a subsidiary's cost of capital depended on both home- and host-country tax parameters when profits are remitted.

6. This prediction is more suitably applied to firm-level data than to aggregate FDI data, of course. The tax capitalization approach suggests that a mature subsidiary's investment financed by retained earnings is unaffected by the home-country tax rate. This suggestion is not equivalent to a claim that aggregate investment out of retained earnings will not be affected by the home-country tax rate.

7. Hartman intends this last variable to proxy for effects on asset valuation of taxes applying only to U.S. investors. (Changes in the valuation of assets affect the cost of investing for potential foreign investors.)

Using the log of the ratio of FDI to U.S. GNP as the dependent variable,[8] Hartman's results indicate that the FDI-GNP ratio increases as the after-tax rates of return rise and decreases as the relative tax rate on foreigners rises. The variables have the expected sign, though explanatory power was much better for investment financed by subsidiary retained earnings. These suggestive findings indicate that taxes are an important determinant of FDI.

Hartman's study provoked many subsequent rounds of replication and refinement. Employing the rate-of-return series calculated by Feldstein and Jun (1987), Boskin and Gale (1987) reestimate Hartman's model using data over the period 1956–84. While their results vary across specifications and time periods, they are qualitatively consistent with Hartman's original findings.

In his dissertation, Newlon (1987) reconsiders and extends the earlier analyses of Hartman and of Boskin and Gale (1987). After correcting miscalculations in the FDI data from the BEA (for the years 1965–73), Newlon reestimates the specifications used by earlier authors and finds that the model relating the log of the FDI-GNP ratio to after-tax rates of return on transfers of funds fits better, though the model for investment financed by retained earnings fits more poorly. When Newlon uses data over the 1956–84 period, his results depart from those of Hartman and Boskin and Gale. He finds no statistically significant estimated coefficient that explains FDI financed by transfers of funds.

These studies are important advances in our understanding of the effects of taxation on FDI. A number of concerns arise, however. An obvious one relates to problems of inference using reduced-form models and highly aggregated data; we return to this in section 5.3 and 5.4. A second relates to the omission of home-country tax rates from the analysis (see, e.g., Slemrod 1990, discussed below). Third, nontax determinants of FDI are not explicitly modeled. Fourth, Newlon (1987) and others have noted a problem in interpreting the coefficient on the rate of return on FDI financed by retained earnings. As long as the home-country taxes worldwide income using a foreign tax credit and deferral, a subsidiary is likely to finance investment first by using retained earnings. In this case, when the subsidiary's desired investment exceeds its retained earnings, the subsidiary will retain all of its income; that is, required earnings and income will be equal. This could lead to a spurious correlation between investment financed out of retained earnings and the rate of return (where the numerator of the latter is effectively retained earnings).[9] Finally, the FDI data supplied by the BEA suffer two drawbacks, even accepting their level of

8. Young (1988) relaxes the assumption that the GNP elasticity of U.S. inbound FDI is unity. With this modification, and using revised data over the 1956–84 period, he estimates a smaller (though still statistically significant) response of FDI financed by retained earnings to the after-tax rate of return, confirming Hartman's result. Young finds no evidence that taxes affect FDI financed by transfers of new funds.

9. The problem is even more general; the spurious correlation can arise even in cases where the subsidiary follows any fixed rule for determining dividend payments out of current earnings, as noted by Newlon (1987).

aggregation: (1) as noted in the introduction, they measure financial flows rather than new capital investment per se;[10] and (2) they are based on periodic benchmark surveys, raising the possibility that FDI flows are more mismeasured the further is the observation from a benchmark year.[11]

Slemrod (1990) addresses some of these concerns, while still relying on the data on FDI provided by the BEA.[12] He disaggregates the data on FDI into the United States by seven countries—Canada, France, Italy, Japan, the Netherlands, the United Kingdom, and (the former) West Germany. He also makes three departures from the approaches used by earlier authors. First, he controls for a richer set of nontax variables, including the ratio of U.S. GDP to the combined GDP of the seven investing countries (to capture impacts of changing market sizes), the prime-age-male unemployment rate in the United States and the weighted average of the unemployment rates in the seven investing countries (to capture impacts on FDI of business cycles), the real effective exchange rate of the U.S. dollar against the GDP-weighted average of the currencies of the seven investing countries (to capture impacts of changes in relative costs of production), and adjustments to address potential measurement error in FDI (see n. 11 above).

Second, he uses measures of effective tax rates on corporate investment in the United States (calculated by Auerbach and Hines 1988) instead of measures of after-tax returns. Third, he includes lagged as well as contemporaneous measures of this tax rate concept (appealing to "time to build" arguments).

Slemrod's principal findings are as follows. Considering the seven countries together, he concludes that: (1) the marginal effective tax rate in the United States has a negative and statistically significant effect on total FDI and transfer-financed FDI; (2) these estimated impacts of the marginal effective tax rate are not robust to the inclusion of the weighted-average foreign unemployment rate (which is itself positively related to FDI into the United States);

10. As constructed by the BEA, FDI includes purchases of existing assets by foreign investors, while it excludes investment raised in the host country or in third countries. The analysis in Auerbach and Hassett (1993) suggests that a significant proportion of U.S. inbound FDI is related to acquisitions.

11. Slemrod (1990) attempts to address the concerns about the official FDI data. To adjust for potential measurements error in FDI on account of the benchmark procedure, he includes in models of FDI (described below) two dummy variables. The first represents the difference between the year for which the data are provided and the year in which the most recent benchmark survey was conducted. The second relates to the post-1974 period as a proxy for once-and-for-all modifications of definitions and concepts relating to FDI carried out by the BEA in 1974.

12. Using aggregate data on FDI over the 1956–84 period considered by earlier authors, Slemrod first reestimates existing models. He then explores effects of pretax rates of return and tax rates separately. For FDI financed by retained earnings, he finds that the estimated coefficients on tax terms are insignificantly different from zero; for FDI financed by transfers of funds, the estimated coefficients on tax terms have the expected sign and are significantly different from zero. These results are the opposite of those in Hartman (1984). When Slemrod uses the marginal effective corporate tax rate on investment calculated by Auerbach and Hines (1988) (instead of the average tax rate), he finds that the marginal effective tax rate has a statistically significant effect on transfer-financed FDI but not on retention-financed FDI.

(3) of the nontax variables, the relative GDP measures, the U.S. unemployment rate, and the FDI measurement adjustment have no statistically significant impact on FDI; and (4) the real effective dollar exchange rate has a negative and statistically significant impact on inbound FDI.[13] When he groups the countries into those with worldwide (foreign tax credit) and those with territorial (exemption) systems, Slemrod's results fail to support predictable differences in the tax sensitivity of FDI between the two groups.[14]

While Slemrod's contribution addresses some of the concerns raised in the empirical literature, it raises others. For example, there are questions about the merits of Slemrod's approach to the problem of spurious correlation between retention-financed FDI and after-tax rates of return (see Hartman 1990). Second, as noted earlier, the BEA data do not allow one to distinguish new investment and acquisitions in FDI. Finally, the approach does not suggest a structural model, which could be used for policy inference.

In the next section, we develop a simple structural model to study new FDI by individual firms. As the reader will likely note in that section and in the following section describing the firm-level panel data we use, our approach also requires many simplifying assumptions. In our view, however, the application of standard, theoretical investment models to firms' decisions offers the best hope of assessing effects of home-country and host-country tax systems on FDI.[15]

5.3   Modeling Effects of Taxes on FDI

5.3.1   Basic Issues

In a world of ideal data, assessing the impact of taxation on firms' FDI decisions would be straightforward.[16] In the q-theory approach, for example, investment I of parent firm i in subsidiary j at time t relative to that subsidiary's capital stock K, under certain conditions,[17] depends linearly on that subsidiary's marginal q, appropriately adjusted for tax considerations.[18] That is,

---

13. While possibly consistent with the low-relative-production-cost explanation offered by Slemrod (see also Pugel 1985), this result is also considered with the capital-market-imperfection explanation offered by Froot and Stein (1991): a low value of the dollar increases the dollar value of foreign investors' net worth, enabling them to offer more collateral and obtain more funds to finance investment in the United States.

14. Such apparent insensitivity could reflect problems in the specification or the tax rate measure, or, in addition, the use of techniques for intertemporal tax minimization.

15. This exercise is similar in spirit to the study of subsidiary dividend repatriation decisions in Hines and Hubbard (1990) and Altshuler, Newlon, and Randolph (chap. 9 in this volume).

16. For the purpose of this analysis, we are ignoring some cost considerations associated with the choice of capacity.

17. The necessary assumptions include perfect competition, constant returns to scale technologies, and quadratic adjustment costs; see, e.g., Hayashi (1982) and Summers (1981).

18.There is nothing special about the q-formulation of the investment demand equation; one could use the cost of capital formulation as well (see, e.g., Cummins, Hassett, and Hubbard 1994). Altshuler and Fulghieri (1990) illustrate the effects of home- and host-country tax parameters and the parent's tax status on a subsidiary's cost of capital.

$$\frac{I_{ijt}}{K_{ij,\,t-1}} = a_{ij} + bq_{ijt} + \varepsilon_{ijt},$$

where a and b are parameters to be estimated and ε is an expectational error.

Home-country and host-country tax parameters have been incorporated in theoretical definitions of the subsidiary's marginal q by Alworth (1988), Altshuler and Fulghieri (1994), Jun (1990), and others, under different assumptions about the taxing regime, dividend policy, and foreign tax credit status of the parent (in countries with worldwide tax systems). In this abstraction, we could estimate a and b, thereby permitting a calculation of elasticities of investment demand with respect to various tax parameters influencing multinational firms' FDI decisions. We could also compare the reasonableness of estimates of a and b with parameters estimated from firm-level data on domestic investment by similarly situated firms in home and host countries.

Unfortunately, this ideal is not particularly useful as a practical guide to estimating effects of taxation on the level of firms' FDI. First, it is difficult to develop a proxy for marginal q under the best of circumstances.[19] For FDI, a further complication arises because location-specific effects on the subsidiary's q cannot be captured by using available data to construct the parent's q, and values of subsidiary-specific q's are not observable.

To reduce these problems, while using the same basic structural strategy as that just described, we use the Euler equation approach to estimate the responsiveness of investment to tax parameters (see, e.g., Abel 1980; Hubbard and Kashyap 1992). As we discuss below, this approach has fewer informational requirements than the conventional q-theory representation used in the empirical investment literature. Nonetheless, it permits estimation of the same structural parameters in the foregoing example so that we can still ask: Given a change in a tax parameter, how does a subsidiary's marginal q change, and how does FDI change? The approach also permits consideration of expounded models in which "net worth" changes can affect FDI (see, e.g., Gertler and Hubbard 1988; Froot and Stein 1991).

5.3.2 Euler Equation Approach

Analyzing investment demand begins with an expression for the value to the parent i of the foreign subsidiary j.[20] The after-tax return to the parent firm at time t reflects capital appreciation and current dividends.[21] In equilibrium, this return equals the return ρ_{ijt}:

$$(1) \qquad \rho_{ijt} = \frac{(1 - t_{it}^{r})[E_t(V_{ij,t+1} - S_{ij,t+1}) - V_{ijt}] + (1 - t_{it}^{d})E_tD_{ij,t+1}}{V_{ijt}},$$

19. See the discussion in Hayashi (1982) and Hubbard and Kashyap (1992).
20. The derivation herein expands on Hubbard and Kashyap (1992) and Hubbard, Kashyap, and Whited (1995).
21. For simplicity, we consider one majority-owned subsidiary per parent; we are thereby abstracting from tax-minimizing strategies available to parent firms with multiple subsidiaries. We are also abstracting from parent investment through third-party conduits located in neither the parent's country nor the subsidiary's country.

where V is the value of the subsidiary at time t, S denotes the value of parent equity transfers, t^r is the effective tax rate on subsidiary earnings retained and invested abroad, and E_t is the expectation operator conditional on information known at time t. (The after-tax capital gain to the parent firm thus consists of the change in the value of the subsidiary less the component of this change due to parent transfers.) Subsidiary j's dividends to its parent i at time $t + 1$ are $D_{ij,t+1}$, and t^d is the tax rate on those dividends. This derivation follows the tax capitalization view of the dividend decision (see the discussion in section 5.2), in which the required rate of return for equity investment in the subsidiary is independent of the subsidiary's dividend policy.

In the absence of any bubbles, solving equation (1) forward yields the following expression for the subsidiary's value at time zero, where β_{ijt} is the appropriate one-period discount factor:

$$(2) \qquad V_{tj0} = E_0 \sum_{t=0}^{\infty} \left(\prod_{j=0}^{t-1} \beta_{ijt} \right) \left[\left(\frac{1 - t_{ijt}^d}{1 - t_{ijt}^r} \right) D_{ijt} - S_{ijt} \right].$$

The subsidiary maximizes equation (2) subject to five constraints.[22] The first is the capital stock accounting identity:

$$(3) \qquad K_{ijt} = I_{ijt} + (1 - \delta) K_{ij,t-1},$$

where K_{ijt} is the capital stock of subsidiary j at time t, I_{ijt} is its investment at time t, and δ is the (assumed constant) rate of economic depreciation.

The second constraint defines dividends. Cash inflows include sales, parent equity transfers, and net borrowing, while cash outflows consist of dividends, variable factor and interest payments, and investment expenditures:

$$(4) \qquad D_{ijt} = (1 - \tau_{jt}) [F(K_{ij,t-1}, N_{ijt}) - w_{jt} N_{ijt} - \psi (I_{ijt}, K_{ij,t-1}) - i_{ij,t-1}$$
$$B_{ij,t-1}] + S_{ijt} + B_{ijt} - (1 - \pi_{jt}^e) B_{ij,t-1} - p_{ijt} (1 - k_{jt} - \tau_{jt} z_{jt}) I_{ijt},$$

where

$N_{ijt} =$ a vector of variable factors of production for subsidiary j at time t;

$w_{jt} =$ a vector of real factor prices for subsidiary j at time t;

$B_{ijt} =$ the real value of net debt outstanding for subsidiary j at time t;[23]

$i_{ijt} =$ nominal interest rate paid on subsidiary j's debt at time t;

$\pi_{jt}^e =$ expected rate of inflation at time t (in currency in which subsidiary j borrows);

$p_{ijt} =$ subsidiary j's price of capital goods at time t relative to the price of output at time t;

22. We are assuming that the parent firm has a controlling interest in the subsidiary.
23. This setup implicitly assumes that the subsidiary's debt can be obtained on identical terms from different sources and that the parent cannot successfully disguise repatriation of profits interest.

$\tau_{jt} =$ corporate income tax rate in the host country for subsidiary j at time t;

$k_{jt} =$ investment tax credit in the host country applying to subsidiary j at time t;

$z_{jt} =$ present value of one dollar of depreciation allowances in the host country applying to subsidiary j at time t;

$F(K_{ij,t-1}, N_{ijt}) =$ subsidiary's real net revenue function ($F_K > 0$, $F_{KK} < 0$); and

$\psi(I_{ijt}, K_{ij,t-1}) =$ real cost of adjusting the capital stock ($\psi_I > 0$, $\psi_{II} > 0$, $\psi_K < 0$, $\psi_{KK} < 0$).

The third and fourth constraints restrict dividends and parent equity transfers, respectively, to be nonnegative:

(5) $$D_{ijt} \geq 0$$

and

(6) $$S_{ijt} \geq 0.$$

The fifth constraint is a transversality condition that prevents the firm from borrowing an infinite amount to pay dividends:

(7) $$\lim_{T \to \infty} \left(\prod_{s=t}^{T-1} \beta_{ijs}\right) B_{ijT} = 0, \text{ for all } t.$$

Let λ_{it} be the series of Lagrange multipliers associated with the constraint (5), and let m_{ijt} represent the ratio $(1 - t^d_{ijt})/(1 - t^r_{ijt})$. Substituting equation (4) into equation (2) for D_{ijt}, and using equation (3) to eliminate I_{ijt} from the problem, the first-order condition for the subsidiary's capital stock (K_{ijt}) can be expressed as

$$E_t \beta_{ijt}\left(\frac{m_{ij,t+1} + \lambda_{ij,t+1}}{m_{ijt} + \lambda_{ijt}}\right)\left\{F_K(K_{ijt}, N_{ij,t+1}) - \psi_K(I_{ij,t+1}, K_{ijt})\right.$$

(8) $$+ (1 - \delta)\left[\psi_I(I_{ij,t+1}, K_{ijt}) + p_{ij,t+1}\left(\frac{1 - k_{j,t+1} - \tau_{j,t+1} z_{j,t+1}}{1 - \tau_{j,t+1}}\right)\right]\right\}$$

$$= \psi_I(I_{ijt}, K_{ij,t-1}) + p_{ijt}\left(\frac{1 - k_{jt} - \tau_{jt} z_{jt}}{1 - \tau_{jt}}\right).$$

To obtain an equation for investment, it is necessary to parameterize the adjustment cost function, $\psi(I_{ijt}, K_{ij,t-1})$. The tradition in the q-theory literature has been to specify adjustment costs that are linearly homogenous in investment and capital, so that marginal and average q are equal (see Hayashi 1982). A convenient parameterization adhering to these constraints is

(9) $$\psi(I_{ijt}, K_{ij,t-1}) = \frac{\alpha}{2}\left(\frac{I_{ijt}}{K_{ij,t-1}} - v_i\right)I_{ijt},$$

where the bliss point in the adjustment cost function is given by v_i. By differentiating equation (9) with respect to I_{ijt} and K_{ijt}, and substituting these results into (8), we obtain

(10)
$$
\begin{aligned}
E_t \beta_{ijt} &\left\{ \left(\frac{m_{ij,t+1} + \lambda_{ij,t+1}}{m_{ijt} + \lambda_{ijt}} \right) F_K(K_{ijt}, N_{ij,t+1}) + \frac{\alpha}{2}\left(\frac{I_{ij,t+1}}{K_{ijt}} \right)^2 \right. \\
&\left. + (1 - \delta) \left[\alpha\left(\frac{I_{ij,t+1}}{K_{ijt}} \right) + p_{ij,t+1}\left(\frac{1 - k_{j,t+1} - \tau_{j,t+1} z_{j,t+1}}{1 - \tau_{j,t+1}} \right) - v_i \right] \right\} \\
&= \alpha\left(\frac{I_{ijt}}{K_{ij,t-1}} \right) + \frac{p_{ijt}(1 - k_{jt} - \tau_{jt} z_{jt})}{1 - \tau_{jt}} - v_i.
\end{aligned}
$$

We assume that expectations are rational and allow for an expectational error, $e_{i,t+1}$, where $E_t(e_{i,t+1}) = 0$ and $E_t(e^2_{i,t+1}) = \sigma_e^2$. The error is uncorrelated with any information known at time t, thereby allowing us to reexpress equation (10) as

(11)
$$
\begin{aligned}
\tilde{\beta}_{ijt} F_K(K_{ijt}, N_{ij,t+1}) &+ \left(\frac{\alpha}{2} \right) \tilde{\beta}_{ijt}\left(\frac{I_{ij,t+1}}{K_{ijt}} \right)^2 + \alpha(1 - \delta)\, \tilde{\beta}_{ijt}\left(\frac{I_{ij,t+1}}{K_{ijt}} \right) \\
&+ (1 - \delta)\tilde{\beta}_{ijt}\left[\frac{p_{ij,t+1}(1 - k_{j,t+1} - \tau_{j,t+1} z_{j,t+1})}{1 - \tau_{j,t+1}} - v_i \right] - \alpha\left(\frac{I_{ijt}}{K_{ij,t-1}} \right) \\
&- \frac{p_{ijt}(1 - k_{jt} - \tau_{jt} z_{jt})}{1 - \tau_{jt}} + v_i = e_{ij,t+1},
\end{aligned}
$$

where

(12)
$$
\tilde{\beta}_{ijt} = \beta_{ijt}\left(\frac{m_{ij,t+1} + \lambda_{ij,t+1}}{m_{ijt} + \lambda_{ijt}} \right).
$$

For the cases mentioned below, we will use the generalized method of moments (GMM) to test for misspecification of equation (11). With a set of instrumental variables that are orthogonal to the error term, the orthogonality conditions should not be rejected for equation (11).

Our strategy is as follows. We estimate the model in equation (11) using data on FDI in foreign subsidiaries of U.S. firms (described below) and proceed in two steps, producing GMM estimates of the underlying parameters under alternative assumptions that tax variables are omitted from or included in the model. Assuming that we have appropriately modeled the subsidiary's investment decision (and chosen appropriate instrumental variables), if tax considerations are important, parameter estimates should be implausible in the "no tax" version, and the model's orthogonality conditions should be rejected. On the other hand, we expect more plausible parameter estimates when tax considerations are properly specified, and the model's orthogonality conditions should not be rejected. Successful estimation of the model's parameters then enables us to return to the q-theoretic experiment suggested in section 5.3: What is the predicted effect on outbound FDI of changes in domestic and foreign tax parameters?

5.3.3   Econometric Estimation

Two general issues arise in the estimation of equation (11). First, the model is nonlinear in both the parameters and the ratio of investment to the capital stock. Moreover, there is a simultaneity problem because of the presence of the expected marginal product of capital in the model. These two considerations argue for GMM estimation.[24]

Second, given the industrial organization considerations discussed in section 5.2, we want to allow for the possibility of firm-specific and time-specific effects. We include year dummies to deal with the latter. Because of the presence of the lagged dependent variable in equation (11), the standard practice of accounting for firm-specific effects by removing the means from the variables in the model will violate the orthogonality conditions used to identify the model. Instead, we first-difference equation (11) and then use twice-lagged instruments, which will still be orthogonal to the moving-average error that the differencing creates.

5.4   The Data

5.4.1   Panel Data on FDI

The data set is constructed from the Compustat Geographic Segment file. Approximately 6,500 companies report information from their foreign operations, segregated by geographic segment. Both U.S.- and foreign-incorporated firms report sales, operating income, and fixed assets. Up to four geographic regions are reported for seven years at a time. We combine two seven-year panels to obtain a data set extending from 1980 to 1991. There is no requirement by either the Financial Accounting Standards Board (FASB) or the SEC regarding the groupings for geographic areas. As a result, the degree of specificity among company reports varies. For example, consider two companies operating in the same countries. Company A might report four different geographic areas: France, Germany, Canada, and Asia. Company B might report two different geographic areas: France and Europe, and "other foreign."

The accounting literature stresses that considerable caution should be exercised in making inferences about data reported for regions and for groups of countries (see, e.g, Pointer and Doupnik 1993). No conclusions about their relative importance can be made from the data. Consider company B again. It is not necessarily the case that one can isolate its French operations since it

---

24. The GMM technique minimizes a quadratic objective function that has an optimal weighting matrix based on initial parameter estimates. The model will be overidentified as long as the number of instrumental variables used exceeds the number of parameters to be estimated. The test is formulated as follows: Under the null hypothesis of orthogonality of the instruments and the error terms, the product of the minimized value of the objective function and the number of observations is distributed as a χ^2 statistic with n degrees of freedom, where n is the difference between the numbers of instruments and parameters. The overidentifying restrictions are rejected if the χ^2 value is higher than a critical value.

reports them first and aggregates all its other European operations. In constructing the panel, we minimize this problem by taking the most conservative course. We include only geographic segments when a single country is reported. While this strategy reduces the number of observations, it increases data quality and accuracy.

A second pitfall in using geographic segment data is that it is sometimes impossible to obtain data in a manner consistent with official definitions because of a company's method of reporting. This is, of course, a problem in constructing any firm-level panel data; it deserves special mention here because companies have more than the usual latitude in what they include in the data. For example, excise taxes might be included in sales, or the value of intangibles might be included in fixed assets. We mitigate the problem by isolating discrepancies from data footnotes. Nevertheless, we emphasize that care is required in constructing variables from these data.

The data are better understood by knowing their genesis. Geographic segment disclosures are mandated by *Statement of Financial Accounting Standards No. 14—Financial Reporting of Segments in a Business Enterprise* (SFAS 14), issued in 1976.[25] SFAS 14 was designed to provide information useful for evaluating the nature of the firm's investment and production decisions but to allow discretion in defining reportable segments and in employing coarse definitions. SFAS 14 requires firms to disclose information about foreign sales, income, and fixed assets if foreign operations account for 10 percent or more of a firm's revenues or assets. The directive became effective for companies with fiscal years ending after December 15, 1976. Two notes should be made about data extending to 1976. Segment data through fiscal years ending in 1979 contain many classification adjustments consistent with a learning process. Moreover, there appears to be little gain from extending samples before 1979, because of the paucity of data. As a result of these considerations, we begin our sample in 1980.

In addition to the pitfalls considered above, two more subtle issues arise in using the geographic segment data. First, as we noted in the introduction, to understand properly the effect of taxes on FDI, the "new investment" component must be separated from the "mergers and acquisitions" component. This is a potentially serious problem in these data, since reporting requirements are broad and data definitions are coarse. While practitioners' advice mitigated our concern,[26] we took two additional steps in the data construction to minimize any potential contamination. First, as is typical in the investment literature, we deleted major capital stock changes to eliminate clear discontinuities in the identity of the firm. Second, the geographic segment file provides a foot-

---

25. See, e.g., the discussions in Senteney and Bazaz (1992) and Pointer and Doupnik (1993).

26. In a private communication, Donald Kirk, chairman of the FASB when SFAS 14 was promulgated, explained to us that firms usually do not record the acquisition of capital through mergers and acquisitions in their geographic segment report. Debbie Compton, senior data manager at Standard & Poor's Compustat, confirmed that Compustat geographic segment data typically do not reflect the results of merger-and-acquisition activity.

note if the data reflect the results of a merger or acquisition; we deleted firms recording this footnote.

A second potential problem is that geographic segment data are reported in U.S. dollars. Since currency fluctuations could misrepresent the value of the foreign subsidiary's data, it is necessary to determine when geographic segment data are converted to dollars. For the purposes of SFAS 14, firms typically convert the data when balance sheets are prepared at fiscal year end.[27]

5.4.2 Constructing Variables Used in the Estimation

We construct the variables used in the econometric estimation as follows. The subsidiary's sales are defined as reported net sales for that geographic segment. The subsidiary's cash flow is defined as the sum of its operating profit and, if available, its depreciation; gross investment is the change in the gross stock of tangible fixed assets. Each of the above variables is divided by the beginning-of-period value of tangible fixed assets. We assume that the subsidiary's capital stock depreciation rate and nominal cost of borrowing is equal to those of its parent firm, which we calculated elsewhere, in Cummins, Hassett, and Hubbard (1994). Host-country tax variables (investment tax credit, depreciation allowances, corporate income tax rate, and withholding tax rate) are taken from Cummins, Harris, and Hassett (chap. 7 in this volume). A detailed discussion of their construction is provided therein with accompanying tables. The price of capital goods is the host country's investment price deflator. All variables are deflated by the host country's GDP deflator.

Tables 5.1–5.4 summarize our data on U.S. firm's outbound FDI; the construction of variables is described therein and below.

Table 5.1 indicates the number of U.S. foreign subsidiaries reporting information in the Compustat data. Countries for which Compustat reports data are Canada, the United Kingdom, (the former West) Germany, France, Japan, and Australia. Data are available over the time period 1980–91. While the number of subsidiaries reporting information varies from year to year (generally growing over the period), we are able to obtain investment and operating information on 282–632 U.S. foreign subsidiaries.

Tables 5.2–5.4 report summary statistics for subsidiary investment, operating income, and sales, respectively. The entries in table 5.2 represent the mean value for year t of the ratio of investment (I_t) to beginning-of-period capital stock (K_{t-1}).[28] The means are calculated using the values of the subsid-

---

27. We thank Donald Kirk for explaining this point to us. Debbie Compton again confirmed that Compustat believes that the data are converted in this way.

28. Since the geographic segment file data are reported in U.S. dollars, one must confront the issue of exchange rate shifts in calculating gross investment as the first-difference in the dollar-valued capital stock. One approach—which is used to generate the estimated results reported in section 5.5—is to construct I/K data from the dollar-valued capital stock data. Alternatively, one could convert the capital stock data into year-end foreign-currency equivalents in constructing I/K. As we describe below in n. 35, our empirical results are not significantly affected by this change. Neither approach is precisely correct because, in principle, investment should be valued in foreign-currency terms as it is made over the year.

Table 5.1   Number of U.S. Foreign Subsidiaries in Sample

Year	Canada	United Kingdom	Germany	France	Japan	Australia	Total
1980	225	25	12	3	4	13	282
1981	224	36	12	4	5	12	293
1982	242	45	11	5	7	14	324
1983	254	54	10	5	10	13	346
1984	272	58	13	6	15	14	378
1985	307	81	16	10	19	18	451
1986	320	94	19	11	23	24	491
1987	346	105	22	11	26	23	533
1988	362	104	21	11	24	24	546
1989	394	113	20	11	25	26	589
1990	403	121	32	15	29	32	632
1991	366	119	29	17	25	26	582

Source: Authors' calculations.

Table 5.2   Mean I_t/K_{t-1} of U.S. Foreign Subsidiaries

Year	Canada	United Kingdom	Germany	France	Japan	Australia	Total
1981	.142	.124	.018	.072	.093	.152	.136
1982	.077	.101	.021	.339	.046	.128	.080
1983	.108	.077	.019	.013	.220	.211	.110
1984	.069	.120	.016	.306	.163	.056	.077
1985	.122	.327	.309	.213	.224	.321	.170
1986	.125	.248	.320	.283	.412	.066	.179
1987	.181	.351	.451	.497	.344	.296	.253
1988	.202	.193	.149	.082	.270	.318	.208
1989	.145	.135	.135	.222	.136	.201	.146
1990	.117	.195	.195	.275	.222	.138	.168
1991	.084	.130	.138	.138	.249	.109	.119

Source: Authors' calculations.
Note: I_t is gross investment.

iary capital stocks as weights. The "operating income" entries in table 5.3 represent the (capital-stock-weighted) mean values of the ratio of operating income to the beginning-of-period capital stock for the various years and countries. The "sales" entries in table 5.4 represent the (capital-stock-weighted) mean values of the ratio of sales to the beginning-of-period capital stock for the various years and countries.

We used three alternative approaches to constructing $\tilde{\beta}$. First, we assumed that $\beta = 0.95$, that is, an implicit real after-tax annual required rate of return of 5.3 percent. (Setting β equal to 0.90 or 0.99 did not significantly affect our

Table 5.3   **Mean *Cash Flow*$_t$/K_{t-1} of U.S. Foreign Subsidiaries**

Year	Canada	United Kingdom	Germany	France	Japan	Australia	Total
1981	.141	.029	.032	.012	.120	.199	.123
1982	.122	.098	.125	.021	.022	.188	.118
1983	.127	.105	.064	.086	.087	.115	.119
1984	.133	.143	.044	.454	.128	.055	.131
1985	.130	.078	.078	.463	.370	.124	.134
1986	.131	.125	.255	.102	.092	.030	.128
1987	.169	.131	.152	.113	.167	.450	.170
1988	.168	.157	.014	.270	.364	.134	.171
1989	.107	.096	.041	.110	.246	.133	.112
1990	.102	.109	.092	.355	.276	.091	.111
1991	.073	.087	.063	.431	.221	.053	.091

Source: Authors' calculations.
Note: Cash flow$_t$ is the sum of operating profit and, if available, depreciation.

Table 5.4   **Mean *Sales*$_t$/K_{t-1} of U.S. Foreign Subsidiaries**

Year	Canada	United Kingdom	Germany	France	Japan	Australia	Total
1981	1.55	1.37	1.40	1.50	.808	1.23	1.51
1982	1.29	1.52	1.42	1.33	1.59	1.54	1.34
1983	1.44	1.48	1.49	.476	1.63	1.30	1.43
1984	1.49	1.38	1.61	1.15	1.96	1.08	1.47
1985	1.46	1.46	1.82	2.03	2.19	1.12	1.50
1986	1.57	1.71	2.09	1.47	1.97	1.27	1.62
1987	1.60	1.50	1.69	1.29	1.85	.935	1.57
1988	1.55	1.33	1.43	1.88	2.07	1.38	1.53
1989	1.46	1.62	1.96	1.69	1.68	1.31	1.52
1990	1.38	1.71	1.76	2.03	1.72	.992	1.47
1991	1.36	1.44	1.23	1.80	1.80	.948	1.37

Source: Authors' calculations.
Note: Sales$_t$ is net sales.

results.) Second, we used data on firms' interest rates, aggregate surveys of expected inflation, and corporate tax rates to construct data on β. Finally, we treated β as a parameter to be estimated.

Because the data we used contain no information about subsidiary dividend repatriations, we begin by assuming that subsidiaries are repatriating dividends, so that $\lambda = 0$. We also examine separately a subset of subsidiaries in the data over the entire period (as a proxy for "mature" subsidiaries, for which our "$\lambda = 0$" assumption may be more innocuous).

Finally, to construct m, we use values for the tax on current repatriations t^d

Table 5.5   **Tax Rate on Repatriations of Overseas Earnings from U.S. FDI, t^d**

Tax System[a]	t^d
Classical	
Excess limit parent	$(\tau_{US} - \tau_j)/(l - \tau_j)$
Excess credit parent	w_j
Split-rate	
Excess limit parent	$(\tau_{US} - \tau_j)(l - \tau_j) + \tau_d - \tau_u + d\,(\tau_d - \tau_u)\,(l - \tau_{US})/(l - \tau_j)^2$
Excess credit parent	$\tau_d - \tau_u + w_j$
Imputation	
Excess limit parent	$(l + a_j)\,\{(\tau_{US} - \tau_j)/[l - \tau_j - a_j d_j(l - \tau_{US})]/(l - \tau_j)^2\} - a_j$
Excess credit parent	$(l + a_j)\,w_j - a_j$

Notes: τ_{US} = U.S. corporate tax rate, τ_j = corporate tax rate in host country j, w_j = withholding tax rate in host country j, d_j = dividend payout rate for subsidiary in host country j, τ_u = tax rate on undistributed profits in host country j, τ_d = tax rate on distributed profits in host country j, a_j = tax credit given for advanced corporation tax in host country j.

[a]For the purpose of this grouping, Canada has a classical system, because benefits of corporate tax integration are not extended to controlling U.S. shareholders. The United Kingdom, under its imputation system, provides a partial credit to controlling U.S. shareholders for payment of its "advanced corporation tax." The German corporate tax system is a mixture of imputation and split-rate systems. Germany does not grant an imputation credit to U.S. shareholders, so we treat the German system as a split-rate system in constructing the tax price of individual repatriations. Under France's imputation credit system, the imputation credit (*avoir fiscal*) is not refundable to controlling U.S. shareholders. Japan had a split-rate tax system until 1989, at which time it switched to a classical system. In its imputation system, Australia does not impose a withholding tax on dividends that have borne the (statutory) Australian corporate tax. For a summary of the corporate tax systems in the countries in our sample, see U.S. Department of the Treasury (1992, appendix B).

implied by the tax prices of repatriations summarized in table 5.5 (see also Altshuler and Newlon 1993).[29] The value of t^d depends on whether the U.S. parent is in an excess limit or excess credit position. Parent firms in an excess limit position owe U.S. corporate tax if the U.S. corporate tax rate exceeds the applicable foreign tax rate. Parent firms in an excess credit position owe no U.S. corporate tax. Because we do not have access to the parents' U.S. income tax returns, we cannot describe precisely whether the foreign tax credit limitation is binding. Instead, we assume that firms with average foreign tax rates above the U.S. corporate tax rate have excess foreign tax credits; firms with average foreign tax rates less than or equal to the U.S. corporate tax rate are assumed to be in an excess limit position.[30] We assume that the accrual-

29. In principle, this measure should reflect the *expected* tax price, because, in particular, parent firms may expect to transit between excess limit and excess credit status in the next period. (Evidence on the empirical significance of such transitions is presented in Altshuler et al. [chap. 9 in this volume].) With data on parent firms' stocks of foreign tax credits, one could attempt to approximate the likelihood of a transition between credit states, with attendant effects on the tax price of repatriations. Lacking parent tax return data, we were unable to do this, however.

30. This assumption is quite imperfect in practice, as shown in the comparison with tax data in Altshuler and Newlon (1993).

Table 5.6   **FDI Euler Equation Models (full sample)**

	Adjustment Cost Parameter α		Test of Overidentifying Restrictions χ^2_9	
Model	Fixed β	Variable β	Fixed β	Variable β
No-tax model	.422	.254	24.36	32.63
	(.395)	(.406)	(.004)	(.001)
Tax model	2.01	1.86	10.23	10.61
	(.612)	(.628)	(.332)	(.303)

Notes: The fixed β is set equal to 0.95; the variable β is defined in the text. Standard errors, in parentheses, are computed from a heteroskedastic-consistent matrix. Significance levels of Hansen's test of overidentifying restrictions are in parentheses beneath the statistic.

The sample contains 1,047 firms. The number of parent firms which report for one subsidiary is 786, for two subsidiaries is 109, for three subsidiaries is 13, and a single parent reports for four subsidiaries.

The instrument set used for estimates above is: $(I/K)_{t-3}$, $(I/K)_{t-4}$, $(I/K)_{t-5}$, $(I/K)^2_{t-3}$, $(I/K)^2_{t-4}$, $(I/K)^2_{t-5}$, $(sales/K)_{t-2}$, $(cash\,flow/K)_{t-2}$, $(k+\tau z)_{t-2}$, $(k+\tau z)^2_{t-2}$. The instruments $(I/K)_{t-2}$, and $(I/K)^2_{t-2}$ are excluded from the set because both were found to be correlated with the error term. Estimates are robust to the exclusion of lags of (I/K) and $(I/K)^2$ dated before $t-3$ and to the exclusion of $(cash\,flow/K)_{t-2}$. Estimates are robust to the inclusion of further lags of those instruments dated $t-2$.

Estimation of β and α in the tax model using the instrument set above produced a point estimate on β of 0.699 with standard error 0.212 and on α of 1.97 with standard error 0.568. The significance level for the test of overidentifying restrictions was 0.390. Estimation of the no tax model (with variable β) using an instrument set without tax terms produced a point estimate on α of 0.155 with standard error of 0.496. The significance level for the test of overidentifying restrictions was 0.002.

equivalent tax rate on (overseas) reinvested earnings, t^r, is constant over time, allowing us to focus on changes in t^d.[31]

5.5   Estimation Results

Our estimates of the adjustment cost parameter α and the tests of the model's overidentifying restrictions are reported in table 5.6. Four sets of results are reported in the table, according to whether the home-country and host-country tax parameters are included in the model in equation (11), and according to whether we hold β constant ("fixed β") or use data to construct β ("variable β"). In all cases, the model is estimated using the panel data on investment by U.S. subsidiaries in Canada, the United Kingdom, Germany, France, Australia, and Japan described earlier.[32] The instrumental variables used are described in the table notes.

31. We also estimated the model assuming that $t^r = t^d/2$ and obtained results similar to those reported below.

32. The results presented in table 5.6 are robust to dividing the sample into Canadian and non-Canadian subsamples.

The first row reports the results under the assumption that "taxes don't matter"—that is, all of the home-country and host-country tax parameters are set equal to zero.[33] The estimated values of α of 0.42 (fixed-β case) and 0.25 (variable-β case) are not statistically different from zero, implying implausibly small costs of adjusting the capital stock. Moreover, the model's overidentifying restrictions are rejected at less than the 1 percent level.[34]

The second row reports the results when the tax parameters are included in the estimation equation. In contrast to the results just discussed, the estimated values of α are now 2.01 (fixed-β case) and 1.86 (variable-β case) and are statistically significantly different from zero. The point estimates are qualitatively similar to those reported in studies using Euler equation models to study U.S. investment (see, e.g., Hubbard and Kashyap 1992; Hubbard et al. 1995) and to those reported by Cummins et al. (chap. 7 in this volume) for domestic investment in a set of European countries. Also in contrast to the "taxes don't matter" case, the complete model's overidentifying restrictions are not rejected. We interpret the improvement in estimating the model as evidence of the importance of tax considerations in U.S. firms' outbound FDI decisions. Estimation of β and α in the tax model (using the same set of instruments) produces a point estimate of β of 0.699, with a standard error of 0.212, and a point estimate of α of 1.97, with a standard error of 0.568. The significance level for the test of overidentifying restrictions is 0.390.

Table 5.7 reproduces the results presented in table 5.6 for the subsample of subsidiaries in the sample for all years. The estimated values of α are similar to those reported for comparable cases for the full sample in table 5.6; the standard errors are larger owing to the much smaller sample of subsidiaries. Estimation of β and α in the tax model (using the same set of instruments) produces a point estimate of β of 0.665, with a standard error of 0.250, and a point estimate of α of 1.56, with a standard error of 0.753. The significance level for the test of overidentifying restrictions is 0.120. Hence, our results are supportive of the basic model derived in section 5.3.[35]

33. This test analyses whether host-country cost-of-capital terms (i.e., $(1 - k_j - \tau_j z_j)/(1 - \tau_j)$) and "international tax" parameters (i.e., $m_{ij,t+1}/m_{ijt}$) jointly matter. When we set $m_{ij,t+1}/m_{ijt}$ equal to unity—in order to examine consequences of ignoring only the "international tax" parameters—the estimated value of the adjustment cost parameter α is 1.88 (with a standard error of 0.701), and the p-value for the test of overidentifying restrictions is 0.222. Given that our calculations of m are necessarily approximations (since, without access to tax data, we are unable to verify the foreign tax credit status of parent firms), the failure to reject the model's overidentifying restrictions in this experiment is not surprising.

34. One must exercise some caution in relying solely on Hansen's (1982) J-test to judge the adequacy of the Euler equation representation of the investment problem. Newey (1985), Ghysels and Hall (1990), and Oliner, Rudebusch, and Sichel (1993) have offered other diagnostic tests. These alternatives have generally addressed the issue of structural stability of coefficient estimates in time-series models. Applying these tests in the panel-data context is a topic on which we are currently working in this research program.

35. Following up on n. 28, we also estimated the model converting the capital stock data into foreign-currency equivalents to construct I/K. In this case (using the fixed-β assumption in the

Table 5.7   **FDI Euler Equation Models (balanced panel sample)**

Model	Adjustment Cost Parameter α		Test of Overidentifying Restrictions χ_9^2	
	Fixed β	Variable β	Fixed β	Variable β
No-tax model	.339	.253	12.08	12.48
	(.401)	(.338)	(.209)	(.188)
Tax model	1.49	1.31	9.40	9.97
	(.611)	(.598)	(.405)	(.353)

Notes: The fixed β is set equal to 0.95; the variable β is defined in the text. Standard errors, in parentheses, are computed from a heteroskedastic-consistent matrix. Significance levels of Hansen's test of overidentifying restrictions are in parentheses beneath the statistic.

The sample contains 103 firms. The number of parent firms which report for one subsidiary is 93, and for two subsidiaries is 5.

The instrument set for the tax model is the same as for the full sample. Estimates are robust to the exclusion of lags of (I/K) and $(I/K)^2$ dated before $t - 3$ and to the exclusion of $(cash\ flow/K)_{t-2}$. Estimates are robust to the inclusion of further lags of those instruments dated $t - 2$.

Estimation of β and α in the tax model using the instrument set above produced a point estimate on β of 0.665 with standard error 0.250 and on α of 1.56 with standard error 0.753. The significance level for the test of overidentifying restrictions was 0.120.

5.6 Discussion

The estimation results presented in section 5.5 offer two implications for analysis of tax policy beyond the simple conclusion that firms take tax incentives into account in the way suggested by standard economic theory in making their investments. The first implication relates to the usefulness of models such as equation (11) in measuring effects of home- and host-country tax changes on firms' FDI. The second addresses the debate over whether the U.S. system of taxing corporate foreign-source income satisfies capital-export neutrality or capital-import neutrality.

5.6.1 Measuring Tax Effects on FDI

Using the assumptions about adjustment costs associated with new investment employed in deriving equation (11), we can return to the initial experiment posed in section 5.2: How do changes in tax parameters affect FDI through their impact on the tax-adjusted q associated with that investment? While we cannot observe the marginal q's to estimate this effect directly, we can infer the coefficient on marginal q (in a regression of I/K on q) from the results summarized in table 5.6. In particular, the coefficient on marginal q in such a regression can be interpreted as the reciprocal of the adjustment cost

---

taxes-included case), the estimated value of the adjustment cost parameter α is 1.62 (with a standard error of 0.640), and the p-value for the test of overidentifying restrictions is 0.516.

parameter α; the point estimate for α of about 2 implies a "q-coefficent" of about 0.5. That is, an increase in a subsidiary's q of 0.10 would increase the contemporaneous (foreign direct) investment-capital ratio by 0.05, a significant effect given the mean values for the investment-capital ratio summarized in table 5.2.

Tax-induced changes in the subsidiary's q reflect changes in host-country tax rates and investment incentives and home-country tax parameters to the extent that the subsidiary is expected to change its dividend-paying status or the parent's foreign tax credit position (i.e., excess credit or excess limit) is expected to change. The marginal q for new investment by a mature (dividend-paying) subsidiary of a parent in a stationary foreign tax credit position will not be affected by permanent changes in home-country tax parameters.[36]

5.6.2   Assessing Capital-Export-Neutral and Capital-Import-Neutral Features of the U.S. System

The failure to reject the investment model derived under the assumptions of the tax capitalization analysis of subsidiaries' dividend policy suggests that we can use that analysis to study effects of home- and host-country tax parameters on the cost of capital for FDI.[37] In that regard, we can offer some observations for equity-financed investments in mature subsidiaries. First, if the home-country tax system is based on the residence principle with a foreign tax credit subject to a limitation and deferral of tax on earnings retained overseas (as in the case for the United States), the home-country tax on repatriations has no effect on subsidiaries' investments financed out of retained earnings—as long as the parent's foreign tax credit position does not change.[38] This relationship

36. This is not strictly true if the definition of taxable income differs across countries or if the home-country tax authority can tax pure profits earned abroad through effective policing of royalty payments and transfer-pricing arrangements (see Leechor and Mintz 1993; and Hines 1994).

37. For analysis of the implications of the tax capitalization approach for subsidiaries' dividend repatriations, see Hines and Hubbard (1990), Altshuler and Newlon (1993), and Altshuler et al. (chap. 9 in this volume). Because Altshuler et al. used panel data from tax returns, they were able to test for differences in the responsiveness of repatriations to temporary and permanent changes in the home-country tax price on repatriations. They find that dividend repatriations are significantly more responsive to temporary tax price changes than to permanent tax price changes, a result consistent with Hartman's application of the tax capitalization approach.

38. To see this, note that the cost of capital $\rho_{ijt}/(1 - \tau_{jt})$ for a marginal investment by parent i in mature subsidiary j at time t solves

$$(1 - \tau_{jt})F_{K,ijt} = \rho_{ijt},$$

where

$$\rho_{ijt} = \left(\frac{m_{ijt}}{m_{ij,t-1}}\right)\beta_{ijt}^{-1} - 1.$$

Under the assumption used in section 5.5 that r is expected to be constant, if the home- and host-country tax rates and the parent's foreign tax credit position do not change, $m_{ijt} = m_{ij,t+1}$, and the cost of capital is independent of the home-country tax rate.

corresponds to capital-import neutrality for investments by mature subsidiaries of U.S. parent firms. In its most basic form, this result was first noted by Hartman (1981, 1984, 1985); Altshuler and Fulghieri (1994) generalized it to incorporate the possibility of changes over time in parents' foreign tax credit positions. Second, the capital-import neutrality implication does not carry over to the case of expected changes in foreign tax credit status. If, on the one hand, the parent firm expected to make a once-and-for-all transition from excess limit status to excess credit status, the subsidiary's cost of capital rises or falls relative to the stationary credit case according to whether $\tau_{US} < \tau_j$ or $\tau_{US} > \tau_j$, respectively.[39] If, on the other hand, the parent firm is expected to make a once-and-for-all transition from excess credit status to excess limit status, the cost of capital (ignoring withholding taxes) is independent of host-country tax parameters, a capital-export-neutral result.[40] Hence, the U.S. residence-based tax system with a foreign tax credit is capital-export neutral in those examples only in a very limited case—for mature subsidiaries that pay no withholding taxes on dividend repatriations and whose parent firms are in an excess limit position in the period in which an investment is made and in an excess credit position thereafter.

One can present similar examples (again assuming all equity finance) for "immature" subsidiaries, those financing initial investment using parent equity transfers. If the subsidiary eventually repatriates dividends, its cost of capital depends in part on the parent's expected future foreign tax credit status when the repatriation occurs. If the parent is in an excess credit position at that time, the home-country tax rate does not affect investment, a capital-import-neutral result. If the parent is in an excess limit position at that time, the cost of capital will depend on both home- and host-country tax parameters.

While these examples are only illustrative (see also the more detailed cases considered by Altshuler and Fulghieri 1990), they suggest the potential usefulness of firm-level panel data to test the appropriateness of the tax capitalization approach's predictions about the responsiveness of subsidiary dividend and investment decisions to tax changes.

---

39. To see this, note that the cost of capital (under the assumptions described in n. 38) is given by

$$(1 - \tau_{jt})^{-1}\rho_{ijt} = (1 - \tau_{jt})^{-1}\left[\left(\frac{m_{ijt}}{m_{ij,t+1}}\right)\beta_{ijt}^{-1}\right] - 1 = (1 - \tau_{jt})^{-1}\left[\left(\frac{1 - \tau_{US,t}}{1 - \tau_{jt}}\right)\beta_{ijt}^{-1}\right] - 1.$$

Hence, if $\tau_{US} > \tau_j$, the cost of capital falls relative to the stationary credit case; if $\tau_{US} < \tau_j$, the cost of capital rises relative to the stationary credit case. For example, given the increase in the likelihood of parents' moving from an excess limit position to an excess credit position after the cut in τ_{US} in the Tax Reform Act of 1986, U.S. FDI would be expected to increase in high-tax countries and decrease in low-tax countries, ceteris paribus.

40. To see this, note the cost of capital (under the assumptions described in n. 38) is given by

$$(1 - \tau_{jt})^{-1}\,\rho_{ijt} = (1 - \tau_{jt})^{-1}\left[\left(\frac{1 - \tau_{jt}}{1 - \tau_{US,t}}\right)\beta_{ijt}^{-1}\right] - 1,$$

which is independent of the host-country tax rate.

5.7 Conclusions

This paper represents a first step in a research program to use microdata on multinational firms' overseas investment decisions to study the determinants of FDI, especially those related to tax policy. In that sense, our exercise is in the spirit of an attempt to use microdata to test models of the effects of tax parameters on subsidiaries' dividend repatriation decisions. The panel data that we use on FDI of subsidiaries of U.S. firms permit us to focus on "new investment," something not possible with the more commonly studied aggregate data. These data also allow us to test structural models of investment decisions, thereby giving us potentially informative estimates of the effects of tax parameters on FDI.

We believe we have been successful in two respects. First, we have extended conventional investment models to accommodate a wide range of tax influences on FDI decisions. Second, our empirical results cast significant doubt on the simplest notion that "taxes don't matter" for U.S. firms' FDI decisions. Tax parameters influence FDI in precisely the ways indicated by neoclassical models. Our results also lend support to the application of the tax capitalization model to the study of dividend repatriation and FDI decisions.

Much work remains, however. First, because of data limitations, we were forced to make a number of simplifying assumptions in estimating our model. In future work, we plan to test the sensitivity of our findings to plausible alternative assumptions. Second, we are working to extend our analysis to study effects of tax policy on U.S. inbound FDI. Third, we plan to test whether shifts in the host-country currency value of firms' investments affect firms' FDI, holding constant other determinants of FDI. Finally, we would like to incorporate imperfect competition and intangible assets in our approach.

References

Abel, Andrew B. 1980. Empirical investment equations: An integrative framework. *Carnegie-Rochester Conference Series on Public Policy* 12 (Spring): 39–91.

Altshuler, Rosanne, and Paolo Fulghieri. 1994. Incentive effects of foreign tax credits on multinationals. *National Tax Journal* 47, no. 2 (June): 349–61.

Altshuler, Rosanne, and T. Scott Newlon. 1993. The effects of U.S. tax policy on the income repatriation patterns of U.S. multinational corporations. In *Studies in international taxation,* ed. Alberto Giovannini, R. Glenn Hubbard, and Joel Slemrod, 77–115. Chicago: University of Chicago Press.

Alworth, Julian S. 1988. *The finance, investment and taxation decisions of multinationals.* Oxford: Basil Blackwell.

Auerbach, Alan J. 1979. Wealth maximization and the cost of capital. *Quarterly Journal of Economics* 93 (August): 433–45.

Auerbach, Alan J., and Kevin A. Hassett. 1993. Taxation and foreign direct investment in the United States: A reconsideration of the evidence. In *Studies in international taxation,* ed. Alberto Giovannini, R. Glenn Hubbard, and Joel Slemrod. Chicago: University of Chicago Press.

Auerbach, Alan J., and James R. Hines, Jr. 1988. Investment tax incentives and frequent tax reforms. *American Economic Review* 78 (May): 211–16.

Ault, Hugh J., and David F. Bradford. 1990. Taxing international income: An analysis of the U.S. system and its economic premises. In *Taxation in the global economy,* ed. Assaf Razin and Joel Slemrod. Chicago: University of Chicago Press.

Boskin, Michael J., and William G. Gale. 1987. New results on the effects of tax policy on the international location of investment. In *The effects of taxation on capital accumulation,* ed. Martin Feldstein. Chicago: University of Chicago Press.

Bradford, David F. 1981. The incidence and allocation effects of a tax on corporate distributions. *Journal of Public Economics* 15 (February): 1–22.

Caves, Richard E. 1982. *Multinational enterprises and economic analysis.* Cambridge: Cambridge University Press.

Cummins, Jason G., Kevin A. Hassett, and R. Glenn Hubbard. 1994. A reconsideration of investment behavior using tax reforms as natural experiments. *Brookings Papers on Economic Activity,* no. 2: 1–74.

Dunning, John H., ed. 1985. *Multinational enterprises, economic structure, and international competitiveness.* Chichester: Wiley.

Feldstein, Martin, and Joosung Jun. 1987. The effect of tax rules on nonresidential fixed investment: Some preliminary evidence from the 1980s. In *The effects of taxation on capital accumulation,* ed. Martin Feldstein, 101–62. Chicago: University of Chicago Press.

Frisch, Daniel J. 1990. The economics of international tax policy: Some old and new approaches. *Tax Notes* (April 30).

Froot, Kenneth A., and Jeremy C. Stein. 1991. Exchange rates and foreign direct investment: An imperfect capital markets approach. *Quarterly Journal of Economics* 106 (November): 1191–1219.

Gersovitz, Mark. 1987. The effects of domestic taxes on foreign private investment. In *The theory of taxation for developing countries,* ed. David M. G. Newbery and Nicholas Stern. New York: Oxford University Press.

Gertler, Mark, and R. Glenn Hubbard. 1988. Financial factors in business fluctuations. In *Financial market volatility.* Kansas City: Federal Reserve Bank of Kansas City.

Ghysels, Eric, and Alastair Hall. 1990. Are consumption-based international capital asset pricing models structural? *Journal of Econometrics* 45:121–39.

Hansen, Lars P. 1982. Large sample properties of generalized method of moments estimators. *Econometrica* 50:1029–54.

Hartman, David G. 1981. Domestic tax policy and foreign investment: Some evidence. NBER Working Paper no. 784. Cambridge, Mass.: National Bureau of Economic Research.

———. 1984. Tax policy and foreign direct investment in the United States. *National Tax Journal* 37 (December): 475–87.

———. 1985. Tax policy and foreign direct investment. *Journal of Public Economics* 26 (February): 107–21.

———. 1990. Comment on "Tax effects on foreign direct investment in the United States: Evidence from a cross-country comparison." In *Taxation in the global economy,* ed. Assaf Razin and Joel B. Slemrod. Chicago: University of Chicago Press.

Hayashi, Fumio. 1982. Tobin's marginal q and average q: A neoclassical interpretation. *Econometrica* 50 (January): 213–24.

Hines, James R., Jr. 1994. Credit and deferral as international investment incentives. *Journal of Public Economics* 55 (October): 323–47.

Hines, James R., Jr., and R. Glenn Hubbard. 1990. Coming home to America: Dividend repatriation decisions of U.S. multinationals. In *Taxation in the global economy*, ed. Assaf Razin and Joel Slemrod. Chicago: University of Chicago Press.

Horst, Thomas. 1977. American taxation of multinational firms. *American Economic Review* 67 (June): 376–89.

Hubbard, R. Glenn, and Anil K. Kashyap. 1992. Internal net worth and the investment process: An application to U.S. agriculture. *Journal of Political Economy* 100 (June): 506–34.

Hubbard, R. Glenn, Anil K. Kashyap, and Toni M. Whited. 1995. Internal finance and firm investment. *Journal of Money, Credit, and Banking* 27 (August).

Jun, Joosung. 1990. U.S. tax policy and direct investment abroad. In *Taxation in the global economy*, ed. Assaf Razin and Joel Slemrod. Chicago: University of Chicago Press.

King, Mervyn A. 1977. *Public policy and the corporation.* London: Chapman and Hall.

King, Mervyn A., and Don Fullerton, eds. 1984. *The taxation of income from capital: A comparative study of the United States, United Kingdom, Sweden, and West Germany.* Chicago: University of Chicago Press.

Leechor, Chad, and Jack Mintz. 1993. On the taxation of multinational corporate investment when the deferral method is used by the capital exporting country. *Journal of Public Economics* 51:75–96.

Newey, Whitney K. 1985. Generalized method of moments specification testing. *Journal of Econometrics* 29:229–56.

Newlon, T. Scott. 1987. Tax policy and the multinational firm's financial policy and investment decisions: Ph.D. dissertation, Princeton University.

Oliner, Stephen, Glenn Rudebusch, and Daniel Sichel. 1993. The Lucas critique revisited: Assessing the stability of empirical Euler equations for investment. Mimeograph, Board of Governors of the Federal Reserve System, Washington, D.C.

Pointer, Martha M., and Timothy S. Doupnik. 1993. An empirical examination of international portfolio theory and SFAS 14 geographical segment disclosures. Mimeograph, University of South Carolina.

Pugel, Thomas. 1985. The United States. In *Multinational enterprises, economic structure, and international competitiveness,* ed. John H. Dunning, Chichester: Wiley.

Senteney, David L., and Mohammad S. Bazaz. 1992. The impact of SFAS 14 geographic segment disclosures on the information content of U.S.-based MNE's earnings releases. *International Journal of Accounting* 27:267–79.

Sinn, Hanns-Werner. 1984. Die bedeutung de accelerated cost recovery system für den internationalen kapitalverkehr. *Kyklos* 37:542–76.

———. 1987. *Capital income taxation and resource allocation.* Amsterdam: North-Holland.

Slemrod, Joel. 1990. Tax effects on foreign direct investment in the United States: Evidence from a cross-country comparison. In *Taxation in the global economy*, ed. Assaf Razin and Joel Slemrod. Chicago: University of Chicago Press.

Summers, Lawrence H. 1981. Taxation and corporate investment: A q-theory approach. *Brookings Papers on Economic Activity,* no. 1: 67–127.

U.S. Department of the Treasury. 1992. *Integration of the individual and corporate tax systems.* Washington, D.C.: Government Printing Office, January.

U.S. Department of the Treasury. Office of Tax Policy. 1993. *International tax reform: An interim report.* Washington, D.C.: Department of the Treasury, January.

U.S. Joint Committee on Taxation. 1990. *Background and issues relating to the taxation*

of foreign investment in the United States. Washington, D.C.: Government Printing Office, January 23.
———. 1991. *Factors affecting the international competitiveness of the United States.* Washington, D.C.: Government Printing Office, May 30.
Wilson, G. Peter. 1993. The role of taxes in location and sourcing decisions. In *Studies in international taxation,* ed. Alberto Giovannini, R. Glenn Hubbard, and Joel B. Slemrod. Chicago: University of Chicago Press.
Young, Kan H. 1988. The effects of taxes and rates of return on foreign direct investment in the United States. *National Tax Journal* 41 (March): 109–21.

Comment   David G. Hartman

When asked to comment on this ambitious paper, which I like very much, I had to first decide whether to comment as the author of Hartman (1984), to which these authors were very generous in their discussion, or in my 1994 role as an advisor to companies in setting global business strategy. I chose the latter, at the expense of the former. I intend to point out some puzzles in the data and then provide some (I hope, realistic) parables about business decisions that might explain the puzzles. In doing so, I aim to cast doubt on the strength of the empirical results, but any criticism will reflect badly on my own previous work. Finally, I will discuss the possibility that exchange rate translation is driving the paper's empirical results.

As introduction, I want to make a point about the very simple short-time-series analysis of Hartman (1984) and the "subsequent rounds of replication and refinement" cited by the authors. In the 1970s only a few economists, including Robert Lipsey and Martin Feldstein at NBER, were interested in foreign direct investment (FDI). That was not surprising, since FDI was small, and though growing was doing so only moderately. Most particularly, it was plausible at that time that the historical pattern in FDI was the result of an equilibrium process of some kind. Around the end of the time periods I was researching, a quite different dynamic took over. FDI, both inward and outward, grew at an extraordinary pace, culminating in the situation in 1994 of nearly every company seeing global expansion as its key to growth. It should have been anticipated that the empirical literature, which takes as its point of departure responses to changes in the marginal profitability of international operations, would be unsuccessful in linking this later period of incredible growth with the earlier period of small and relatively stable FDI. In other words, history provides one major discontinuity to explain, and the existing models provide little hope of explaining it. I sometimes wonder whether in-

David G. Hartman is executive vice president of ICF Kaiser International Consulting. Previously he was executive director of the National Bureau of Economic Research.

cluding a time series of the number of times "globalization" appears in *Business Week* might be the answer.

That brings me to the distinction between the paper's conceptual model and some business decisions that I believe are incorporated in the data. The paper's model describes a rather simple world. This is a world in which FDI increases or declines as companies adjust to a new equilibrium rate of return available in a specific location.

Alternatively, one can view the foreign investment decision as a lumpy process of one-time strategic decisions on how to serve an emerging market or change the locus of production. Since the data the authors carefully construct look like the aggregation of a series of investment surges, one must be concerned about just this kind of issue. If the empirical investigation deals with firms observed in their startup phase or in a major building phase, the predicted relationship between investment and observed rates of return should be quite different. But before getting into details, I want to comment on some of the puzzles raised by the data.

Puzzles

To explain why I think that a more "realistic" model of a start-up foreign subsidiary is needed, I refer to the volatility and the timing of the data included in the paper. Even looking at averages by country, we find that it is not uncommon for the capital stock to grow by 10 percent one year and 40+ percent the next, or for the cash flow as a fraction of invested capital to go from 10 to 30+ percent and then back to 10 percent over three years. This volatility is puzzling unless these data reflect start-up operations, or unless some other phenomenon (such as a foreign exchange effect) is at work, a point I will return to later.

The timing of movements in the data, even at a crude aggregate level, is even more puzzling. For example, the aggregate of the German subsidiaries included in the data had a great year in 1982, a recessionary year and a time of poor performance across a broad range of indigenous German companies. While it is not a fair criticism to take the authors' model literally, it seems legitimate to question why, in an equilibrium model of investment, U.S.-owned companies would in aggregate have a pattern of return and investment so dissimilar to that of indigenous German firms.

It is also interesting that in nearly all of the countries examined, the naked eye can tell from a simple graph that aggregate sales lead aggregate investment, usually by a year (see fig. 5C.1). I have trouble thinking of the traditional investment model being consistent with this pattern when the changes in sales are so large. In the neoclassical model, improved sales increase capacity utilization and encourage investment, but it is hard to imagine stretching capacity so far. The answer, of course, is that the German subsidiary is only a part of the company's operation and sales in Germany can easily increase without extra production in Germany. In light of the voltality of the data, it is easy to speculate that the company is deciding to serve a rapidly growing market by in-

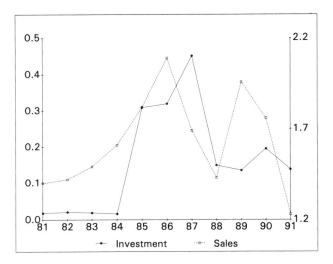

Fig. 5C.1   Investment and sales: German subsidiaries
Source: Cummins and Hubbard (chap. 5 in this volume, tables 5.2 and 5.4).

vesting to establish a substantial local presence for the first time or to dramatically increase its size. This phenomenon might be consistent with what the authors are hoping to capture, though a more appropriate model would be one that weighs the cash-flow effects of producing in different locations, rather than treating the German subsidiary in isolation. Most important is whether this calls into question the empirical conclusions about taxes. That depends critically on how a company making such strategic moves would report its investment and cash flow in the "separate, new" market, as I will discuss.

Parables

One possible conclusion is that the data are describing a set of investment surges representing new operations or major increases in the size of existing foreign operations. We would expect most truly new foreign ventures to begin with an unprofitable investment period, quite probably lasting for years, followed by a payback period. If that is what we are observing, we should be surprised not to get perverse results from regressions of investment on profitability or cash flow.

To see how the "confirming" results reported here could arise, we can turn to several business parables. In one fairly common situation, a "separate, new" foreign operation might be set up to provide better service to an established base of sales. As opposed to our expectation of an initial period of losses in a true start-up operation, we would not necessarily be surprised to see this type of FDI accompanied by high rates of return, as the existing sales base is assigned to a subsidiary that supports a partially independent set of company functions. This would also be consistent with the fact that sales lead investment.

Similarly, successful managers are often given responsibility for a wider geographic area. Thus, on average a profitable operation tends to be assigned responsibility for making and managing new investments. With a sample so limited in detail about a firm's multiple operations in a region, this possibility is difficult to evaluate.

We could continue to speculate but the point is that there are many possibilities besides the phenomenon being modeled here to explain the association of profitability and investment, and they might do better in explaining some of the puzzles in the data.

Foreign Exchange

A more straightforward concern is the impact of exchange rates. The authors have addressed whether the companies' translation of subsidiary data into dollars was done at consistent points in time. But the much more important question is whether the act of translating into dollars has itself produced a spurious association between investment and cash flow.

The dollar was of course highly volatile in the decade of the 1980s, apparently having had a major impact on the observations used in this paper. Looking at table 5.2, for example, we see the dollar-denominated capital stock in Germany staying flat as the dollar soared in the early 1980s, surging as the dollar plunged during 1985–87, and growing at a reasonable, modest pace thereafter as the dollar stabilized. We would need to know more than we or the authors do about the original currency of denomination of the companies' books and the details of their operations to be certain, but this series has all the earmarks of a capital stock that grew steadily at just about 15 percent per year in deutsche marks. That is, virtually all of the year-to-year change in the capital stock (i.e., the variation in investment) could apparently have been produced by exchange rate changes.

The authors indicate in footnote 35 that they have been able to address the most obvious problem—creating an investment series by differencing capital stocks already translated into dollars. Though the authors' alternative estimates are not described in detail, it would appear that foreign exchange effects could still be driving the investment data. Changing the dollar-reported capital stock into "foreign-currency equivalents" before differencing it to construct investment is a good check, since it should reduce the potential for the most extreme spurious volatility in investment caused by the dollar. But even translating a perfect deutsche mark–denominated *investment* series into dollars would still incorporate the dollar's movement in measured investment. In addition, any adjustment back to foreign currencies of figures that are reported in dollars by the companies is dangerous, since we have little information about their translation process. The data also provide only general guidance about where the capital is located and where the profits are earned (firms report the country in which the "subsidiary is located"). So, any currency adjustment undertaken by researchers in constructing investment series is highly problematic.

Knowing how exchange rates affect the cash flow of these operations is even more of a question. We cannot tell the difference even between the two extremes: a subsidiary that incurs local costs to produce products sold in the United States and a subsidiary that sells locally those products produced in the United States. It is at least plausible, though, that translating cash flow in deutsche marks into dollars has created a spurious pattern of movement closely related to a spurious pattern of movement in investment.

I would conclude that the set of results in the main body of the text shows distinct signs of being driven by exchange rate translation. As I have noted, the authors report some additional work done to mitigate the most obvious problem, but I would hardly call the case closed. That having been said, the problem is the common one of trying to make the most of very crude data; I can only admire the authors' clever leveraging of the poor information available and applaud their attempts to verify their results.

Taxes

So far none of my comments relate to the most striking part of the paper: that the measures incorporating taxes work, and work significantly better than those without. This lends support to the importance of taxes and to the tax capitalization model that is so near to my heart.

Much as I support the authors' strategy of plunging ahead with limited information, the tax measures are obviously crude. First, they are country specific but in large measure neither industry nor financing specific. Previous work has shown tax rates to vary far more by industry and by financing method than by country (or, for that matter, through time for most countries). It is remarkable, then, that rather crude measures (again, however, the best that can be done with the data available) are so successful in explaining company behavior.

Is there any obvious alternative explanation of why these measured tax rates "work"? Without seeing the detail of the tax rates, it is hard to speculate, but we do know some things. First, 1986 was the big event in terms of variation in rates over time. The U.S. tax reform made a striking change toward excess credit status for most firms. That year also coincided with major exchange rate realignments, so there is a superficial plausibility to some coincident exchange rate effect having been captured by taxes. To carry speculation further, the tax change was least significant for operations in Canada, where tax rates followed the U.S. rates down in the 1980s. Canada was also the only country with only minor exchange rate changes.

The more important point is that even before reading the paper we knew that the 1986 tax change did indeed coincide with the beginning of a big surge in U.S. investment abroad. But it also coincided with the beginning of a *worldwide* surge in foreign investment that has been the subject of a great deal of speculation and little convincing explanation. That global surge was clearly unconnected with the U.S. tax reform. It is a mystery that if solved might shed some light on whether there is some other phenomenon at work here . . . one that simply coincides with the U.S. tax reform.

The final comment is that my criticisms are directed toward the specific period under study and the potential problems related to the time-series aspects of the analysis. In fact, this work is an important beginning with firm-level panel data that has potential to bring a qualitative improvement in our understanding of the foreign investment process. Additional tests may prove that the time-series dimension of the data (especially exchange rate changes and the maturing of subsidiaries) is not driving the results. I hope that it does. In any event, this promising line of work is extremely time consuming but also path breaking, in a field that has been focused on simple time-series models. Previous simple time-series analysis cannot hope to shed light on this phenomenon that has obviously undergone some dramatic and little-understood shift during the interval of observation. This paper makes real progress toward better understanding.

Reference

Hartman, David G. 1984. Tax policy and foreign direct investment in the United States. *National Tax Journal* 37 (December): 475–87.

6   The Alternative Minimum Tax and the Behavior of Multinational Corporations

Andrew B. Lyon and Gerald Silverstein

6.1   Introduction

The alternative minimum tax (AMT) was designed as part of the Tax Reform Act of 1986 in response to concerns that a number of firms that reported positive "book" profits to their shareholders paid no corporate tax to the federal government. A corporation is required to calculate its tax liability under both the regular tax rules and the AMT rules, and it pays tax according to the system that results in the largest income tax liability.

The AMT rules potentially affect multinational corporations (MNCs) in a manner quite different from their effect on domestic corporations. First, the taxable income of domestic corporations (and that of the domestic operations of MNCs) is generally increased due to restrictions on deductions under the AMT and the inclusion of certain income that would be excluded from taxation under the regular tax. However, for foreign operations, deductions are quite similar for AMT and regular tax purposes.

Second, although the domestic tax base is generally larger under the AMT than under the regular tax, the tax rate on all AMT income is 20 percent rather than the 34 or 35 percent rate that generally applies to corporations under the regular tax system.[1] As a result, whether a firm pays tax under the AMT de-

Andrew B. Lyon is associate professor of economics at the University of Maryland and a faculty research fellow of the National Bureau of Economic Research. Gerald Silverstein is an economist in the Office of Tax Analysis of the U.S. Department of Treasury.

The authors are grateful to Alan Auerbach, Jim Hines, Glenn Hubbard, and seminar participants at the National Bureau of Economic Research and the Office of Tax Analysis for helpful discussions and comments.

1. The 1993 Omnibus Reconciliation Act increased the regular corporate tax rate to 35 percent for firms with taxable income in excess of $10 million, effective January 1, 1993. The 34 percent tax rate from the prior law continues to begin at a taxable income of $75,000. Phaseouts of the benefit of lower graduated rates under the regular tax create marginal tax rates of 39 and 38 percent for certain narrow ranges of income. There is no change in the AMT tax rate for corporations.

pends on the particular sources of income and types of deductions received by the firm. For U.S.-based MNCs, the lower marginal rate of taxation under the AMT may present the firm a timing opportunity to repatriate income from low-tax foreign countries. Repatriated income is less likely to be subject to U.S. tax, or will be subject to a smaller amount of tax, because foreign tax credits can shelter a greater percentage of taxable income.

Third, a separate AMT provision limits the total amount of tax that may be offset through foreign tax credits. For a firm for which this provision is a binding constraint, positive amounts of U.S. tax will be paid on repatriated dividends even if the firm would otherwise have excess foreign tax credits.

The AMT affects a significant number of firms.[2] In 1990 the corporate AMT accounted for 8.5 percent of corporate tax receipts, or $8.1 billion.[3] Including regular taxes paid by these AMT firms, AMT firms paid 21.4 percent of all corporate income tax. Approximately 25 percent of corporations with assets in excess of $50 million paid AMT. Among the largest firms, those with assets in excess of $500 million, the proportion of firms paying AMT was 30.6 percent.

Among multinational firms, AMT incidence is slightly more prevalent. This is partly due to the correlation between firm size and AMT liability and the fact that the largest firms are more likely to receive foreign-source income.[4] Among firms in 1990 filing form 1118—the form on which foreign tax credits are calculated—28 percent of those with assets in excess of $50 million paid AMT. Among these multinationals with assets in excess of $500 million, 33.3 percent paid AMT. Of all form 1118 filers, 53 percent of all assets and 56 percent of all foreign-source income was accounted for by corporations paying AMT.

The existence of the AMT can affect a multinational firm in a number of different ways, from the design of dividend repatriation strategies to locational choice of real investment. In this paper we outline how incentives can be affected by the AMT and present data suggestive of how important these effects may be.

The next section of the paper describes the mechanics of calculating AMT and the limitations placed on the use of foreign tax credits against AMT. Section 6.3 considers the relative investment incentives for locating investment domestically and abroad for an AMT firm. Section 6.4 examines the incentives

2. Gerardi, Milner, and Silverstein (1994) present data on the coverage of the corporate AMT from 1987 to 1991.

3. The actual effect on revenues may be greater because most business credits (such as the R&D tax credit) may not be claimed by firms on the AMT, and regular tax firms may not use these credits or the AMT credit to reduce their regular tax liability below the floor created by the AMT. The denied credits do not show up in the data as additional tax payments, but are carried forward into future years by the firms. As discussed in Lyon (1991), the AMT also affects total revenue collections by changing behavior. To the extent that tax-favored investments are discouraged relative to other investments, total revenue collections may be higher under the regular tax.

4. E.g., even in the largest asset category, form 1118 filers constitute 24.1 percent of the corporations, but account for 47.7 percent of the assets in the largest asset category.

for repatriating foreign-source income under the AMT. In section 6.5, tax return data of corporations are examined to analyze the prevalence of AMT status among U.S.-based multinationals, their receipt of foreign-source income, and the tax prices faced by these firms on additional repatriations of foreign-source income. A concluding section summarizes the findings and suggests directions for continuing research in this area.

6.2 Determination of AMT

A firm calculates its AMT by making a number of modifications to its taxable income reported for regular tax purposes. Here we briefly describe the steps in calculating AMT (summarized in table 6.1). More detail on the most important modifications is provided below.

The starting point for computation of the AMT is the firm's regular taxable income before any deduction for net operating losses (NOL). To this amount, the firm adds back a number of deductions that are restricted under the AMT and certain sources of income not taxable under the regular tax rules (adjustments and preferences). NOL deductions may offset up to 90 percent of this sum. Subtracting allowable NOL deductions results in alternative minimum taxable income (AMTI). AMTI is then reduced by subtracting an exemption amount (a maximum amount of $40,000, phased out ratably to zero for firms with AMTI between $150,000 and $310,000). Tax is calculated by multiplying this net amount by the 20 percent AMT tax rate. Tax may be reduced by a limited amount of AMT foreign tax credits, as described in more detail below. This yields the firm's tentative minimum tax. Tentative minimum tax is com-

Table 6.1   **AMT Calculation**

Line	Quantity
1.	Regular taxable income, before NOL
2.	+ Adjustments and preferences (including ACE)
3.	= Taxable income before NOL
4.	− AMT NOL (up to 90 percent of line 3)
5.	= AMTI
6.	− Exemption amount
7.	= AMTI net of exemptions
8.	× 20 percent
9.	= AMT before credits
10.	− Allowable AMT foreign tax credits
	(i) U.S. tax × (Foreign income)/(Worldwide income)
	(ii) 90 percent limitation
11.	= Tentative minimum tax
12.	− Regular tax (before all credits except foreign tax credit and possessions tax credit)
13.	= AMT

pared to regular income tax before all credits except the foreign tax credit and the possessions tax credit. If tentative minimum tax exceeds this amount of regular tax liability, the excess is payable as AMT, in addition to the firm's payment of its regular tax liability. Each dollar of AMT payments creates a dollar of AMT credits that may be used in future years only against regular income tax liability. AMT credits may not be used to reduce regular tax liability below tentative minimum tax.

6.2.1 Adjustments and Preferences

A number of adjustments and preferences are added back to regular taxable income to derive AMTI. The most notable of these are the adjustments for depreciation and adjusted current earnings (ACE). These two adjustments are examined in detail. Other adjustments and preferences include amortization of pollution control facilities, amortization of mining and development costs, basis adjustments in determining gain or loss from the sale of property, income from long-term contracts and installment sales, merchant marine capital construction funds, depletion deductions, certain tax-exempt interest income, intangible drilling costs, and bad debt reserves of financial institutions.

Depreciation

For domestic assets placed in service after 1986, recovery periods under the AMT are equal to the asset's class life (asset depreciation range [ADR] midpoint). These recovery periods can be up to twice as long as those provided under the regular tax. Depreciation deductions for equipment are calculated using the 150 percent declining-balance method switching to straight line. Under the regular tax, most equipment qualifies for the more accelerated depreciation method of 200 percent declining balance switching to straight line. Depreciation deductions under the AMT are also limited by the adjustment for ACE, described below.

For property used abroad by a branch or a foreign subsidiary, depreciation deductions are the same for regular tax and AMT purposes. Foreign-use property of a branch is depreciated using the straight-line method over the asset's class life. For property held by a foreign subsidiary, the "earnings and profits" method is used under both the AMT and regular tax (this method results in depreciation allowances similar to those used for a foreign branch).[5]

Adjusted Current Earnings

The adjustment for ACE is based on the calculation of earnings and profits. For taxable years after 1989, if ACE exceeds AMTI before NOL and before the ACE adjustment, AMTI is increased by 75 percent of the difference.[6]

---

5. Earnings and profits is a separate measure of income used to determine the portion of a dividend deemed to be paid out of earnings and the portion paid out of capital. Earnings and profits is also used in the calculation of the ACE adjustment as explained below.

6. If ACE is less than AMTI, AMTI may be reduced by 75 percent of this difference, but not by

ACE includes items of income not included in AMTI, such as tax-exempt interest, and ACE does not allow certain deductions, such as the dividends-received deduction.

For domestic property placed in service in 1990–93, depreciation is calculated using the straight-line method over the asset's class life. There is no additional ACE depreciation adjustment for foreign-use property.

Prior to 1990, a book income adjustment was used instead of ACE. Under the book income adjustment, taxable income was increased by 50 percent of the difference between book income and AMTI calculated without regard to the book income adjustment and before NOL.

6.2.2   Allowable AMT Foreign Tax Credit

AMT foreign tax credits differ from the foreign tax credits claimed by the taxpayer against regular income tax, although the process of calculating them is similar. Under both the regular tax and the AMT, the foreign tax credit that may be claimed in a given year is limited to the amount of U.S. tax that would have been paid on the foreign income. This limitation is calculated separately for each income category or "basket."

The U.S. tax that would have been paid on the foreign income is calculated by multiplying (1) the ratio of *foreign income* to *worldwide income* by (2) the taxpayer's *U.S. tax liability* (before use of foreign tax credits). Under the AMT, *foreign income, worldwide income,* and *U.S. tax liability* used in this calculation are all calculated using the AMT rules. The U.S. component of worldwide income will differ from that used in the regular tax computation chiefly because of the various adjustments and preferences described above. Foreign income will vary to a lesser extent because the depreciation deductions taken for foreign-use property under the regular tax rules are the same as under the AMT. Differences in the apportionment of certain expenses jointly allocable between domestic and foreign-source income may cause other differences in the ratio of foreign income to worldwide income under the AMT. For example, interest expense is generally allocated in proportion to the tax basis of domestic and foreign assets. The tax basis of domestic assets will be higher under the AMT than under the regular tax since depreciation deductions are taken more slowly. The tax basis of foreign assets is generally the same under the AMT as under the regular tax. As a result, a greater share of interest expense is domestically sourced under the AMT than under the regular tax.[7]

---

more than the amount by which AMTI was increased in prior years due to the ACE adjustment. The 1993 act repeals the ACE depreciation adjustment beginning in 1994.

7. The characterization of income across the limitation categories differs between the AMT and the regular tax for certain types of passive income. Certain income that would otherwise be placed in the passive income category is placed in the general limitation category if it is highly taxed. Income is determined to be highly taxed if the foreign tax rate on such income exceeds the regular corporate tax rate (for purposes of regular tax computation) or the AMT tax rate (for purposes of AMT calculation).

After computing the foreign tax credits for each separate limitation category using AMT rules, a second, overall limitation is applied on the amount of foreign tax credits that may be used against AMT. The combined use of NOL deductions and AMT foreign tax credits may not reduce tentative minimum tax by more than 90 percent. AMT foreign tax credits denied as a result of the 90 percent limitation are treated like other excess foreign tax credits, and may be carried back two years and carried forward five years to offset tentative minimum tax.

The following example illustrates the operation of the 90 percent limitation under the AMT. Assume the firm has regular tax liability before any credits of $510,000 and regular foreign tax credits of $500,000. In the absence of the AMT the firm would have total U.S. tax liability of $10,000. Now assume that for AMT purposes, the firm has AMT NOL deductions of $250,000 (line 4 of table 6.1), AMT before credits of $450,000 (line 9 of table 6.1), and AMT foreign tax credits before application of the 90 percent limitation of $410,000. Together the use of AMT NOL deductions and AMT foreign tax credits cannot reduce the firm's tentative minimum tax by more than 90 percent of the amount that would occur in the absence of NOLs and foreign tax credits. The AMT NOL deductions have the effect of reducing the firm's tentative minimum tax by $50,000 ($250,000 × 0.20), so that in the absence of NOLs and foreign tax credits, tentative minimum tax would be $500,000. The combined use of NOLs and foreign tax credits may not reduce tentative minimum tax below $50,000 (a 90 percent reduction). As a result, only $400,000 of AMT foreign tax credits may be used. Tentative minimum tax is $50,000, and AMT payment is $40,000 in addition to the $10,000 payment of regular tax liability.

AMT payment does not change the characterization of the firm's regular foreign tax credits. The firm is assumed to have used $500,000 in regular foreign tax credits, creating neither a carryback nor a carryforward situation for regular tax purposes. Any of the firm's AMT foreign tax credits denied as a result of either the operation of the separate limitations or the 90 percent limitation may be carried back two years to offset prior years' tentative minimum tax and up to five years forward to offset future tentative minimum tax. The AMT payment of $40,000 creates $40,000 in AMT credits that may be used in future years to offset regular tax.

6.3   Incentives Affecting Capital Investment

As described above, the depreciation deduction for foreign-use property is the same for both regular tax and AMT purposes. Whereas for domestic property the AMT generally creates a tax penalty for new investment undertaken by an AMT firm relative to the incentives faced by a regular tax firm, the opposite may be the case for foreign-use property.[8] Under the AMT, a firm claims

8. While firms currently on the AMT are likely to have reduced incentives for domestic investment, the overall effect of the AMT on domestic investment is more difficult to ascertain. This is

the same depreciation deductions as it would for regular tax purposes for foreign-use property, but income generated by the investment can be taxed at only 20 percent under the AMT rather than the 34 or 35 percent tax rate applying under the regular tax system. If this were the only difference between the regular and AMT systems, a firm permanently on the AMT must have a lower cost of capital for foreign-use property than a regular tax firm: The taxable income of the property is the same, but the AMT rate is lower.

As a result, under these assumptions, foreign-use property is treated more favorably under the AMT than under the regular tax, while domestic property is treated less favorably under the AMT than under the regular tax. The AMT rules thus create an unambiguous reduction in the price of investment in foreign-use equipment relative to domestic-use equipment.

Several elaborations to this analysis can be made. First, if the foreign country's rate of tax on the investment exceeds the U.S. regular rate of tax, then the foreign investment creates excess tax credits. For a firm permanently in an excess credit position, the foreign country's tax rate is the effective rate of tax on this investment. However, because domestic investment is still discouraged under the AMT relative to the regular tax, the price of foreign-use equipment relative to domestic-use equipment is still lower for an AMT firm than for a regular tax firm.

Second, the cost of financing investment for an AMT firm is likely to be higher than for a regular tax firm when debt finance is used. This is because interest payments are deductible at the corporate statutory tax rate (34 or 35 percent for a regular tax firm and 20 percent for an AMT firm). The after-tax cost of a dollar of interest payments thus rises from 65 or 66 cents to 80 cents on the AMT.[9] Thus, while the absolute cost of debt-financed investment is higher on the AMT, the price of foreign investment relative to U.S. investment is still lower for the AMT firm.

The price of foreign investment relative to domestic investment can be calculated for an AMT firm and for a regular tax firm. Because the assumption of permanent AMT liability is likely to be an extreme one, the relative incentives for domestic and foreign investment for firms only temporarily on the AMT should be compared with the incentives faced by regular tax firms.[10] The calcu-

---

because the AMT also has an effect on firms that are currently paying regular tax but that anticipate a future period of AMT liability. These firms may have greater investment incentives currently than if they were to remain permanently on the regular tax. See Lyon (1990) for a discussion. The example discussed in the text considers incentives of firms currently subject to the AMT.

9. The loss in the value of the interest deductions under the AMT serves to increase the AMT credit a firm may claim in the future.

10. Gerardi et al. (1994) present data on the duration of AMT liability for firms between 1987 and 1991. Among a selected panel of AMT payers, 70 percent of taxpayers had AMT liability for two or fewer years of the five years in the panel. This calculation tends to understate the time period over which firms are affected by the incentives of the AMT for two reasons. First, many firms incurred liability in 1990 and 1991, and the length of time these firms will remain on the AMT is still unknown. Second, AMT credits may not be used to reduce regular tax liability below tentative minimum tax liability. Firms unable to fully use AMT credits against regular tax effec-

Table 6.2   **Marginal Effective Tax Rates for Domestic (U.S.) and Foreign-Use Property (%)**

Asset (1)	Location (2)	Regular Tax (3)	Five-Year Temporary AMT (4)	Ten-Year Temporary AMT (5)
Equipment	U.S.	26.8	32.5	33.0
	Foreign-use	38.3	36.8	33.3
Structures	U.S.	35.6	35.0	33.3
	Foreign-use	37.8	36.9	35.0

Source: Authors' calculations.
Note: See text for assumptions.

lations below assume that the firm is in excess limitation status for foreign tax credits, that the investment is equity financed so that there is no change in the firm's discount rate, and that all income flows (both receipts and deductions) on the foreign investment are immediately repatriated to the U.S. parent (as would occur if the property were held by a foreign branch). The corporate marginal effective tax rate is calculated separately for an aggregate category of equipment and for commercial structures using the tax rules in effect from 1990 to 1992.[11]

Table 6.2 compares the corporate marginal effective tax rates for equipment and structures under permanent regular tax status and temporary five-year or ten-year initial periods of AMT liability.[12] For equipment located in the United States, a regular tax firm faces a marginal effective tax rate of 26.8 percent. The same investment located abroad faces a 38.3 percent effective tax rate under the regular tax system. In terms of the cost of capital net of depreciation, this is an increase of 18.6 percent. For a firm with an initial five-year period of AMT liability, equipment located in the United States has a marginal effective tax rate of 32.5 percent. For this AMT firm, the effective tax rate on foreign-use equipment is 36.8 percent. The cost of capital net of depreciation for the foreign investment relative to the domestic investment increases by 6.8 percent.

---

tively face the same marginal incentives as firms paying AMT. Between 1987 and 1990, $17.2 billion was paid in AMT, but AMT credits claimed between 1988 and 1991 totaled only $3.4 billion.

11. It is assumed that economic depreciation of the investment follows a geometric pattern, so that returns on the investment each period are proportional to its remaining value. Rates of depreciation are based on estimates by Hulten and Wykoff (1981). Annual inflation is assumed to be 3.8 percent, and the after-tax real rate of return is 5 percent. The cost of capital for equipment is based on a capital-stock weighted average of the cost of capital for 31 types of equipment. These and other assumptions follow Lyon (1990). The corporate marginal effective tax rate is calculated as $(\rho - s)/\rho$, where ρ is the cost of capital net of depreciation and s is the after-tax real return.

12. The period of temporary AMT liability includes both the period during which the firm is paying AMT and the period during which it uses up its AMT credits. Because AMT credits may not reduce regular tax liability below tentative minimum tax, a firm does not face the incentives of the regular tax system until past AMT credits are exhausted.

Finally, for the firm facing a ten-year temporary period of AMT liability, the marginal effective tax rate for domestic equipment is 33.0 percent, while it is 33.3 percent for foreign-use equipment. The cost of capital net of depreciation for foreign-use property relative to domestic-use property is only 0.45 percent higher for this firm.

This analysis suggests that the AMT creates a *relative* incentive to locate investment abroad rather than in the United States. Of course, it can also be seen from the table that foreign-use property is always treated less preferentially than domestic property for a firm facing a *given* tax system. Thus, it is not correct to say that the AMT creates an *absolute* incentive to invest abroad rather than domestically. Rather, it is the incentive *relative* to the regular tax system that favors foreign-use equipment investment over domestic investment.

Table 6.2 shows that for investments in structures, the marginal effective tax rate is very similar for both AMT firms and regular tax firms. Even here, the increase in the cost of capital for foreign investment relative to domestic investment is slightly smaller for AMT firms than for regular tax firms, reinforcing the results found for equipment investment.

Finally, it is worth emphasizing that the cost-of-capital calculations presented here are based on a specific set of assumptions that may not be generally applicable. In particular, it was assumed that earnings of the foreign subsidiary were repatriated immediately. Because such income may be deferred for U.S. tax purposes, the tax status of the firm at the time of the investment may not affect the cost of capital of foreign-use property. Rather, the tax rate of the firm at the time of repatriation may be more relevant.[13] However, even in the case where the cost of capital of foreign-use equipment is the same for regular and AMT purposes, the fact that the cost of capital of domestic-use equipment is increased on the AMT relative to the regular tax creates a relative incentive for AMT firms to undertake investment abroad at the expense of domestic investment.

6.4   Income Repatriation Incentives

The differences in statutory rates and foreign tax credit calculations create the potential for AMT firms to face different incentives for the receipt of foreign-source income than if they were subject to only the regular tax. Hines and Hubbard (1990), Altshuler and Newlon (1993), and Altshuler, Newlon, and Randolph (chap. 9 in this volume) have shown that firms take advantage of deferral and timing opportunities to reduce their global tax liabilities on foreign-source income. This section considers the different tax positions faced by an AMT firm and its incentive to receive foreign-source income.

---

13. The next section examines whether the AMT presents an opportunity for repatriating such income.

A number of potential tax situations might be considered in evaluating the incentive for dividend repatriation and deferral. The variety of tax situations is somewhat larger under the AMT than for regular tax purposes, because the firm's regular foreign tax credit position—i.e., whether it is in excess credit or excess limit—may not be the same as its position under the AMT. In addition, the firm may be in an excess credit position under the AMT due to either the separate income category limitations or the 90 percent limitation, each of which may result in a different incentive for repatriation.

Before considering the foreign tax implications of the AMT, it may be useful to examine the effects of an AMT firm earning additional income in the absence of foreign tax interactions. Consider a firm that receives an additional dollar of income that is fully included in both minimum taxable income and regular taxable income. The net effect of this income on overall current-year tax liabilities is an increase in tax payments of 20 cents, and a *decrease* in the firm's AMT credits of 14 cents. This result can be derived as follows: The additional dollar of income increases the firm's regular tax liability by 34 cents (assuming it is subject to the 34 percent marginal tax rate) and increases the firm's tentative minimum tax by 20 cents. Because AMT is defined as the difference between regular tax payments and tentative minimum tax, AMT falls by 14 cents. The net increase of 20 cents is the sum of the increase in regular tax liability and the decrease in AMT.

Now consider the same situation, but in addition assume that the firm had AMT NOL deductions that were restricted by the 90 percent limitation. In this case, an additional dollar of income would cause the firm's net tax payments to increase by 2 cents. This is because the firm's regular tax would increase by 34 cents (assuming the firm is subject to this regular tax rate), but the firm's tentative minimum tax would increase by only 2 cents. (The dollar of additional taxable income would allow the use of an additional 90 cents in AMT NOLs. AMTI would increase by 10 cents, and tentative minimum tax would increase by 0.20×10 cents.) AMT would decline by 32 cents, reducing future AMT credits by 32 cents.[14]

Next we consider foreign tax credit interactions and their effect on AMT liabilities.

6.4.1 Excess Credit Positions

Initially we assume the firm is in an excess credit position for both regular tax and AMT calculations. An AMT firm could be in excess credit either because of the conventional limitation on foreign tax credits based on the ratio

---

14. If the firm had a tax loss for regular tax purposes, current tax liability would still increase by 2 cents. In this case the 2 cents would be from the AMT payment, so AMT credits would increase by 2 cents. The additional dollar of income would not change regular tax liability, but it would reduce by one dollar the amount of regular NOL carried forward. The reduction in regular NOL carryforwards can be thought to increase future regular tax liability by 34 cents, provided the NOL carryforward period would not have otherwise expired.

Table 6.3   **Tax Cost of Dividend Repatriation: Excess Credit Position on Regular Tax**

Position	Current Tax Price	Regular FTC Carryforwards	AMT Credit	AMT FTC Carryforwards
1. Regular tax firm	0	$T^* - .34$	n.a.	n.a.
AMT position				
2. Excess credit	0	$T^* - .34$	0	$T^* - .20$
3. 90 Percent limitation	.02	$T^* - .34$	.02	$T^* - .18$
4. Excess limit	$.20 - T^*$	$T^* - .34$	$.20 - T^*$	n.a.

of foreign to worldwide income or because of the 90 percent limitation. We consider both cases below.

Ninety Percent Limitation Not Binding

We assume that for regular tax purposes the firm is subject to the 34 percent tax rate. Under the regular tax, an additional dollar of earnings repatriated results in no additional regular tax payments, and the stock of regular foreign tax credits carried to another year increases by $T^* - 0.34$, where T^* is the foreign tax payment on this income.[15]

Similarly for AMT purposes, assuming the 90 percent limitation is not binding, the additional dollar of earnings repatriations results in no additional AMT and the stock of AMT foreign tax credits carried to another year increases by $T^* - 0.20$.

If the firm was also in excess credit for the previous two years, the foreign tax credits must be carried forward for up to five years. If T^* is less than 0.34, the firm has reduced the amount of regular tax credits it must carry forward. If T^* is greater than 0.34, the only cost to a regular tax firm of the earnings repatriation is if the additional regular foreign tax credit carryforward created will not be used in the next five years. In this case, the firm might have been better off deferring receipt of the foreign earnings until a time when the foreign tax credit could offset regular tax. The same incentives should generally guide an AMT firm. The AMT firm, however, should consider its ability to use both its regular and AMT foreign tax carryforwards in future years.[16]

Rows 1 and 2 of table 6.3 summarize these tax price effects for firms in an excess credit position under both the regular tax and the AMT.

15. It is assumed that the foreign country has a classical corporate income tax system. See Altshuler and Newlon (1993) for variations on the tax price measure under split-rate and imputation corporate tax systems. The effect on worldwide tax liability of withholding taxes, which may be imposed by the foreign country when income is repatriated, is not specifically considered here. Tax prices examined in this section are based on tax payments to the United States.

16. The scenario becomes a little more complicated for a firm in an excess credit position under only one of the two parallel tax systems. This possibility is examined in more detail later.

Ninety Percent Limit Binding

The firm is assumed to be in excess credit for regular tax purposes. For AMT purposes, the firm is assumed to be marginally constrained from using additional AMT foreign tax credits because of the 90 percent limitation.[17] For regular tax purposes, the effect of an additional dollar of earnings repatriated is the same as above, resulting in no current tax liability. Under the AMT, however, the additional dollar of repatriated earnings increases AMT before credits (line 9 of table 6.1) by 20 cents. Only an additional 18 cents of AMT foreign tax credits may be used to offset this tax, so tentative minimum tax increases by 2 cents. Because current regular tax liability is unchanged by the receipt of these earnings, AMT increases by 2 cents and a 2-cent AMT credit is generated. AMT foreign tax credits carried to another year increase by $T^* - 0.18$.

Relative to the case in which the 90 percent limitation is not binding, there is a diminished incentive to repatriate earnings. This is true regardless of whether the marginal dividend is from a high-tax country or a low-tax country.

One case in which an AMT firm facing the 90 percent limitation would still have a tax incentive to repatriate earnings is if it had regular NOL carryforwards that would otherwise expire unused.[18] (In this case the firm's regular marginal tax rate is zero rather than 34 percent.) By repatriating an additional dollar of foreign earnings, the firm can essentially convert the expiring tax shield into a regular foreign tax credit with a new five-year carryforward period. The cost to the firm of preserving this tax shield is the 2-cent payment of AMT today, less the present value of the 2-cent AMT credit the firm will claim in a future year.

Rows 1 and 3 of table 6.3 summarize the tax cost of earnings repatriations for firms in an excess credit position for regular tax purposes but subject to the 90 percent limitation for the AMT.

6.4.2   Excess Limit Positions

We initially assume the firm is in an excess limit position for both the regular tax and the AMT. Under the regular tax, an additional dollar of earnings repatriations reduces regular tax liability by $T^* - 0.34$ (assuming the firm is subject to the 34 percent regular tax rate). Earnings repatriated from high-tax countries ($T^* > 0.34$) thus lower current regular tax liability.

For a firm on the AMT, tentative minimum tax is reduced by $T^* - 0.20$ from the additional earnings. Since AMT reflects the difference between regular tax liability and tentative minimum tax, AMT declines by 14 cents. Total cur-

---

17. The firm could be marginally constrained on its use of NOL deductions due to the 90 percent limitation. In this case, the following description of the change in AMT liability continues to hold, but AMT NOL deductions carried to another year would decline by 90 cents and AMT foreign tax credits carried to another year would increase by T^*.

18. A similar incentive exists if AMT NOLs would expire. Regular tax and AMT NOL deductions may be carried back three years and carried forward fifteen years.

rent tax liability, the sum of regular tax liability and AMT, thus declines by $T^* - 0.20$.

The incentive for earnings repatriation is greater for a firm on the AMT. The reduction in current tax payments is 14 cents larger than for a firm facing only the regular tax. Current tax payments decline for any $T^* > 0.20$. The additional 14-cent savings today comes at a cost of a 14-cent reduction in the AMT credit that could be claimed at a later date.

The first two rows of table 6.4 summarize the tax cost of earnings repatriations for firms in an excess limit position for regular tax purposes.

6.4.3   Different Regular and AMT Credit Positions

The incentive to repatriate earnings while in an excess limit position could lead to a situation in which a firm is in an excess limit position for regular tax purposes, but is in an excess credit position on the AMT due to either the conventional limitation or the 90 percent limitation on foreign tax credits. As explained below, it is also possible for the firm to be in excess credit for regular tax purposes but excess limit for the AMT.

First, we consider the case of a firm that is in an excess limit position for regular tax purposes, but is in excess credit under the AMT due to the conventional limit. Such a firm lowers its regular tax liability by $T^* - 0.34$ from an additional dollar of earnings, but its tentative minimum tax liability is unchanged. Since AMT is the difference between tentative minimum tax and regular tax, AMT rises by $T^* - 0.34$, leaving total current tax liability—the sum of regular tax and AMT—unchanged. The additional AMT results in AMT credits of $T^* - 0.34$. A firm in this position faces no current cost for earnings repatriations. Foreign tax credits limited under the AMT may be carried to another year. The only cost of earnings repatriation is if the firm anticipates prolonged AMT status and expects to be in an AMT excess credit position in these years. In this instance, if $T^* > 0.20$, the AMT foreign tax credit carryforwards might expire unused, and the firm might have been better off deferring these earnings until it could make use of the AMT foreign tax credits. (If $T^* < 0.20$, the AMT firm benefits from using up AMT foreign tax credits that would otherwise have expired unused.)

Table 6.4   Tax Cost of Dividend Repatriation: Excess Limit Position on Regular Tax

Position	Current Tax Price	AMT Credit	AMT FTC Carryforwards
1. Regular tax firm	$.34 - T^*$	n.a.	n.a.
AMT position			
2. Excess limit	$.20 - T^*$	$-.14$	n.a.
3. Excess credit	0	$T^* - .34$	$T^* - .20$
4. 90 Percent limitation	$.02$	$T^* - .34 + .02$	$T^* - .18$

Second, we consider the 90 percent limitation. An additional dollar of foreign earnings affects regular tax liability as described above for an excess limit firm, decreasing regular tax liability by $T^* - 0.34$. Under the AMT, the additional earnings will *increase* tentative minimum tax by 2 cents. This occurs because only 90 percent of the additional minimum tax liability may be offset with AMT foreign tax credits. As a result, total current tax liability increases by 2 cents. The savings in current tax liability relative to the regular tax are $0.32 - T^*$. As a result, AMT credits decline by this amount. Relative to the firm's regular excess limit tax status, the AMT provides the firm a low-cost opportunity to repatriate earnings from foreign countries with low T^* (i.e., $T^* < 0.32$).

These two cases are summarized in rows 3 and 4 of table 6.4.

Finally, we consider the case of a firm that is in an excess credit position for regular tax purposes but is in an excess limit position under the AMT. This situation could arise where the firm has regular foreign tax credit carryforwards (or NOL deductions) but these carryforwards do not exist under the AMT. Such a firm faces no increase in regular tax liability from an additional dollar of foreign earnings. AMT liability increases by $0.20 - T^*$. As a result, earnings repatriated from countries with $T^* > 0.20$ can lower current AMT liability. The reduction in AMT reduces the firm's AMT credit by an equivalent amount. This case is considered in row 4 of table 6.3.

6.4.4   Summary of Repatriation Incentives

In summary, this section has identified a number of cases under which earnings repatriation is favored for AMT status relative to regular tax status. Table 6.5 provides a side-by-side comparison of the possible current tax prices faced by regular tax and AMT firms. For firms with AMT status, the incentive for earnings repatriation relative to regular tax status is noted in parentheses beneath the tax price.[19]

In only one of the six possible combinations of tax prices is the AMT tax price greater than the regular tax price for all possible foreign tax rates (T^*): where the firm faces the 90 percent limitation on foreign tax credits under the AMT but for regular tax purposes is in an excess credit position. Even in this case, the firm faces only a 2-cent tax per dollar of repatriated earnings.

In four cases, the AMT tax price is less than the regular tax price for some foreign tax rates. In the remaining case, the tax prices are identical.

The analysis in this section suggests that in general the AMT offers firms

---

19. Because the AMT only alters the timing of tax payments by the firm (AMT credits may be carried forward for an unlimited duration), the present value of the deviation between the regular tax price and the AMT tax price is a function of both the current tax price and the present value of the change in AMT credits (as well as the change in foreign tax credit carryforwards). Deviations in the current tax price are therefore more meaningful the longer the period that a firm remains subject to the AMT and the longer the firm's foreign tax credit position for regular tax purposes remains unchanged.

Table 6.5   **Summary of Current Tax Prices and Incentives for Dividend Repatriation Relative to Regular Tax Status**

	Regular Tax Position	
AMT Position	Excess Limit	Excess Credit
No AMT liability	$.34 - T^*$	0
Excess limit	$.20 - T^*$ (advantageous)	$.20 - T^*$ (advantageous for $T^* > .20$)
90 Percent limitation	.02 (advantageous for $T^* < .32$)	.02 (slight penalty)
Excess credit	0 (advantageous for $T^* < .34$)	0 (neutral)

the opportunity for low-cost earnings repatriations. The next section presents data on the extent of AMT liability among multinationals and on their foreign earnings repatriations while on the AMT.

6.5   Tax Return Data of MNCs

Using Internal Revenue Service tax return information, we are able to examine the prevalence of AMT status among MNCs. We are further able to examine the receipt of foreign-source income by these multinationals to explore the possibility that these firms alter their pattern of income repatriation to take advantage of the timing opportunities made possible by AMT status.

6.5.1   Data Description

The data used in this analysis are from the 1990 Internal Revenue Service Statistics of Income microdata files. Two primary files are used. Data concerning general characteristics of firms such as assets and tax liabilities are obtained from the corporate 1120 file. Data relating to foreign-source income and the credit position of firms with foreign tax credits are from the corporate 1118 file. Both files contain tax information prior to audit or amendment of the return.

The 1120 file consists of a stratified sample of the corporate population. Pass-through entities such as S-corporations, regulated investment companies, and real estate investment trusts are excluded from our analysis.[20] Firms with partial-year returns are also excluded. The remaining data represent 2,040,110 corporations consisting of approximately 55,000 actual observations. All corporations with more than $250 million in assets are included in the sample, while corporations in lower asset categories are sampled at a rate varying from

---

20. Pass-through entities do not pay minimum tax, although the recipients of the income may owe minimum tax based on their own taxable income from all sources.

50 to 0.25 percent. The sample includes taxpayers filing returns with accounting periods ending between July 1990 and June 1991.

Corporations included in the 1118 file consist of those corporations on the 1120 file that additionally claimed a foreign tax credit on form 1118.[21] An AMT firm that claims foreign tax credits against its regular tax liability will file a form 1118. A separate form indicating foreign tax credits used against AMT is not required to be filed. We estimate the foreign tax credit position for AMT purposes by substituting the appropriate AMT variables for the regular tax counterparts in the limitation calculation of form 1118. The AMT variables are taken from the AMT tax form, form 4626.

A number of corporations that receive foreign-source income do not file a form 1118. Such firms may be in a net operating loss position or may have other credits or NOL carryforwards that reduce their tax liability to zero, even before the use of foreign tax credits. The data in this paper regarding repatriated foreign-source income consist only of those firms that claimed a foreign tax credit.

6.5.2   AMT Status of Recipients of Foreign-Source Income

Table 6.6 shows AMT incidence for all corporations and for form 1118–filing corporations in 1990. While only 1–2 percent of all corporations incur AMT liability, a significantly higher percentage of larger corporations pay AMT. Of corporations with assets in excess of $50 million, 24.6 percent paid AMT. Among form 1118 filers with assets in excess of $50 million, 28.1 percent paid AMT. AMT incidence is even more prevalent among the largest-asset category, those with assets in excess of $500 million. Among all corporations in this largest-asset category, 30.6 percent paid AMT. Of form 1118 filers in this largest-asset category, 33.3 percent paid AMT.[22]

Table 6.7 presents the same information, but weights each firm by its reported assets.[23] Because AMT incidence is increasing with asset size, a larger fraction of total assets is affected by the AMT than suggested by the number of firms paying AMT. Nearly 40 percent of all assets reported by corporations are owned by firms paying AMT. Among form 1118 filers, AMT incidence is

21. Recall that the 1120 file is a stratified sample, but includes all firms with greater than $250 million in assets. Firms in this asset category account for over 90 percent of foreign tax credits. As a result, the stratification method is unlikely to result in significant sampling error of foreign-source income.

22. Nonfinancial corporations and corporations in finance and real estate were also examined separately. Among nonfinancial corporations with more than $500 million in assets and filing a form 1118, 31.2 percent paid AMT. Of the financial corporations in this asset category filing a form 1118, 38.8 percent paid AMT.

23. It should be noted that for corporations with foreign subsidiaries, reported assets deviate even more substantially from replacement cost than for domestic firms. This is because the value of the foreign subsidiary is carried by the parent firm at the historic cost of the equity in the subsidiary. In addition to the deviation between current cost and historic cost of the original physical assets in the subsidiary, the value of accumulated retained earnings within the foreign subsidiary is not accounted for in the parent's books.

Table 6.6   Counts of Corporations by Size, AMT Status, and Form 1118 Status, 1990 (counts in units)

Asset Size Class[a] (thousand $)	All Corporations Total Number	Form 1118 Filers Number	Form 1118 Filers Percentage of Total	AMT Payers Total Number	AMT Payers Form 1118 Filers Number	AMT Payers Form 1118 Filers Percentage of Total	AMT Incidence: Percentage of AMT Payers Among All Corporations	AMT Incidence: Percentage of AMT Payers Among Form 1118 Filers
0–100	1,039,755	324	.03	1,109	1	.00	.11	.31
100–250	376,082	233	.06	1,097	0	.00	.29	.00
250–500	236,695	488	.21	2,329	91	3.89	.98	18.55
500–1,000	163,416	495	.30	4,426	42	.95	2.71	8.49
1,000–10,000	183,975	1,144	.62	14,297	131	.91	7.77	11.42
10,000–50,000	25,055	690	2.75	4,482	153	3.41	17.89	22.13
50,000–100,000	5,958	255	4.27	1,335	58	4.35	22.41	22.81
100,000–250,000	4,687	366	7.82	1,101	88	7.98	23.50	24.00
250,000–500,000	1,805	208	11.52	462	54	11.69	25.60	25.96
500,000+	2,682	646	24.09	822	215	26.16	30.65	33.28
Total	2,040,110	4,848	.24	31,459	832	2.64	1.54	17.16

[a]Classes consist of asset sizes greater than or equal to the lower limit and strictly less than the upper limit.

Table 6.7   Assets of Corporations by Size, AMT Status, and Form 1118 Status, 1990 (billion $)

Asset Size Class[a] (thousand $)	All Corporations			AMT Payers			AMT Incidence: Percentage of AMT Payers	
	Total Assets	Form 1118 Filers		Total Assets	Form 1118 Filers		Among All Corporations	Among Form 1118 Filers
		Assets	Percentage of Total		Assets	Percentage of Total		
0–100	31.7	.0	.04	.0	.0	.00	.00	.00
100–250	61.4	.0	.05	.2	.0	.00	.29	.00
250–500	84.3	.2	.22	.9	.0	4.25	1.06	20.21
500–1,000	116.1	.3	.30	3.3	.0	1.01	2.81	9.57
1,000–10,000	492.0	3.9	.79	48.0	.6	1.18	9.75	14.56
10,000–50,000	559.1	17.0	3.05	103.5	3.7	3.62	18.52	21.98
50,000–100,000	420.8	18.2	4.32	95.2	4.4	4.62	22.63	24.16
100,000–250,000	728.5	58.6	8.04	172.4	14.3	8.31	23.67	24.47
250,000–500,000	633.4	74.7	11.79	162.5	19.5	12.03	25.65	26.17
500,000+	12,809.5	6,110.3	47.70	5,736.3	3,290.0	57.35	44.78	53.84
Total	15,936.8	6,283.2	39.43	6,322.2	3,332.7	52.71	39.67	53.04

[a]See table 6.6 for definition of asset size classes.

significantly greater when weighted by assets. Fifty-three percent of assets owned by form 1118 filers are owned by those paying AMT. While only about 830 form 1118 filers pay AMT, their assets account for just under 53 percent of the assets owned by AMT payers.[24]

The upper panel of table 6.8 shows foreign-source income and foreign-source income as a share of assets for form 1118 filers paying regular tax and paying AMT. In total, 56 percent of all foreign-source income is earned by AMT firms. As a result, incentives for the receipt of the majority of foreign-source income are governed by the rules and tax rates affecting the AMT rather than the regular tax.

The upper panel of table 6.8 can also be used to examine whether a greater share of foreign-source income is reported by form 1118 filers subject to the AMT than would be expected based on the share of assets reported by these firms. As noted earlier, the measure of assets used here may understate the current value of foreign subsidiary assets. In addition, because the measure of assets also includes the book value of domestic assets, the ratio of foreign-source income to assets should not be interpreted as the return on a firm's foreign assets.

In aggregate, there does not appear to be a significant difference in the ratio of foreign-source income to assets between AMT firms and non-AMT firms. For example, foreign-source income constitutes 1.31 percent of assets for non-AMT payers and 1.49 percent of assets for AMT payers, a difference of only 14 percent. Of form 1118 filers with assets less than $500 million, however, foreign-source income of non-AMT firms constitutes 2.47 percent of assets, while for the AMT firms foreign-source income constitutes 6.48 percent of assets, a strikingly large difference of more than 150 percent.

The bottom panel of table 6.8 presents the same data for foreign-source dividends (except deemed dividends).[25] Foreign-source dividends can be viewed as a relatively more discretionary component of foreign income and therefore may better represent the voluntary repatriation of income by the U.S. parent. A story similar to that in the top panel holds. In aggregate, foreign-source dividends account for 0.86 percent of assets for non-AMT corporations and for only 0.72 percent of assets for AMT firms. The fact that dividends compose a higher percentage of assets for non-AMT firms than for AMT firms is entirely the result of dividends received by the highest asset category. When

---

24. Of nonfinancial corporations filing a form 1118, 50.0 percent of the assets were owned by AMT payers. Of the financial corporations filing a form 1118, 55.8 percent of the assets were owned by AMT payers.

25. Deemed dividends are nondiscretionary in the sense that they must be reported by the parent. (Firms have some planning opportunity on whether to choose to earn income that would be classified as a deemed dividend.) Nondeemed dividends may therefore represent the income flow over which the parent has the most control. Note that in certain asset categories the quantity of dividends reported in the bottom panel of table 6.8 significantly exceeds the net foreign-source income reported in the top panel. This appears to be due to the reporting of expenses that reduce foreign-source income below the amount of dividends received.

Table 6.8   Foreign-Source Income and Foreign-Source Dividends (except deemed) of Form 1118 Filers by Size and AMT Status

| | Foreign-Source Income of Form 1118 Filers (million $) | | | | | Foreign-Source Income/Assets (%) | | | | |
Asset Size Class[a] (thousand $)	All Corporations	Non-AMT Payers	AMT Payers Total	At 90% Limit	Other	All Corporations	Non-AMT Payers	AMT Payers Total	At 90% Limit	Other
0–50,000	967	524	443	386	57	4.50	3.06	10.10	32.78	1.76
50,000–100,000	488	240	249	222	27	2.68	1.74	5.65	12.44	1.02
100,000–250,000	1,664	1,148	516	420	97	2.84	2.60	3.60	8.80	1.01
250,000–500,000	2,860	1,304	1,556	1,394	162	3.83	2.37	7.96	17.21	1.41
0–500,000	5,979	3,216	2,763	2,422	341	3.46	2.47	6.48	15.30	1.27
500,000+	82,423	35,556	46,867	16,968	29,899	1.35	1.26	1.42	2.04	1.22
Total	88,402	38,772	49,630	19,390	30,240	1.41	1.31	1.49	2.29	1.22

| | Foreign-Source Dividends (except deemed) (million $) | | | | | Foreign-Source Dividends (except deemed)/Assets (%) | | | | |
Asset Size Class[a] (thousand $)	All Corporations	Non-AMT Payers	AMT Payers Total	At 90% Limit	Other	All Corporations	Non-AMT Payers	AMT Payers Total	At 90% Limit	Other
0–50,000	346	97	249	141	107	6.48	2.47	17.68	30.18	11.44
50,000–100,000	145	57	89	58	30	2.42	1.34	4.92	6.28	3.47
100,000–250,000	530	327	202	158	44	2.15	1.77	.00	5.62	1.33
250,000–500,000	1,300	620	681	563	118	3.45	2.18	7.33	12.01	2.55
0–500,000	2,320	1,100	1,220	921	299	3.15	2.00	6.55	10.34	3.08
500,000+	36,463	17,618	18,845	9,603	9,242	.75	.83	.68	1.18	.47
Total	38,784	18,719	20,065	10,524	9,541	.78	.86	.72	1.28	.49

[a]See table 6.6 for definition of asset size classes.

only form 1118 firms with less than $500 million in assets are examined, dividends are found to constitute 2.00 percent of assets for the non-AMT firms and 6.55 percent of assets for the AMT firms, or a rate more than 200 percent higher for the AMT firms.

One would like to examine the form 1118 filers in more detail, together with better information on their foreign subsidiary assets, before reaching definitive conclusions on how the AMT changes their behavior regarding the receipt of foreign income. For example, in the case of the smaller form 1118 filers, we need to distinguish between two hypotheses: (1) because these firms were subject to the AMT they increased their receipt of foreign income versus (2) these firms were subject to the AMT, but for reasons exogenous to the AMT treatment of foreign-source income chose to repatriate income. The second hypothesis may be true for a number of reasons. Consider the possibility that AMT status is indicative of low earnings and that these firms may be cash-flow constrained. It might not be unreasonable to expect that a cash-flow-constrained firm would seek to increase its repatriation of foreign income. The fact that low cash flow and AMT status are correlated may falsely imply that the AMT status encouraged repatriations.[26]

6.5.3   Foreign Credit Position of AMT Taxpayers

As described in section 6.4, the tax price of foreign-source income for AMT firms, and the advantage of dividend repatriation while subject to the AMT relative to the regular tax system, depends on both the foreign tax credit position for regular tax purposes and that for the AMT. As summarized earlier in table 6.5, six potential tax price differentials exist for a firm subject to the AMT. In table 6.9, we group form 1118 filers into these six AMT cells (and two regular tax cells for non-AMT taxpayers)[27] based on the foreign tax credit position of the firms. The chart separates firms with zero regular taxable income from those with positive regular taxable income. Firms with current losses or NOLs are "generically" excess credit firms for regular tax purposes (an additional dollar of foreign-source income will not give rise to regular tax liability) and thus face the same incentives as any other excess credit firms for regular taxes, but it is useful to distinguish among these firms for AMT purposes. The foreign tax credit position shown in table 6.9 is for the basket category accounting for the largest share of the firm's foreign-source income.[28] The

---

26. Using other data, Hines and Hubbard (1990) find a strong correlation between foreign subsidiary dividend payments and parent dividend payments that might be suggested by a cash-flow constraint of the parent firm. Altshuler and Newlon (1993) find that the relationship of foreign subsidiary dividend payments to the parent is accounted for by a fixed effect for the parent, rather than by the level of parent dividend payments.

27. Note that even regular taxpayers can face the same incentives as an AMT payer to the extent that they are prevented from using AMT credits or other business credits to reduce regular tax liability below tentative AMT. We hope to separately identify these firms in later work.

28. For parent firms that are classified as nonfinancial firms, this basket is nearly always the general limitation basket. This basket accounts for about 90 percent of the foreign-source income

Table 6.9   **Foreign Tax Credit Position of Form 1118 Filers, 1990**

	Position for Regular Taxes			
		Excess Credit		
AMT Position	Excess Limit	No Regular Taxes	Regular Taxes	Total
No AMT liability	1.743	366	1,908	4,017
	35.95	7.55	39.36	
Excess limit	120	28	0	148
	2.48	.58	.00	
At 90 percent limit	12	114	42	168
	.25	2.35	.87	
Excess credit	60	112	343	515
	1.24	2.31	7.08	
Total	1,935	620	2,293	4,848

Note: Top number in cell is count in units; bottom number is count as a percentage of total number of form 1118 filers.

credit position is based on the last dollar of foreign-source income received for the basket.

First, we consider firms with a regular tax excess credit position and with a positive amount of regular tax. None of these firms are in an excess limit position for the AMT, as anticipated given the lower AMT statutory rate. Approximately 90 percent of these firms that face AMT liability also have excess credits for purposes of the AMT and thus face the same marginal incentives for dividend repatriation (343 of 385 firms). The remaining 10 percent of these firms that pay AMT (42 firms) are subject to the 90 percent limitation. These firms pay an extra tax of 2 cents at the margin for each dollar of foreign-source income, relative to their regular tax liability.

Table 6.10 displays the amount of foreign-source income for the same cells as shown in table 6.9. The 42 firms subject to the 90 percent limitation account for approximately 13 percent of all foreign-source income earned by form 1118 corporations ($11.34 billion/$88.40 billion) and 23 percent of the foreign-source income received by AMT payers. A maximum of $227 million in extra current-year AMT tax payments are made by these firms because of the 90 percent limitation (0.02 times $11.34 billion), since these firms would otherwise be in an excess credit position.[29] Firms in an excess credit position

---

received by nonfinancial firms. Most of the remaining income for these firms appears in the passive basket. For financial firms, the basket selected is the financial services income basket. This basket accounts for 88 percent of the foreign-source income received by these firms.

29. This amount is a maximum cost because some of the foreign-source income may be fully shielded by foreign tax credits. It is only true at the margin that an additional dollar of foreign-source income increases tax liability by 2 cents. Additional analysis indicates that the firms with foreign-source income facing the 90 percent limitation on the use of foreign tax credits against

Table 6.10   **Foreign-Source Income of Form 1118 Filers by Foreign Tax Credit Position, 1990**

| | | Position for Regular Taxes | | |
| | | Excess Credit | | |
AMT Position	Excess Limit	No Regular Taxes	Regular Taxes	Total
	22,995	207	15,570	38,772
No AMT liability	26.01	.23	17.61	
	4,225	536	0	4,761
Excess limit	4.78	.61	.00	
	2,657	4,013	11,343	18,012
At 90 percent limit	3.01	4.54	12.83	
	2,785	568	23,505	26,858
Excess credit	3.15	.64	26.59	
Total	32,662	5,323	50,417	88,402

Note: Top number in each cell is foreign-source income in million dollars; bottom number is this income as a percentage of total foreign-source income earned by form 1118 filers.

for both AMT and regular tax purposes account for 27 percent of all foreign-source income and 47 percent of the foreign-source income earned by AMT payers.

Next we consider firms with zero regular taxable income and positive AMT liability. A small number—about 11 percent, or 28 firms—are in an excess limit position for the AMT. These firms have an incentive to repatriate income from countries with $T^* > 0.20$. Less than 1 percent of foreign-source income is attributable to these 28 firms. A larger number of firms and amount of foreign-source income is subject to the 90 percent limitation. About 4.5 percent of total foreign-source income and 8 percent of the foreign-source income of AMT payers is in this cell. Extra tax payments resulting from this limitation are a maximum of $80 million.

Finally, we consider firms in an excess limit position for regular tax purposes. A significant number of these firms also are in an excess limit position under the AMT. By being subject to the AMT, these firms save in the current year 14 cents per dollar of foreign-source income received. About 9 percent of the foreign-source income received by AMT payers accrues to these firms. These firms save approximately $590 million in current-year taxes on their foreign-source income as a result of being subject to the lower AMT tax rate. Another significant group of the firms in excess limit for regular tax purposes, accounting for about 6 percent of the foreign-source income received by AMT payers, is in an excess credit position under the AMT. This group of firms saves

---

AMT are facing the constraint primarily because of the large amount of foreign tax credits available to the firms rather than the existence of NOLs.

the difference between 34 percent and their average foreign tax credit rate (a number in excess of 20 percent) on each dollar of foreign-source income received. Finally, a slightly smaller share of the excess limit firms for regular tax purposes, 5 percent of the foreign-source income received by AMT payers, is subject to the 90 percent limitation on foreign tax credits. The 90 percent limitation still results in lower U.S. tax payments, by the amount that the average foreign tax rate is less than 32 percent per dollar of foreign-source income received.

In sum, it appears that total payments of tax on foreign-source income are lower for AMT firms than if they were subject to the regular tax rules. The analysis, however, has been unable to determine whether the increased incentive to receive foreign-source income actually significantly affects repatriation behavior. While the data in table 6.8 indicate that smaller firms on the AMT appear to have higher rates of repatriation of foreign income, it is indeterminate whether this is the result of a tax price advantage of AMT status or whether higher rates of repatriation are correlated with other factors leading to AMT status. Extension of the single-period analysis over a number of years for firms in our sample and linking the parent-firm tax returns with information returns on the foreign subsidiaries (form 5471) will allow us to better examine alternative hypotheses.

6.6   Conclusions

This paper has shown the extent to which incentives of U.S.-based MNCs are affected by the AMT. More than half of all foreign-source income in 1990 was received by corporations subject to the AMT. As a result, the tax prices on foreign-source income created by the AMT may be at least as important as those created by the regular tax. While data shown in Gerardi et al. (1994) indicate that AMT incidence for the largest corporations in 1990 was approximately 25 percent greater than in 1989 or 1991, the large stock of unclaimed AMT credits accumulated by corporations suggests that the incentives created by the AMT will continue to be an important factor in the future. As shown in section 6.3, the AMT may create an incentive for AMT firms to invest abroad rather than domestically. For firms interested in repatriating income from abroad, the AMT may create a temporary timing opportunity that allows repatriation of this income at a lower cost than if the firms were subject to the rules of the regular tax system. These two different incentives may have an ambiguous overall effect on U.S. domestic investment if repatriated income is retained by the parent in the United States. Alternatively, the two incentives together may suggest that the AMT provides an opportunity for firms to repatriate income from foreign locations with poor reinvestment opportunities and to reinvest the funds abroad in different foreign locations with better opportunities to take advantage of the temporary relatively lower cost of capital.

Section 6.5 presents data on the different repatriation patterns of AMT firms and non-AMT firms. There is a general tendency for both AMT firms and non-AMT firms with assets under $500 million to repatriate a larger amount of foreign-source income (relative to the assets of the firm) than for the largest MNCs. The smaller AMT firms, however, receive a significantly higher share of foreign-source income than their non-AMT counterparts. It appears that larger firms, those with assets in excess of $500 million, may find permanent deferral of foreign-source income more advantageous than the temporary timing advantage offered by the AMT. The differences in behavior between the largest firms and the smaller firms may be consistent with the view that the smaller firms face cash-flow constraints on their investment opportunities while the larger firms either have sufficient cash flow to undertake new investment or can raise outside funds at a relatively low cost. We hope in future research to examine more closely the differences in repatriation behavior between AMT firms and non-AMT firms, and to make use of information reported by the foreign subsidiaries of the U.S. parents to determine whether the pattern of repatriation from these subsidiaries is consistent with predictions about tax-minimizing behavior of the parent firms.

References

Altshuler, Rosanne, and T. Scott Newlon. 1993. The effects of U.S. tax policy on the income repatriation patterns of U.S. multinational corporations. In *Studies in international taxation,* ed. Alberto Giovannini, R. Glenn Hubbard, and Joel Slemrod, 77–115. Chicago: University of Chicago Press.

Gerardi, Geraldine, Hudson Milner, and Gerald Silverstein. 1994. The effects of the corporate alternative minimum tax: Additional results from panel data for 1987–1991. In *National Tax Association—Tax Institute of America, Proceedings of the eighty-sixth annual conference, 1993.* Columbus, Ohio: National Tax Association.

Hines, James R., and R. Glenn Hubbard. 1990. Coming home to America: Dividend repatriations by U.S. multinationals. In *Taxation in the global economy,* ed. Assaf Razin and Joel Slemrod, 161–207. Chicago: University of Chicago Press.

Hulten, Charles R., and Frank C. Wykoff. 1981. The measurement of economic depreciation. In *Depreciation, inflation, and the taxation of income from capital,* ed. Charles R. Hulten, 81–125. Washington, D.C.: Urban Institute Press.

Lyon, Andrew B. 1990. Investment incentives under the alternative minimum tax. *National Tax Journal* 43:451–65.

———. 1991. The alternative minimum tax: Equity, efficiency, and incentive effects. In *Economic effects of the corporate alternative minimum tax,* 51–82. Washington, D.C.: American Council for Capital Formation.

———. 1992. Tax neutrality under parallel tax systems. *Public Finance Quarterly* 20:338–58.

Comment   Alan J. Auerbach

In terms of its own language, this paper asks the following question: What should the impact of the AMT on MNCs be, in light of ACE and NOLs? In short, it considers the simultaneous impact of several complications to the corporate income tax on the behavior of U.S. multinational corporations (MNCs) with investments abroad. For a reader not totally immersed in the arcana of the tax code, this is a head-spinning journey. But we cannot blame the authors for this; they are simply trying to analyze a set of issues made very complicated by those who have given us the federal tax code.

Lyon and Silverstein are to be commended for their careful description of how the provisions of the alternative minimum tax (AMT) interact with the treatment of foreign-source income. Because the paper does devote so much effort to getting the institutional analysis right, let me step backward and offer a broad summary of what they are up to. The incentives faced by multinationals under the regular income tax are quite complicated and have been the subject of study by several authors. Lyon and Silverstein, in the first part of their paper, consider how two incentives, to invest abroad and to repatriate earnings from abroad, are influenced by the presence of the corporate AMT. They then go on to consider the extent to which the second of these decisions is actually influenced in practice, by looking at patterns of income repatriation by AMT status.

The two most important features of the AMT relevant to the current investigation are its treatment of depreciation and its nominal tax rate. The AMT provisions regarding depreciation are less generous for domestic investment, but not for foreign investment, than those of the regular income tax. Thus, firms under the AMT are encouraged to invest relatively more abroad. Second, the AMT rate is lower than the regular corporate rate—20 versus 34 percent during the time period analyzed. Thus, firms that are not already in an excess credit position under the regular income tax, and hence are facing additional taxes on repatriated income, will pay lower taxes on marginal repatriated income under the AMT.

There are, of course, many additional complications. Some, such as the AMT's limit on the use of credits to offset taxable income, the authors treat explicitly. Others, such as the dynamics of carrying AMT credits forward, they mention but ignore. Still, the basic conclusions seem robust to these complications. The key question is how important these incentives are in the very complicated world of international investment and finance. This proves to be a very difficult question to answer.

The authors begin their empirical analysis by illustrating, in tables 6.6 and 6.7, that the AMT could be an important factor, in that it affects a large number of firms operating abroad. Weighted by total corporate assets, over half of all firms reporting foreign activity are subject to the AMT. It is striking how much

Alan J. Auerbach is the Robert D. Burch Professor of Economics and Law at the University of California, Berkeley, and a research associate of the National Bureau of Economic Research.

the AMT is related to size and foreign activity. Indeed, this highlights one of the difficulties the authors face. Their analysis implicitly takes AMT status as given, but it clearly is not a random occurrence. To the extent that AMT status is correlated with the behavior being considered, this presents problems of interpretation.

A good illustration of this problem comes from the analysis of foreign-source income in table 6.8. The authors argue, based on the theory described above, that foreign-source income and, in particular, foreign-source dividends should be higher for firms subject to the AMT than those not subject to the AMT. They find that, at least as a share of firm assets, this is not the case for the groups as a whole, but is true for smaller firms. But recall that smaller firms are less likely to be subject to the AMT, so there is clearly a sample selection issue here. Moreover, smaller firms (with assets less than $50 million), both those subject to the AMT and those that are not, have much higher ratios of repatriated dividends to assets (17.68 and 2.47 percent, respectively) than do firms of all sizes (0.86 and 0.78 percent), suggesting that there is much more behind the curtain than on stage.

A second, related problem with this analysis is the denominator it uses to measure how much income firms are repatriating. The assets to which foreign-source dividends and income are being compared are the multinational's total assets, not its foreign assets. Unless foreign assets as a share of total assets is independent of AMT status—which is doubtful given how the AMT works— it is not clear how the comparative ratios should be interpreted.

The preceding analysis looks at different firms and asks whether those under the AMT repatriate more income than those not subject to the AMT. The implication is that AMT firms face a lower tax on repatriations than otherwise identical firms not under the AMT would. However, the paper's final set of statistics, in tables 6.9 and 6.10, casts doubt on this assumption.

This conclusion can be demonstrated most clearly by the density in the lower right-hand corner of table 6.10, which weights by firm size. This table indicates that most firms subject to the AMT are already in an excess credit position under the regular income tax—they pay no taxes on marginal repatriations of income. Virtually all such firms either remain in this position under the AMT or actually face limits on the use of credits to offset income, causing marginal taxes to rise slightly above zero. Hence, for the bulk of multinational firms subject to the AMT—about 80 percent, weighted by foreign-source income—falling under the AMT delivers no tax incentive at all for repatriations.

In summary, the paper has made an important contribution in carefully indicating the potential incentives for the generation and repatriation of foreign-source income. By showing how large a share of the corporate sector falls under the AMT, particularly those firms operating abroad, it offers convincing proof that we need to think more about the AMT than many of us have in the past. However, the empirical results still leave plenty of room for argument about what the behavioral effects of the AMT actually are in practice.

7   Accounting Standards, Information Flow, and Firm Investment Behavior

Jason G. Cummins, Trevor S. Harris, and Kevin A. Hassett

7.1   Introduction

In many countries, capital markets provide the major source of external financing for firms. In these countries, a financial accounting system has developed over time that seeks to fulfill a regulatory objective of providing relevant and reliable information about the financial position and profitability of the firm to shareholders and lenders. In other countries, capital markets have played a less crucial role, and the information objectives have been less well defined.

Tax authorities have also developed reporting requirements that facilitate the accurate calculation of tax liabilities. In the United States and several other countries the two sets of information are largely distinct ("two-book" countries); one book is designed to accurately describe the firm's tax liability, and one is designed to convey to the market essential information for assessing the firm's profitability.[1] The existence of two sets of books reflects the different objectives of financial-market participants and policymakers. The most effec-

Jason G. Cummins is assistant professor of economics at New York University and John M. Olin Fellow at Columbia University. Trevor S. Harris is professor of accounting at the Graduate School of Business of Columbia University. Kevin A. Hassett is associate professor of economics and finance at the Graduate School of Business of Columbia University and economist at the Board of Governors of the Federal Reserve System.

Cummins's research was funded by the Center for International Business Education (CIBE) and the Chazen Institute at Columbia University. Harris's research was partially funded by the CIBE and the Rudolph Schoenheimer Fellowship. The authors thank Valerie Amerkhail, Rusty Goldin, R. Glenn Hubbard, Steve Oliner, Pete Wilson, and Penelope Winkle for helpful discussions and Samuel Coffin for able research assistance. The views expressed in this paper are those of the authors and do not necessarily represent those of the Board of Governors of the Federal Reserve System.

1. As discussed in section 7.2, the designation "two-book" does not imply that all measures differ for accounting and tax purposes. Rather, it refers to the regulatory environment that separates accounting and tax reporting.

tive rules to enforce tax regulations may not be the same rules that induce efficient transmission of information about the firm to the market.

Many countries do not have a two-book system similar to that in the United States. Instead, these countries typically require firms to match their tax and accounting statements for each taxable entity. Under tax conformity (in "one-book" countries), firms may only take tax deductions if they have been recognized in reports to shareholders either before or concurrent with tax recognition. Firms operating in these countries face a fundamentally different environment in which signals of the firm's profitability to external investors are intermeshed, perhaps inextricably, with the firm's tax accounts.[2]

For the most part, tax research has ignored differences in accounting regimes. In this paper, we carefully document some of the institutional details of one-book and two-book countries, with the goal of identifying significant differences between the two regimes. We then explore the extent to which accounting regimes might be expected to affect the interaction between tax policy and real behavior.[3]

If information flows less smoothly to the market in one-book countries, one would expect several consequences. First, firms may have relative difficulty raising funds in equity markets if they cannot provide reliable information to shareholders. As a result, one-book firms may have relatively more capital supplied by and closer relationships with banks, which could, in principle, provide the careful monitoring necessary in a world without particularly useful accounting information. As we discuss below, there is already some limited evidence suggesting that this is the case (see, e.g., Hoshi, Kashyap, and Scharfstein 1991).[4] Second, while firms in the United States may freely act to minimize their tax burdens by availing themselves of all legal tax benefits, as we discuss below, firms in one-book countries may have to equate the benefit of tax minimization strategies, which effectively reduce their reported taxable income, with two potential costs: lower reported income may inadvertently signal that the firm's prospects have worsened and may, in addition, reduce the pool of funds that can be legally distributed to shareholders. These tradeoffs may make firm investment in this environment much less sensitive to tax policy than is the case in the United States.

These arguments suggest that multinationals based in one-book countries

---

2. Firms everywhere must keep a careful account of their assets in order to operate efficiently. This set of "operating books" could also be quite useful for information purposes (e.g., during a friendly takeover or to banks with insider holdings). Technically, this means that we should be referring to "two-book" and "three-book" countries. Since the operating books are not constrained by law (and thus their value is difficult to assess), and are generally unavailable for applied research, we will continue with our terminology.

3. It is not the purpose of this paper to model the equilibrium between the accounting system and the institutional environment or to explain the evolution of a country's system.

4. The direction of causality could well be the opposite. The demand for external equity capital may be low where close relationships with banks are allowed. In this case, low demand for information may explain the lack of a second set of financial accounts.

may be at a disadvantage when investing in countries with generous tax incentives. A necessary but not sufficient condition for this to occur is for firms in one-book countries to demonstrate less responsiveness to domestic tax incentives. By induction, if one-book firms do not utilize domestic tax benefits, they also may not utilize those earned abroad. Using panel data drawn from the Global Vantage database, we explore this question below and show that investment is in some cases less sensitive to tax policy in one-book countries.

The paper proceeds as follows: In section 7.2, we provide a description of the major differences in accounting systems across countries. In section 7.3, we develop a structural model in order to formalize and explore the implication that in countries with one-book accounting standards domestic firm-level investment may be less sensitive to tax law changes. In section 7.4, we introduce a multicountry firm-level panel data set that, combined with panels of tax information, allows us to estimate the model derived in section 7.3. Section 7.5 summarizes our results. Three appendices provide additional detail on the accounting system in each country of the sample, the data set, and the tax parameters.

7.2   The Different Accounting Regimes

There are certain generic attributes that apply in several countries that illustrate the key differences between national accounting regimes. We first focus on two countries, the United States and Germany, and then discuss in appendix A how other countries vary from the two benchmarks. It is crucial to understand from the outset that these regimes are not static and that national accounting systems are moving toward a more global equilibrium as global capital markets evolve. Hence, we relate some historical detail to develop an understanding of the dynamics of the environment over the period we consider.

7.2.1   The United States: A "Two-Book" Case

U.S. public companies are required to provide periodic published financial statements in conformity with generally accepted accounting principles (GAAP). While the requirement for publicly available annual financial statements derives from specific laws, the precise features of GAAP are determined by private-sector organizations, primarily the Financial Accounting Standard Board (FASB). The FASB operates under the watchful eye of a regulatory agency, the Security and Exchange Commission (SEC), that occasionally prescribes its own rules or interpretations that become part of GAAP. There is an established hierarchy whereby the SEC and FASB rules largely determine U.S. GAAP.

The clearly stated objective of U.S. GAAP is to provide information to investors and creditors to enable them to predict the future cash flows and profitability of an enterprise. The FASB has tried to ensure that it is not perceived to be providing a measure of income that is necessarily useful for meeting the fiscal objectives of tax regulators. In fact, reporting requirements for tax purposes have evolved independently over time.[5] The tax base used for calculating income taxes is determined by the tax code, and differences arise in the valuation criteria and measurement rules applied for tax and financial reporting purposes. For example, tax regulations allow a specific accelerated schedule of depreciation for equipment. U.S. GAAP requires companies to allocate the costs of equipment so as to reflect how it is consumed in the production of revenue. While companies choose among a set of alternatives, often choosing an accelerated method, it is most unlikely that this method would yield the same depreciation schedule used for tax purposes, as the latter is determined by efforts to influence a firm's capital investment practices.

The spirit of financial reporting practice is to reduce the information asymmetries between managers and owners by reflecting the economic activity of the entity. This information can then we used to evaluate how well managers have utilized their resources, allowing shareholders and creditors to determine their investment strategies based on expected profitability. By maintaining a dual valuation and measurement system the potentially conflicting objectives of information revelation and fiscal policy can each be achieved independently.

Of course, accurate forecasts of tax liabilities are crucial for evaluating a firm's prospects. To aid in reconciliation of the two sets of books, U.S. GAAP requires a detailed explanation of material differences between tax payable on the basis of tax law and a hypothetical tax expense based on the product of accounting income and the federal tax code.

The separation of the two sets of books is the rule, but there are exceptions that help shed light on the forces that may govern behavior in one-book countries. The case of accounting for inventory provides an interesting example. Under U.S. tax regulations, companies may adopt a last-in-first-out (LIFO) policy to account for inventory. This practice will usually lead to higher expenses, and hence lower taxable income when prices of inputs rise. At the time LIFO was first allowed, the tax regulations required that companies adopting LIFO for tax purposes also use the method for financial reporting purposes. Thus, LIFO is the primary example of tax conformity in the United States. Initially, companies were not permitted to provide information about the value of inventory accounted for using other methods, such as the first-in-first-out (FIFO) method. However, this was perceived by managers and shareholders as creating biases in the information system. As a result, many managers chose not to adopt LIFO practices, even though such adoption would have significantly reduced tax liabilities. Eventually, firms lobbied for rules that allow for supplementary disclosures of the more current (and, presumably, more informative) measures of inventory. While extensive research has been performed

---

5. The alternative minimum tax (AMT) was an attempt to partially bridge the gap. To ensure that GAAP did not become tax driven, the FASB lobbied against making taxable income or AMT based on U.S. GAAP.

analyzing why many companies choose not to adopt LIFO, it seems reasonable to assume that, given rational investors and managers, the benefits from information based on unbiased measures outweighed the costs of forgone potential tax savings in this episode.[6]

To summarize, U.S. GAAP utilizes a broad proprietary concept that assumes shareholders and to an extent creditors are the focal point for resource allocation decisions and the corporate entity is the vehicle for the efficient use of the allocated resources. It is also widely presumed that profit maximization is the goal of both managers and shareholders, so that by providing information about the use of resources, investors can ensure their efficient allocation. Tax-reporting rules have evolved independently over time. In the one recent case where conformity of the books was required by law, some U.S. firms, surprisingly, chose not to use LIFO, even though this decision increased tax liabilities.

7.2.2   Germany: A "One-Book" Case

The U.S. perspective contrasts to the traditional German approach to accounting. The primary source of German accounting regulation has been the Commercial Code, Handelsgesetzbuch (HGB), which was revised in 1985 to incorporate the Fourth and Seventh Directives of the European Community.[7] In addition, there are several other laws that influence accounting practice, including the income tax law.

We shall describe the relationship between tax and accounting regulation in some detail, but initially it is useful to understand that the accounting laws have, from the beginning, been oriented toward a determination of what income is available for distribution to stakeholders (shareholders, tax authorities, and employees) with the clear objective of protecting creditors and "ensuring" the maintenance of the entity as an operating unit. German law and the institutional framework are oriented toward protecting and developing the capital base of each entity. The accounting system reflects a similar objective and utilizes an entity concept as the core framework. This creates fundamental differences relative to the proprietary approach adopted in the United States, where the purpose of reporting rules is less conservative.

The emphasis on capital maintenance and *minimization* of distributable income is manifested in the legally dictated dominance of the application of prudence for measuring assets and liabilities. Asset accruals are governed by

---

6. Recent examples of research in this area include Jennings, Mest, and Thompson (1992).

7. The Fourth Directive defined the format of financial statements, defined basic concepts and valuation principles, and required the accounts to be evaluated in terms of providing a "true and fair" view of the firm's financial position. However, within each of these categories, flexibility was permitted to reflect different jurisdictional preferences. The Seventh Directive focused on the requirement to present fully consolidated financial statements for groups of companies forming a single economic entity.

the "imparity principle" (*Imparitätsprinzip*), requiring recognition of both realized and unrealized losses (e.g., on foreign exchange contracts) but disallowing recognition of any unrealized gains.[8] This introduces a conservative bias in the reported net asset measure. As in the United States, German income is essentially equal to the change in cum dividend net assets. However, German taxable income is measured directly from the tax balance sheets, whereas U.S. taxable income is derived from revenue and expense flows.

Traditionally, Germany has also required a close conformity between tax and financial reporting measures. As explained, the legally based accounting rules are formulated on the basis of determining what income can be distributed. Ordelheide and Pfaff (1993) argue that the tax law takes a similar perspective as it is based on taxing the earnings that can be distributed by an enterprise while maintaining the productive capacity of the income source. Hence, in Germany there has been a symmetry in the objectives of tax and financial reporting that does not exist in the United States. This leads to the observation that both German tax and financial reporting regulations focus on long-run maintenance of the capital base, and therefore of the source of income, even if this may not lead to profit maximization in a neoclassical sense. The imposition of prudence has a noticeable effect on the pattern of German returns. German companies have lower average reported profitability than their U.S. counterparts, but there is also less cross-sectional variation in the reported profitability (see, e.g., Harris, Lang, and Möller 1993).

The similarity between tax and financial reporting systems is not only the result of confluent objectives. The German tax computation is based on balance sheets prepared in accordance with GAAP. This is known as the "authoritative principle" (*Massgeblichkeitsprinzip*), and the direction of causality is from accounting to tax. While this is the initial direction of the relation, there is a second effect that goes in the opposite direction and is known as the "reverse authoritative principle" (*umgekehrte Massgeblichkeitsprinzip*). The latter generally allows companies to use the tax rules to determine certain accounting policies when no specific policy is prescribed by the accounting law. The tax law requires companies to take the expense for accounting purposes in order to have it deducted for tax purposes, much like LIFO in the United States, and hence the two sets of books are virtually identical.[9]

The discussion so far describes how the German laws facilitate a lower tax base to restrict distributable and taxable income. However, once the base is determined the tax law creates an incentive to distribute the income by the differential rates applied to distributed and retained current income (see appendix C).

Another significant difference between the German and U.S. systems is the

---

8. In contrast, U.S. firms must recognize unrealized gains and losses in certain cases, such as foreign exchange contracts.
9. This explains the "one-book" nomenclature.

treatment of consolidation. German income tax is largely applied at the level of the legal entity, with investments in subsidiaries measured at acquisition cost or lower. The HGB of 1985 required companies to present fully consolidated financial statements.[10] To some extent, the HGB of 1985 permits companies to apply different accounting standards in their consolidated statements than they use for the legal entity tax-conforming financial statements. Consequently, to the extent that German companies perceive a cost created by tax conformity requirements they can choose a two-book approach if they have to present group accounts. While this may appear to create a system similar to that found in the United States, this is unlikely to be the case for several reasons. First, the information and accounting systems in place generate data for each of the individual, legal entity tax-conforming statements. The consolidated statements are compiled from these, and to the extent that the legal entity statements are uninformative because of their basis in tax law, this would also apply to the consolidated statements. The basic reporting practice is still governed by tax regulations. Second, users of financial statement, have, presumably, developed an understanding of how to interpret the individual legal entity reports or have created mechanisms to reduce information asymmetries. Thus, the marginal benefit of a change in accounting practice is probably less than it would be if the information set consisted solely of the financial statements. Nevertheless, since both types of firms appear in our sample, in the empirical tests of the model we consider controlling for these factors by differentiating between companies that applied full consolidation and those that do not.

If reports are perceived to be somewhat uninformative, alternative sources may emerge if the benefits of additional information are perceived to be high by market participants. In Germany, financial analysts have developed a process to yield an adjusted earnings measure that is meant to be more useful for making cross-sectional and time-series comparisons. Some firms voluntarily supply the information, and if it is not supplied, analysts attempt to impute it. The measure, known as the DVFA/SG earnings, does not adjust specifically for tax-oriented items; however, to the extent that a tax-based valuation measure makes earnings less comparable it will be adjusted in the calculation.[11]

In sum, the one-book basis of accounting in Germany arises from a common objective of capital maintenance for tax and reporting. This objective is weighted more heavily than profit maximization, which is a dominant objective in the United States. While the reasons for the German system having evolved in this manner are outside the scope of this paper, they are clearly related to the sources of capital available to firms, the history and institutional framework of the country, including the use of bearer shares, the lack of large amounts of institutional capital outside of banks, the acceptance of weaker antitrust regula-

10. After 1990, all German companies satisfied this requirement, but before then only a subset did.
11. Busse von Colbe et al. (1991) provide a useful discussion of the DVFA/SG earnings measure.

tion, and the lack of regulation of insider trading. However, increasing demand for international sources of capital is shifting the institutional structure toward a two-book system.

7.2.3   Summary of Accounting Differences

Figures 7.1 and 7.2 summarize the basic features of the U.S. and German accounting regimes, respectively. In the United States, the tax and financial reports are governed by separate bodies. The subsidiaries' information is consolidated by the parent into two separate statements, one prepared for the IRS and one for the SEC.

In Germany, the organization is more complicated. All reporting is based on the HBG, which governs unconsolidated tax returns filed by the parent and each subsidiary. These returns are filed with the Ministry of Finance. To some extent the tax rules feed back into the reporting practice via the *umgekehrte Massgeblichkeitsprinzip*. Finally, parents prepare consolidated statements that are mostly based on the same accounting rules that govern the tax returns.

7.3   Accounting Regimes and Firm Investment

In this section, we develop a structural model to help explore a precise implication of our descriptive analysis: the responsiveness of domestic investment to changes in the domestic tax code may also depend on the accounting regime. The reluctance of domestic investors to utilize tax incentives will drive a wedge between the costs of capital faced by investors from different countries. In our view, this investigation is a crucial precursor to the analysis of the effects of accounting regimes on foreign capital flows.

To derive testable implications from a model with varying information revelation by firms, we begin with the standard Euler equation model for investment.[12] The firm maximizes the present discounted value of after-tax dividends. The firm's production function is assumed to be Cobb-Douglas with constant returns to scale:

$$(1) \qquad Y_{i,t} = F(K_{i,t-1}, N_{i,t}) = A K_{i,t-1}^{\theta} N_{i,t}^{1-\theta},$$

where Y is output, K is the capital stock, N is labor input, i is the firm index, and t is the time index. Investment in capital, I, which depreciates at a constant geometric rate, δ, is assumed to be subject to quadratic adjustment costs:

$$(2) \qquad C(I_{i,t}, K_{i,t-1}) = \frac{\alpha_0}{2} \left(\frac{I_{i,t}}{K_{i,t-1}} - \delta_i \right)^2 K_{i,t-1}.$$

In addition, we assume that in countries relying on only one set of books, the market participants employ an independent monitor, which verifies that the

---

12. Oliner, Rudebusch, and Sichel (1993) provide an excellent review of these models.

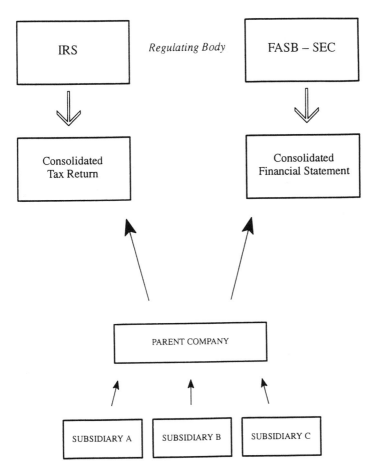

Fig. 7.1   Schematic of U.S. accounting regime

firm is actually investing at the level of *I*. One could think of these as costs incurred by the shareholder in order to gain an accurate description of firm activity.[13] These costs result from the fact that high deductions lower the firm's tax base, and the market requires that this type of reduction be distinguishable from a reduction due to lower profitability. In a two-book country, higher tax benefits are endnoted in the financial statement, and so should be desirable from the perspective of the firm. In a one-book country, this may not be the

13. The DVFA/SG earnings report is an example of the type of monitoring that we are attempting to model. Kanniainen and Södersten (1994) use such monitoring costs to develop a model in which a firm chooses not to maximize its tax debt, because higher tax debt would lead to higher marginal monitoring costs.

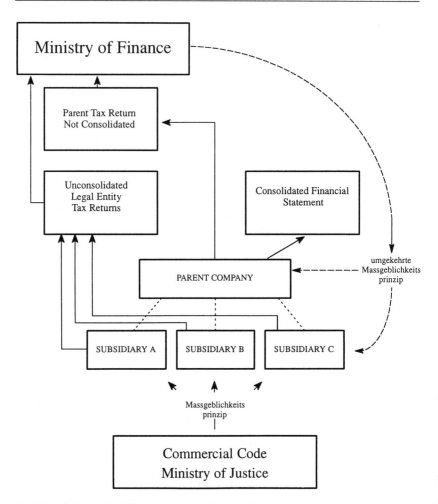

Fig. 7.2   Schematic of German accounting regime

case. Tax benefits that are large relative to earnings may require significant additional information costs.[14] Specifically, we assume that the firm faces an additional information revelation cost function;

$$(3) \qquad \Omega(I_{i,t}, K_{i,t-1}) = \frac{\alpha_1}{2} \left(\Gamma_{i,t} \frac{I_{i,t}}{K_{i,t-1}} \right)^2 K_{i,t-1},$$

where $\Gamma_{i,t}$ describes the tax benefit of investing, which, in the United States, is defined as

14. In a one-book country with few investment incentives, these costs should be inconsequential. But in all the countries in our sample, investment incentives exist (especially for depreciation) and are, in general, generous (see appendix C).

(4) $$\Gamma_{i,t} = k_t + \sum_{s=t}^{\infty} (1 + \rho_s + \pi_s^e)^{-t} \tau_{i,s} \mathrm{Dep}_{i,s}(s - t),$$

where k is the investment tax credit, ρ is the real required rate of return, τ is the marginal corporate tax rate, and $\mathrm{Dep}(a)$ is the depreciation allowance permitted an asset of age a discounted at a nominal rate that includes the inflation rate expected, π^e. This expression may be defined slightly differently depending on the tax code.[15] We use the detailed information on each country's tax code (contained in appendix C) to calculate the above expression. This function has the desirable properties that the marginal cost of revelation increases with the tax benefits and that these costs have a lower bound of zero if tax benefits are also zero. The assumption that these costs are quadratic is somewhat restrictive, but simplifies our estimation problem significantly.[16]

The firm is assumed to be a price-taker in the prices of output, p, capital goods, g, and labor, w. To simplify the exposition, the price of output is normalized to equal unity, so that the purchase price of capital and labor are relative prices and the relative price of capital goods to output is simply g.

The firm chooses investment to maximize the expected present discounted value of after-tax dividends

(5) $$V_{i,t} = E_t \sum_{s=t}^{\infty} \left(\prod_{j=t}^{s} \beta_{i,j} \right) D_{i,s},$$

where

(6) $$\begin{aligned} D_{i,s} &= (1 - \tau_{i,s})[F(K_{i,s-1}, N_{i,s}) - C(I_{i,s}, K_{i,s-1}) - \Omega(I_{i,s}, K_{i,s-1})] \\ &= g_{i,s}(1 - \Gamma_{i,s})I_{i,s}, \end{aligned}$$

subject to the capital accumulation constraint

(7) $$K_{i,s} = (1 - \delta_i)K_{i,s-1} + I_{i,s},$$

where E_t is the expectations operator conditional on information available at time t and $\beta_{i,j}$ is the period-j discount factor for firm i. The derivational details and resulting Euler equations that incorporate equity and debt issuance are omitted here for expositional simplicity. Their addition generates few additional insights into the issues on which we have focused.

To derive the Euler equation for investment, set the derivatives of the Lagrangian that results from equations (5) through (7) to zero at time t:

(8) $$(1 - \tau_{i,t})\left[g_{i,t}\left(\frac{1 - \Gamma_{i,t}}{1 - \tau_{i,t}}\right) + C_{I_t} + \Omega_{I_t} \right] = \lambda_{i,t},$$

(9) $$E_t[\beta_{i,t+1}(1 - \tau_{i,t+1})(F_{K_t} - C_{K_t} - \Omega_{K_t}) + (1 - \delta_i)\lambda_{i,t+1}] = \lambda_{i,t}.$$

15. E.g., a slight redefinition would be necessary for those countries in our sample that have different rules for basis adjustment.
16. The monitoring adjustment cost is not a function of the depreciation rate because we believe that information costs are high when tax benefits are high relative to earnings.

Equation (8) is the first-order condition that equates the marginal cost of acquiring capital and the shadow value, $\lambda_{i,t}$, of an increase in the capital stock at time t. Equation (9) indicates that it is optimal to set the return in period $t + 1$ of a marginal unit of capital equal to the cost of capital in period $t + 1$. To derive the equation we estimate, we use equation (8), and equation (8) rolled forward one period, to substitute out for the unobservables, $\lambda_{i,t}$ and $\lambda_{i,t+1}$:

$$(10) \quad E_t\beta_{i,t+1}(1 - \tau_{i,t+1})\left\{(F_{K_t} - C_{K_t} - \Omega_{K_t}) + (1 - \delta_i)\left[C_{I_{t+1}} + \Omega_{I_{t+1}}\right.\right.$$
$$\left.\left. + g_{i,t+1}\left(\frac{1 - \Gamma_{i,t+1}}{1 - \tau_{i,t+1}}\right)\right]\right\} = (1 - \tau_{i,t})\left[C_{I_t} + \Omega_{I_t} + g_{i,t}\left(\frac{1 - \Gamma_{i,t}}{1 - \tau_{i,t}}\right)\right].$$

Substituting in the specific functional forms for C, Ω, and F:

$$(11) \quad C_{I_t} = \alpha_0\left(\frac{I_{i,t}}{K_{i,t-1}} - \delta_i\right),$$

$$(12) \quad \Omega_{I_t} = \alpha_1\Gamma_{i,t}^2 \frac{I_{i,t}}{K_{i,t-1}},$$

$$(13) \quad C_{K_t} = \frac{\alpha_0}{2}\left(\frac{I_{i,t+1}}{K_{i,t}} - \delta_i\right)^2 - \alpha_0\left(\frac{I_{i,t+1}}{K_{i,t}} - \delta_i\right)\frac{I_{i,t+1}}{K_{i,t}},$$

$$(14) \quad \Omega_{K_t} = -\frac{\alpha_1}{2}\left(\Gamma_{i,t+1}\frac{I_{i,t+1}}{K_{i,t}}\right)^2.$$

After rearranging terms, simplifying, imposing rational expectations to eliminate the expectations operator, and generalizing the expectations error to account for the panel nature of our data, we obtain

$$(15) \quad \beta_{i,t+1}(1 - \tau_{i,t+1})\left\{\theta\frac{Y_{i,t+1}}{K_{i,t}} + \frac{\alpha_0}{2}\left(\frac{I_{i,t+1}}{K_{i,t}}\right)^2 + \frac{\alpha_1}{2}\left(\Gamma_{i,t+1}\frac{I_{i,t+1}}{K_{i,t}}\right)^2\right.$$
$$+ \alpha_0(1 - \delta_i)\left(\frac{I_{i,t+1}}{K_{i,t}}\right) + (1 - \delta_i)\left[g_{i,t+1}\left(\frac{1 - \Gamma_{i,t+1}}{1 - \tau_{i,t+1}}\right)\right.$$
$$\left.\left. + \alpha_1\Gamma_{i,t+1}^2\frac{I_{i,t+1}}{K_{i,t}}\right] - \alpha_0\left(\delta_i - \frac{\delta_i^2}{2}\right)\right\} - (1 - \tau_{i,t})\left[\alpha_0\left(\frac{I_{i,t}}{K_{i,t-1}} - \delta_i\right)\right.$$
$$\left. + g_{i,t}\left(\frac{1 - \Gamma_{i,t}}{1 - \tau_{i,t}}\right) + \alpha_1\Gamma_{i,t}^2\frac{I_{i,t}}{K_{i,t-1}}\right] = u_i + v_{t+1} + e_{i,t+1}.$$

The first error term on the right-hand side of equation (15), u_i, is a firm-specific measurement error in the levels of the left-hand-side variables. This error is assumed to be approximately constant over time. The last two error terms, v_{t+1} and $e_{i,t+1}$, are expectational errors, where $E_t(v_{t+1} + e_{i,t+1}) = 0$. The Euler equation we estimate follows directly from this equation. Equation (15) is first differenced to remove the first error term and estimated by the generalized method of moments (GMM) with time dummies. The GMM estimator accommodates conditional heteroskedasticity of unknown form in the error term $e_{i,t+1}$, and the time dummies estimate v_{t+1} in each period.[17] While the model is somewhat stylized, it does provide a structural test for the importance of accounting regimes for domestic investment behavior. Strictly speaking, for firms in two-book countries, α_1 should be equal to zero, and for firms operating in one-book countries, α_1 should be greater than zero. To the extent that firms in one-book countries are able to avoid information restrictions, α_1 may be zero even in one-book countries.

7.4   Empirical Analysis

In this section we present estimates of our model. For estimation, we use the Global Vantage data set and panels of tax information, described in detail in appendices B and C, to estimate the first difference of equation (15) for one-book and two-book countries. As we indicated above, in many countries mechanisms have emerged that attempt to provide a second set of books for some firms in one-book countries. In addition to the most basic split between one- and two-book countries, we also explore the extent to which consolidation helps firms in one-book countries avoid signaling problems. To briefly fore-shadow the results, we will show that we can identify large differences in investment behavior between one- and two-book firms when we only include in our sample firms that can clearly be classified as one or two book. Simply classifying by country, which ignores additional information about firm-specific accounting practices, leads to inconclusive results.

The discussion of accounting regimes raises serious measurement issues that will affect any empirical studies that use the Global Vantage database. When constructing the model, we have specific variables for output, taxes, and capital. The extent to which the variables recorded in our database conform to these definitions varies considerably across and within countries. Nowhere is the measure as precise as we would like. These measurement problems are serious in every country in our sample, but it is important to note that one should not conclude from our accounting discussion that measurement error, in the classical regression sense, is higher in one-book countries. The theme of our discussion is that the information reported by firms in one-book countries is not as comprehensive and relevant for assessing future profitability as it is in two-book countries. The principal advantage of the second set of books is their ability to provide a signal of current earnings and hence profitability to external capital markets, perhaps better than tax accounts could. The degree to which specific variables are measured well or poorly is highly idiosyncratic, however. For example, the tax books may well be the best tool for measuring

---

17. The moving average error introduced by first-differencing is treated by using instruments dated before $t - 1$ and by a Bartlett spectral density kernel to correct the GMM weighting matrix.

the impact of a change in the tax law on a specific firm. These effects may appear larger in one-book countries if the variables reported in Global Vantage are based on tax conformity.

To help minimize the problems of measurement error, we pay careful attention to the source of each data item. Within our one-book countries, data for different firms are based on different levels of consolidation. To aid in a more precise mapping of accounting effects and econometric estimation, Global Vantage identifies the firm's accounting standard (see appendix B). The tax rules in many countries apply at the level of the legal entity. In the Global Vantage database, recorded data are frequently drawn from consolidated reports, which may have little correlation with the variables that go into the tax calculation. Moreover, these consolidated reports also may include foreign investments, which in many countries fall outside of the sphere of domestic tax policy. Global Vantage identifies whether the annual financial statements represent the legal entity report, a holding company report (rarely used), a domestic consolidation report, or full consolidation report.[18] Over our sample period, consolidation becomes increasingly prevalent, and we are able to explore the impact on our results of restricting our sample to firms whose data are drawn from consolidated and unconsolidated reports. In general, consolidation causes the most problems for our empirical analysis when it incorporates substantial foreign assets that are not covered by domestic tax laws. When this occurs, the measure of investment includes investment not necessarily covered by domestic law, which can bias tax coefficients severely.[19]

Tables 7.1 and 7.2 contain the tax variables that we use in our empirical work. Details of variable construction are contained in appendix B. Table 7.3 provides the means and standard deviations for the some of the variables we use. In addition, the number of observations available for estimation is reported in each cell.

The structural model developed in section 7.3 has many antecedents. Specifically, if α_1 is set equal to zero, so that the Ω adjustment function (eq. [3]) has no effect, equation (15) reduces to a standard investment Euler equation (see, e.g., Abel 1980; Cummins and Hubbard, chap. 5 in this volume; Himmelberg 1990; Hubbard and Kashyap 1992). This standard investment equation has been estimated on many different data sets under a wide variety of different assumptions. To provide a link to this literature and to introduce the model in this paper, the estimates of the standard investment Euler equation are provided in table 7.4.

For one-book countries, α_0, the investment adjustment cost parameter, is estimated to be 1.21 with standard error 0.499. For two-book countries, the estimate is 2.32 with standard error 0.771. The test of the overidentifying re-

18. Harris et al. (1993) provide a discussion of this issue for German companies.
19. For any single firm-year there is only one of the reports within the database. Hence, while it would be useful to discriminate between the legal entity (one-book) and consolidated (possible two-book) reports for a given firm-year, this is not possible with Global Vantage.

Table 7.1   **Marginal Corporate Income Tax Rates**

Country	1981	1982	1983	1984	1985	1986	1987	1988	1989	1990	1991	1992
Australia[a]	.46	.46	.46	.46	.46	.49	.49	.39	.39	.39	.39	.39
Belgium[b]	.48	.45	.45	.45	.45	.45	.43	.43	.43	.41	.39	.39
Canada[c,d]	.483	.483	.472	.46	.483	.483	.464	.391	.391	.391	.391	.391
Denmark	.40	.40	.40	.40	.50	.50	.50	.50	.50	.40	.38	.38
France[e]	.50	.50	.50	.50	.50	.45	.45	.42	.39	.37	.34	.34
Germany[f]	.56	.56	.56	.56	.56	.56	.56	.56	.56	.50	.519	.519
Ireland[d]	.45	.50	.50	.50	.50	.50	.50	.47	.43	.43	.40	.40
Italy[c]	.363	.413	.413	.464	.464	.464	.464	.464	.464	.464	.478	.552
Japan[c,g]	.42	.42	.42	.433	.433	.433	.42	.42	.40	.375	.384	.384
Netherlands	.48	.48	.48	.43	.43	.42	.42	.42	.35	.35	.35	.35
New Zealand	.45	.45	.45	.45	.45	.48	.48	.28	.33	.33	.33	.33
Norway[h]	.508	.508	.508	.508	.508	.508	.508	.508	.508	.508	.508	.28
Spain	.33	.33	.35	.35	.35	.35	.35	.35	.35	.35	.35	.35
Sweden[i]	.58	.58	.58	.52	.52	.52	.52	.52	.52	.40	.30	.30
Switzerland[j]	.098	.098	.098	.098	.098	.098	.098	.098	.098	.098	.098	.098
United Kingdom	.52	.52	.52	.45	.40	.35	.35	.35	.35	.35	.33	.33
United States[c]	.46	.46	.46	.46	.46	.46	.40	.34	.34	.34	.34	.34

[a]Undistributed profits were taxed at the rate of .50 until an imputation system came into operation July 1987.

[b]Excess profits surtax at the rate of .04 applied until 1982.

[c]Additional corporate income tax levied by state and/or municipal government which is rebated or deductible at the federal level.

[d]Corporate income tax is levied at a lower rate on manufacturing firms.

[e]Split-rate system, which applied a higher tax rate to distributed profits, was in effect from 1989 until 1992.

[f]Distributed profits taxed at a lower rate of .36.

[g]Distributed profits were taxed at a .10 lower rate until 1988. In 1989, distributed profits were taxed at a .05 lower rate. The split-rate system was permanently abolished in 1990.

[h]Additional corporate income taxes were levied at the municipal level and for a "tax equalization fund" resulting in a combined rate of .23 which was not deductible from the federal rate of .278. Effective 1992, the federal corporate income tax was abolished, the municipal rate was lowered to .11, and the tax equalization fund rate was increased to .17.

[i]Additional corporate income tax levied at the municipal level, which was deductible at the federal level, was abolished in 1985.

[j]Federal, cantonal, and municipal corporate income taxes, which are typically partially deductible against one another, are levied at graduated rates based on the proportion of taxable profits to equity capital. Top federal rate reported.

strictions rejects the model, at standard confidence levels, for one-book countries and does not reject it for two-book countries. Both parameter estimates are within the range reported in previous research using U.S. firm-level panel data (see, most recently, Hubbard, Kashyap, and Whited 1995).

To the extent that these results conform with previous estimates, we feel confident that the data will allow extension to incorporate the features of the model derived in section 7.3. However, we advise caution in interpreting the estimates of the standard model literally, and especially in interpreting the test

Table 7.2		Investment Incentives										
Country	1981	1982	1983	1984	1985	1986	1987	1988	1989	1990	1991	1992
Australia[a]	.18	.18	.18	.18	.18	0	0	0	0	0	0	0
Belgium[b]	.05	.05	.05	.05	.05	.05	.05	.05	.05	.04	.03	0
Canada[c]	.07	.07	.07	.07	.07	.07	.05	.03	0	0	0	0
Denmark[d]	0	0	0	0	0	0	0	0	0	0	0	0
France[a]	.10	.15	0	0	0	0	0	0	0	0	0	0
Germany	0	0	0	0	0	0	0	0	0	0	0	0
Ireland	0	0	0	0	0	0	0	0	0	0	0	0
Italy	0	0	0	0	0	0	0	0	0	0	0	0
Japan	0	0	0	0	0	0	0	0	0	0	0	0
Netherlands[e]	.12	.12	.12	.125	.125	.125	.125	0	0	0	0	0
New Zealand	0	0	0	0	0	0	0	0	0	0	0	0
Norway	0	0	0	0	0	0	0	0	0	0	0	0
Spain[f]	.15	.15	.15	.15	.15	.15	.15	.10	.05	.05	.05	.05
Sweden[h]	.10	.10	.10	0	0	0	0	0	0	0	0	0
Switzerland	0	0	0	0	0	0	0	0	0	0	0	0
United Kingdom	0	0	0	0	0	0	0	0	0	0	0	0
United States[c]	.1	.08	.08	.08	.08	.08	0	0	0	0	0	0

Note: All 17 countries have investment incentives for specific regions or industries, for certain types of business fixed investment, or for research and development which are not reported.

[a]Investment incentive was a deduction.

[b]Investment incentive was a deduction. Before 1982, the incentive was an investment reserve.

[c]Investment incentive was an investment tax credit (ITC). In Canada, regional and some asset ITCs were retained at reduced rates after 1988.

[d]A limited investment reserve is available. See footnote g below for a description.

[e]Investment incentive was an ITC (called "WIR"). In 1984, the various WIR rates were combined into one uniform rate; before 1984 the rate reported is that for most fixed assets. Beginning in 1990, an investment deduction is available at degressive rates ranging from .18 to .02 for relatively small scale investment; no deduction is allowed after the cutoff total is reached.

[f]Investment incentive is an ITC. In 1985, a statutory rate for fixed assets was instituted; before 1985 the rate reported is that for the typical investment grant.

[g]Investment incentive was an investment allowance. Until 1990, an investment reserve program was also available. It allowed companies to set aside and deduct, at their own discretion, up to 50 percent of their pretax profits for future investments in a countercyclical fund. The benefit of the fund was that it could be used for immediate depreciation of new assets acquired.

of the overidentifying restrictions. While it is usual in this literature to "accept" a model if the test statistic is less than the critical value, the test is only of the orthogonality of the instruments and the error terms. This may pose a more serious problem than usual in this data set since we have argued throughout that there are a wide number of measurement error problems in the variables that we use for instruments and in the estimation. We have attempted to alleviate these potential biases in constructing the variables and in estimating the model, but we, necessarily, remain agnostic about the degree to which these efforts are successful.[20]

20. The range of point estimates and their standard errors was relatively tight, but we found that wild swings in the χ^2 statistic could result from seemingly innocuous changes in the instrument set.

Table 7.3   **Sample Statistics**

Country	$\dfrac{I_t}{K_{t-1}}$	$\dfrac{\text{sales}_t}{K_{t-1}}$	$\dfrac{\text{cash flow}_t}{K_{t-1}}$	$\dfrac{\text{debt}_t}{\text{assets}_t}$	Number of Firms (1991)
Australia	.17	2.58	.26	.25	120
	(.21)	(1.93)	(.57)	(.21)	
Belgium	.27	3.95	.48	.39	51
	(.23)	(1.85)	(.55)	(.25)	
Canada	.18	2.18	.21	.34	299
	(.19)	(2.02)	(.41)	(.25)	
Denmark	.23	3.70	.30	.36	64
	(.19)	(1.85)	(.32)	(.24)	
France	.29	4.40	.48	.29	201
	(.19)	(2.06)	(.51)	(.20)	
Germany	.30	4.23	.40	.23	237
	(.19)	(1.97)	(.34)	(.22)	
Ireland	.17	3.35	.29	.27	45
	(.22)	(1.96)	(.62)	(.22)	
Italy	.24	3.25	.44	.34	79
	(.22)	(1.87)	(.48)	(.23)	
Japan	.24	4.02	.31	.26	336
	(.16)	(1.84)	(.23)	(.19)	
Netherlands	.21	3.61	.38	.33	101
	(.16)	(1.89)	(.38)	(.25)	
New Zealand	.18	3.20	.24	.37	21
	(.24)	(1.85)	(.37)	(.22)	
Norway	.22	2.81	.19	.50	45
	(.21)	(1.85)	(.32)	(.22)	
Spain	.12	2.03	.24	.31	75
	(.19)	(1.92)	(.33)	(.27)	
Sweden	.22	3.67	.31	.49	68
	(.20)	(1.84)	(.32)	(.25)	
Switzerland	.24	3.41	.38	.40	107
	(.19)	(1.78)	(.40)	(.23)	
United Kingdom	.21	3.71	.43	.21	598
	(.22)	(2.00)	(.48)	(.18)	
United States	.21	3.28	.32	.30	2486
	(.20)	(2.14)	(.66)	(.25)	

Note: Standard deviations are in parentheses below the means.

Table 7.5 presents estimates of α_0 and α_1 in equation (15). The investment adjustment cost parameter, α_0, in both samples is positive and significant. For one-book countries, it is estimated to be 0.739 with standard error 0.351. For two-book countries, it is estimated to be 0.998 with standard error 0.265. Both these estimates are within the range of adjustment costs—although somewhat lower than—estimated using the Euler equation formulation. An estimate of 0.998 implies that an extra dollar of investment will lead to about 0.05 dollars of adjustment costs.[21]

21. Interpretation of the size of the adjustment costs depends on the proximity to the steady state. Near the steady state, most of investment is replacement investment, which does not incur

Table 7.4   **Standard Euler Equation Estimates**

Regime	Investment Adjustment Cost Parameter ρ_0	Test of Overidentifying Restrictions χ^2_{13}
One-book countries	1.21	22.23
	(.499)	(.039)
Two-book countries	2.32	19.65
	(.771)	(.104)

Notes: The standard Euler equation sets α_1 equal to zero in eq. (15).

One-book countries are Belgium, Denmark, France, Germany, Italy, Japan, Norway, Spain, Sweden, and Switzerland. Two-book countries are Australia, Canada, Ireland, Netherlands, New Zealand, the United Kingdom, and the United States.

Standard errors, in parentheses, are computed from a heteroskedastic-consistent matrix. Significance levels of Hansen's test of overidentifying restrictions are in parentheses beneath the statistic.

The one-book sample contains 1,890 firms. The two-book sample contains 4,420 firms. The instrument set used for estimation includes: $(I/K)_{t-2}$, $(I/K)_{t-3}$, $(I/K)^2_{t-2}$, $(I/K)^2_{t-3}$, (cash flow/K)$_{t-2}$, (cash flow/K)$_{t-3}$, (sales/K)$_{t-2}$, (sales/K)$_{t-3}$, (depreciation/K)$_{t-2}$, (dividends/operating income)$_{t-2}$, (debt/assets)$_{t-2}$, (interest/K)$_{t-2}$, (taxes/K)$_{t-2}$, $(k + \tau z)_{t-2}$, and $(k + \tau z)^2_{t-2}$.

Table 7.5   **Euler Equation Estimates**

Regime	Investment Adjustment Cost Parameter α_0	Accounting Adjustment Cost Parameter α_1	Test of Overidentifying Restrictions χ^2_{12}
One-book countries	.739	−.696	45.33
	(.351)	(.489)	(9.05×10^{-6})
Two-book countries	.998	−4.84	77.09
	(.265)	(1.36)	(1.48×10^{-11})

Notes: One-book countries are Belgium, Denmark, France, Germany, Italy, Japan, Norway, Spain, Sweden, and Switzerland. Two-book countries are Australia, Canada, Ireland, Netherlands, New Zealand, the United Kingdom, and the United States.

Standard errors, in parentheses, are computed from a heteroskedastic-consistent matrix. Significance levels of Hansen's test of overidentifying restrictions are in parentheses beneath the statistic.

The sample sizes and instrument set are the same as reported in table 7.4

To provide additional insight into these estimates it is useful to compare them to those reported in closed-form q-model formulations. These estimates are substantially smaller than ones implied by closed-form q-formulations esti-

---

any adjustment costs in the model. For the first few dollars over and above depreciation, marginal adjustment costs are low, by the convexity assumption. Far away from the steady state, marginal adjustment costs can be very high, even given our parameter estimates. For the comparison reported in the text, we applied the sample means of the investment-to-capital ratio and depreciation rate (0.21 and 0.16, respectively) in order to gauge the relative adjustment costs.

mated with either U.S. firm-level panel data (see, e.g., Gilchrist and Himmelberg 1991) or with U.K. firm-level panel data (see, e.g., Blundell et al. 1992).[22] The small estimates reported in the q-studies implied unreasonably large adjustment costs, implying that the scale of the adjustment cost is substantially larger than that of the purchase cost of the investment good. The estimates above indicate significantly lower adjustment costs.

The accounting adjustment cost parameter α_1 in table 7.5 is negative and insignificant in the one-book sample, and negative, substantially larger, and significant in the two-book sample. For one-book countries, the estimate is -0.696 with standard error 0.489. For two-book countries, the estimate is -4.84 with standard error 1.36. However, we should not overemphasize the precision of these results: the tests of overidentifying restrictions are rejected in both models (with tiny implied p-values). Both estimates have the incorrect sign. An extra dollar of investment leads to 0.03 dollars more in total adjustment costs in the one-book sample, and 0.003 dollars less in adjustment costs in the two-book sample, given the sample means of the relevant parameters (see n. 21).

There are a variety of reasons why this result may not be spurious, in spite of the fact that it confounds the intuition outlined in the description of the countries' institutional features and the assumptions in deriving the model. However, we believe the crude one-book/two-book distinction may not be what the model captures. In section 7.2, we outlined how firms, even in one-book countries, can avoid restrictions placed on them by the tax authority and how they attempt to mitigate the information costs associated with their home countries' particular institutional features. Perhaps the estimation results were not illuminating because we incorrectly grouped firms; one-book/two-book may not be the exact partitioning between firms facing low information revelation costs and those facing high ones.

There are a number of different subsamples that might provide evidence on this point. In table 7.6, we consider two polar opposites that seem to confirm the analysis of why one-book/two-book is too coarse a distinction. Table 7.6 presents estimates for two subsamples. The first is one-book firms that report only in accordance with domestic accounting standards *and* are not fully consolidated (i.e., report as legal entities). The second is one-book firms that report in accordance with U.S. GAAP (nearly all of whom are fully consolidated). The groupings incorporate firms from many different countries.[23]

In the first subsample, both adjustment cost parameters are positive and significant. In the second, similar to the result in two-book countries reported in table 7.3, the investment adjustment cost parameter is positive and significant,

---

22. See Cummins, Hassett, and Hubbard (1994), who use the q-model but estimate much smaller adjustment costs, in line with those reported above.

23. The largest number of firms in the first subsample is from Germany, and in the second from Japan.

Table 7.6   Euler Equation Estimates (one-book country subsamples)

Subsample	Investment Adjustment Cost Parameter α_0	Accounting Adjustment Cost Parameter α_1	Test of Overidentifying Restrictions χ^2_{12}
Domestic accounting standards and domestic consolidation	.520 (.219)	3.64 (1.02)	17.81 (.122)
Domestic accounting standards in accordance with U.S. GAAP	1.91 (.683)	−7.55 (4.52)	56.17 (1.12×10^{-7})

Notes: One-book countries are Belgium, Denmark, France, Germany, Italy, Japan, Norway, Spain, Sweden, and Switzerland. Standard errors, in parentheses, are computed from a heteroskedastic-consistent matrix. Significance levels of Hansen's test of overidentifying restrictions are in parentheses beneath the statistic.

The first subsample contains 790 firms. The second subsample contains 381 firms. The instrument set used for estimation is the same as reported in table 7.4.

while the accounting adjustment cost parameter is negative and not significant. In the first subsample, α_0 is estimated to be 0.520 with standard error 0.219 and α_1 is estimated to be 3.64 with standard error 1.02. These estimates imply that an extra dollar of investment leads to a total of 0.07 dollars of adjustment costs, with 0.05 dollars of that attributable to the accounting adjustment costs, given the sample means of the relevant parameters. In addition, the model cannot be rejected at standard confidence levels.

In the second subsample, α_0 is estimated to be 1.91 with standard error 0.683 and α_1 is estimated to be -7.55 with standard error 4.52. The test of the over-identifying restrictions is rejected conclusively. These estimates accord closely with those reported for two-book firms in table 7.3, providing some evidence that firms that report according to U.S. GAAP face adjustment costs similar to those faced in two-book countries. The total of the two adjustment costs is roughly zero. The investment adjustment cost parameter is plausible, the accounting adjustment parameter is negative, and the test of the orthogonality conditions is decisive.

The results in table 7.6 seem to confirm the hypothesis that additional costs can be associated with the taking of tax benefits in one-book countries and that this cost is largely avoided by a portion of firms even in one-book countries. Monitoring costs appear to be important, and their size depends critically on identifying which firms are likely to be subject to them within one-book countries. The size of the monitoring costs is at the high end of estimates for the investment adjustment cost parameters in the Euler equation literature and dominate investment adjustment costs in our model. Firms in one-book countries that prepare accounts according to U.S. GAAP appear to be qualitatively similar to firms in two-book countries.

7.5 Conclusions

We describe two different accounting regimes that govern reporting practice in most developed countries. We provide a structural model that formalizes a testable implication of our discussion: that domestic firm-level investment in one-book countries may face additional adjustment costs and, as a result, be less sensitive to tax law changes than is investment in two-book countries. In our discussion of the accounting regimes, we indicate that over time mechanisms have emerged in one-book countries that allow some firms to provide information in alternative ways. Our econometric estimates suggest that accounting regime differences play an important role in describing the domestic investment pattern across countries. In particular, firms that operate under a "pure" one-book system behave as if they face an additional cost when utilizing investment incentives. The firms appearing most constrained are those that do not file consolidated statements according to U.S. GAAP. Firms in one-book countries filing according to U.S. GAAP behave much more like U.S. firms. Since most multinationals face some type of consolidation requirement, our evidence suggests that the playing field for multinationals is probably roughly even with respect to ability to claim tax benefits. Information costs may have driven a wedge in historical user costs of capital, but these forces are likely diminishing today; many one-book countries are gradually moving toward two-book systems, as exemplified by the Fourth and Seventh Directives of the European Community.

Our results, taken at face value, suggest one should not study international taxation in isolation. The institutional environment in which multinationals operate may be crucial to their decision making. We have studied one particular aspect of this interaction, but there are many others. In work in progress, we are exploring whether international capital flows have become more efficient over time in response to the gradual easing of information asymmetries imposed by accounting regimes.

Appendix A
Summaries of Country-Specific Accounting Practices

Canada

Canada has a two-book system with financial reporting accounting standards based on a proprietary approach prescribed by the Canadian Institute of Chartered Accountants. There is a close similarity to U.S. GAAP that is evidenced by the SEC allowing mutual recognition of Canadian accounting standards for Canadian firms listing in the United States. However, Canadian GAAP does not provide the detailed reconciliation of tax expense for tax and financial reporting purposes that we find in the United States. Canadian taxes are applied on the consolidated results but on a territorial basis.

United Kingdom and Ireland

The United Kingdom has had a two-book system since the corporation tax was first introduced. The basic financial reporting requirements derive from the Companies Act first issued in the mid-nineteenth century and amended many times since then. The Companies Acts of 1985 and 1989 are the key regulatory items currently in force. The Companies Acts require audited financial statements to present a "true and fair view" in conformity with GAAP. GAAP has been outlined by various private bodies in a similar manner to that found in the United States. The most recent standard-setting body is the Accounting Standards Board, which is structured on a basis very close to the FASB.

Two distinctions between the United Kingdom and the United States are worth noting. First, there is no SEC equivalent to provide a tight regulatory link. Second, the existing codification of U.K. GAAP is much less detailed and less comprehensive than in the United States. There are also distinctions between U.K. and U.S. GAAP, some of which are relevant to the issues considered in this paper. The first distinction is that U.K. managers may revalue their assets periodically.[24] These asset revaluations are discretionary, and the gains and losses are not taxable, nor are they reported in current reported income. Thus, gross investment in assets measured from Global Vantage using tangible fixed assets (see appendix B) is measured with error as in some cases it includes revaluation adjustments (see, e.g., Easton, Eddey, and Harris 1993). The second distinction is that U.K. tax law does not permit the use of LIFO for inventory valuation. Thus, while LIFO is permitted by U.K. GAAP, it is not used. Third, the accounting treatment for temporary differences in the timing of tax and accounting revenues or expenses is usually different in the United Kingdom, relative to the United States. In the United Kingdom, companies have the option to accrue only for those differences which are expected to be realized ("crystallize") within a five-year period. In the United States, all temporary differences must be accounted for. The alternative treatments may cause a difference in reported debt, equity, and income measures.

The U.K. financial reporting system follows the proprietary approach, with equity being a major source of capital. Taxable income is determined by tax rules which are not bound by U.K. GAAP, so it is a two-book case.

Australia and New Zealand

The roots of accounting and tax practice for these countries lie in the United Kingdom, with the United States playing a greater role in more recent times. Both countries adopt a proprietary approach to their financial reporting practices and have established capital markets as the major source of capital for large firms. As in the United Kingdom, discretionary revaluations of assets are permitted and occur. Easton et al. (1993) find that these revaluations are value relevant but also demonstrate the potential errors in extracting this level of information from the aggregated data in Global Vantage, as we noted in the discussion of the U.K. practice. Hence, we note that our gross investment proxy is knowingly measured with error, in part because of the idiosyncrasies in the accounting systems.

Netherlands

The Netherlands provides another example of a two-book system. Historically, the Netherlands had an essentially laissez-faire system with companies

---

24. Asset revaluations in different forms occur in many countries in our sample. See appendix C for whether and to what extent countries allow revaluations.

applying generally acceptable accounting standards. While various laws have been enacted since the first Accounting Act, effective since 1971, for most of the time listed companies have usually followed accounting principles oriented toward representing the economic substance of transactions.

The tax law has its own specific requirements but requires taxable income to be based on sound business practice. So there is an implicit, but no direct link to financial reporting requirements.

The accounting law was amended to incorporate the Fourth Directive of the European Community with an effective date of January 1984 and the Seventh Directive of the European Community effective from January 1990. However, both of these amendments were more in form than substance as listed Dutch companies were already complying with most of the standards.

As in the case of Australia, New Zealand, and the United Kingdom, Dutch companies may revalue their assets or apply a full current cost system. In such cases, as the tax system continues to be based on historical costs, the depreciation charge may be higher for accounting purposes for certain assets.

In general, in the Netherlands we expect the differences between tax and accounting income to be less than for several other two-book systems.

Japan

The accounting system originates in the German Commercial Code (HGB), which was "imported" at the time of the Meiji Restoration, and was revised on the basis of changes in Germany's Commercial Code through 1938 (Ballon and Tomita 1988). Following World War II, revisions of the Commercial Code and the first Securities Exchange Law (1948) were based on U.S. practices. Hence, the Japanese system is a mix of our two benchmark systems. The focus of both tax and financial reporting has been the legal entity, as we find in Germany. Currently, tax is still applied on the legal entity results rather than the consolidated group accounts.

An example which helps to illustrate the legal versus consolidated entity aspect of taxation is the often misunderstood issue of the tax deductibility of goodwill. The tax law allows goodwill to be amortized over five years and deducted in the calculation of taxable income. But this goodwill is generally not the goodwill found in consolidated financial statements which arises from investments in the equity of subsidiaries. For such investments, there is no goodwill separately reported in the legal entity statements. The taxable goodwill that arises is from an asset purchase made at a premium to market value. On consolidation the two goodwill measures are accounted for in the same manner, but in the legal entity reports they are treated differently and hence are not taxed in the same manner.

To better understand the relationship between tax and financial reporting in Japan, it is useful to be aware of some of the regulatory influences and the evolution and perceived relevance of consolidated reporting. The foundation of financial and tax reporting is the Commercial Code which applies to all legal entities and is under the jurisdiction of the Ministry of Justice. On the other hand, the Securities Exchange Law applies to listed companies, and is the source of regulations for consolidated reports. The Securities Exchange Law is administered by the Ministry of Finance, which is the *de facto* source of GAAP for listed companies despite the existence of advisory committees like the Business Accounting Deliberation Council. Measurement rules used to obtain taxable net income are largely based on GAAP for financial reporting purposes, at least as applied to the legal entity level. Thus, expenses such as depreciation and cost of goods sold conform in the tax and accounting income measures.

Differences arise in the two sets of books as a result of certain tax-exempt or disallowed items or when a company chooses to take expenses in excess of those allowed for tax purposes. A common example is in the accrual for employee postemployment benefits. The tax law allows a deduction equal to 40 percent of the amount payable at the fiscal year end. Many companies accrue between 40 and 100 percent of this amount. As we might expect from rational tax minimization strategies, we know of no instances of companies that accrue less than 40 percent. There are other examples where the tax-based reserve is usually in excess of what would be required under an information-oriented system. A simple example is the reserve for bad debts which is based on a percentage of total receivables plus allowances for specific doubtful customers.

There is a growing body of evidence that the reports which result from this hybrid system interact in idiosyncratic ways with market indicators. First, there is both anecdotal (see Viner 1988) and empirical evidence that the primary accounting information source in Japan is the legal entity rather than consolidated report (see, e.g., Darrough and Harris 1991; Hall, Hamao, and Harris 1993). Second, French and Poterba (1991) and Hall et al. (1993) show that equity prices are not related to accounting data in any manner that is consistent with what is found in the United States. This finding is consistent with what we might expect in a one-book country.

As we argued earlier, if the books are unreliable signals of the market performance of firms, alternative information sources may well emerge which attempt to fill the gap. As is the case in Germany, such alternative conduits have also emerged in Japan. Japanese companies began to access capital in the international markets in the 1960s. Many of these companies (e.g., SONY) sought capital in the United States but only had legal entity financial statements. Consequently, they "voluntarily" prepared consolidated statements in conformity with U.S. GAAP to comply with U.S. regulations. In 1983, Japan required fully consolidated financial statements for the first time for all listed companies. Those companies already preparing their consolidated statements under U.S. GAAP were allowed to use these for Japanese purposes too. Hence, to some extent, a two-book system has existed for some Japanese multinationals.

In addition, managers systematically provide forecasts of operating profits and sales. Darrough and Harris (1991) shows that these forecasts have information content, particularly at the legal entity level.

In sum, Japan has a one-book system applying to the majority of corporations. However, both via application of U.S. GAAP for certain companies' consolidated statements, and via supplementary information, investors receive additional information for valuation purposes.

France and Belgium

Traditionally, French companies have followed a one-book system, and this persists for legal entities. The French have a long tradition of a codified accounting system. There is a legally defined chart of accounts (from the Plan Comptable Général) which is followed for both financial reporting and taxation purposes, at least at the legal entity level.

Requirements for additional information oriented toward investors first occurred in 1967 with the creation of a stock exchange regulatory authority, the Commission des Operations de Bourse (COB), which encouraged companies to reveal more investor-oriented information. As consolidated accounts were urged by COB but had no legal basis, several large companies adopted their own approaches, with several choosing U.S. GAAP or International Accounting Standards (IAS). France adopted the EC's Seventh Directive, which required consolidated accounts for listed companies, and from 1986, companies were allowed not to apply French GAAP at the consolidated level. Hence, we find that there is a mix of accounting approaches applied for the French companies in our sample.

An interesting example of how French groups take a flexible approach to their group accounts is in the treatment of premia on acquisitions of other companies. Since the 1980s this "goodwill" has frequently been capitalized and labeled "market share" with no amortization generally applied. There is no tax consequence to this treatment.

The tax regulations use the legal entity reports in a manner similar to what we have described in other one-book countries. However, at least since the mid-1980s many French companies have deviated from the valuation rules applied for tax purposes, at least for their consolidated accounts.

Scandinavia

We describe Sweden as representative of the Scandinavian countries in our sample, which include Denmark and Norway. Tax law in Sweden has allowed a series of tax-free reserves which historically must be reflected in the published financial statements. These reserves have included an inventory reserve, investment reserves, and special depreciation reserves. Thus, while the tax rate has been relatively high, this has been compensated for by a lower base. Recent tax reforms have eliminated many of the tax-free reserves (see appendix C).[25]

Scandinavian systems have been influenced by the German system and have a one-book approach. Nevertheless, to facilitate some separation of the tax-free reserve data, the annual adjustments have been reflected as a separate part of the income statement and the cumulative amounts are reported as a nondistributable reserve in the balance sheet. Hence, while the one-book model applies, the information related to specific tax-oriented adjustments can be largely differentiated.

Italy

Italy has a one-book system with roots in a Napoleonic Civil Code. The Italian system is perceived to be strongly tax driven, which may have led to the fact that it was unable to pass legislation to incorporate the Fourth and Seventh Directives of the European Community until the 1990s. The new directives are irrelevant for our sample of companies.

However, similar to France, Italy created a regulatory body to oversee the stock exchange and listed companies. This body, known as CONSOB (Commissions Nazionale per la Societe la Borsa), required listed companies to apply IAS as no domestic standards oriented toward investor information existed. Prior to the recently approved amendments, IAS allowed several options. Hence, it is likely that the financial reports even under IAS will closely mirror the legal entity statements that are based on the tax conformity principle.

Spain

The Spanish system was also based on the French system, but until the 1980s the system was almost entirely tax driven. Spain incorporated the Fourth and Seventh Directives in 1989 and 1990, so most companies will not meet these new reporting requirements during our sample period.

Switzerland

Historically, the only legal obligation for Swiss companies has been to prepare legal entity balance sheets and income statements. While many large companies have provided additional information, historically there has been no common approach by these companies. In the last few years there has been a trend by Swiss companies to adopt IAS, although not always in a uniform manner.

---

25. Denmark has a narrower investment reserve, and Norway none at all (see appendix C). In general, Denmark has the most investor-oriented system.

The tax system cannot be described in a concise manner as there is no single federal tax rate and the federal taxes need not even be the most significant (see appendix C). There are canton, municipal, and sometimes church taxes applied to varying degrees. Furthermore, the tax rates are often based on average income, so taxes may be applicable to income in years after the income is earned.

Appendix B
Data Description

The data set we use in an 11-year (1982–92) unbalanced panel of firms for 17 countries from the Global Vantage industrial database.[26] This database contains information on approximately 6,650 companies from 31 countries. Data for most companies are available since 1982. Comprehensive balance sheet and income statement data are provided. Definitions are standardized to insure intracompany data consistency between different accounting periods and intercompany data consistency within and across countries. However, Global Vantage does not adjust data for accounting differences. Instead, it provides extensive additional information on relevant accounting standards, data definitions, and available firm-specific disclosures to enable the user to make whatever adjustments are necessary. OECD member countries with more than 20 firms reporting data are chosen for analysis. Unlike the Compustat database, Global Vantage has relatively few firm entrants and exist, making the data set nearly balanced.

The variables used are defined as follows. To facilitate replication and extension of our empirical results and to aid researchers in data construction on this relatively unfamiliar data set, we provide the data item numbers in parentheses after each variable. Gross investment is the sum of the change in the net stock of tangible fixed assets (data item 76) and depreciation (data item 11).[27] A more precise estimate of depreciation can be obtained (data item 12), but we choose the one above since most firms do not separately report the more precise figure. The definition of economic depreciation used is the same as used in previous research with the Compustat database (see, e.g., Cummins et al. 1994). The investment variable is divided by the value of its own beginning-of-period capital stock. Output is defined as net sales/turnover (data item 1) and is also di-

---

26. See table 7.5 for a list of all the countries.

27. Defining gross investment as the change in the gross stock of tangible fixed assets (data item 77) is not feasible since that data item is frequently not reported by firms, or was not required to be reported by firms (e.g., German firms did not report the gross stock of fixed assets until the HGB of 1985). There is no data item in Global Vantage comparable to the capital expenditures data item in Compustat.

vided by the value of its own beginning-of-period capital stock. The Euler equation model we derived has a parsimonious specification so that the above variables are the only ones we need construct from Global Vantage.

In addition to those variables above we construct several others to use in the instrument set for econometric estimation. Operating income is defined exactly as such (data item 14). Net income is defined as income before extraordinary items (data item 32). Economists usually define cash flow as the sum of net income and depreciation (defined above). This definition is, at best, a coarse measure. The accounting literature stresses that better measures are available. We experiment with an alternative definition of cash flow derived from this literature. Alternative cash flow is defined as the sum of net income, depreciation, deferred taxes (data item 180), transfers to provisions (data item 182), gain (loss) on sale of fixed assets (data item 181), transfers to (from) reserves (data item 22), and the change in current liabilities (data item 104) minus the change in inventory (data item 66) and the change in accounts receivable (data item 63). The efficacy of this alternative measure was unclear in our empirical work, perhaps because the usual definition of cash flow is only another measure of income (whereas the alternative better measures free cash flow) or because the alternative definition is available less frequently or subject to more serious measurement error. Total income tax is defined exactly as such (data item 23). These variables are also divided by their beginning-of-period capital stocks. The dividend payout rate is defined as the ratio of common dividends (data item 36) to operating income (defined above). Alternative definitions of the payout ratio have no qualitative affect on the empirical results. We chose the above definition because it limited the number of negative observations. Total debt is defined as the sum of short-term debt (data item 94) and long-term debt (data item 106). The debt-to-asset ratio is defined as total debt divided by the sum of the equity value of the firm and total debt. The equity value of the firm is complicated to calculate in Global Vantage. There is no single shares outstanding variable to match with one stock market price variable. Instead, a separate database (called the issues file) contains market-related data items, which include multiple issues with multiple prices for firms in several countries (reflecting the differences across countries in capital markets.) The equity value of the firm is defined in the standard manner (end-of-year stock price multiplied by stock outstanding) when one issue exists.[28] When more than one issue exists, the value of each is calculated in the standard manner and all the issue values are summed. The firm's average interest rate is defined as the ratio of interest expense (data item 15) to total debt. All variables are deflated by the country's GDP deflator.

Firm-specific depreciation rates are constructed using the method in Cum-

---

28. The issues file uses descriptors instead of data item numbers.

mins et al. (1995). Past studies using foreign firm-level data have relied on the one-digit SIC code depreciation rates constructed from Hulten and Wykoff (1981) and capital stock weights.[29] We feel that the Euler equation model requires the more precise firm-specific depreciation rate and that, while the assumption of homogeneous capital stocks may be appropriate for some very large countries, it is inadequate for our sample of 17 countries.

The present value of tax savings from depreciation allowances is constructed from those tax parameters following Salinger and Summers (1983). The discount rate, β, is defined as $1/[1 + (1 - \tau) i - \pi^e]$, where i is the nominal interest rate, calculated as firm's average interest rate. Alternatively, fixing β at values between 0.90 and 0.99 did not qualitatively affect our empirical results. Finally, GDP deflators and investment price deflators (i.e., the price of capital goods) are from the OECD National Accounts tables.

Global Vantage provides information particularly well suited to the model derived in this paper. There are data that potentially allow precise identification of the accounting information that we have hypothesized have real effects. We use two period descriptors for additional identification of the model in our empirical work. Global Vantage provides a descriptor each period of the firm's accounting standard. Most usefully, the data reflect a domestic standard if a company omits a reference to a specific standard. When reported, the standards include: domestic standards; domestic standards in accordance with U.S. GAAP; domestic standards generally in accordance with OECD or International Accounting Standards Committee (IASC) guidelines; domestic standards for parents and domestic subsidiaries, native country or U.S. standards for overseas subsidiaries; modified U.S. standards (Japanese companies' financial statements translated into English); and U.S. standards. Another useful variable for our empirical analysis is the level of consolidation. This period descriptor identifies whether a company's financial statements represent consolidated or unconsolidated information. Applicable categories identified are: only domestic subsidiaries are consolidated, fully consolidated (parent company and subsidiary), nonconsolidated holding company, and nonconsolidated holding company (parent company only).

This appendix concludes with several caveats which may help guide applied researchers using Global Vantage in the future. Global Vantage offers a wealth of data that, in many ways, improve on more familiar firm-level panel data sets such as Compustat, Datastream, and Value-Line. There are, however, several negative features of the data set. The data set is split into four different files: industrial, financial services, issues, and currency.[30] The financial services file is superior to the industrial file in coverage and detail, reflecting the fact that

---

29. See, e.g., Hayashi and Inoue (1991).
30. The currency file contains exchange rates and cross-rate tables for designated currencies to facilitate cross-country analysis.

it was compiled after the industrial file. For example, equipment-and-structures capital stock data are provided in the financial services file but not in the industrial file. The biggest defect not easily overcome is that there is no way to seamlessly move between the industrial or financial services file and the issues file because there is no common reference variable across files. The issues file is in itself difficult to use because of the multiple equity issues discussed above. Finally, perhaps the most subtle and potentially important feature of the data is that the variables are scaled within each country. For example, data are reported in billions of yen or lira and in thousands of pound sterling. In addition, the scaling is not consistent *within* each country. For example, data for the British company BP are reported in millions of pound sterling, while most of the other companies in the U.K. sample are reported in thousands of pound sterling. Failure to account for this reporting difference causes data to be incorrect at three orders of magnitude with obvious consequences.

The programs used for data extraction and construction and for estimation are available from the authors on request.

Appendix C
Tax Parameters

This appendix details the tax parameters we use and relevant features of each country's tax code. It is divided into four sections. The first provides the marginal corporate income tax rate, τ. The second provides the investment incentive (credit or deduction), k. These first two sections consist primarily of two tables, annotated, where appropriate, to reflect particularly important features of the country's tax code. For additional detail we refer the interested reader to Cummins, Hassett, and Hubbard (1994), which specifically addresses the effects of tax reform on firm investment behavior. The next two sections provide depreciation and inventory valuation rules. Neither one of these sections of the tax code is easily or accurately summarized in a table, so we provide a detailed description for each country. Descriptions for the United States are omitted (see, e.g., Auerbach 1982, 1983; Hulten and Wykoff 1981; Salinger and Summers 1983; Shoven and Bulow 1975). While depreciation and inventory valuation rules change much less frequently than corporate tax rates and tax credits, they do change over our sample period. We will note particularly significant changes below, but again, we refer the interested reader to Cummins et al. (1995) for additional detail.

There are four data sources for this appendix. The primary source for current tax law is the loose-leaf services of the International Bureau of Fiscal Documentation (IBFD). The IBFD publishes guides to taxation in separate services for Europe (*Guide to European Taxation. Volume 2, The Taxation of Companies in Europe*), Asia and the Pacific (*Taxes and Investment in Asia and the Pacific. Part 2, Countries*), and Canada (*Taxes and Investment in Canada*).[31] These services do not, in general, contain the historical detail necessary to construct a time series of changes in tax law. For that purpose, we use the IBFD's *Tax News Service,* which is a weekly periodical containing every significant tax law change. Some of the detail in the *Tax News Service* is contained in the IBFD's *Annual Report* and in its *European Tax Handbook.*

Two other sources are useful to validate and further illuminate the above sources. Neither provide sufficient detail, or, in some cases, accurate information, on relevant tax parameters. The OECD's *Taxing Profits in a Global Economy: Domestic and International Issues,* which tries to extend the King and Fullerton (1984) methodology, provides an annex which contains summaries of individual countries' tax laws. The summaries contain broad detail on each country's tax law but caution is advised. The data sources are undocumented, and several items were found to be incorrect. Coopers & Lybrand's *International Tax Summaries* and *International Accounting Summaries* provide concise and accurate yearly descriptions of countries' tax laws. The volumes sometimes lack sufficient detail on depreciation and inventory valuation rules and on the timing of tax changes.

Marginal Corporate Tax Rates

Table 7.1 reports the statutory marginal corporate income tax rates for the 17 countries in our sample over 1981–92. Close attention must be paid to the notes since no single rate completely summarizes the wide variation in the countries' tax systems. Two regularities are obvious. Rates vary widely and have steadily declined in nearly every country.

Investment Incentives

Table 7.2 reports the investment tax credits and deductions for the countries in our sample. Interestingly, only a few countries provide broad-based statutory investment incentives. However, all countries in our sample have investment incentives for specific regions or industries, for certain types of business fixed investment, or for research and development which are not reported. These special incentives tend to be extremely complex, and in many cases, they cannot be summarized because they are essentially negotiated between the taxpayer and tax authority.

---

31. In addition, the IBFD also publishes guides to taxation in Africa, the Middle East, China, Latin America, and the Caribbean.

Depreciation Rules[32]

Australia

Depreciation of assets is calculated on the cost price and the useful life of the assets (which before 1991 was estimated by the tax authority), which the taxpayer estimates based on the statutory definition. The tax authority continues to publish recommended depreciation rates which the taxpayer may elect over estimating useful life. Plant and machinery may be depreciated on either a straight-line (SL) or declining-balance (DB) basis. In the absence of a formal election for the SL method, the DB method is used. Most assets acquired after 1992 are depreciable by reference to a six-rate schedule, with useful lives ranging from three to more than thirty years and DB rates ranging from 10 to 60 percent. SL rates are two-thirds of DB rates. Assets may be depreciated at a lower rate at the option of the taxpayer. Assets with an effective life of less than three years or low-cost assets may be depreciated immediately. Structures may be depreciated at 2.5 percent per year if construction commenced after September 1987, 4 if construction commenced between August 1984 and September 1987, and 2.5 if construction commenced before August 1984. The period over which the depreciation may be claimed is 40 years for structures subject to the 2.5 percent rate and 25 years for structures subject to the 4 percent rate.

Belgium

Depreciation of assets is calculated on the cost price and the useful life of the assets and is allowed as of the financial year in which they were acquired or produced and must be applied every year. The law allows only SL and DB methods. SL is the normal method. The depreciation periods and the corresponding rates are normally fixed by agreement between the taxpayer and the tax authority, although for certain assets the rates are set by administrative ruling (e.g., commercial buildings 3 percent; industrial buildings 5; machinery and equipment 10 or 30; and rolling stock 20). DB is optional, as is a combination of both methods—if in a certain year the amount of depreciation computed by applying DB is lower than that computed according to SL, then a company can switch to the latter method. Accelerated depreciation (AD) is available for certain assets based on administrative ruling (e.g., ships and scientific equipment).

Canada

The capital cost allowance system groups depreciable assets into various classes (similar to the method used in the United States). Each class is depre-

---

32. Unless otherwise noted, assets may be revalued in conformity with the relevant tax law.

ciable at a specific rate, generally on a DB basis. In the year of acquisition, only half the normal rate may be claimed on that asset. The depreciation allowances are elective, allowing the taxpayer to claim any desired amount (subject to the maximum). The following sets out some of the more common types of depreciable assets with the applicable DB rates: structures 4 percent, machinery and equipment 30, and autos and computers 30. Asset revaluation is not allowed.

Denmark

SL depreciation for business structures is permitted. For most types of buildings the depreciation rate is 6 percent of cost during the first 10 years, and 2 percent thereafter (a lower rate is applied to service buildings of 4 and 1 percent, and a higher rate to building installations of 8 and 4 percent). Between 1982 and 1990, the depreciable base was adjusted annually for inflation. For equipment, DB depreciation is allowed on a collective basis. The rate may be chosen by the taxpayer but may not exceed 30 percent in any year. Tax depreciation is not allowed for accounting purposes.

France

Depreciation is normally computed by the SL method. However, the law provides for other methods, namely, DB and AD. The SL method may be applied without restriction. The rates are computed by dividing the expenditure by the estimated useful life of the asset as determined in accordance with accepted business practice. Taxpayers may opt for a varying depreciation rate based on a different useful-life estimation but this will be accepted only if the difference is within 20 percent of customary practice. The DB method is allowed on a more limited scale. It may not be applied to assets whose useful life is less than three years nor to many classes of assets. The rate is computed by multiplying the rate of SL depreciation by 1.5 if the useful life is three or four years, by 2 if the life is five or six years, and by 2.5 if the life exceeds six years. AD in the form of an initial deduction is available for certain assets (e.g., environmental protection equipment). Only limited asset revaluation is permitted.

Germany

Systems of depreciation allowed by law are the SL, DB, and certain other methods (e.g., sum of the years' digits). A switchover from DB to SL is permitted, but not vice versa. The rates of depreciation for buildings are set out in the law and for other assets in the official recommended tables (over 90 tables) that are issued by the various tax authorities. The taxpayer may deviate from them in individual cases on reasonable grounds. For business structures, the annual SL rate is 4 percent. The corresponding DB rates are, 10 percent for the first four years, 5 for the following three years, and 2.5 for the remaining 18 years. For fixed assets a general table applies SL rates of 10 percent for machinery, 20 for office equipment, 10 for office furniture, 20 for computers, and 20 for motor vehicles. If the assets are depreciated according to DB the annual rate is limited to three times the SL rate with an allowable maximum of 30 percent. AD is allowed for certain special assets (e.g., those in development areas or private hospitals) and if justified by excessive wear and tear. Asset revaluation is not allowed.

Ireland

Depreciation is granted for structures and plant and equipment (which has a relatively wide meaning). The SL method is typically used. Rates for principal depreciable assets are 4 percent for industrial structures, 10 for commercial structures, 10 for machinery and equipment, 20 for motor vehicles (DB method used), and 100 for research expenditure.

Italy

Depreciation of tangible assets is permitted on a SL basis. Depreciation is determined by applying the coefficients established by the tax authority, reduced by half for the first fiscal year. These coefficients are established for categories of assets based on normal wear and tear in various productive sectors (rates for structures vary from 3 to 7 percent, and for machinery and equipment from 20 to 25 percent). AD is also allowed. In addition to normal depreciation, the deductible amount may be increased by 200 percent in the year in which the asset is acquired and in one of the following two years. Moreover, normal depreciation may always be increased in proportion to more intense use of the asset (intensive depreciation). The amount of depreciation may be less than normal depreciation, and the difference may be spread over subsequent fiscal years. Only limited asset revaluation is permitted.

Japan

The amount depreciable on assets per year is computed on the assumption that their salvage value is 10 percent of the acquisition cost. However, companies may claim depreciation until the residual value of the asset reaches 5 percent (i.e., up to 95 percent of acquisition costs). The statutory useful lives of assets are prescribed by the tax authority. They range from 4 years (for motor vehicles) to 65 years (for office buildings). Special depreciation is available for assets subject to abnormal wear and tear and due to extraordinary circumstances. AD is also available for designated assets and industries (e.g., environmental protection equipment and ships.) Initial-year depreciation rates range from 8 to 30 percent and further AD can follow. Asset revaluation is not allowed.

Netherlands

Depreciation of assets is compulsory whether the company is profitable or not. Assets with a low cost can be fully depreciated in the year of acquisition.

All systems of depreciation are permitted provided that the system is in accordance with sound business practices and that it is consistently applied. This means that changes in the system will not be allowed when a change is made just for tax purposes. Depreciation is based on historic cost price, useful life, and the salvage value of the asset. No official guidelines for depreciation exist. In practice, the rates are agreed upon between the taxpayer and the tax authority.

New Zealand

A new depreciation regime became law in April 1993. The pivotal difference between the old and new regimes is that under the latter the taxpayer has a statutory right to a deduction for depreciation. Previous depreciation deductions were at the tax authority's discretion. The taxpayer may choose SL or DB methods. The method may be changed from year to year. Depreciation rates are calculated from a formula that accounts for acquisition cost, market value, and useful life. The tax authority provides a very extensive schedule of estimated useful lives (ranging from 4 to 50 years), with applicable DB and SL rates. Application for special rates may be made in certain circumstances. Previously, the tax authority mandated choice of SL or DB methods and depreciation rates.

Norway

The DB method of depreciation is mandatory. The 1992 tax reform has influenced the system of depreciation by changing the division of business assets into a smaller number of classes and by generally reducing the maximum rates allowed. Depreciable assets are divided into eight classes (maximum rates follow in parentheses): (1) office machines (30 percent), (2) goodwill (30), (3) motor vehicles (25), (4) equipment (20), (5) ships (20), (6) aircraft (20), (7) industrial structures (5), and (8) commercial structures (2). Assets in classes 1–4 are written down on a collective basis; classes 5–8 are depreciated individually. AD for ships, aircraft, and certain structures has been abolished as of 1992. Assets with an estimated life of less than three years and low cost assets may be depreciated immediately.

Spain

Depreciation is allowed on all tangible and intangible fixed assets on the basis of their normal useful life. Depreciation may be calculated by the SL method. In certain cases (e.g., industrial machinery and computers), the DB method is permitted. Rates for depreciation are contained in official tables. Examples of general maximum SL rates follow (with the minimum rate following in parentheses): Industrial structures 3 percent (2 percent), commercial structures 2 (1.33), machinery 8 (5.6), tools 20 (12.5), office furniture 10 (6.67), computers 25 (16.7), and motor vehicles 14 (9.1). Assets intensively used may be depreciated at a maximum rate increased by 33 percent for each additional shift. Under the DB method, the annual depreciation rate is increased by 50 percent (if the useful life is less than five years), or by 150 percent (if the useful life is eight years or more). The tax authorities can accept, at their discretion, special AD (or even free depreciation) for certain assets and industries. Asset revaluation is not permitted.

Sweden

Machinery and equipment are normally depreciated by the DB method. The maximum depreciation allowance is 30 percent of the aggregate book value of all assets at the beginning of the tax year, plus the cost of assets acquired, less the amount received for assets sold during the year. Should a SL depreciation of 20 percent per year on all assets result in a lower book value in any year, the annual depreciation may be increased correspondingly. If the taxpayer can prove that the real value of machinery and equipment is lower than that resulting from the above-mentioned depreciation methods, the depreciation may be allowed in an amount resulting in the value. Assets with a useful life not exceeding three years and low-cost assets may be depreciated immediately. For buildings, only the SL method is permitted. In general, depreciation is based on cost and useful life. The rates vary between 1.5 and 5 percent per year as agreed by the taxpayer and the tax authority.

Switzerland

The SL and DB methods are allowed, but depreciation must conform to usual business practice. Official guidelines for depreciation are published, but they are not obligatory. In practice, depreciation rates vary among the cantons. AD (up to 80 percent) is allowed in certain cantons. Asset revaluation is not permitted.

United Kingdom

Industrial structures are eligible for 4 percent annual depreciation on the SL method. There are no allowances for commercial structures. Plant and equipment (which has a relatively wide meaning) is eligible for 25 percent annual depreciation on the DB method.

Inventory Valuation[33]

Australia

For valuation of stock, the tax authority accepts average cost (AC), standard cost (SC), specific identification (SI), and FIFO. LIFO and base-stock methods are not allowed.

---

33. Unless otherwise noted, stock is valued at the lower of cost or market value.

Belgium

The tax code does not contain special provisions for the valuation of stock. The tax authority therefore requires that the stock be valued at cost or market value, whichever is lower. As for methods, AC, SI, FIFO, and LIFO methods are accepted but the base-stock method is not.

Canada

Permissible inventory valuation methods include AC and FIFO. In some circumstances, the tax authority will accept the SC method. The LIFO method is not accepted.

Denmark

The AC, SI, FIFO, and SC methods are considered appropriate; LIFO is acceptable but rarely used.

France

The FIFO and AC methods are usually used. The LIFO method is not generally permitted except when used in consolidated financial statements.

Germany

From the assessment year 1990, LIFO is allowed. AC and SI are typical methods; FIFO is not allowed unless it approximates actual physical flows.

Ireland

FIFO, AC, or any similar method is allowed; LIFO is not acceptable.

Italy

Any system of inventory valuation is permitted provided it is not less than if the LIFO method is used.

Japan

For valuation of stock, the tax authority accepts AC, SI, LIFO, and FIFO. The method should be applied consistently and not distort the computation of the income of a corporation.

Netherlands

Under the sound business practice principle, many systems of inventory valuation are allowed (e.g., LIFO, FIFO, or base-stock methods). The system must be applied consistently.

New Zealand

The tax authority accepts the AC, SC, or FIFO methods of inventory valuation. LIFO and base-stock methods are not allowed.

Norway

The FIFO method must be used for inventory valuation.

Spain

Accepted methods for inventory valuation are AC (in practice, the generally applied method) and FIFO. The LIFO and base-stock methods are not accepted for tax purposes.

Sweden

Prior to 1991, inventories were frequently carried at an amount lower than the maximum amount permitted by the lower of cost or market value, due to tax incentives. In determining inventory valuation, the FIFO method should be applied.

Switzerland

Acceptable inventory valuation methods include AC, SC, and FIFO. LIFO is not permitted.

United Kingdom

FIFO, AC, or any similar method is allowed. LIFO is not acceptable.

References

Abel, Andrew B. 1980. Empirical investment equations: An integrative framework. *Carnegie-Rochester Conference Series on Public Policy* 12 (Spring): 39–91.

Auerbach, Alan J. 1982. The new economics of accelerated depreciation. *Boston College Law Review* 23 (September): 1327–55.

————. 1983. Taxation, corporate financial policy, and the cost of capital. *Journal of Economic Literature* 21: 905–40.

Ballon, R. J., and I. Tomita. 1988. *The financial behavior of Japanese corporations.* Tokyo: Kodansha.

Blundell, Richard, Stephen Bond, Michael Devereux, and Fabio Schiantarelli. 1992. Investment and tobin's *Q:* Evidence from company panel data. *Journal of Econometrics* 51 (January/February): 233–58.

Busse von Colbe, W., K. Geiger, H. Haase, H. Reinhard, and G. Schmitt. 1991. *Ergebnis nach DVFA/SG.* Dusseldorf: Schaffer.

Coopers & Lybrand. Various years. *International accounting summaries.* New York: Wiley.

————. Various years. *International tax summaries.* New York: Wiley.

Cummins, Jason G., and Kevin A. Hassett. 1992. The effects of taxation on investment: New evidence from firm-level panel data. *National Tax Journal* 45 (September): 243–52.

Cummins, Jason G., Kevin A. Hassett, and R. Glenn Hubbard. 1994. A reconsideration of investment behavior using tax reforms as natural experiments. *Brookings Papers on Economic Activity,* no. 2:1–74.

————. 1995. An international comparison of the effects of tax reforms on business fixed investment. Mimeograph, Columbia University.

Darrough, M., and T. S. Harris. 1991. Do management forecasts of earnings affect stock prices in Japan? In *Japanese financial market research,* ed. W. T. Ziemba, W. Bailey, and Y. Hamao. New York: Elsevier.

Easton, P. D., P. Eddey, and T. S. Harris. 1993. An investigation of revaluations of tangible long-lived assets. *Journal of Accounting Research* 31 (supplement): 1–38.

French, K., and J. Poterba. 1991. Are Japanese stock prices too high? *Journal of Financial Economics* 29 (October): 337–363.

Gilchrist, Simon, and Charles P. Himmelberg. 1991. Evidence on the role of cash flow in reduced-form investment equations. Mimeograph, New York University.

Hall, C., Y. Hamao, and T. S. Harris. 1993. A comparison of relations between security market prices, returns, and accounting measures in Japan and the United States. *Journal of International Financial Management and Accounting* 5 (February): 47–73.

Harris, T. S., M. Lang, and H. P. Möller. 1993. The value-relevance of German accounting measures: An empirical analysis. Mimeograph, Columbia University.

Hayashi, Fumio, and Tohru Inoue. 1991. The relation between firm growth and Q with multiple capital goods: Theory and evidence from panel data on Japanese firms. *Econometrica* 59 (May): 731–53.

Himmelberg, Charles P. 1990. A dynamic analysis of dividend and investment behavior under borrowing constraints. Mimeograph, New York University.

Hoshi, Takeo, Anil Kashyap, and David Scharfstein. 1991. Corporate capital structure, liquidity and investment: Evidence from Japanese industrial groups. *Quarterly Journal of Economics* 106 (February): 33–60.

Hubbard, R. Glenn, and Anil K. Kashyap. 1992. Internal net worth and the investment process: An application to U.S. agriculture. *Journal of Political Economy* 100 (June): 506–34.

Hubbard, R. Glenn, Anil K. Kashyap, and Toni M. Whited. 1995. Internal finance and firm investment. *Journal of Money, Credit, and Banking,* forthcoming.

Hulten, Charles R., and Frank C. Wykoff. 1981. The measurement of economic Depreciation. In *Depreciation, inflation, and the taxation of income from capital,* ed. Charles R. Hulten, 81–125. Washington, D.C.: Urban Institute Press.

International Bureau of Fiscal Documentation. Various issues. *Annual report.* Amsterdam: International Bureau of Fiscal Documentation.

————. Various issues. *European tax handbook.* Amsterdam: International Bureau of Fiscal Documentation.

————. Various issues. *Tax news service.* Amsterdam: International Bureau of Fiscal Documentation.

————. 1993. *Guide to European taxation. Volume 2, The taxation of companies in Europe.* Amsterdam: International Bureau of Fiscal Documentation.

————. 1993. *Taxes and investment in Asia and the Pacific. Part 2, Countries.* Amsterdam: International Bureau of Fiscal Documentation.

————. 1993. *Taxes and investment in Canada.* Amsterdam: International Bureau of Fiscal Documentation.

Jennings, R., D. P. Mest, and R. B. Thompson. 1992. Investor reaction to disclosures of 1974–75 LIFO adoption decisions. *Accounting Review* 67 (April): 337–54.

King, Mervyn A., and Don Fullerton, eds. 1984. *The taxation of income from capital: A comparative study of the United States, United Kingdom, Sweden, and West Germany.* Chicago: University of Chicago Press.

Kanniainen, Vesa, and Jan Södersten. 1994. Costs of monitoring and corporate taxation. *Journal of Public Economics* 55: 307–21.

OECD (Organisation for Economic Co-operation and Development). 1991. *Taxing profits in a global economy: Domestic and international issues.* Paris: OECD.

Oliner, S., G. Rudebusch, and D. Sichel. 1993. New and old models of business investment: A comparison of forecasting performance. Mimeograph, Board of Governors of the Federal Reserve System, Washington, D.C.

Ordelheide, D., and M. Pfaff. 1993. *German financial reporting*. London: Routledge.

Salinger, Michael, and Lawrence H. Summers. 1983. Tax reform and corporate investment: A microeconomic simulation study. In *Behavioral simulation models of tax policy analysis*, ed. Martin Feldstein. Chicago: University of Chicago Press.

Shoven, J., and J. Bulow. 1975. Inflation accounting and nonfinancial corporate profits: Physical assets. *Brookings Papers on Economic Activity*, no. 2: 557–98.

Tax Bureau, Ministry of Finance. 1990. *An outline of Japanese taxes: 1990*. Tokyo: Ministry of Finance.

Viner, Aron. 1988. *Inside Japanese financial markets*. New York: Dow Jones, Irwin.

Comment   G. Peter Wilson

The Cummins, Harris, and Hassett paper differs from the typical offering in the international accounting literature because the authors test hypotheses using a rigorous model of economic behavior. This contrasts with the prevalent approach in the accounting literature, which is to use ordinary least squares to test for statistical relationships that are consistent with hypothesized behavior. I suspect the paper also differs from the usual offering in the economics literature in that the authors' hypotheses more fully exploit institutional aspects of international accounting. Thus, as we might expect from this research team, the paper significantly extends two literatures.

The authors examine an important research question: Are firms' investment decisions influenced by whether they are required to use essentially the same accounting for tax and financial reporting? In the United States, the accounting rules for recording many economic events differ significantly for tax and financial reporting because the authorities responsible for these rules recognize that their reporting objectives differ. The stated objective of financial reporting is to provide information that is useful for predicting future cash flows. In contrast, the objectives of tax reporting are subordinate to the broader social and economic objectives of the tax system, which include, among other things, raising revenue, redistributing income, and promoting certain kinds of economic activity.

The authors refer to the United States and other countries where there is little conformity between tax and financial reporting as "two-book" countries. They refer to countries where almost complete conformity is mandated for financial and tax accounting as "one-book" countries. Typically, one-book countries have congruent objectives for financial and tax reporting. For ex-

G. Peter Wilson is visiting associate professor of management at the Massachusetts Institute of Technology.

ample, in Germany, the ultimate one-book country, the objectives of the tax and financial reporting systems are essentially the same—to maintain capital.

The authors proffer that firms in one-book countries are disadvantaged, relative to their two-book counterparts, when they make tax-advantaged investments. The reason, they argue, is that the one-book firms must recognize the related accelerated depreciation deductions for both financial and tax purposes. In contrast, the two-book firms can use straight-line depreciation for financial reporting and, thus, report higher financial income. To the extent that profitability has the same impact on the cost of capital in both regimes, firms in one-book countries could face a higher cost of capital to finance new projects.

However, I question whether profitability is as important in the one-book regimes. For example, if the providers of German capital and the German tax authorities are both more interested in capital maintenance than in profitability, as the authors suggest, then why do the providers of capital care if financial reporting income is reduced to make investments that preserve capital? My concern here only makes the empirical question of whether the cost of capital is higher in one-book countries more interesting.

The authors cleverly model this additional cost of capital as the cost a one-book firm incurs to signal that its reduction in income is due to prudent tax planning rather than to poor operating performance. As indicated in equation (3), the cost of this revelation signal, Ω, which is treated as an additional adjustment cost in the standard investment model used by Cummins and Hubbard (chap. 5 in this volume), depends nonlinearly on the size of the tax benefit per dollar of investment, the amount invested, and the capital in place at the start of the year. This is a keen modeling insight, and I believe that it is the only point where the analytic and econometric analysis differs substantively from the Cummins and Hubbard paper. Thus, many of the discussant's comments about the Cummins and Hubbard paper are also appropriate here.

The signaling cost, Ω, is assumed to increase quadratically in the size of the tax benefits. On the one hand, this seems intuitive because we might expect firms with lower reported income to have to work harder to convince analysts that income is low because of good tax planning. On the other hand, if a one-book firm started using a second set of books (as some of the sample firms do), the cost of producing and distributing reports from these second books would not depend on the size of the tax break.

In a related matter, as the authors acknowledge, the model is silent as to whether the signaling cost is incurred by the firm or by shareholders in the form of additional monitoring fees. Another option is that these costs are paid to shareholders in the form of risk premiums that could possibly be reduced by additional disclosure. Accounting academics would like to know how these costs, which are variable in the model, compare to the fixed costs of establishing two sets of books or setting up business as an external intermediary such as the DVFA/SA. If firms or outside intermediaries cannot achieve the economies of scale to cover these fixed costs and firms cannot credibly convey their private information to the capital markets, then the result could be a higher cost of capital in the form of risk premiums.

The results are mixed for the primary tests reported in table 7.5, which partition the data into one- and two-book countries. For both samples, the signaling cost parameter, α_1, has the wrong sign and the model's overidentifying restrictions are rejected. However, I agree with the authors that the most interesting results are reported in table 7.6. These are based on a subpartition of the one-book firms that produces a more powerful test of the authors' economic intuition. Firms are partitioned into (1) "pure" one-book firms that report in accordance with domestic accounting standards and are not fully consolidated and (2) not-so-pure one-book firms that voluntarily issue supplementary reports that conform to U.S. GAAP, presumably because they are accessing global capital markets. These latter firms do not incur revelation signaling costs because their U.S. GAAP numbers already reveal their profitability. The authors find that the signaling costs are significant and that the model is not rejected for the pure one-book firms. This is a nice result, and more generally, this paper is excellent research.

My only negative comment is that there are some disconnections between the appendices and the exposition in the main text. In particular, the authors could have explained more clearly how the various accounting procedures documented by country in the appendices affect the estimation of the model and the interpretation of the results. For example, they could have distinguished the accounting procedures that affect the variable's measurement errors from those that affect the accuracy of the sample partition. Aside from these minor concerns with the exposition, I think that this is superb work that demonstrates the gains that can be achieved when accountants and economists collaborate.

8   Taxes, Technology Transfer, and the R&D Activities of Multinational Firms

James R. Hines, Jr.

8.1 Introduction

Many governments encourage the development and use of new technologies within the borders of their countries. It is not difficult to understand why they do so. It is widely believed that the positive correlation between local economic affluence and the presence of technologically advanced industries implies that the use of new technologies enhances overall productivity. More direct evidence generally supports the conclusion that the economic benefits of research and development (R&D) activity extend to local firms other than those undertaking the R&D.[1] Since there are reasons to expect that externality-generating R&D activities may be underprovided by markets in which developers of new technologies do not capture all of the economic benefits that the technologies provide, various governments offer R&D-related tax subsidies.[2] Governments that do not offer R&D tax subsidies are often concerned that

James R. Hines, Jr., is associate professor of public policy at the John F. Kennedy School of Government, Harvard University, and a faculty research fellow of the National Bureau of Economic Research.

The author thanks Jeffrey Geppert for outstanding research assistance, and Adam Jaffe and James Poterba for helpful comments on an earlier draft. Financial support from the National Science Foundation (grant SES-9209373) and the National Bureau of Economic Research is gratefully acknowledged.

1. See Griliches (1991) and Nadiri (1993) for surveys of empirical measures of productivity spillovers from R&D activities.

2. In theory, the welfare consequences of subsidizing R&D are ambiguous because competitive pressures might generate too much R&D in certain industries in the absence of a subsidy and because foreign competitors may benefit from domestic subsidies (or in other ways influence the domestic market). See Dixit (1988) and Reinganum (1989) for surveys of the theory. The United States introduced the research and experimentation tax credit, and increased the tax deductibility of the R&D expenses of certain multinational corporations, in the Economic Recovery Tax Act of 1981. This legislation appears to have been motivated by consideration of economic externalities, though the focus of congressional sentiment as described in U.S. Joint Committee on Taxation (1981) is on comparisons of U.S. research intensity with the research intensities of other countries.

perhaps they should. There are, however, many open questions about the impact of tax policy on the level of R&D.

Tax systems influence the level and content of R&D activity through a variety of channels. This paper focuses on R&D by multinational firms, and on the impact of one particular set of taxes: withholding taxes on cross-border royalty payments. Firms that develop new technologies in their home countries and use the technologies in foreign locations are required to pay royalties from foreign affiliates to domestic parent companies. Governments tax these royalty payments. High tax rates make royalties, and the technology imports that they accompany, more expensive for the foreign affiliates that pay the taxes.

In theory, higher costs of imported technology might encourage or discourage local R&D by affiliates of multinational corporations. If local R&D is complementary with imported technology, then high royalty tax rates should discourage local R&D, while if local R&D is a substitute for imported technology, then high royalty tax rates should encourage local R&D.

This paper has two objectives. The first is to identify the degree to which R&D activity by multinational firms is sensitive to local tax conditions. The second objective is to determine whether imported technology and local R&D are complements or substitutes.

The results suggest that R&D responds significantly to local tax rates, and that local R&D is a substitute for imported technology. These results appear both in the behavior of American investors in other countries and in the behavior of foreign investors in the United States. Firms appear to react to high royalty tax rates by paying fewer royalties and performing additional R&D locally. To the extent that royalty payments reflect actual technology transfer (rather than adept accounting practices), the behavior of multinational firms implies that local R&D is a substitute for imported technology.

Section 8.2 of the paper briefly describes the tax treatment of multinational firms, paying particular attention to technology-related issues. Section 8.3 describes a simple model of firm behavior that traces the link between taxation and the degree of complementarity or substitutability of local R&D and imported technology. Section 8.4 describes the data that serve as the basis of the empirical work. Section 8.5 presents evidence on the relationship between royalty tax rates in foreign countries and the R&D intensities of local affiliates of American multinational firms. Section 8.6 examines the same relationship for foreign firms investing in the United States. Section 8.7 is the conclusion.

8.2   Multinational Firms, Taxation, and International Technology Transfer

This section examines the role of multinational firms in international technology transfer and reviews the tax treatment of R&D expenditures and royalty receipts by multinational firms.

8.2.1   International Technology Transfer

There is considerable interest in understanding the role that multinational firms play in transferring technologies across borders. There are two methods by which multinational firms provide new technologies to the countries in which they invest. The first method is to develop new technologies locally, through R&D or other similar types of activity. The second method is to import technologies produced elsewhere.

The foreign affiliates of American firms use both methods to bring technologies to the countries in which they operate, and there exists sufficient information to assess quantitatively the relative significance of each method. Direct information on the R&D activities of the foreign affiliates of U.S. firms is reported in surveys conducted by the U.S. Commerce Department. Information on technology imports by these affiliates is considerably sketchier. One can, however, infer the approximate magnitude of technology imports from royalties paid by the affiliates to U.S. parent firms and third parties in other countries, since royalty payments should, in principle, reflect the values of imported technologies.

Table 8.1 reports detailed information about the aggregate technology-related behavior of the foreign affiliates of U.S. firms in 1982 and 1989. It is noteworthy that these affiliates paid more in royalties to their parent firms ($9.8 billion in 1989) than they spent on R&D ($7.9 billion in 1989), though, as the table indicates, there was extensive use of both methods of technology acquisition. The survey distinguishes two categories of R&D expenditure: R&D by affiliates for themselves and R&D by affiliates for others (the latter of which is R&D performed on a contract basis). R&D by affiliates for themselves constitutes roughly 80 percent of their total R&D expenditures.

American firms spend a considerable amount of money on R&D performed in foreign countries, but in recent years, foreign-owned firms in the United States have spent even more than that on R&D performed here. Figure 8.1 illustrates the R&D expenditure levels of foreign affiliates of U.S. firms and foreign-owned firms in the United States over the 1977–90 period. Due to the R&D intensity of the U.S. economy relative to the rest of the world, and the strength of foreign direct investment into the United States since 1973, foreign firms have spent more on R&D inside the United States than American firms have spent on R&D outside the United States in every year since 1982, and the gap between the two expenditure levels is widening (see fig. 8.1).[3]

There is considerable interest in the role of multinational firms in transfer-

---

3. Exchange rate fluctuations can confound the interpretation of fig. 8.1 since changes in the value of the dollar relative to foreign currencies affect the dollar-denominated relative magnitudes of R&D performed in the United States and abroad, even if nominal expenditures are unchanged. This consideration is not significant in this case, however, since a simple adjustment for the changing value of the dollar relative to a trade-weighted average of foreign currencies produces a figure that very closely resembles fig. 8.1.

Table 8.1   R&D and Royalty Activity of Foreign Affiliates of U.S. Multinationals

Activity	1982	1989
R&D expenditures, total	3,851	7,922
By affiliate for itself	3,073	6,307
By affiliate for others	778	1,615
Royalty receipts, total	435	1,461
From U.S. parents	36	54
From other foreign affiliates	193	656
From unaffiliated Americans	26	97
From unaffiliated foreigners	180	654
Royalty payments, total	4,308	12,472
To U.S. parents	3,663	9,839
To other foreign affiliates	354	1,488
To unaffiliated Americans	102	660
To unaffiliated foreigners	189	485

Source: U.S. Department of Commerce (1985, 1992).

Note: Amounts are millions of current dollars. Data cover majority-owned foreign affiliates of U.S. multinational firms.

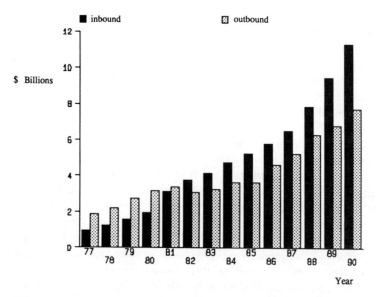

Fig. 8.1   R&D by foreign firms in the United States and by American firms abroad, 1977–90

Sources: U.S. Department of Commerce (various issues); National Science Foundation (1993).
Note: The vertical scale measures billions of current dollars of annual R&D expenditures. Darkly shaded bars represent total R&D expenditures of foreign-owned firms in the United States. Lightly shaded bars represent total R&D expenditures of foreign affiliates of American firms.

ring technology across borders, and the impact that government policy can have on the rate and direction of technology transfer. Though these issues have been extensively studied,[4] one of the open questions is the degree to which imported technology is a substitute or complement for local R&D.

8.2.2   U.S. Taxation of Foreign Income[5]

The United States taxes income on a "residence" basis, meaning that American corporations and individuals owe taxes to the U.S. government on all of their worldwide income, whether earned in the United States or not. The top U.S. corporate tax rate is now 35 percent. Since foreign profits are usually taxed in host countries, U.S. law provides a foreign tax credit for income taxes (and related taxes) paid to foreign governments, in order not to subject American multinationals to double taxation. The foreign tax credit mechanism provides that an American corporation earning $100 in a foreign country with a 12 percent tax rate (and a foreign tax obligation of $12) pays only $23 to the U.S. government, since its U.S. corporate tax liability of $35 (35 percent of $100) is reduced to $23 by the foreign tax credit of $12. The foreign tax credit is, however, limited to U.S. tax liability on foreign income; if, in the example, the foreign tax rate were 50 percent, then the firm pays $50 to the foreign government but its U.S. foreign tax credit is limited to $35. Hence, an American firm receives full tax credits for its foreign taxes paid only when it is in a "deficit credit" position, i.e., when its average foreign tax rate is less than its tax rate on domestic operations. A firm has "excess credits" if its available foreign tax credits exceed U.S. tax liability on its foreign income. Firms average together their taxable incomes and taxes paid in all of their foreign operations in calculating their foreign tax credits and the foreign tax credit limit.[6]

Deferral of U.S. taxation of certain foreign earnings is another important feature of the U.S. international tax system. An American parent firm is taxed on its subsidiaries' foreign income only when returned ("repatriated") to the

---

4. See, e.g., Teece (1976), Germidis (1977), Mansfield, Teece, and Romeo (1979), Mansfield and Romeo (1980), Davidson and McFetridge (1984), Lipsey, Blomstrom, and Kravis (1990), Zejan (1990), Blomstrom (1991), Ethier and Markusen (1991), Wang and Blomstrom (1992), and Blomstrom and Kokko (1993). These studies together consider the effect of a large number of variables on technology transfer and R&D activity, though they do not consider the effect of royalty tax rates on local R&D intensities.

5. Parts of this brief description of the tax system are excerpted from Hines (1991).

6. In order to qualify for the foreign tax credit, firms must own at least 10 percent of a foreign affiliate, and only those taxes that qualify as income taxes are creditable. Furthermore, income is broken into different functional "baskets" in the calculation of applicable credits and limits. Income earned and taxes paid in the conduct of most types of active foreign business operations are grouped in one basket; petroleum industry income is grouped in a separate basket; and there are separate baskets for items such as passive income earned abroad. The basket distinctions imply that a firm might simultaneously have excess foreign tax credits in the petroleum basket (which is common, since foreign tax rates on oil income are typically quite high) and deficit foreign tax credits in the active income basket. Such a firm would have to pay some U.S. tax on its active foreign income, even though it has excess foreign tax credits on its petroleum income.

parent corporation. This type of deferral is available only to foreign operations that are separately incorporated in foreign countries ("subsidiaries" of the parent) and not to consolidated ("branch") operations. The U.S. government taxes branch profits as they are earned, just as it would profits earned within the United States.

The deferral of U.S. taxation may create incentives for firms with lightly taxed foreign earnings to delay repatriating dividends from their foreign subsidiaries.[7] This incentive arises in those cases in which firms expect never to repatriate their foreign earnings, or in which they anticipate that future years will be more attractive for repatriation (either because domestic tax rates will be lower or because future sources of foreign income will generate excess foreign tax credits that can be used to offset U.S. tax liability on the dividends).[8] It appears that, in practice, American multinationals tend to pay dividends out of their more heavily taxed foreign earnings first.[9] Consequently, the average tax rate that firms face on their foreign income need not exactly equal the average foreign tax rate faced by their branches and subsidiaries abroad.

Branch earnings and dividends from subsidiaries represent only two forms of foreign income for U.S. income tax purposes. Interest received from foreign sources also represents foreign income, though foreign interest receipts are often classified within their own basket and hence are not averaged with other income in calculating the foreign tax credit. Royalty income received from foreigners, including foreign affiliates of U.S. firms, is also foreign-source income. Foreign governments often impose moderate taxes on dividend, interest, and royalty payments from foreign affiliates to their American parent companies; these withholding[10] taxes are fully creditable against an American taxpayer's U.S. tax liability on foreign income.

7. The incentive to defer repatriation of lightly taxed subsidiary earnings is attenuated by the Subpart F provisions, introduced into U.S. law in 1962, that treat a subsidiary's passive income, and income invested in U.S. property, as if it were distributed to its American owners, thereby subjecting it to immediate U.S. taxation. The Subpart F rules apply to controlled foreign corporations, which are foreign corporations owned at least 50 percent by American persons holding stakes of at least 10 percent each. Controlled foreign corporations that reinvest their foreign earnings in active businesses can continue to defer their U.S. tax liability on those earnings. See Hines (1994a), Hines and Rice (1994), and Scholes and Wolfson (1992) for the behavioral implications of these rules.

8. It is interesting to note that the deferral of U.S. tax liability does not itself create an incentive to delay paying dividends from foreign subsidiaries since the U.S. tax must be paid eventually. See Hartman (1985).

9. See the evidence presented in Hines and Hubbard (1990).

10. Taxes on cross-border flows, such as dividends, interest, and royalties, are known as "withholding" taxes because of some of the specifics of their administration. Strictly speaking, these taxes represent obligations of the recipients of the cross-border flows and not the payors; this arrangement permits immediate full crediting of withholding taxes by recipients who are eligible to claim foreign tax credits. The taxes are called "withholding" taxes because the local payor is the withholding agent for the tax and is therefore liable to its host government for full payment of the taxes.

8.2.3   The Tax Treatment of R&D Expenditures and Royalty Receipts

American multinational firms that perform R&D in the United States intending to use the resulting technology both in the United States and abroad face a complex tax treatment of their transactions. Since passage of the Tax Reform Act of 1986, American multinationals are no longer allowed to deduct 100 percent of their U.S. R&D expenses against their U.S. tax liabilities. Instead, U.S. law requires American firms to allocate R&D expenses between U.S. and foreign source based on the fraction of a firm's sales that are foreign.[11] The practical importance of this system is that firms with excess foreign tax credits receive usable tax deductions for only a fraction (equal to the ratio of domestic sales to total worldwide sales) of their U.S. R&D expenses. This system is based on the idea that multinational firms performing R&D in the United States use only a fraction of the output of their R&D activities to enhance their sales in the United States and, consequently, that only a fraction of their R&D costs should be deductible against U.S.-source income.

Royalties received by American parent firms for R&D used abroad represent taxable foreign-source income of the American firms. American firms with deficit foreign tax credits must pay U.S. income tax on these royalty receipts, while firms with excess foreign tax credits can apply the excess credits against U.S. taxes due on the royalties, thereby eliminating the U.S. tax liability created by the royalty receipts.

Most of the world's governments impose withholding taxes on cross-border royalty payments from affiliates located within their countries. These royalty tax rates are frequently reduced according to the terms of bilateral tax treaties. For example, the United States imposes a 30 percent tax on royalties paid to foreign corporations, but this tax rate is often reduced, in some cases to zero, when recipients of royalty payments are located in countries with whom the United States has a tax treaty in force.

8.3   Framework for Analysis

This section analyzes the implications of systems of international taxation for the R&D behavior of multinational firms.

Consider a multinational firm that establishes a foreign affiliate to produce and sell goods in the foreign country in which the affiliate is located.[12] The affiliate generates sales using local inputs of capital, labor, and intermediate products; in addition, the affiliate uses technology from its parent and the technology it generates on its own to produce goods for sale. The reduced-form

---

11. See Hines (1993, 1994b) for descriptions of the precise formulas used and quantitative assessments of their impact on R&D spending levels.

12. This analysis abstracts from the possibility that the activities of a foreign affiliate directly enhance the sales of its domestic parent firm. One of the practical difficulties that American firms encounter in such situations is that royalties paid by U.S. parents to their foreign affiliates are severely tax disadvantaged. See Hines (1994b) for a discussion of this issue.

function that describes the impact of technologies on the affiliate's sales can be formalized as $S(R, R^*, \phi)$, in which S denotes sales in the local (foreign) market, R is technology provided by the parent firm to the affiliate in this market, R^* is the technology that the affiliate generates on its own, and ϕ denotes other features of the local market (as well as the affiliate's profit-maximizing employment of local factors).

American tax law and the tax laws of most other countries[13] require that foreign affiliates pay rents or royalties to their parent firms for the fair market value of technologies transferred from the parent firms to the affiliates. Of course, in practice it is frequently difficult to establish the fair market value of technology transferred from one party to another within a controlled group since there may exist no market prices for the types of technology in question. In such circumstances, tax-avoiding firms that transfer technology from the parent to its foreign affiliates often have incentives to select royalty payments that transfer taxable income out of high-tax jurisdictions and into low-tax jurisdictions. Governments are aware of this incentive and try to use their enforcement power to prevent royalties from deviating too greatly from reasonable values.[14]

One way to describe government enforcement efforts is to introduce an additional cost that firms bear when royalties deviate from market values. The cost includes the cost that firms incur in justifying their royalty declarations to tax authorities. If this adjustment cost rises sufficiently with the size of the deviation of reported royalties from market values, it will ultimately limit the degree to which firms modify royalty payments simply for tax purposes.

A quadratic model of adjustment costs provides a convenient framework to use in analyzing the impact of government enforcement efforts. One can distinguish R, the true value of transferred technology, from r, the royalty paid to the parent firm by the affiliate receiving the technology. If the rate of adjustment cost is quadratic in the deviation of declared royalties from the technology's market value, then adjustment costs equal $\alpha[(R - r)^2/R^2]$ for each unit of technology transferred. The parameter α is taken to be constant. Total adjustment costs equal the product of R and this term, or $\alpha(R - r)^2/R$.

The affiliate's technology-related taxable income represents the difference between sales revenue generated by the technology and the affiliate's costs. These costs include the affiliate's own R&D expenditures, the royalties it pays to the parent firm, and the adjustment cost.[15] The parent firm receives a royalty

---

13. Of the 25 industrialized countries surveyed by Lawlor (1985), 24 apply the arm's-length principle to the taxation of related-party transactions; Hong Kong is the lone exception.

14. For evidence on the overall effectiveness of transfer price enforcement, see Kopits (1976), Grubert and Mutti (1991), Harris et al. (1993), and Hines and Rice (1994).

15. This treatment of the foreign affiliate abstracts from its activities that are unaffected by R&D activities or technology imports. The affiliate, and not the parent firm, is assumed to bear the adjustment cost because doing so simplifies the algebra that follows. A more general treatment that allocates adjustment costs between affiliates and parent firms yields qualitatively similar results. See e.g., the treatment of adjustment costs in Hines and Rice (1994).

from its affiliate and may incur a cost of producing the technology that it transfers to the affiliate. In order to fix ideas for the analysis that follows, the model describes the behavior of a multinational firm that has excess foreign tax credits and that values on a one-for-one basis its after-tax profits in foreign subsidiaries.[16] The multinational firm maximizes after-tax profits, π:

(1) $$\pi = (1 - \tau^*)[S(R, R^*, \phi) - R^* - r - \alpha(R - r)^2/R] + (1 - w^*)r - cR,$$

in which τ^* is the foreign statutory tax rate, w^* is the withholding tax rate imposed by the foreign government on outgoing royalty payments, and c is the per unit cost incurred by the parent firm to develop and/or transfer the technology represented by R. The first term in expression (1) represents the after-foreign-tax profits earned by the affiliate; the second term is the parent firm's after-withholding-tax royalty receipts; and the third term is the parent firm's cost of developing the technology that it transfers to the affiliate. In some cases, parent firms costlessly transfer to their subsidiaries technologies developed for other purposes, so it is possible that $c = 0$.

The first-order condition describing the firm's optimal choice of r is

(2) $$(1 - \tau^*)[2\alpha(R - r)/R - 1] + (1 - w^*) = 0,$$

which yields

(3) $$r = R\{1 + (\tau^* - w^*)/[2\alpha(1 - \tau^*)]\}.$$

The first-order condition describing the firm's optimal choice of R is

(4) $$(1 - \tau^*)[\partial S/\partial R - \alpha(R - r)(R + r)/R^2] - c = 0.$$

Imposing equation (3) and simplfying yields

(5) $\partial S/\partial R = c/(1 - \tau^*) + (w^* - \tau^*)/(1 - \tau^*) - (w^* - \tau^*)^2/[4\alpha(1 - \tau^*)^2].$

The first-order condition describing the firm's optimal choice of R^* is considerably simpler:

(6) $$\partial S/\partial R^* = 1.$$

16. A firm values its subsidiaries' profits on a one-for-basis either if there is no tax due upon repatriation or if the firm can use deferral strategies of the type described in Hines and Rice (1994) to reduce the present value of repatriation taxes. A firm with deficit foreign tax credits maximizes an expression that is similar to equation (1), with the difference that the terms $1 - \tau^*$ and $1 - w^*$ are replaced by $1 - \tau$, in which τ is the home country tax rate. The first-order conditions describing the behavior of such a firm imply that the firm sets $r = R$, and that, in this static setting, host country tax rates do not influence its behavior. In practice, the behavior of American multinational firms should reflect some kind of average of these two extremes. The analysis that follows assumes that all American firms have excess foreign tax credits, so, to the extent that many firms do not, the empirical estimates *understate* the responsiveness of the affected group to local tax conditions. The home countries of foreign investors in the United States have tax systems that differ considerably in their treatments of R&D expenditures and royalty and dividend income from foreign sources. The empirical work in this paper distinguishes home-country tax systems only by whether firms are permitted to claim foreign tax credits, which omits some more subtle distinctions and may, thereby, introduce measurement error in the tax variables.

The conditions (3), (5), and (6) characterize the multinational firm's optimal interior choices of R, R^*, and r. Inspection of equations (5) and (6) indicates that taxation does not affect the required marginal productivity of R&D performed in the foreign location, while taxation does affect the required marginal productivity of R&D performed in the home country. Consequently, as long as tax rates are set in a manner that is exogenous to the unobservable factors that determine R&D intensity, it is possible to use the tax variables that appear on the right-hand side of equation (5) to estimate the extent to which domestic technology is a substitute or complement for foreign R&D.

8.4   Data

There are two available sources of detailed information on the R&D activities of multinational firms located in a large number of countries. The first source is the 1989 Benchmark Survey of the Bureau of Economic Analysis (BEA) of the U.S. Department of Commerce. This survey, the results of which are reported in U.S. Department of Commerce (1992), is the most recent comprehensive survey of the activities of the foreign affiliates of American multinational firms. The survey covers activities during 1989. In order to protect the confidentiality of survey respondents, BEA does not divulge the responses of individual firms and reports country aggregates only for those countries in which there are sufficient numbers of U.S. firms with sizable activities that aggregate figures do not reveal information about individual firms. Useful R&D and royalty data are available for affiliates in 43 foreign countries for 1989.

The second source of information is the 1987 survey of foreign direct investment in the United States, reported in U.S. Department of Commerce (1990). This survey describes the activities of foreign-owned firms in the United States during 1987. Because of data suppressions and other limitations, useful data are available on investors from 27 different countries during 1987.

The goal of the statistical work is to examine the relationship between royalty tax rates and levels of R&D activity, both for American firms investing in foreign countries and for foreign firms investing in the United States. The difficulty that such a study encounters is that R&D levels differ for reasons that have nothing to do with tax rates. One nontax factor that is clearly associated with R&D spending is the degree of R&D intensity in the countries in which multinational firms have operations. The foreign affiliates of American multinationals located in countries whose economies are R&D intensive tend to perform more R&D than do affiliates located in other countries. Similarly, foreign-owned affiliates in the United States tend to invest more in R&D if their parent firms are located in technologically intensive countries.[17]

17. At a first pass, this association is suggestive of a complementary relationship between local R&D and imported technology, since affiliates of multinational firms headquartered in R&D-intensive countries probably face lower real costs of importing technology than do affiliates of firms from other countries. But differences in the technological intensities of parent firms also reflect heterogeneity between affiliates that can invalidate such an inference.

Information is available from the National Science Foundation (1992) on the R&D intensities of a large number of countries. The National Science Foundation constructs indices that reflect national R&D/GNP ratios; because of data limitations, these ratios are not all calculated using data for the same year, though most observations represent the period 1986–88.[18] In the empirical work that follows, the variables that influence R&D demand are interacted with these country-level measures of R&D intensity. This procedure represents a simple, if rather unsubtle, adjustment for heterogeneity among countries in the extent to which their firms undertake R&D. Local R&D intensity can have an important impact on the demand for imported technology as well, so the R&D intensity variable appears in the royalty equations. Since R&D intensity is likely to have a less direct impact on royalties than it does on R&D expenditures, the R&D intensity variable enters the royalty equations independent of the other explanatory variables.

Information on tax systems and tax rates is reported by Price Waterhouse (various issues). In the empirical work that follows, firms are assumed to face effective tax rates on their technology-related activities equal to statutory corporate tax rates in host countries. Tables 8.3 and 8.4 report means and standard deviations of the variables used in the empirical work.

8.5   Foreign Affiliates of American Multinational Corporations

The model described by equations (1)–(6) carries the implication that technology-related royalty payments and R&D spending levels should respond to local tax rates. Specifically, the model predicts that higher withholding taxes on royalties will reduce royalty payments both by discouraging technology transfers and by reducing the ratio of reported royalties to the values of technologies transferred.

The regressions reported in table 8.5 test these implications on the data that describe the behavior of the foreign affiliates of American multinational corporations for the year 1989. Table 8.5 presents estimates of the coefficients that correspond to the implied specification of the royalty demand equation that emerges from equations (3) and (5). The dependent variable is a ratio, the numerator of which is royalties paid by the foreign affiliates of U.S. firms to their parent companies, and the denominator of which is total sales by the affiliates.[19] Data represent country aggregates.

18. R&D/GNP ratios change little from year to year, as evidenced by the time-series data on France, Germany, Japan, the United Kingdom, and the United States presented in table 8.2. These economies, which are among the most R&D intensive in the world, exhibit only gradual movements in R&D intensity relative to each other. This pattern suggests that time-invariant cross-sectional differences in R&D intensity are likely to be much more important than any differences created by the asynchronous nature of the data reported by the National Science Foundation.

19. The equations reported in table 8.5 were all rerun using total royalties paid in place of royalties paid to U.S. parents, with very similar results (and not surprisingly, since, as table 8.1 indicates, 80 percent of all royalties paid by the foreign affiliates of American firms go to the parent companies of the affiliates paying the royalties). The regressions reported in table 8.5 use

Table 8.2   **R&D Expenditure as a Percentage of GNP, 1961–89**

Year	France	West Germany	Japan	United Kingdom	United States
1961	1.4	–	1.4	2.5	2.7
1962	1.5	1.2	1.5	–	2.7
1963	1.6	1.4	1.5	–	2.8
1964	1.8	1.6	1.5	2.3	2.9
1965	2.0	1.7	1.6	–	2.8
1966	2.1	1.8	1.5	2.3	2.8
1967	2.2	2.0	1.6	2.3	2.8
1968	2.1	2.0	1.7	2.2	2.8
1969	2.0	1.8	1.7	2.3	2.7
1970	1.9	2.1	1.9	–	2.6
1971	1.9	2.2	1.9	–	2.4
1972	1.9	2.2	1.9	2.1	2.4
1973	1.8	2.1	2.0	–	2.3
1974	1.8	2.1	2.0	–	2.2
1975	1.8	2.2	2.0	2.1	2.2
1976	1.8	2.1	2.0	–	2.2
1977	1.8	2.1	2.0	–	2.2
1978	1.8	2.2	2.0	2.2	2.1
1979	1.8	2.4	2.1	–	2.2
1980	1.8	2.4	2.2	–	2.3
1981	2.0	2.5	2.3	2.4	2.4
1982	2.1	2.6	2.4	–	2.5
1983	2.1	2.6	2.6	2.2	2.6
1984	2.2	2.6	2.6	–	2.7
1985	2.3	2.8	2.8	2.3	2.8
1986	2.3	2.8	2.8	2.4	2.8
1987	2.3	2.9	2.8	2.3	2.8
1988	2.3	2.9	2.9	2.2	2.7
1989	2.3	2.9	3.0	2.0	2.7

Source: National Science Foundation (1991).

Note: French data are based on gross domestic product (GDP); consequently, percentages may be slightly overstated compared to GNP. Omissions (–) indicate that R&D data are unavilable.

The estimates reported in column (1) of table 8.5 imply that royalty payments respond negatively to royalty tax rates and are close to unaffected by statutory tax rates. The coefficients indicate that, at a statutory tax rate of 35 percent, a 10 percent reduction in the withholding tax rate on royalties stimulates additional royalty payments equal to 0.1 percent of sales. The implied elasticity of royalty payments with respect to the royalty tax rate, calculated using these estimates and mean values of the variables as reported in table 8.3,

---

royalties paid to parent companies because only for those royalties is it clear at what rate the royalties will be taxed.

Table 8.3   **Variable Means and Standard Deviations: Foreign Affiliates of U.S. Corporations, 1989**

Variable	Mean	Standard Deviation	N
Parent royalties/Sales	0.00774	0.00693	41
R&D/Labor compensation	0.05370	0.06317	43
R&D for affiliate/Total R&D	0.89466	0.16576	38
R&D/GDP	0.01080	0.00878	41
$w^*/(1 - \tau^*)$	0.42149	0.54876	41
$\tau^*/(1 - \tau^*)$	0.65270	0.29224	41
$(w^* - \tau^*)/1 - \tau^*)$	−0.23121	0.46387	41
$[(w^* - \tau^*)/(1 - \tau^*)]^2$	0.26339	0.27492	41
$1/(1 - \tau^*)$	1.65270	0.29224	41
w^*	0.20784	0.25274	38
τ^*	0.37666	0.09167	38
$[w^*/(1 - \tau^*)](\text{R&D/GNP})$	0.00263	0.00446	43
$[\tau^*/(1 - \tau^*)](\text{R&D/GNP})$	0.00737	0.00797	43
$[(w^* - \tau^*)/(1 - \tau^*)](\text{R&D/GNP})$	−0.00475	0.00752	43
$[(w^* - \tau^*)/(1 - \tau^*)]^2(\text{R&D/GNP})$	0.00388	0.00641	43
$[1/(1 - \tau^*)](\text{R&D/GNP})$	0.01793	0.01602	43

Note: The regressions reported in tables 8.5–8.7 use these variables. The first three represent country-level aggregate activities of foreign affiliates of U.S. corporations in 1989, as reported in U.S. Department of Commerce (1992). The variable R&D/GNP represents country R&D/GNP ratios reported by the National Science Foundation (1991). The variable τ^* represents local statutory corporate tax rates, and w^* represents withholding tax rates imposed by foreign countries on royalty payments to the United States. Observations are country-level aggregates of the behavior of all U.S.-owned affiliates.

Table 8.4   **Variable Means and Standard Deviations: Foreign-Owned Affiliates in the United States, 1987**

Variable	Mean	Standard Deviation	N
Royalties/Sales	0.00759	0.00936	27
R&D/Labor compensation	0.08749	0.13590	27
R&D/GNP	0.01511	0.00932	27
w	0.12037	0.12805	27
$w(1 - \text{FTC})$	0.06481	0.11752	27
w^2	0.03028	0.03998	27
$w^2(1 - \text{FTC})$	0.01750	0.03532	27
$w(\text{R&D/GNP})$	0.00120	0.00190	27
$w(1 - \text{FTC})(\text{R&D/GNP})$	0.00068	0.00181	27
$w^2(\text{R&D/GNP})$	0.00028	0.00056	27
$w^2(1 - \text{FTC})(\text{R&D/GNP})$	0.00017	0.00054	27

Note: The regressions reported in tables 8.8 and 8.9 use these variables. The first two variables represent country-level aggregate activities of foreign-owned affiliates in the United States in 1987, as reported in U.S. Department of Commerce (1990). The variable R&D/GNP represents country R&D/GNP ratios reported by the National Science Foundation (1991). The variable w represents the withholding tax rate imposed by the United States on royalty payments from the United States. The variable FTC equals unity if an investor's home country taxes worldwide income and grants foreign tax credits to its residents, and equals zero otherwise. Observations are country-level aggregates of the behavior of all U.S.-owned affiliates.

Table 8.5   **Royalty Tax Rates and Royalty Payments by Foreign Affiliates of U.S. Corporations, 1989**

Variable	(1)	(2)	(3)	(4)	(5)
Constant	0.0060	0.0014	0.0142	0.0016	0.0176
	(0.0027)	(0.0014)	(0.0067)	(0.0015)	(0.0078)
R&D/GNP	0.4310	0.4023	0.4310	0.4310	0.4002
	(0.1201)	(0.1215)	(0.1201)	(0.1282)	(0.1240)
$w^*/(1 - \tau^*)$	−0.0068				
	(0.0027)				
$\tau^*/(1 - \tau^*)$	−0.0013				
	(0.0042)				
$(w^* - \tau^*)/(1 - \tau^*)$		−0.0061	−0.0068	−0.0063	−0.0066
		(0.0025)	(0.0027)	(0.0025)	(0.0027)
$[(w^* - \tau^*)/(1 - \tau^*)]^2$				−0.0027	0.0039
				(0.0037)	(0.0046)
$1/(1 - \tau^*)$			−0.0082		−0.0107
			(0.0042)		(0.0052)
$\hat{\sigma}$	0.0053	0.0055	0.0053	0.0055	0.0052
	(0.0007)	(0.0007)	(0.0007)	(0.0007)	(0.0006)
log L	125.0988	122.8083	125.0988	123.0681	125.4541
N	41	41	41	41	41

Note: The columns report coefficients from Tobit regressions in which the dependent variable is the ratio of royalties paid by foreign affiliates of U.S. corporations to their parent companies to the affiliates' total sales. The variable R&D/GNP represents country R&D/GNP ratios reported by the National Science Foundation (1991). The variable τ^* represents local statutory corporate tax rates, and w^* represents withholding tax rates imposed by foreign countries on royalty payments to the United States. Observations are country-level aggregates of the behavior of all U.S.-owned affiliates. Standard errors are in parentheses.

is approximately −0.4.[20] If sales are unaffected by changes in royalty tax rates, then this figure implies that doubling the royalty tax rate reduces royalties by 40 percent, a sizable fraction.

Since sales may respond to tax rate changes, this calculation may understate the responsiveness of royalties, but nevertheless strongly suggests that the true elasticity lies between zero and −1. It is, however, important to note that the aggregate nature of the data may introduce considerable measurement error that biases the estimated coefficient toward zero. The sign of any bias introduced by omitted variables is ambiguous, though the magnitude could be large.

The results presented in column (2) of table 8.5 indicate that royalties also respond significantly to differences between royalty withholding tax rates and statutory tax rates. As predicted, the local R&D/GNP ratio is positively correlated with royalty payments. Alternative specifications reported in columns (3)–(5) of table 8.5 yield similar conclusions: high tax rates on royalties are associated with lower ratios of royalty payments to total sales.

20. Exercises such as this one are fraught with dangers, since variables may exhibit considerable differences between their conditional and unconditional means. The calculation in the text is meant only to be illustrative.

The specifications used to obtain the results described in table 8.5 were changed in a number of ways, in every case generating similar results. One specification issue concerns the appropriate choice of denominator for the dependent variable. Specifications in which labor compensation replaces sales as the denominator of the dependent variable yield results that are almost identical to those reported in table 8.5. Due to the somewhat heterogeneous nature of royalties, it seems most appropriate to scale this variable by sales. In the regressions reported in tables 8.6 and 8.9, the dependent variables that represent R&D expenditures are scaled by labor compensation in manufacturing for somewhat different reasons. Manufacturing affiliates account for approximately 90 percent of the R&D activity of foreign-owned affiliates in the U.S. and of the foreign affiliates of U.S. firms. Labor expenditures share with R&D expenditures the feature of immediate deductibility for tax purposes[21] and are more reasonably thought of as the product of firm choices than are sales, which may be functions of R&D. All of the R&D demand equations in reported in tables 8.6 and 8.9 were rerun scaling the dependent variable by labor expenditures, with results that are very similar to those reported in the tables.

8.5.1   A First Approach to Estimating the Impact of Taxes on R&D

The results reported in table 8.5 indicate that royalty payments by the foreign affiliates of U.S. multinational firms respond to tax rates in the predicted manner. The model described in equations (1)–(6) does not, however, carry a prediction about the sign of the effect of tax rates on R&D expenditure levels, and the object of the regressions reported in tables 8.6 and 8.7 is to measure the sign of any effect that may be present. The regressions reported in tables 8.6 and 8.7 address this measurement problem using very different methodologies—though, as it happens, the results point to conclusions that are quite similar.

Table 8.6 presents regressions that estimate of the impact of the tax treatment of royalties on the R&D intensities of foreign affiliates of U.S. firms, using specifications drawn from the model described in equations (1)–(6). The dependent variable is the ratio of R&D expenditures in 1989 to manufacturing labor compensation in 1989. The results in the table are strongly suggestive of an important impact of royalty taxes on R&D activity, but not all of the estimated coefficients in the table are significant. The strongest and most parsimonious specification is presented in column (2) of table 8.6, and here the estimated coefficients suggest that an unfavorable tax climate for royalties is associated with greater R&D activity. Imported technology and local R&D appear to be substitutes.

21. Of course, some countries (including the United States) offer tax credits and other inducements to firms that perform R&D (and in some cases to firms that hire labor). A brief survey of country practices indicates, however, that sizable R&D subsidies are rare (e.g., see Hall 1993 for an analysis of the magnitude of the marginal subsidy provided R&D in the United States by the research and experimentation tax credit), and that the primary subsidy comes from the immediate deductibility of R&D expenses that almost all industrialized countries provide.

Table 8.6   Local Tax Rates and R&D Intensities of Foreign Affiliates of U.S.
Corporations, 1989

Variable	(1)	(2)	(3)	(4)	(5)
Constant	−0.0260	−0.0274	−0.0260	−0.0208	−0.0209
	(0.0146)	(0.0150)	(0.0146)	(0.0146)	(0.0147)
R&D/GNP	10.0631	8.8330	12.7071	8.0861	8.5018
	(2.0237)	(1.8161)	(3.4801)	(1.7744)	(4.7042)
$[w^*/(1 - \tau^*)] \cdot$ (R&D/GNP)	3.1769				
	(2.1870)				
$[\tau^*/(1 - \tau^*)] \cdot$ (R&D/GNP)	−5.8209				
	(2.3508)				
$[(w^* - \tau^*)/(1 - \tau^*)] \cdot$ (R&D/GNP)		4.2941	3.1769	0.3143	0.3981
		(2.0724)	(2.1870)	(2.9011)	(3.0308)
$[(w^* - \tau^*)/(1 - \tau^*)]^2 \cdot$ (R&D/ GNP)				−4.4628	−4.2460
				(2.4171)	(3.3159)
$[1/(1 - \tau^*)] \cdot$ (R&D/GNP)			−2.6440		−2.2590
			(2.0200)		(2.7136)
$\hat{\sigma}$	0.0497	0.0509	0.0497	0.0487	0.0487
	(0.0062)	(0.0063)	(0.0062)	(0.0060)	(0.0060)
log L	47.1507	46.3131	47.1507	47.9522	47.9568
N	43	43	43	43	43

Note: The columns report coefficients from Tobit regressions in which the dependent variable is the ratio of R&D expenditures by foreign affiliates of U.S. corporations to the affiliates' expenditures on labor compensation in manufcturing. The variable R&D/GNP represents country R&D/GNP ratios reported by the National Science Foundation (1991). The variable τ^* represents local statutory corporate tax rates, and w^* represents withholding tax rates imposed by foreign countries on royalty payments to the United States. Observations are country-level aggregates of the behavior of all U.S.-owned affiliates. Standard errors are in parentheses.

Columns (3)–(5) of table 8.6 report the results of alternative specifications of the model. Two aspects of these results are noteworthy. The first is that the estimated coefficients on the variable $[1/(1 - \tau^*)] \cdot$ (R&D/GNP) are always insignificant. This variable appears as one part of the first term on the right-hand side of equation (5), and the estimated coefficient captures the effect of c, the cost of developing technology at home to transfer to affiliates abroad. The insignificance of the estimated coefficient implies either that firms transfer nonrival technologies to their affiliates, so $c = 0$, or that the estimating methodology is not powerful enough to identify an important effect. The second noteworthy aspect of the results is that the specifications that include quadratic tax terms generate insignificant results. These results may reflect the limited ability of the estimators to distinguish the effects of collinear variables in a small sample.

Using the coefficient estimate from the equation presented in column (1) of table 8.6, the implied elasticity of R&D activity with respect to the withholding tax rate on royalties (evaluating all variables at their sample means) is approximately 0.16. This figure is smaller than the implied royalty elasticity calculated from table 8.5, which is reassuring because own-price elasticities are usually stronger than cross-price elasticities. This estimated elasticity suggests that local R&D is a mild substitute for imported technology, but it is helpful to consider additional evidence before drawing any conclusions.

8.5.2   A Second Approach to Estimating the Impact of Taxes on R&D

One difficulty that arises in estimating the impact of royalty tax rates on local R&D levels is that many omitted variables influence R&D spending. It is possible that these variables are correlated with royalty withholding tax rates in a way that biases the estimated tax rate coefficients and generates a misleading conclusion concerning the substitutability of R&D for imported technology. The regressions reported in table 8.6 control for local technological environments simply by interacting the tax variables with the R&D/GNP measure.

An alternative approach is to use available information that distinguishes the R&D activity of foreign affiliates of American firms for their own purposes from R&D activity that they undertake on behalf of others. Both types of R&D activity are likely to be influenced by local economic and technological conditions. It is, however, possible that the latter type of contract-style R&D performed for others is generally unaffected by the availability of technology imports from parent firms. If not, then R&D performed for others serves as a control group with which to compare R&D performed by affiliates for their own purposes. Under the hypothesis that R&D performed for others is unaffected by technology imports, the fraction of an affiliate's total R&D activity undertaken for itself is a positive function of royalty taxes if local R&D and imported technology are substitutes, and a negative function of royalty taxes if local R&D and imported technology are complements.

There are 38 countries in the sample for which the BEA data distinguish R&D performed by affiliates for themselves from R&D performed by affiliates for others. Table 8.7 presents estimated coefficients from regressions in which the dependent variable is the ratio of R&D performed by affiliates for themselves to total R&D by affiliates. The results once again suggest that local R&D is a substitute for imported technology. In the regression reported in column (1) of table 8.7, the estimated coefficient on royalty withholding tax rates is positive and significant; the same is true of the coefficient on the difference between withholding and statutory tax rates reported in column (2). The coefficient estimates reported in column (2) indicate that a 10 percent change in the difference between foreign withholding and statutory tax rates (normalized by one minus the foreign statutory tax rate) is associated with a 2.6 percent change in the intensity of R&D activity by affiliates for themselves.

Columns (3)–(5) of table 8.7 report the results of alternative specifications of the R&D demand equation. The coefficient estimates from these specifications are consistent with those reported in columns (1) and (2) and are also consistent with the results reported in table 8.6. In particular, the estimated

Table 8.7   **Local Tax Rates and the Own-Intensity of R&D by Foreign Affiliates of U.S. Corporations, 1989**

Variable	(1)	(2)	(3)	(4)	(5)
Constant	0.9644	0.9294	0.9750	0.9447	0.8776
	(0.1273)	(0.0685)	(0.3608)	(0.2065)	(0.4103)
$w^*/(1 - \tau^*)$	0.2654				
	(0.1333)				
$\tau^*/(1 - \tau^*)$	−0.2048				
	(0.2028)				
$(w^* - \tau^*)/(1 - \tau^*)$		0.2562	0.2654		0.2362
		(0.1256)	(0.1333)		(0.1509)
w^*				0.4378	
				(0.2333)	
τ^*				−0.3872	
				(0.5543)	
$[(w^* - \tau^*)/(1 - \tau^*)]^2$					−0.1071
					(0.2982)
$1/(1 - \tau^*)$			0.0606		0.1311
			(0.1923)		(0.2766)
$\hat{\sigma}$	0.2527	0.2527	0.2527	0.2550	0.2525
	(0.0435)	(0.0434)	(0.0435)	(0.0439)	(0.0434)
log L	−12.1006	−12.1524	−12.1006	−12.5287	−12.0370
N	38	38	38	38	38

Note: The columns report coefficients from Tobit regressions in which the dependent variable is the ratio of R&D expenditures by foreign affiliates of U.S. corporations for their own use to the affiliates' total R&D expenditures. The variable τ^* represents local statutory corporate tax rates, and w^* represents withholding tax rates imposed by foreign countries on royalty payments to the United States. Observations are country-level aggregates of the behavior of all U.S.-owned affiliates. Standard errors are in parentheses.

coefficient of the variable $1/(1 - \tau^*)$ is again insignificant. The estimates reported in column (1) of table 8.7 imply that the elasticity of R&D spending with respect to royalty withholding taxes (evaluating all variables at their sample means) is approximately 0.11, which resembles the elasticity calculated from estimates reported in table 8.6.

The regressions reported in tables 8.6 and 8.7 offer consistent evidence that the aggregate behavior of the foreign affiliates of American multinational firms exhibits substitution of local R&D for imported technology. It is important to note, however, that there can be more than one interpretation of this pattern at the level of individual firms. One possibility is that tax differences influence the behavior of firms located in different countries. A second possibility is that tax differences encourage specific firms to locate in certain countries and not in others, *without* influencing the R&D intensities of individual firms.[22] A third,

22. Lipsey et al. (1990) examine the impact of host country characteristics on the attributes—particularly R&D intensities—of multinational firms choosing to locate within the country. They do not, however, consider the impact of tax policies.

and perhaps the most likely, possibility represents some combination of the first two. The use of aggregate data makes it impossible to use the observed pattern of behavior to distinguish these explanations; however, for many purposes, it may not be necessary to distinguish them.

8.6   Foreign-Owned Affiliates in the United States

The behavior of foreign-owned affiliates in the United States offers additional evidence on the responsiveness of R&D activity to royalty tax rates. This evidence must, however, be interpreted with caution, owing to heterogeneous circumstances of foreign firms that invest in the United States and the small sample size of 27 foreign countries for which sufficient data are available.

Home country tax treatments of foreign multinational firms that invest in the United States differ according to individual circumstances and national law. There are two dimensions along which the variation between investors is most important. The home governments of some foreign investors tax the worldwide incomes of their residents while granting credits for foreign taxes paid, while other governments exempt all foreign-source income from tax.[23] A second dimension along which tax systems differ concerns the degree of integration of personal and corporate taxes. For some countries, their corporation taxes largely represent advanced withholding taxes against personal tax liabilities.

The specification of royalty equations corresponding to the system described by equations (1)–(6) is somewhat different in the case of foreign investors in the United States than it is in the regressions reported in table 8.5. To start, the tax rate τ^* is the U.S. tax rate, which is the same for all foreign investors. The value of c, the cost of producing technology for export, need not be similar for different foreign investors and is captured in the estimating equations by the inclusion of R&D/GNP as an explanatory variable. And there may be important differences between the incentives facing investors from foreign tax credit countries and those facing investors from countries that do not grant foreign tax credits.

Table 8.8 presents estimates of the determinants of royalty payments by foreign-owned affiliates in the United States in 1987. The coefficient on the withholding tax rate in the regression presented in the column (2) of table 8.8 implies that raising the tax rate by 10 percent reduces the royalty/sales ratio by 0.74 percent. The estimated coefficient lies just at the margin of statistical significance. To understand its magnitude in a different way, the implied elasticity of royalties/sales, evaluating all variables at their population means, is approximately -0.12. If sales are unaffected by changes in royalty tax rates, then this figure implies that doubling the royalty tax rates reduces royalties by 12 percent.

23. Of course, this dichotomous breakdown greatly oversimplifies the many distinctions and subtleties that foreign tax systems exhibit.

Table 8.8   Royalty Tax Rates and Royalty Payments by Foreign-Owned
               Affiliates in the United States, 1987

Variable	(1)	(2)	(3)	(4)	(5)
Constant	−0.0012	0.0005	−0.0004	0.0007	−0.0003
	(0.0008)	(0.0011)	(0.0008)	(0.0011)	(0.0008)
R&D/GNP	0.1100	0.0541	0.0834	0.0529	0.0831
	(0.0432)	(0.0471)	(0.0418)	(0.0458)	(0.0413)
w		−0.0074		−0.0174	
		(0.0036)		(0.0116)	
$w(1 - \text{FTC})$			−0.0073		−0.0151
			(0.0038)		(0.0187)
w^2				0.0342	
				(0.0375)	
$w^2(1 - \text{FTC})$					0.0269
					(0.0630)
$\hat{\sigma}$	0.0018	0.0016	0.0016	0.0016	0.0016
	(0.0003)	(0.0003)	(0.0003)	(0.0003)	(0.0003)
$\log L$	77.1371	79.3389	79.1162	79.7464	79.2077
N	27	27	27	27	27

Note: The columns report coefficients from Tobit regressions in which the dependent variable is the ratio of royalties paid by foreign-owned affiliates to the affiliates' total U.S. sales in 1987. The variable R&D/GNP represents country R&D/GNP ratios reported by the National Science Foundation (1991). The variable w represents the withholding tax rate imposed by the United States on royalty payments from the United States. The variable FTC equals unity if an investor's home country taxes worldwide income and grants foreign tax credits to its residents, and equals zero otherwise. Observations are country-level aggregates of the behavior of all foreign-owned affiliates. Standard errors are in parentheses.

Column (3) of table 8.8 presents the same regression in which the withholding tax rate is now transformed to be zero for all investors from foreign tax credit countries. The results are very similar to those reported in column (2). Columns (4) and (5) report results of regressions in which squares of the withholding tax rates are introduced; the coefficient estimates are insignificant, reflecting the multicollinearity of the two tax rate variables and the limited amount of variation in a sample of this size.

Table 8.9 presents estimated coefficients from regressions that investigate the correlation between the R&D intensity of foreign-owned affiliates in the United States and the tax variables that influence the cost of imported technology. One striking feature of all of the regressions presented in table 8.9 is the strong correlation between the R&D intensity of foreign-owned affiliates in the United States and the R&D intensity of the countries in which their parent firms are located. Column (2) presents the simplest specification that includes tax rate variables; the estimated coefficient on the interaction between the withholding tax rate and home country R&D intensity is positive and significant. The implied elasticity of R&D with respect to the cost of imported technology (evaluated at sample means) is approximately 0.3. This is a very sizable

Table 8.9   **Royalty Tax Rates and R&D Intensities of Foreign-Owned Affiliates in the United States, 1987**

Variable	(1)	(2)	(3)	(4)	(5)
Constant	−0.1844	−0.1716	−0.1345	−0.1625	−0.1387
	(0.0697)	(0.0565)	(0.0456)	(0.0547)	(0.0472)
R&D/GNP	14.6146	12.1191	10.5524	12.2114	10.6242
	(3.5479)	(2.9640)	(2.3883)	(2.8594)	(2.4134)
w(R&D/GNP)		30.8403		−5.6039	
		(11.9140)		(42.1940)	
$w(1 - FTC) \cdot$(R&D/GNP)			45.4557		72.9530
			(10.0257)		(63.4897)
w^2(R&D/GNP)				128.6451	
				(142.4354)	
$w^2(1 - FTC) \cdot$(R&D/GNP)					−93.2700
					(212.7782)
$\hat{\sigma}$		0.1335	0.1094	0.0891	0.1060	0.0892
		(0.0225)	(0.0190)	(0.0153)	(0.0185)	(0.0154)
log L		6.7117	9.2883	13.0824	9.6807	13.1794
N		27	27	27	27	27

Note: The columns report coefficients from Tobit regressions in which the dependent variable is the ratio of the U.S. R&D expenditures of foreign-owned affiliates to the affiliates' total U.S. manufacturing labor compensation in 1987. The variable R&D/GNP represents country R&D/GNP ratios reported by the National Science Foundation (1991). The variable w represents the withholding tax rate imposed by the United States on royalty payments from the United States. The variable FTC equals unity if an investor's home country taxes worldwide income and grants foreign tax credits to its residents, and equals zero otherwise. Observations are country-level aggregates of the behavior of all foreign-owned affiliates. Standard errors are in parentheses.

elasticity, particularly in view of the smaller own-price elasticity of royalties implied by the estimates reported in table 8.8. Furthermore, the responsiveness of royalties to withholding tax rates reflects changes in reporting behavior in addition to changes in amounts of technology transferred. The elasticity implies that, in the absence of an effect arising through the scale of operations, doubling the withholding tax rate raises R&D expenditures by 30 percent. This estimated response magnitude is very large and may reflect the imprecision of estimates drawn from so small a sample. Nevertheless, it is striking that the pattern of substitutability between R&D and imported technology appears for foreign investors in the United States as well as for American investors in other countries.[24]

Column (3) of table 8.9 presents estimates from the specification in which the withholding tax rate is interacted with a variable that equals zero if the investor's parent company is located in a foreign tax credit country, and equals

24. Unfortunately, BEA does not require foreign-owned firms in the United States to distinguish the R&D they perform for their own use from R&D that they perform for others, so it is not possible to estimate equations of the type reported in table 8.7 for foreign investors in the United States.

one otherwise. The results are qualitatively very similar to those presented in column (2), with the difference that the estimated R&D appears in this specification to be even more responsive to withholding tax rates. Columns (4) and (5) present regression results for specifications that include quadratic withholding tax rate terms, which again exhibit symptoms of multicollinearity.

Evidence on the behavior of foreign owned affiliates in the United States suggests conclusions that are very similar to those that emerge from the behavior of the foreign affiliates of American corporations. Foreign investors in the United States pay fewer royalties, and use more R&D-intensive operations, when facing higher tax rates on royalties paid to their home countries. The restricted size of the sample of investing foreign countries makes statistical inference difficult, but the estimated coefficients indicate a responsiveness that is somewhat greater than that for the foreign affiliates of American corporations.

8.7   Conclusion

This paper uses information on the behavior of the foreign affiliates of U.S. firms and foreign-owned affiliates in the United States to estimate the relationship between technology imports and local R&D. The idea is to use the tax treatment of royalty payments to identify the degree of substitutability between these sources of technology. Evidence from the actions of American and foreign firms indicates that R&D expenditures respond to local tax rates, and that technology imports and local R&D are substitutes. The substitutability of these two sources of technology carries numerous implications for the impact of tax policy on R&D activity, particularly when contrasted with the complementarity that is sometimes thought to characterize their relationship.

References

Blomstrom, Magnus. 1991. Host country benefits of foreign investment. NBER Working Paper no. 3615. Cambridge, Mass.: National Bureau of Economic Research, February.

Blomstrom, Magnus, and Ari Kokko. 1993. Policies to encourage inflows of technology through foreign multinationals. NBER Working Paper no. 4289. Cambridge, Mass.: National Bureau of Economic Research, March.

Davidson, W. H., and Donald G. McFetridge. 1984. International technology transactions and the theory of the firm. *Journal of Industrial Economics* 32:253–64.

Dixit, Avinash. 1988. International R&D competition and policy. In *International competitiveness,* ed. A. Michael Spence and Heather A. Hazard, 149–71. Cambridge: Ballinger.

Ethier, Wilfred J., and James R. Markusen. 1991. Multinational firms, technology diffusion and trade. NBER Working Paper no. 3825. Cambridge, Mass.: National Bureau of Economic Research, August.

Germidis, Dimitri, ed. 1977. *Transfer of technology by multinational corporations* Paris: Organisation for Economic Co-operation and Development.

Griliches, Zvi. 1991. The search for R&D spillovers. NBER Working Paper no. 3768. Cambridge, Mass.: National Bureau of Economic Research, July.

Grubert, Harry, and John Mutti. 1991. Taxes, tariffs, and transfer pricing in multinational corporate decision making. *Review of Economics and Statistics* 73:285–93.

Hall, Bronwyn H. 1993. R&D tax policy during the 1980s: Success or failure? In *Tax policy and the economy,* vol. 7, ed. James M. Poterba, 1–35. Cambridge: MIT Press.

Harris, David, Randall Morck, Joel Slemrod, and Bernard Yeung. 1993. Income shifting in U.S. multinational corporations. In *Studies in international taxation,* ed. Alberto Giovannini, R. Glenn Hubbard, and Joel Slemrod, 277–302. Chicago: University of Chicago Press.

Hartman, David G. 1985. Tax policy and foreign direct investment. *Journal of Public Economics* 26:107–21.

Hines, James R., Jr. 1991. The flight paths of migratory corporations. *Journal of Accounting, Auditing and Finance* 6:447–79.

———. 1993. On the sensitivity of R&D to delicate tax changes: The behavior of U.S. multinationals in the 1980s. In *Studies in international taxation,* ed. Alberto Giovannini, R. Glenn Hubbard, and Joel Slemrod, 149–87. Chicago: University of Chicago Press.

———. 1994a. Credit and deferral as international investment incentives. *Journal of Public Economics* 55:323–47.

———. 1994b. No place like home: Tax incentives and the location of R&D by American multinationals. In *Tax policy and the economy,* vol. 8, ed. James M. Poterba, 65–104. Cambridge: MIT Press.

Hines, James R., Jr., and R. Glenn Hubbard. 1990. Coming home to America: Dividend repatriations by U.S. multinationals. In *Taxation in the global economy,* ed. Assaf Razin and Joel Slemrod, 161–200. Chicago: University of Chicago Press.

Hines, James R., Jr., and Eric M. Rice. 1994. Fiscal paradise: Foreign tax havens and American business. *Quarterly Journal of Economics* 109:149–82.

Kopits, George F. 1976. Intra-firm royalties crossing frontiers and transfer-pricing behaviour. *Economic Journal* 86:791–805.

Lawlor, William R., ed. 1985. *Cross-border transactions between related companies: A summary of tax rules.* Deventer, Netherlands: Kluwer.

Lipsey, Robert E., Magnus Blomstrom, and Irving B. Kravis. 1990. R&D by multinational firms and host country exports. In *Science and technology: Lessons for development policy,* ed. Robert E. Evenson and Gustav Ranis, 271–300. Boulder, Colo.: Westview.

Mansfield, Edwin, and Anthony Romeo. 1980. Technology transfer to overseas subsidiaries by U.S.-based firms. *Quarterly Journal of Economics* 95:737–50.

Mansfield, Edwin, David Teece, and Anthony Romeo. 1979. Overseas research and development by U.S.-based firms. *Economica* 46:187–96.

Nadiri, M. Ishaq. 1993. Innovations and technological spillovers. NBER Working Paper no. 4423. Cambridge, Mass.: National Bureau of Economic Research, August.

National Science Foundation. 1991. *International science and technology data update: 1991* (NSF 91-309). Washington, D.C.: National Science Foundation.

———. 1993. *Selected data on research and development in industry: 1991.* Washington, D.C.: National Science Foundation.

Price Waterhouse. Various issues. *Corporate taxes—A worldwide summary.* New York: Price Waterhouse.

Reinganum, Jennifer F. 1989. The timing of innovation: Research, development, and diffusion. In *Handbook of industrial organization,* vol. 1, ed. Richard Schmalensee and Robert D. Willig. Amsterdam: North-Holland.

Scholes, Myron S., and Mark A. Wolfson. 1992. *Taxes and business strategy: A planning approach.* Englewood Cliffs, N.J.: Prentice Hall.

Teece, David J. 1976. *The multinational corporation and the resource cost of international technology transfer.* Cambridge, Mass.: Ballinger.

U.S. Department of Commerce. Bureau of Economic Analysis. Various issues. *Foreign direct investment in the United States.* Washington, D.C.: Government Printing Office.

———. 1985. *U.S. direct investment abroad: 1982 Benchmark Survey data.* Washington, D.C.: Government Printing Office.

———. 1990. *Foreign direct investment in the United States: 1987 Benchmark Survey, final results.* Washington, D.C.: Government Printing Office.

———. 1992. *U.S. direct investment abroad: 1989 Benchmark Survey, final results.* Washington, D.C.: Government Printing Office.

U.S. Joint Committee on Taxation. 1981. *General explanation of the Economic Recovery Tax Act of 1981* Washington, D.C.: Government Printing Office.

Wang, Jian-Ye, and Magnus Blomstrom. 1992. Foreign investment and technology transfer: A simple model. *European Economic Review* 36:137–55.

Zejan, Mario C. 1990. R&D activities in affiliates of Swedish multinational enterprises. *Scandinavian Journal of Economics* 92:487–500.

Comment   Adam B. Jaffe

This paper examines the effect of the tax treatment of royalties paid by foreign affiliates for the use of their parents' technology both on the magnitude of such royalties paid and on the expenditures by the affiliates on research and development (R&D). The paper finds that royalty payments do respond negatively to tax rates, and that affiliate R&D is *increased* by higher taxes on royalties, which implies that affiliate R&D and imported technology from the corporate parent are substitutes rather than complements in generating net revenues for the affiliate. The first result is probably satisfying to tax economists, but is of limited significance because we cannot tell how much of the effect corresponds to changes in the use of technology and how much represents changes in the valuation of technology for royalty tax purposes. The second result, however, is a provocative one that is contrary to most people's prior beliefs. If it is true that affiliate R&D is a substitute for parent technology, this would have important implications for understanding multinational corporations and for the design of domestic policy. My comment will address why this result is significant, and then go on to consider how convincing the paper is about the complementarity question.

Significance of the Result

There are a number of reasons why we care about whether parent and affiliate R&D are complements or substitutes. First, there is the important industrial

Adam B. Jaffe is associate professor of economics at Brandeis University and a research associate of the National Bureau of Economic Research.

organization question of how companies decide whether to start operations overseas, and what the role of R&D is in that process. A standard view of why companies engage in overseas investment is that they have intangible assets, such as technology, that are at least partially nonrival across countries, but that it is difficult to capture the returns to these assets through arm's-length transactions such as technology licenses. Hence, establishing overseas operations captures quasi rents to these assets that would otherwise be lost. A puzzle within this view is why companies would then engage in research *at* the affiliate location. A potential answer to this puzzle is that such research is complementary to the home research, either because it is more easily focused on specific conditions of the host-country market (or input markets) or because local R&D allows the parent to benefit from spillovers from the R&D performed in the host country. If parent and affiliate research are *not* complements, then the puzzle of why affiliates do research reappears.[1]

The second reason why complementarity matters is that governments may wish to encourage R&D within their borders because of a belief that R&D generates positive externalities. As Hines discusses, the tax treatment of royalty payments might be an instrument to encourage local R&D, but the instrument can only be used if we know whether raising the cost of "buying" technology from the parent company increases or decreases the incentive to do R&D locally, that is, whether affiliate and parent technology are complements or substitutes.

This policy conundrum is, however, actually more complicated than simply asking whether raising the cost of importing technology stimulates or inhibits local R&D. If the location of R&D matters at all, it has to be the case that R&D spillovers are geographically localized, that is, that technology developed at home creates greater external benefits for domestic firms than does technology developed abroad.[2] This implies that domestic firms are not fully benefiting from technology developed in other countries. It is plausible that the importation of that technology for use by an affiliate might bring with it the spillovers that otherwise would not be readily available to domestic firms. Thus, there is a crucial policy question that is logically prior to the question of whether taxing technology imports encourages or discourages local R&D. That is: Which creates more local externalities, the import of technology from abroad or the production of technology at home? This would seem to turn on the question of whether the spillovers are generated by the process of the creation of technology or by its use. Both the theoretical and empirical literature on spillovers appears to be silent on this question, largely because creation and use are typically thought of as occurring in the same place.

1. I return to this issue below.
2. As the paper mentions, the primary analytical justification for policies to encourage R&D is the belief that R&D generates positive externalities to other firms. If such externalities are *not* geographically localized, then they cannot be a source of differences in growth rates across countries and policymakers should not care whether R&D is done at home or abroad. See Jaffe, Henderson, and Trajtenberg (1993) for evidence on the extent of geographic localization of research spillovers.

An interesting observation derives from the combination of the results that affiliate and parent R&D are substitutes, while parent R&D appears to be "free," that is, sufficiently nonrival across countries that the incremental cost of using parent technology in another affiliate is zero (table 8.6 and related discussion). If both results are correct, then, in the absence of tax distortions, it seems unlikely that affiliates would do R&D (since affiliate R&D is merely a substitute for something that is free). In the presence of taxes, this result no longer holds. It is possible that affiliates would choose to perform what is essentially duplicative R&D, merely to avoid paying withholding taxes on the transfer of the parent's already created knowledge. This result might appear to be highly wasteful from a social point of view, but that is unclear given that the affiliate's R&D will generate spillovers.

Convincingness of the Result on Complementarity

Within the confines of the paper itself, the finding that affiliate and parent R&D appear to be substitutes is quite robust. The paper takes three distinct cuts at the issue: it shows that foreign affiliates of U.S. corporations do more R&D in countries with high withholding rates (table 8.6), that affiliates of foreign corporations do more R&D in the United States if their parents are in countries whose tax treaties with the United States result in higher withholding rates on royalties emanating from the United States (table 8.9), and that foreign affiliates (of U.S. corporations) that operate in high-withholding-rate countries have a higher *fraction* of their R&D that is for their own purposes rather than for contract research (table 8.7).

I do have reservations about two aspects of these results. First, as the paper points out, the effect of the withholding rate on the U.S. R&D of foreign firms is implausibly large, suggesting that affiliate R&D responds *more* to the royalty tax rate than do the royalties themselves, despite the fact that the royalty effect is the sum of a real effect and an effect from the incentive to undervalue technology to reduce the tax. This suggests that some kind of spurious correlation may be at work.

My second reservation derives from the fact that in table 8.6 and table 8.9 (though *not* in table 8.7) the royalty tax effect is estimated from the interaction of the withholding tax rate variable with the R&D intensity of the host country (in the case of foreign affiliates of U.S. firms) or the parent country (in the case of U.S. affiliates of foreign firms). This interaction is motivated by the need to allow for the effects of unobserved differences in the R&D incentives in different countries. Such differences are likely to be important, and the interaction effect is plausible. It is also the case, however, that the R&D/GNP variables are extremely significant on their own in both tables 8.6 and 8.9. It is very likely that the effects of R&D intensity, even ignoring any tax effects, are nonlinear and vary depending on economic and institutional features of the countries involved. This makes it hard to know for sure whether the coefficient on the interaction term is really picking up the effect attributed to it by the model, or whether it is simply picking up additional aspects of the R&D intensity effect.

Overall, whether these results are convincing depends on one's prior belief regarding the complementarity of affiliate R&D and imported technology from the parent. I have a strong prior that they are complements. First, analyses of the relationship between different kinds of R&D in other settings have generally found complementarity. Jaffe (1986) shows that spillovers from the R&D of a technologically related firm can increase another firm's patents, profits, and market value, but the effectiveness of such spillovers is itself a function of how much R&D the spillover-receiving firm performs. That is, firms' own R&D and spillovers from other firms are complements in the generation of economically useful new knowledge. Cohen and Levinthal (1989) find that firms must undertake their own R&D in order to learn about research results produced elsewhere, again suggesting complementarity. Though it is possible that the affiliate and parent R&D combine in a way that is wholly different from how knowledge inside and outside the firm combine, it is unclear why this should be so.

A second reason to expect complementarity is that affiliate R&D ought to facilitate the absorption of locally generated R&D spillovers from other firms. If it is true that R&D spillovers are geographically localized, then one reason to enter a foreign country (particularly an R&D-intensive one such as the United States) would be to absorb its R&D spillovers. If Cohen and Levinthal are right and you have to do your own R&D to absorb spillovers, it seems likely that you have to have a local R&D presence to benefit from local spillovers. To the extent that such spillovers are complements with own R&D, then own local R&D ought to be complementary with parent R&D.

Finally, Hines's paper itself contains results that seem to suggest complementarity. Among firms in the United States that are foreign owned, the strongest predictor of R&D intensity is the R&D intensity of their parent countries. The paper explains this as reflecting differences in the *nature* of the firms established here by parents from different origins, and this is plausible. But it also can be interpreted as saying that firms whose parents have a strong technology base do more R&D here, which would suggest complementarity.

One possibility is that these complementarity effects are masked in the country aggregates. It could be that, for any given firm, affiliate and parent R&D are substitutes for some values of affiliate R&D and complements for others. For example, it seems plausible that some small scale of affiliate research is necessary to combine what the parent knows with locally available knowledge about both supply-side factors (e.g., the characteristics of locally available inputs) and demand-side factors (local tastes and availability of complementary products). Beyond this small scale, perhaps incremental affiliate R&D is merely a substitute for parent technology. If this is true, we could find that the country aggregates act like substitutes despite features of complementarity at the micro level.

References

Cohen, W., and D. Levinthal. 1989. Innovation and learning: The two faces of R&D. *Economic Journal* (September).

Jaffe, A. 1986. Technological opportunity and spillovers of R&D: Evidence from firms' patents, profits and market value. *American Economic Review* (December).

Jaffe, A., R. Henderson, and M. Trajtenberg. 1993. Geographic localization of knowledge spillovers as evidenced by patent citations. *Quarterly Journal of Economics* (August).

9   Do Repatriation Taxes Matter?
Evidence from the Tax Returns
of U.S. Multinationals

Rosanne Altshuler, T. Scott Newlon, and
William C. Randolph

An open question in the literature on the taxation of multinational corporations is whether taxes due on repatriation of foreign-source income influence whether the profits of foreign subsidiaries are repatriated or reinvested abroad. Theoretical arguments by Hartman (1985) suggest that dividend payments by foreign subsidiaries should not be influenced by such repatriation taxes. Under this view, which is analogous to the "new view" of dividend taxation applied to domestic firms, taxes due upon repatriation are unavoidable costs for "mature" foreign subsidiaries that finance investment out of retained earnings.[1] As a result, investment and dividend payment decisions are unaffected by those taxes. The results of recent empirical work that used cross-sectional data on U.S. multinationals seem to contradict Hartman's theoretical result. These studies indicate that dividend remittances are sensitive to repatriation taxes. This presents a puzzle.

Hartman's analysis (and the new view of dividend taxation) is based on the assumption that taxes on dividends are constant over time. This paper investigates whether the empirical evidence can be reconciled with the theoretical results by recognizing that repatriation taxes on dividends may vary over time. This variability may provide firms with an incentive to repatriate relatively more profits from a subsidiary when the tax cost of doing so is temporarily

Rosanne Altshuler is assistant professor of economics at Rutgers University and a faculty research fellow of the National Bureau of Economic Research. T. Scott Newlon is an economist in the Office of Tax Analysis of the U.S. Department of Treasury. William C. Randolph is an economist in the Congressional Budget Office.

The authors are grateful to Gordon Wilson for his assistance in using the Treasury tax data. They thank Bill Gentry and other conference participants for valuable comments. They also thank seminar participants at the University of Pennsylvania, the University of Toronto, and the 1993 NBER Summer Institute for helpful comments. Any views expressed in this paper are those of the authors and do not necessarily represent those of the U.S. Treasury Department or the Congressional Budget Office.

1. See King (1977), Auerbach (1979), and Bradford (1981).

relatively lower than normal, and to retain more profits when the tax cost of repatriation is higher than normal.[2] Such timing behavior could be revealed in cross-sectional data by a relationship between dividend payout levels and the current level of the tax cost of dividend payments, when the actual relationship is between dividend payout levels and the current level of the tax cost *relative* to its normal level. If timing opportunities are important to dividend payout decisions, it becomes difficult to interpret the tax effects estimated in previous papers. In particular, these estimates will tend to confuse the effects of permanent tax changes, as would occur due to changes in statutory tax rates, with the effects of tax changes due to transitory changes in the situation of the taxpayer.

It is important to distinguish whether cross-sectional differences between subsidiaries in dividend payout behavior are due to the current level of the tax cost of paying dividends or to the difference between the current and the normal, or expected future, tax cost. Making this distinction will help us evaluate the effects of tax policy on the location of investment, the form of finance, and tax revenues. More specifically, it has implications for the evaluation of policies such as the reduction of withholding tax rates in bilateral tax treaties and the repeal of the deferred taxation that foreign profits generally enjoy in the United States. The policy implications of this work are discussed in more detail in the final section of the paper.

Microdata can be used to distinguish the effects of transitory variation in tax costs from the effects of permanent differences in tax costs. This paper uses a recently created data set containing U.S. tax return information for a large sample of U.S. corporations and their foreign subsidiaries. For some of our empirical work, we link the subsidiary-specific data across time to create a panel data set. To our knowledge, this is the largest panel data set in existence that contains tax information on multinationals. It is also the only panel data set that has detailed tax information on both the parent corporations and their foreign subsidiaries.

We use information about cross-country differences in tax rates to estimate separate effects for the permanent and transitory components of the tax price of dividend repatriation. The idea is that variations across countries in average repatriation tax prices or in statutory tax rates will be correlated with the permanent component of tax price variation, but uncorrelated with transitory variations. Using these measures to construct instrumental variables for the tax price allows us to separately identify permanent and transitory tax price effects. Our estimation strategy is similar to that of Burman and Randolph (1994), who used state tax rates as instruments to separate permanent from transitory effects of taxes on capital gains realizations.

To preview our results, we find that the permanent tax price effect is signifi-

---

2. The term "normal" is used here to imply that there is some permanent, or long-run average, repatriation tax cost that the multinational faces. By "normal" tax cost we really mean expected future tax cost.

cantly different from the transitory price effect and is not significantly different from zero, while the transitory tax price effect is negative and significant. This suggests that previous cross-sectional analysis has measured the effect of timing behavior, either through tax planning that affects both the tax price and dividend payments or through companies timing their repatriations to take advantage of exogenous transitory variations in tax prices.

The remainder of the paper is organized as follows. Section 9.1 briefly reviews Hartman's analysis, the related empirical literature, and some more recent theoretical work in this area. Section 9.2 derives the tax price of a dividend repatriation, section 9.3 presents the empirical model, and section 9.4 describes the data. Results are presented in section 9.5, followed by concluding remarks.

9.1 Hartman Analysis and Subsequent Studies

The U.S. system for taxing the income earned by the foreign subsidiaries of U.S. corporations defers taxation of foreign income until it is brought back to the United States and provides a credit for foreign taxes paid.[3] Under this credit and deferral system, the two main forms of repatriation tax that a firm incurs on income remitted from a foreign subsidiary are the residual home-country tax liability (if any) not offset by the foreign tax credit and any withholding tax imposed by the source country. Hartman (1985) argued that, under a credit and deferral tax system, the repatriation tax on foreign-source income is irrelevant to the investment and dividend payment decisions of foreign subsidiaries that are financed through retained earnings ("mature" subsidiaries). Hartman's insight was that, since the repatriation tax is unavoidable, it reduces the opportunity cost of investment and the return to investment by the same amount. As a result, the tax does not affect a mature subsidiary's choice between reinvesting its foreign earnings and repatriating funds to its parent.[4] His analysis is essentially an application of the "new view" or "tax capitalization view" of dividend taxation put forward by King (1977), Auerbach (1979), and Bradford (1981). The new view holds that taxes on dividends (if constant over time) have no distortionary effects on the real decisions of domestic corporations. Although Hartman's analysis pertains to the residual U.S. tax on foreign income, it applies equally well to withholding taxes.

Several empirical studies using cross sections of tax return data appear to contradict Hartman's theoretical result. Mutti (1981) used U.S. tax return data from 1972 to estimate the effect of tax costs on the choice of income remittance channels. He found significant tax effects in estimates of the parameters

---

3. The Subpart F provisions of the tax code provide for accrual basis taxation on certain foreign income.

4. Note that this result does not imply that home- and host-country taxes have no effect on the repatriation decision. They do have an impact due to their effect on home- and host-country after-tax rates of return, but not through the tax on repatriation.

of a dividend equation. Goodspeed and Frisch (1989) and Hines and Hubbard (1990) both used 1984 tax return data of large samples of U.S. corporations and their foreign subsidiaries to investigate tax effects on foreign income remittances. Goodspeed and Frisch matched data on parent corporations with country-specific information on their foreign subsidiaries in an attempt to quantify income repatriation incentives created by the U.S. tax system. By further disaggregating the 1984 tax return data, Hines and Hubbard were able to study income repatriation behavior using a data set that matched subsidiary-specific information to parent corporation data. Both studies found significant evidence of tax effects on income repatriation. Altshuler and Newlon (1993) used U.S. tax return data from 1986 to investigate tax effects on dividend remittances from foreign subsidiaries to their U.S. parent corporations. This paper improved on previous work by providing a more accurate specification of the tax incentives facing firms. Results from estimates of dividend equations indicated a somewhat larger and more significant tax effect than had been previously estimated.

Recognizing that Hartman's theoretical analysis did not allow repatriation taxes to vary over time may help to reconcile it with the empirical results from the above studies. There are at least two different ways in which the repatriation tax may vary. First, it may vary over time due to differences between the tax base definitions of the United States and the host country of the foreign subsidiary. The U.S. foreign tax credit is based on the average foreign tax rate of the subsidiary, where the average is calculated with respect to the U.S. definition of the tax base. Differences in tax base definitions may vary over time, for example, if capital cost allowances differ, causing the average foreign tax rate as defined by the United States to vary. This variation in the average foreign tax rate causes the foreign tax credit allowed for a given dividend payment to vary over time as well. Such variations in the average foreign tax rate may be planned. For example, to the extent that the timing of deductions and credits is discretionary, a foreign subsidiary may shift them from years in which it is remitting income to years in which it is not remitting income, thereby maximizing the foreign tax credit. This device is known as the "rhythm method" in the tax-planning jargon.[5]

The second cause of variation in the repatriation tax is movement by the parent company between being in "excess credit," that is, having more foreign tax credits available than are needed to offset potential U.S. tax liability on foreign-source income, and being in "excess limitation," the opposite condi-

---

5. The rhythm method was a more useful tax-planning device for U.S. multinationals prior to the Tax Reform Act of 1986, when the foreign tax credit was calculated year by year. The 1986 act switched to a system in which the foreign tax credit is calculated based on the pool of previously unremitted foreign earnings and uncredited taxes, and therefore shifting the year in which tax credits and deductions are taken has much less effect on the foreign tax rate for U.S. foreign tax credit purposes.

tion. Since the U.S. foreign tax credit operates, to some extent, on an overall basis, excess foreign tax credits generated from one source of foreign income can be used to offset potential U.S. tax on another source of foreign income that generates insufficient foreign tax credits. If the parent corporation is in excess credit, there is no additional U.S. tax cost to repatriating foreign income. If the parent is in excess limitation, the U.S. tax cost of repatriating income from a subsidiary may be positive or negative, depending on the average foreign tax rate of the subsidiary.

Several recent theoretical contributions have incorporated a repatriation tax that may vary over time and that may be endogenous to the investment and financial decisions of subsidiaries and parent corporations. Hines (1994) shows that U.S. tax payments on foreign-source income are affected by differences in the way the United States and host countries determine taxable income. In his model, the repatriation tax is a function of the ratio of U.S.-defined income to foreign-defined income. He points out that this ratio may vary over time and may be affected by investment decisions. As a result, investment incentives may be influenced by the repatriation tax. Leechor and Mintz (1993) make a similar argument. In their model, the repatriation tax is also endogenous and the Hartman result obtains only when host and home country tax bases, adjusted for inflation, are proportional to each other.

Altshuler and Fulghieri (1994) offer a model in which parent corporations may switch into and out of the excess credit position. This model shows that the Hartman result obtains only when the credit position is stationary. The insight here is that switching between credit states breaks down the equivalence between the impact of repatriation taxes on the opportunity cost of capital and on the returns to investment.

In one sense, none of these recent theoretical contributions has departed from the Hartman result: the level of the repatriation tax does not by itself affect the incentive to repatriate income rather than reinvest it. Instead, it is the variation over time in the level of the repatriation tax that affects the incentive to repatriate income, because this variation provides parent corporations with the opportunity to time remittances so that they occur in years when repatriation tax rates are relatively low. If these theoretical predictions are correct, then failure to distinguish between the effects of permanent and transitory variation in the tax price when estimating tax effects on repatriation of foreign income could lead to incorrect results. The effect of permanent variation in the tax price might be overstated, since the estimates would confound the effects of permanent and transitory variation in the tax price.

9.2 Tax Price of Dividend Repatriations

In this section we specify a measure of the tax price of repatriating foreign income in the form of dividends and we briefly discuss the factors that may cause that tax price to vary over time.[6] To understand how these tax prices are derived, some background information on the foreign tax credit is useful. The discussion here borrows heavily from Altshuler and Newlon (1993).

The foreign tax credit has two components. The first, called the "direct credit," is a credit for foreign taxes paid directly on income as it is received by a U.S. taxpayer. Foreign taxes eligible for the direct credit include withholding taxes on remittances to the U.S. taxpayer such as dividends, interest, and royalties, and also income taxes on foreign branch operations. The second component, called the "deemed-paid" or "indirect credit," is a credit for foreign income taxes paid on the income out of which a dividend distribution is made to the U.S. taxpayer. The deemed-paid credit is generally a credit for foreign corporate income taxes.

The deemed-paid credit for a dividend remittance from a foreign subsidiary is calculated by grossing up the dividend to reflect the foreign tax deemed paid on that dividend income.[7] To illustrate, suppose subsidiary i makes a dividend payment, D_i, to its parent corporation. The grossed-up dividend is

$$(1) \qquad\qquad D_i + T_i D_i/(Y_i - T_i),$$

where T_i denotes the total foreign income tax paid by subsidiary i and Y_i denotes the subsidiary's pretax income from the U.S. perspective, which is the subsidiary's book earnings and profits. Equation (1) can be rewritten as $D_i/(1 - \tau_i)$, where τ_i represents the average subsidiary tax rate, T_i/Y_i, on foreign earnings from the U.S. perspective. The U.S. tax on the dividend before credits is $\tau D_i/(1 - \tau_i)$, where τ denotes the U.S. rate of tax. The United States considers that creditable foreign tax was paid on the dividend in the amount of $\tau_i D_i/(1 - \tau_i)$. The U.S. tax liability on the dividend payment after the deemed-paid credit is therefore $D_i(\tau - \tau_i)/(1 - \tau_i)$.

The amount of foreign tax credit that can actually be used is limited, however, to the amount of U.S. tax payable on foreign income. Therefore, if the foreign tax rate, τ_i, exceeds the U.S. tax rate, τ, excess credits are created in the amount of $D_i(\tau_i - \tau)/(1 - \tau_i)$. If the foreign tax rate is less than the U.S. tax rate, then a U.S. tax liability of $D_i(\tau - \tau_i)/(1 - \tau_i)$ accrues, and the remitted foreign income is said to be creating excess limitation.

As noted above, the limitation on the foreign tax credit operates to some extent on an overall basis. This means that excess credits accruing from one source of foreign income can often be used to offset U.S. tax (excess limita-

6. Although we focus on dividend payments, income may be remitted to parent companies in the form of interest, rents, and royalty payments. Previous work by Altshuler and Newlon (1993) suggests that dividend payments are the most important channel for income remittances, making up over 60 percent of the total foreign income derived by U.S. parents from their foreign subsidiaries in 1986.

7. As mentioned above, for tax years beginning in 1987, the amount of foreign tax credit associated with a dividend payment is based on the accumulated value of earnings and profits. Although this changes the gross-up formula in the text, it is not relevant for our analysis since our data are taken from years prior to 1986.

tion) on foreign income from another source. This is called cross-crediting or averaging of foreign income. The ability to cross-credit means that the effect of repatriating foreign income from a particular source may be positive, negative, or zero.[8]

9.2.1 Derivation of Tax Prices

We define the tax price of a dividend remittance as the additional global tax liability arising from an incremental dollar's worth of dividend repatriations. To derive the tax price we must take into account both the incremental U.S. and source country taxes on a dollar of dividends. The U.S. tax liability generated by dividend payments before the foreign tax credit equals $\tau D_i/(1 - \tau_i)$. The foreign taxes creditable against U.S. tax liability are deemed-paid taxes plus withholding taxes, or

$$(2) \qquad \tau_i D_i/(1 - \tau_i) + \omega_i D_i,$$

where ω_i denotes the withholding tax rate in the host country. If the parent is in excess credit, any U.S. tax liability on a dollar of dividends is offset by the foreign tax credit. If the parent is in excess limitation, the U.S. tax liability equals

$$(3) \qquad (\tau - \tau_i)D_i/(1 - \tau_i) - \omega_i D_i.$$

To compute the global tax price of a dollar of dividends we add the source-country effect to the U.S. tax effect. Under a classical corporate income tax system,[9] the total source-country tax liability on subsidiary i equals,

$$(4) \qquad T_i = \tau_i Y_i + \omega_i D_i.$$

As a result, the only host-country tax consequences of a dividend remittance are the associated withholding taxes. If the parent is in excess credit, there is no U.S. tax consequence and therefore the global tax price is ω_i. If the parent is in excess limitation, the global tax price, p, is

$$(5) \qquad p = (\tau - \tau_i)/(1 - \tau_i).$$

---

8. Congress has restricted cross-crediting by creating "baskets" of different types of foreign income to each of which a separate foreign tax credit limitation applies. Before the 1986 act, the period which our study covers, there were five separate baskets: (1) one for investment interest income, (2) one for "domestic international sales corporation" dividend income, (3) one for the foreign trade income of a "foreign sales corporation," (4) another for distributions from a foreign sales corporation, and (5) one for all other foreign-source income, which we will call general limitation income. The 1986 act decreased the potential for cross-crediting further by increasing the number of separate limitation baskets to nine.

9. For simplicity we focus our discussion in this section on the derivation of the tax price of a dividend remittance from a foreign subsidiary operating in a country that uses a classical corporate tax system. In our empirical work we also take details of host-country tax systems into account, since our sample includes subsidiaries that operate in countries with split-rate and imputation systems. The derivation of the tax prices for these types of tax systems is discussed in detail in Altshuler and Newlon (1993).

The withholding tax has no net effect on global taxes because the extra withholding tax paid on the dividend remittance is offset by a reduction of U.S. tax of an equal amount. Due to cross-crediting, the global tax price may be negative and dividend payments may reduce the firm's global tax liability.[10]

Expression (5) shows that, if the parent corporation is in excess limitation, the tax price of a dividend remittance is inversely related to the subsidiary's average tax rate, τ_i. As noted previously, to the extent that these variations in τ_i are endogenous, for example, because the timing of deductions and credits is elective, they can become a part of tax-planning strategies for repatriating foreign-source income. Even if a subsidiary's average tax rate is relatively constant, the tax price of remittances will fluctuate significantly when the subsidiary's parent switches credit position. Consider a subsidiary with an average tax rate above the U.S. corporate rate. When the parent is in excess limitation, the tax price of a dividend remittance is negative $((\tau - \tau_i)/(1 - \tau_i) < 0)$. When the parent is in excess credit, the tax price equals the withholding tax rate. As a result, tax prices for some subsidiaries can be negative in some years and positive in others. These changes in tax prices may also be endogenous if parents can control their foreign tax credit positions through careful structuring of remittances from foreign subsidiaries. The next section presents an estimation strategy to separate the effect of these transitory components of tax prices from the effect of changes in the permanent component.

9.3 Empirical Model of Dividend Repatriations

Previous work by Hines and Hubbard (1990) and Altshuler and Newlon (1993) has estimated a simple empirical model of dividend repatriations. For subsidiaries paying a dividend, the model takes the following basic form:

$$(6) \qquad d = a_0 + a_1 P + br + XA + \varepsilon,$$

where d is the dividend payout expressed as the ratio of subsidiary dividends to assets, P is the current tax price of dividend repatriation,[11] r is the after-tax rate of return for the subsidiary, and X is a vector of characteristics of subsidiary and parent. Equation (6) is not derived explicitly from the firm's optimization problem, but can be considered a reduced form suitable for testing the general implications of theoretical models such as Hartman's. It is similar to

---

10. We neglect here the cases in which the parent corporation has tax losses, since, as in earlier papers by Hines and Hubbard (1990) and Altshuler and Newlon (1993), we include in our sample only those U.S. corporations with positive worldwide taxable income. Corporations with tax losses are excluded here for simplicity's sake, since the carryover rules for tax losses and foreign tax credits can interact in ways that may complicate the incentives for income repatriation of these firms.

11. Altshuler and Newlon (1993) also use a measure of the "expected" tax price that attempts to take into account the fact that excess foreign tax credits can be carried back to several prior years or forward to several future years to offset taxes in those years.

the empirical models used to explain dividend payments in a purely domestic context.

In these previous papers, P was expected to have a negative coefficient since higher tax prices were expected to reduce the attractiveness of repatriation. The after-tax rate of return, r, may have an ambiguous effect on the dividend payout. On the one hand, if dividend payments are a residual, then higher earnings, which would increase the measured rate of return, could be expected *ceteris paribus* to increase the dividend payout. On the other hand, a higher after-tax rate of return would increase desired investment, having the effect of increasing retained earnings and reducing the dividend payout. Other relevant variables are included in X, the most important of which is perhaps the age of the subsidiary. Some of the theoretical literature (such as Newlon 1987 and Sinn 1990) suggests that older subsidiaries should have higher dividend payout ratios. This prediction is a direct consequence of the value of deferral when there is a repatriation tax; that is, if there is deferral, then dividend payouts will on average be an increasing function of age, other things constant.

As noted already, by using the current tax price, P, the above model may confound the potentially different effects of permanent and transitory components of the tax price. It is beyond the scope of this paper to derive a theoretical model that explicitly incorporates intertemporal variation in repatriation tax prices. Instead, we use a reduced-form empirical model to test the general implications that could be expected from any such model. In particular, a transitory decrease (increase) in the tax price reduces the current tax price relative to future tax prices and thus enables the firm to increase the value of its foreign-source income by accelerating (delaying) dividend repatriations. But a permanent change in the tax price does not change the relative prices of current and future repatriation. Therefore, one would expect dividend repatriations to be affected more by transitory than by permanent changes in tax prices. And Hartman's (1985) work would indicate that permanent changes in tax prices should have no effect at all on dividend repatriations.

Based on these considerations, our empirical model generalizes equation (6) to allow for differences in transitory and permanent tax price effects:

$$(7) \qquad d = a_0 + a_1(P - P^*) + a_2 P^* + br + XA + \varepsilon,$$

where P^* is the permanent component of the tax price and hence $P - P^*$ is the transitory component. We estimate this in a slightly different form:

$$(8) \qquad d = a_0 + a_1 P + (a_2 - a_1)P^* + br + XA + \varepsilon.$$

One difficulty in estimating equation (8) is that the permanent component of the tax price, P^*, is unobservable. To capture the effect of P^* we use an instrumental variables approach in which we instrument the tax price on a variable, P^i, that we expect to be correlated with the permanent component of the tax price but uncorrelated with its transitory component. This essentially involves replacing P^* in equation (8) with its predicted value,

$$\hat{P}* = \hat{b}_0 + \hat{b}_1 P^i + \hat{b}_2 r + X\hat{B},$$

where the coefficients are derived from the regression

$$P* = b_0 + b_1 P^i + b_2 r + XB + \xi.$$

We experiment with two alternative instruments for the permanent component of the tax price, the country average tax price and the country statutory withholding tax rate. These instruments reflect cross-country variation in taxes that should also be reflected in the permanent component of the tax price but not in the purely transitory component.

For estimation of equation (8), we use a Tobit procedure because dividend payments are censored at zero. On the surface, this may appear unnecessary since actual dividend payments are, by definition, nonnegative. However, the desired level of dividend payments could be negative. This result would obtain if, as suggested by the theoretical work in this area, foreign retained earnings were the preferred source of finance for foreign investment but foreign investment exceeded foreign earnings. Our use of a Tobit procedure implicitly assumes that we have modeled desired dividends, but only observe actual dividends.

9.4 Data

Our data set contains information from three sets of tax and information forms filed by a large sample of nonfinancial U.S. multinational corporations. Subsidiary data are obtained from information returns, called 5471 forms, filed for each foreign subsidiary of a U.S. taxpayer. Form 5471 includes balance sheet and income statement variables along with detailed information on remittances to U.S. parent corporations. For the purposes of this study, we needed to append information on the taxable income and foreign tax credit position of parent corporations to the subsidiary specific data from the form 5471's. We obtained income data from corporate income tax returns filed by the U.S. parent corporations. We calculated foreign tax credit positions using data from the forms filed in support of foreign tax credit claims. Detailed data from foreign tax credit forms and data from 5471 forms is compiled only in even years and were available to us for only the years 1980, 1982, 1984, and 1986.

Calculating subsidiary-specific tax prices for dividend remittances for each sample year also requires knowledge of the host-country withholding tax rates, the appropriate foreign corporate tax rates, and details of host-country tax systems. To develop a list of country-specific withholding tax rates for each sample year, we used the Price Waterhouse (1980, 1982, 1984, 1986) guides and tax treaties. These guides also provided the appropriate statutory tax rates for the countries in our sample with nonclassical (e.g., split-rate and imputation) corporate tax systems. Finally, in each year of the sample we used the subsidiary's average foreign tax rate to measure the corporate tax rate τ_i at which dividends are grossed up and foreign tax credits are calculated. To calculate this rate we divided foreign tax payments by before-tax earnings and profits, both obtained from the 5471 form data.

In some situations, calculating average tax rates in this manner may lead to an unsatisfactory approximation of τ_i. In particular, problems arise when subsidiaries report negative earnings and profits, receive tax refunds from host countries, repatriate dividends in excess of current earnings and profits, and receive dividends from subsidiaries of their own. Where feasible, adjustments were made in these cases to arrive at a more satisfactory measure of τ_i.[12] Various screens were also applied to the data to eliminate observations for which the data were suspect. After these deductions the total number of observations in the sample was 22,906.

Some of the estimation required linking subsidiaries in two consecutive sample years to form a panel. This was done largely through an algorithm that matched subsidiaries based on their U.S. parent corporation, company name, date of incorporation, and country of residence. Many subsidiaries could not be matched on this basis, and they therefore could not be included in the panel. The total number of observations in the panel was 7,118.

Table 9.1 presents for each country represented in the sample the mean dividend-asset ratio, the mean tax price, the standard deviation of the tax price, and the statutory withholding tax rate for the subsidiaries located in that country for 1984. This table provides information that may be valuable in evaluating the usefulness of country mean tax prices and statutory withholding tax rates as instruments for the permanent component of the tax price. First, note that there is substantial variation in country mean tax prices and in statutory withholding tax rates. Mean country tax prices range from -0.21 for Germany to 0.38 for Greece. Statutory withholding tax rates range from zero for a number of tax haven countries to 55 percent for Mexico. This degree of variation across countries means that these variables may be useful instruments, since the cross-country variation is presumably correlated with variation in the permanent component of the tax price.

Note also that within each country the standard deviation of the tax price is relatively large, in no case less than 0.14. This demonstrates that there is a substantial portion of variation in tax prices not explained by differences in country statutory dividend withholding and corporate income tax rates. Finally, note that no clear relationship between country mean dividend payout ratios and country mean tax prices or statutory withholding rates emerges from inspection of table 9.1. This presages the results presented in the next section.

---

12. See Altshuler and Newlon (1993) for a description of the methodology.

Table 9.1   **Country Averages, 1984**

Country	Mean Dividend-Asset Ratio (%)	Tax Price Mean	Tax Price Standard Deviation	Withholding Tax Rate (%)
West Germany[a]	3.9	−0.21	0.38	15
Japan[a]	2.7	−0.15	0.48	10
Norway[a]	1.6	−0.11	0.19	15
United Kingdom[a]	2.2	−0.10	0.38	5
Austria	4.2	0.02	0.41	6
Sweden	0.7	0.03	0.34	5
France	2.2	0.03	0.34	5
Finland	4.2	0.03	0.47	5
Italy	2.4	0.07	0.26	6
Denmark	1.8	0.07	0.22	6
Luxembourg	1.0	0.08	0.49	6
Malaysia	2.6	0.08	0.29	0
Peru	3.4	0.08	0.79	40
Canada	3.7	0.08	0.26	5
Belgium	2.3	0.13	0.35	15
Singapore	5.1	0.13	0.29	0
Costa Rica	4.8	0.13	0.37	15
Netherlands	2.7	0.14	0.20	5
New Zealand	2.3	0.14	0.22	15
Colombia	4.9	0.15	0.23	20
Australia	2.2	0.16	0.24	15
South Africa	3.9	0.16	0.20	15
Guatemala	3.9	0.17	0.27	13
Thailand	4.7	0.18	0.18	20
Brazil	4.0	0.19	0.51	25
Netherland Antilles	1.0	0.19	0.23	0
Bahamas	3.4	0.19	0.25	0
Ireland	3.6	0.20	0.25	0
Portugal	0.9	0.20	0.22	25
Hong Kong	4.9	0.21	0.21	0
Philippines	1.7	0.22	0.14	20
Bermuda	3.5	0.23	0.23	0
Spain	1.9	0.23	0.14	18
Venezuela	2.0	0.24	0.18	20
Cayman Islands	2.8	0.24	0.23	0
Mexico	2.6	0.25	0.43	55
Chile	5.1	0.25	0.20	30
Argentina	2.8	0.25	0.29	18
Panama	4.6	0.26	0.23	10
Taiwan	3.4	0.27	0.35	35
Liberia	1.2	0.28	0.15	15
Greece[a]	2.0	0.38	0.28	47
All subsidiaries	2.9	0.08	0.34	11

[a]Nonclassical countries.

9.5 Results

Table 9.2 presents the estimation results. Column (1) of the table presents the results of estimating the simple dividend model presented in equation (6) that incorporates only the current tax price of repatriation. These estimates use the full sample of 22,906 observations. They are presented to check that the results with our sample are essentially the same as found by Hines and Hubbard (1990) and Altshuler and Newlon (1993).

The results presented in column (1) are indeed similar to those found in previous work. The coefficient on the tax price is negative and statistically significant and of similar magnitude to the estimates in previous papers. To gauge the economic significance of this coefficient, note that it implies that a reduction in tax price of one standard deviation (0.34) implies an increase in the overall dividend payout ratio (including those that pay dividends and those that do not) of about 0.004, which is equal to about 11 percent of the mean dividend payout ratio of 0.036. Thus, moving the tax price from one standard deviation above the mean to one standard deviation below the mean implies an increase in the dividend payout ratio equal to about 22 percent of the mean dividend payout ratio.

The coefficient on the after-tax rate of return is positive, significant, and less than one. This is plausible, since it implies that an increase in earnings increases dividend payments. Because it is significantly less than one, the coefficient also suggests that an increase in the after-tax rate of return increases retained earnings. Also as expected, the coefficient on subsidiary age is positive and significant.

Column (2) and the remaining columns of the table present the results of estimating the model in equation (8) that distinguishes between permanent and transitory tax price effects. To interpret the tax price coefficient estimates in these columns, recall that in equation (8) the effect of the transitory component of the tax price is captured by the coefficient on the current tax price, while the coefficient on the permanent tax price equals the difference between the permanent and transitory tax price effects. Thus, the coefficient estimates in the first row of the table represent transitory tax price effects, the second-row coefficient estimates represent the difference between the permanent and transitory tax price effects, and the coefficient estimates in the third row, which are sums of the coefficients in the first two rows, represent permanent tax price effects.

Column (2) of table 9.2 shows estimates, using the full sample, of the basic model in which the country mean tax price is used as an instrument for the permanent component of the tax price. The estimated effect of the transitory component of the tax price (in the first row) is negative and statistically significant. Furthermore, it is larger in absolute magnitude than the estimated effect from the model excluding the permanent tax price effect.[13] This result

---

13. A Hausman test shows that this difference is statistically significant.

Table 9.2   Tobit Model Estimation Results

RHS Variables and Estimation Details	Full Sample		Partial Sample Matched with Two-Year Leads			Full Sample	
	(1)	(2)	(3)	(4)	(5)	(6)	(7)
Current (global) tax price	−0.046	−0.059	−0.066	−0.078	−0.070	−0.047	−0.049
	(.0057)	(.0062)	(.0109)	(.0114)	(.020)	(.0057)	(.0058)
Permanent tax price[a]	—	0.087	0.092	0.089	0.080	0.080	0.13
		(.016)	(.0263)	(.0265)	(.031)	(.076)	(.038)
Sum of tax price coefficients[b]	—	0.027	0.027	0.010	0.010	0.033	0.078
		(.015)	(.024)	(.024)	(.024)	(.076)	(.038)
Subsidiary earnings/assets	0.58	0.55	0.49	0.80	0.80	0.55	0.53
	(.016)	(.016)	(.027)	(.055)	(.055)	(.032)	(.021)
Subsidiary age/100	0.37	0.38	0.33	0.33	0.33	0.38	0.39
	(.017)	(.017)	(.028)	(.028)	(.028)	(.022)	(.018)
Instrumental variable							
Permanent							
Country mean tax price		x	x	x	x	x	
Withholding rate							x[c]

	(1)	(2)	(3)	(4)	(5)	(6)	(7)
Income							
Two-year forward				x	x		
Transitory							
Two-year change in tax price					x		
Intercept (1980)	−0.29	−0.29	−0.24	−0.28	−0.28	−0.26	−0.29
	(.0059)	(.0060)	(.0093)	(.012)	(.012)	(.0051)	(.0064)
1982 dummy	0.026	0.026	0.038	0.039	0.039	0.030	0.026
	(.0051)	(.0051)	(.0071)	(.0073)	(.0073)	(.0054)	(.0051)
1984 dummy	−0.029	−0.030	−0.0037	0.00075	0.00098	−0.030	−0.031
	(.0053)	(.0053)	(.0085)	(.0088)	(.0088)	(.0053)	(.0054)
1986 dummy	−0.012	−0.012	–	–	–	−0.012	−0.013
	(.0065)	(.0065)				(.0066)	(.0066)
Observations	22,906	22,906	7,118	7,118	7,118	22,906	22,906
Paying dividends (%)	28	28	37	37	37	28	28

Note: Dependent variable is ratio of subsidiary dividends to assets. Numbers in parentheses are standard errors.

[a] Measures the difference between effects of changes in permanent and transitory tax prices (transitory tax price = current tax price − permanent tax price).

[b] Measures the effect of permanent tax price changes, holding the transitory tax price constant.

[c] Uses part of withholding rate orthogonal to the foreign statutory and country mean average tax rates.

implies that transitory variation in the tax price has a large effect on the incentive to repatriate income.

The estimated difference between the permanent and transitory tax price effects presented in the second row of column (2) is positive and statistically significant. This implies that the permanent component of the tax price is not only significantly different from the transitory tax price effect, but, since the coefficient is positive, cannot have as large a negative impact on dividend repatriations. In fact, the estimated permanent tax price effect presented in the third row is not significantly different from zero. These results provide support for the hypothesis that the dividend repatriation incentive is affected by transitory but not permanent changes in the tax price of repatriation, a result that is consistent with Hartman's analysis.

One potential problem with the results from the basic model in column (2) arises because the tax incentive to retain earnings abroad should depend on the expected foreign after-tax rate of return, but we use the actual rate for the current year in our estimates. This may bias the coefficient on the after-tax rate of return toward zero. More important, the difference between the current and expected after-tax rates of return will be part of the error term. Consequently, the current tax price and the country mean tax price will both be correlated with the error term because both depend on current foreign taxes and income. This may bias the coefficients on the current and permanent tax prices.

To explore whether this is a significant problem, we used the two-year-lead after-tax rate of return as an instrument for the expected after-tax rate of return. The motivation for this approach is that, under rational expectations, the difference between the future actual and expected after-tax rates of return (the forecast error) should be independent of the current after-tax rate of return, which reflects only current information.

This approach reduces the sample size in two ways. First, use of the two-year lead means that only the first three years of the data can be used. Second, only observations for which matches could be found in the following year of the sample could be used. As mentioned above, these restrictions reduced the sample size to 7,118.

There is some risk that the selection of subsidiaries dropped from the sample by these requirements was not random. For example, current income repatriation might depend on whether there are plans to sell a subsidiary in the future, and subsidiaries sold within two years would be excluded from the sample. Subsidiaries that are being shut down might also be more or less likely to pay dividends, and a subsidiary shut down within two years would be excluded from the sample. If for these or other reasons the selection was significantly nonrandom, selection bias might be induced.

To investigate whether there is any potential selection bias, column (3) of table 9.2 presents the results of estimating the basic model of column (2) using the restricted sample. Note that a higher percentage of the subsidiaries in the restricted sample pay dividends to their U.S. parent corporation. This is consistent, for example, with dividend payments being lower before a subsidiary is sold or shut down. But note that based on Hausman tests on the individual coefficients of interest the regression results do not differ significantly from those obtained using the full sample. Thus, there are no signs of selection bias in the restricted sample.

Column (4) of table 9.2 presents the results of the regression using the two-year-lead after-tax rate of return as an instrument for the expected after-tax rate of return. The coefficient on the after-tax rate of return increases, and the difference is significant based on a Hausman test. This coefficient implies that a higher expected after-tax rate of return is associated with greater retention of earnings, but not by as much as measured in the previous regressions. The tax price coefficients are not significantly different from those in column (2).[14] These results therefore provide no evidence that the permanent tax price coefficients are biased by using the current instead of the expected future foreign after-tax rate of return.

A second potential problem arises because even after controlling for differences in country average tax prices and the other regression variables using the instrumental variables approach, the current tax price may still be correlated with the permanent tax price. This is because the permanent tax price may depend not only on cross-country differences in taxes, but also on the portfolio of subsidiaries held by the U.S. parent corporation, on the parent's U.S. operations, and on expectations about the future. This problem also could bias the tax price coefficients. It would tend to bias the transitory tax price coefficient toward the permanent tax price coefficient and to bias the permanent tax price coefficient (i.e., the estimated difference between the permanent and transitory tax price effects) toward zero.

To determine whether this is a serious problem, we estimated the model using the change in tax price between the current year and the two-year lead as an instrument for the transitory tax price. This approach was adopted because the change in the tax price is likely to be less correlated than the current tax price with the permanent tax price. The results of this estimation are presented in column (5) of table 9.2. There is no significant change in any of the coefficients; they are simply estimated with somewhat less precision. Thus, there is no evidence that the tax price coefficients are biased from a correlation between the current and permanent tax prices.

A third problem may exist because much of the variation in the country mean tax price comes from variations in effective corporate tax rates across countries, but variations in foreign effective corporate tax rates may also affect foreign after-tax rates of return. As a result, it may be difficult to separately identify the effects of variations in foreign effective tax rates as they affect

---

14. The coefficient on the current tax price is just barely significantly different ($T = 2.0$), but the significance is probably overstated since we have not adjusted the standard errors to account for instrumental variables estimation.

repatriation through their effect on the tax price of repatriation and as they affect repatriation through their effects on the foreign after-tax rate of return. For example, a higher foreign corporate tax rate will decrease the tax price of repatriation for the subsidiary of a U.S. corporation that is in excess limitation, but it will also, ceteris paribus, decrease the foreign after-tax rate of return, thereby decreasing the incentive to defer repatriation of foreign income. Although the models we estimate attempt to avoid this problem by controlling separately for the foreign after-tax rate of return, the measure we use is imperfect, and hence there is some possibility of misspecification biasing the tax price results.

Our first approach to testing whether this is a significant problem is to use the country statutory dividend withholding tax rate in place of the country mean tax price as an instrument for the permanent component of the tax price. The statutory withholding tax rate is related to the tax price, but has no direct relation to the corporate tax rate. Column (6) of table 9.2 presents the results of this estimation, using the full sample again. Note that the permanent tax price coefficient changes very little from the basic model estimate in column (2). The difference is not statistically significant based on a Hausman test. This provides some evidence that there is no serious misspecification problem.

The approach used to generate the results presented in column (6) may not provide a conclusive fix for the potential problem, because country statutory withholding tax rates are correlated with country corporate tax rates. To address this additional possible difficulty we remove the correlation from the withholding rate instrument. To do this we regress the withholding rate on the country mean average corporate tax rate and the country statutory tax rate and use the residual from this regression as an instrument for the permanent component of the tax price. In other words, we use as an instrument the part of the withholding tax rate that is orthogonal to the country mean tax rate and the statutory corporate tax rate. The results of this procedure are presented in column (7) of table 9.2. Here again the coefficient on the permanent component of the tax price is not significantly different, based on a Hausman test, from the coefficient obtained in the estimates of the basic model presented in column (2).

9.6 Conclusion

The tax price effects on dividend repatriations found in previous studies using the simple model of dividend repatriations apparently measure largely the effect of the timing of dividend repatriations undertaken to take advantage of intertemporal variation in tax prices. These timing opportunities may arise either endogenously, through tax planning that affects both tax prices and dividend payments, or through exogenously caused variations in tax prices. Therefore, although repatriation taxes seem to affect dividend repatriation behavior, this is apparently only because tax prices vary over time. This result is consistent with the prediction of Hartman's model.

The results presented here should not be construed to imply that the "permanent" levels of host- and home-country taxation do not affect dividend repatriation by foreign subsidiaries. Host- and home-country corporate taxation will of course affect the earnings reinvestment decision, and hence the dividend repatriation decision, through their impacts on host- and home-country after-tax rates of return. The evidence from our estimates merely implies that host- and home-country taxation do not affect repatriation through the permanent component of the repatriation tax.

Our results may have policy implications. The most obvious implications relate to policies on dividend withholding tax rates. For example, many capital-importing countries consider lowering withholding taxes, either unilaterally or in the context of bilateral tax treaty negotiations, to try to attract new equity investment. But some countries may be inhibited by the fear that such a measure would lead to increased flight of the accumulated multinational equity "trapped" by existing high withholding taxes. Our results suggest that, as long as the reduction in the withholding tax rate is viewed as permanent, such fears are unfounded. Permanent changes in dividend withholding tax rates appear likely mainly to attract new equity investment and not to encourage repatriation of equity accumulated from past earnings.[15]

To the extent that these results support the Hartman model, they have implications regarding the incentive effects of the credit and deferral system that the United States uses to tax most foreign income of U.S. multinationals. In particular, if the repatriation tax is irrelevant for the dividend repatriation decision, then, at least as regards retained earnings, the incentives for foreign investment are the same as they would be under a system that exempts foreign income from taxation.

References

Altshuler, Rosanne, and Paolo Fulghieri. 1994. Incentive effects of foreign tax credits on multinationals. *National Tax Journal* 47, no. 2 (June): 349–61.
Altshuler, Rosanne, and T. Scott Newlon. 1993. The effects of U.S. tax policy on the income repatriation patterns of U.S. multinational corporations. In *Studies in international taxation,* ed. A. Giovannini, G. Hubbard, and J. Slemrod, 77–115. Chicago: University of Chicago Press.

15. If a reduction in withholding tax rates is perceived by multinational investors as a signal of more favorable and stable policies toward multinational investment, it may in fact increase reinvestment of earnings.

Auerbach, Alan J. 1979. Wealth maximization and the cost of capital. *Quarterly Journal of Economics* 93:433–45.
Bradford, David. 1981. The incidence and allocation effects of a tax on corporate distributions. *Journal of Public Economics* 15:1–22.
Burman, Leonard and William Randolph. 1994. Distinguishing permanent from transitory effects of capital gains tax changes: New evidence from micro data. *American Economic Review* 84(4): 794–809.
Goodspeed, Timothy and Daniel J. Frisch. 1989. U.S. tax policy and the overseas activities of U.S. multinational corporations: A quantitative assessment. Manuscript, U.S. Treasury Office of Tax Analysis.
Hartman, David. 1985. Tax policy and foreign direct investment. *Journal of Public Economics* 26:107–21.
Hines, James R., Jr. 1994. Credit and deferral as international investment incentives. *Journal of Public Economics* 55, no. 2 (October): 323–47.
Hines, James R., Jr., and R. Glenn Hubbard. 1990. Coming home to America: Dividend repatriations by U.S. multinationals. In *Taxation in the global economy,* ed. A. Razin and J. Slemrod, 161–200. Chicago: University of Chicago Press.
King, Mervyn. 1977. *Public policy and the corporation.* London: Chapman and Hall.
Leechor, Chad, and Jack Mintz. 1993. On the taxation of multinational corporate investment when the deferral method is used by the capital exporting country. *Journal of Public Economics* 51:75–96.
Mutti, John. 1981. Tax incentives and repatriation decisions of U.S. multinational corporations. *National Tax Journal* 34:241–48.
Newlon, T. Scott. 1987. Tax policy and the multinational firm's financial policy and investment decisions. Ph.D. dissertation, Princeton University.
Price Waterhouse. 1980, 1982, 1984, and 1986. *Corporate taxes: A worldwide summary.* New York: Price Waterhouse.
Sinn, Hans Werner. 1990. Taxation and the birth of the foreign subsidiaries. NBER Working Paper no. 3519. Cambridge, Mass.: National Bureau of Economic Research, November.

Comment   William M. Gentry

Recent empirical evidence (Hines and Hubbard 1990; Altshuler and Newlon 1993) on how taxes affect dividend repatriation decisions of U.S. multinational corporations with foreign subsidiaries appears at odds with economic theory. These papers find that the tax consequences of repatriating dividends affect the level of repatriations: firms for which dividends generate little in the way of extra current taxes repatriate more dividends than firms for which dividends would generate more in extra current taxes. While this result seems plausible at face value, it is contrary to the "trapped equity" view of dividend taxation. This theory (see Hartman 1985) suggests that taxes should not affect dividend repatriation decisions provided that a firm faces the same tax rate over time.

Unlike previous empirical work, Altshuler, Newlon, and Randolph address

William M. Gentry is assistant professor of economics and public policy studies at Duke University and a faculty research fellow of the National Bureau of Economic Research.

the issue of whether firms face the same tax rate over time. The authors offer two important innovations over previous empirical work: (1) they incorporate instrumental variable techniques that separate temporary and permanent tax rates, and (2) they have panel data. By separating the tax rate facing a firm into a temporary and a permanent component, the authors can measure tax effects that are much more in the spirit of Hartman's theory. Their results are striking and consistent across specifications: temporary tax rates affect repatriations, but permanent tax rates do not have statistically significant effects on repatriations. Thus, the results are consistent with both Hartman's theory and previous empirical work. Current tax rates affect repatriation decisions, but the permanent component of the tax rate (the object of the Hartman's theory) does not affect repatriations.

My first comments address questions about alternative estimation techniques for separating permanent and temporary tax rates. My later comments address ideas for further study of the interaction between taxes and dividend repatriation.

Separating Permanent and Temporary Components of the Tax Price

The paper's empirical model regresses dividend repatriations (normalized by subsidiary assets) on the current tax price, the permanent tax price, the subsidiary's rate of return, the subsidiary's age, and a set of year effects. The immediate problem for estimating this equation is that the permanent tax price is unobservable. The paper solves this problem by using the predicted value of the current tax rate as the permanent tax rate. This predicted value of the tax rate comes from regressing the current tax price on the other regressors in the main equation plus an instrument. The instrument is typically the mean tax price of other U.S. subsidiaries operating in the same country.

The goal is to separate the current tax price, P, into two components, P^* the permanent tax price and ε the temporary component of the tax price. The paper uses the country mean tax price or the statutory withholding tax rate as the key piece of information for distinguishing the two components. My concern is whether these instruments are adequate for separating the two components. As a somewhat silly example of my concern, consider a country that hosts subsidiaries from two industries, A and B. Subsidiaries in the two industries face different permanent tax prices, P_A^* and P_B^*, and neither industry has a temporary component in its tax price. That is, subsidiaries in each industry face a constant tax price over time. Suppose that industry A has a higher tax price than industry B. If there are an equal number of subsidiaries from the two industries, then the country mean tax price would be $(P_A^* + P_B^*)/2$. In the framework of the paper, each subsidiary would be measured as having a current tax price that differs from the permanent tax price. Subsidiaries in industry A would be measured as having above average tax prices, and those in industry B would be measured as having below average tax prices. If firms in industry A repatriated fewer dividends than firms in industry B, then the approach in the paper would classify this situation as firms responding to temporary fluctuations in the tax price instead of properly classifying it as a response to differences in permanent tax prices.

While this particular example is contrived, the general point is that permanent tax rates may vary across firms within a country. I can suggest two types of sensitivity analysis for the potential problem of misclassifying the components of the current tax price. The first change would be to expand the information set used to predict the permanent component of the tax price. The additional variables should be correlated with the permanent tax price but not correlated with the temporary component of the tax price. These would be things that would be correlated with the permanent situation of the firm but not temporary conditions for the firm. Thus, the subsidiary's industry, its parent, or its mix of assets (equipment vs. structures) might be plausible candidates, but the rate of growth of assets would not be appropriate since it depends on the temporary condition of the firm.

The second change in the measurement of permanent tax prices would make more explicit use of the panel nature of the data. For firms that appear in the data for all of the years, the permanent tax price could be defined as the average tax rate over the four years and the temporary component would be the deviation from this average. This methodology would be similar to Auten and Clotfelter's (1982) work on capital gains realizations. The advantage of this method is that it allows for firm-specific permanent tax rates. Obviously, this method is not without its own flaws. For a firm that truly had a temporarily low tax price in all four of the years, this method would misclassify this temporarily low tax price as a permanent tax price. Also, the sample size might be reduced considerably by the need to match firms across years. If this attrition is not random, the smaller sample might suffer from selection bias. For example, the matched sample used in specifications (3)–(5) in table 9.2 is slightly more likely to pay dividends than the full sample. While the methodology in the paper may in the end be more attractive than using a smaller matched sample, this alternative would provide an interesting check for robustness.

Variance of the Distribution of Tax Prices

Table 9.1 shows that the variance in the distribution of current tax prices differs substantially across countries. These differences are not incorporated in the estimation but may be important for the size of a firm's response to the temporary component in its tax price. For example, in 1984, both Mexico and Chile had a mean tax price of 0.25. However, the standard deviation of the tax price is 0.43 in Mexico and 0.20 in Chile. If firms believed that the distribution of tax prices would be the same in the future and that their current tax price is a random draw from the country's distribution of tax prices, then a current tax price of 0.10 should have less of an effect on firms in Mexico than in Chile. The intuition for this difference comes from search theory. For parent firms of subsidiaries operating in Mexico, the deviation of -0.15 from the mean tax price is a relatively small deviation in the tax price. They would be less willing to pay dividends based on the -0.15 deviation from the mean tax price because they know the probability of an even lower tax price next year is relatively high. That is, parents with Mexican subsidiaries should be more likely to turn down the opportunity to repatriate at a tax price of 0.10 and wait (the equivalent of effortless search) for a lower tax rate in the future.[1]

In terms of estimation, I expect that correcting for the differences in the variance of tax prices would involve weighting the observations based on the variance of the conditional distribution of tax prices of the firm. That is, an observation with a 0.15 deviation in the tax price should receive more weight in the estimation if it is from a country with a tight distribution of tax prices than if it is from a country with a disperse distribution of tax prices.

Endogenous versus Exogenous Variation in Tax Prices

I find the variation in tax prices both within and across countries intriguing. As discussed in Altshuler and Newlon (1993), part of this variation comes from firms moving between excess credit and excess limitation status. Part of the variation comes from fluctuations in the subsidiary's average tax rate created by fluctuations in business conditions. Some of the variation within a country comes from differential taxation of industries and assets. Last, some of the variation across time and across countries results from legislated differences in tax rules. Many of these sources of variation, such as legislated differences in tax codes, are exogenous (at least in the short run) to both the parent firm and the subsidiary. However, other parts of the variation in tax prices depend on the firm's decisions. For example, cross-crediting provisions mean that a parent's decisions for one subsidiary affect the incentives to repatriate income from another subsidiary. The paper does the obvious thing and assumes that tax price fluctuations are exogenous to the firm. At some level, the tax prices and repatriations are endogenously determined by other firm choices. This endogeneity, however, does not lend itself to regression analysis and may be best left for case-study methods on multinational tax planning (see Wilson 1993).

Extensions to Other Questions in International Taxation

The distinction of temporary and permanent components in the tax price is potentially important for a number of other decisions faced by multinational corporations. For example, the choice between structuring a subsidiary such that it will pay dividends instead of rents and royalties may depend on both the level and volatility of tax prices for the different repatriation channels. Another example would be the parent's choice between lending money to the subsidiary and making an equity transfusion. One would expect that these more long-run organizational form choices would be more sensitive to permanent tax rates

---

1. This analogy to search assumes that the firms passively accept the current year's tax price. As discussed below, actual tax prices may be endogenous to the firm's tax planning.

than to current tax rates that include a temporary component. However, the timing of these transactions (such as royalty payments) may be sensitive to the temporary component of tax rates. The challenge for empirical work is to sort through how permanent and temporary components of taxes affect both the level of activity and the timing of activity. I hope that the authors will use their impressive data set to explore some of these issues in future papers.

Concluding Remarks

In conclusion, I found this paper very interesting and insightful. The authors are to be commended for cleverly disentangling the tax incentives for dividend repatriations. In addition to reconciling the apparent differences between economic theory and previous empirical work on how taxes affect multinational dividend repatriation decisions, the paper serves as a reminder that timing issues can be extremely important for how taxes affect business decisions.

References

Altshuler, Rosanne, and T. Scott Newlon. 1993. The effects of U.S. tax policy on the income repatriation patterns of U.S. multinational corporations. In *Studies in international taxation,* ed. A. Giovannini, R. G. Hubbard, and J. Slemrod, 77–115. Chicago: University of Chicago Press.

Auten, Gerald, and Charles T. Clotfelter. 1982. Permanent versus transitory tax effects and the realization of capital gains. *Quarterly Journal of Economics* 97:613–32.

Hartman, David. 1985. Tax policy and foreign direct investment. *Journal of Public Economics* 26:107–21.

Hines, James R., Jr., and R. Glenn Hubbard. 1990. Coming home to America: Dividend repatriations by U.S. multinationals. In *Taxation in the Global Economy,* ed. A. Razin and J. Slemrod, 161–200. Chicago: University of Chicago Press.

Wilson, G. Peter. 1993. The role of taxes in location and sourcing decisions. In *Studies in international taxation,* ed. A. Giovannini, R. G. Hubbard, and J. Slemrod, 195–231. Chicago: University of Chicago Press.

10   Interest Allocation Rules, Financing Patterns, and the Operations of U.S. Multinationals

Kenneth A. Froot and James R. Hines, Jr.

10.1   Introduction

International business operations pose special tax problems for multinational firms as well as for the governments that tax them. Multinational firms often centralize certain activities that generate returns in more than one country. For example, firms may borrow money in one country in order to deploy the funds elsewhere. Firms are entitled to claim tax deductions for interest costs, but countries in which they borrow may not permit all of the associated interest expenses to be deducted against local income for tax purposes. The method used to calculate allowable interest tax deductions can, in turn, affect financing choices and operating decisions.

American tax law permits only incomplete deductibility of the interest expenses of multinational firms. U.S. law specifies rules that determine the extent to which interest costs incurred by multinational firms in the United States can be deducted for tax purposes against U.S. income. These rules are often changed, the last major change occurring in 1986.

This paper examines the impact on firm behavior of the change in the U.S. interest allocation rules introduced by the Tax Reform Act of 1986. The 1986 act significantly reduced the tax deductibility of the U.S. interest expenses of certain American multinational corporations. Congress changed the law in 1986 because it was concerned that some U.S.-based firms received tax deduc-

Kenneth A. Froot is professor of business administration at Harvard Business School and a research associate of the National Bureau of Economic Research. James R. Hines, Jr., is associate professor of public policy at the John F. Kennedy School of Government, Harvard University, and a faculty research fellow of the National Bureau of Economic Research.

The authors are grateful to Paul O'Connell for outstanding research assistance, and to Julie Collins for helpful comments on an earlier draft. Generous research support was provided by the National Bureau of Economic Research, the Division of Research at Harvard Business School, and the National Science Foundation (grant SES-9209373).

tions for interest expenses in the United States that enhanced their profits overseas. The 1986 act introduced a new formula for multinational firms to use in calculating the fraction of their interest expenses that can be deducted against taxable income in the United States.

This tax change increased the tax liabilities of certain American multinationals and made additional borrowing more expensive for these firms. One of the concerns raised during the deliberations over the 1986 act was that this additional cost of borrowing might discourage some firms from investing in new plant and equipment, since a sizable fraction of new investment is financed by borrowing. This paper examines the impact of the tax change on the operations of those multinational firms that were affected by the change in interest allocation rules. To do so, it is necessary to compare the behavior of the affected firms to the behavior of those firms that were unaffected by the interest allocation provisions of the 1986 act.

The results indicate that the change in interest allocation rules significantly influenced the operations of American multinational firms. Firms that were unable to deduct all of their interest expenses against their U.S. tax liabilities issued 4.2 percent less debt between 1986–91 (measured as a fraction of total firm assets), and invested 3.5 percent less in property, plant, and equipment, than did other firms. In addition, the affected firms showed a greater proclivity to lease rather than own capital assets and to reduce the scope of their foreign operations. All of these behavioral responses are consistent with the incentives created by the interest allocation provisions of the Tax Reform Act of 1986.

Section 10.2 describes the U.S. tax treatment of the interest expenses of multinational corporations and analyzes the incentives created by the Tax Reform Act of 1986. Section 10.3 describes the data used to analyze the impact of the 1986 tax change. Section 10.4 presents the results of regressions that estimate the impact of the 1986 tax change on various aspects of the operations of American multinational firms. Section 10.5 is the conclusion.

10.2   Tax Treatment of Interest Expense

This section describes the tax treatment of interest expenses of U.S. corporations, paying special attention to the treatment of multinational corporations. It identifies the incentives created by the Tax Reform Act of 1986, as a prelude to analyzing the impact of the act on the behavior of U.S. firms.

Interest expenses generally are deductible against the taxable income of U.S. corporations. There are, however, two important circumstances in which the deductibility of interest is of limited value to an interest-paying corporation. The first arises when a corporation has negative profits before interest deductions. Since a firm with losses pays no taxes, interest deductions do not reduce its tax liability. Corporations are, however, permitted to carry net operating losses backward up to three years or forward up to fifteen years.[1] The second circumstance is one in which a firm is subject to the corporate alternative minimum tax (AMT); firms paying the AMT face idiosyncratic tax incentives.[2]

10.2.1 Foreign and Domestic Allocation of Interest Deductions

Special problems arise in allocating the interest deductions of multinational firms. The idea that underlies U.S. law is that, when a multinational firm incurs interest expense in the United States, a certain fraction of the expense should be allocated as a deduction against taxable domestic income and the remainder allocated against the firm's foreign income. The respective fractions are determined on the basis of the income-generating capacity created by the loans on which interest is paid. The extreme difficulty that this concept encounters is that it is not always clear to what extent a particular loan generates domestic-source and foreign-source income.

In order to understand the significance of the sourcing of interest deductions, it is necessary to review the treatment of foreign-source income. Due to some peculiarities of the changes in U.S. tax law after 1986, certain firms found that the cost of debt changed significantly between 1986 and 1987. The goal of the empirical work described in section 10.3 is to follow and compare the behavior of firms facing higher costs of debt to that of firms facing unchanged cost of debt.

10.2.2 U.S. Taxation of Foreign Income[3]

The United States taxes income on a "residence" basis, meaning that American corporations and individuals owe taxes to the U.S. government on all of their worldwide income, whether earned in the United States or not. The top U.S. corporate tax rate is now 35 percent. Since foreign profits are usually taxed in host countries, U.S. law provides a foreign tax credit for income taxes (and related taxes) paid to foreign governments, so as not to subject American multinationals to double taxation. With the foreign tax credit, a U.S. corporation that earns $100 in a foreign country with a 12 percent tax rate (and a foreign tax obligation of $12) pays only $23 to the U.S. government, since its U.S. corporate tax liability of $35 (35 percent of $100) is reduced to $23 by the foreign tax credit of $12. The foreign tax credit is, however, limited to U.S. tax liability on foreign income; if, in the example, the foreign tax rate were 50

---

1. Tax loss carryforwards do not accrue interest, a feature that limits their value even to firms that expect to have taxable profits in the future. Scholes and Wolfson (1992) analyze the value of tax loss carryforwards in uncertain environments.

2. For the remainder of the paper, we analyze taxpaying firms that are not subject to the AMT. Lyon and Silverstein (chap. 6 in this volume) report that 30.7 percent of firms with assets over $500 million paid the AMT in 1990.

3. Parts of this brief description of the tax system are excerpted from Hines (1991).

percent, then the firm pays $50 to the foreign government but its U.S. foreign tax credit is limited to $35. Hence, a U.S. firm receives full tax credits for its foreign taxes paid only when it is in a "deficit credit" position, that is, when its average foreign tax rate is lower than its tax rate on domestic operations. A firm has "excess credits" if its available foreign tax credits exceed U.S. tax liability on its foreign income.[4] Firms average together their taxable incomes and taxes paid in all of their foreign operations in calculating foreign tax credits and the foreign tax credit limit.

Deferral of U.S. taxation of certain foreign earnings is another important feature of the U.S. international tax system. A U.S. parent firm is taxed on its subsidiaries' foreign income only when returned ("repatriated") to the parent corporation. This type of deferral is available only to foreign operations that are separately incorporated in foreign countries ("subsidiaries" of the parent) and not to consolidated ("branch") operations. The U.S. government taxes branch profits as they are earned, just as it does profits earned within the United States.

The deferral of U.S. taxation may create incentives for firms with lightly taxed foreign earnings to delay repatriating dividends from their foreign subsidiaries.[5] This incentive arises in those cases in which firms expect never to repatriate their foreign earnings, or in which they anticipate that future years will be more attractive for repatriation (either because domestic tax rates will be lower or because future sources of foreign income will generate excess foreign tax credits that can be used to offset U.S. tax liability on the dividends).[6] It appears that, in practice, U.S. multinationals choose their dividend repatriations selectively, generally paying dividends first out of more heavily taxed foreign earnings.[7] Consequently, the average tax rate that firms face on foreign income need not exactly equal the average foreign tax rate faced by their branches and subsidiaries abroad.

Branch earnings and dividends from subsidiaries represent only two forms of foreign income for U.S. income tax purposes. Interest received from foreign sources also represents foreign income, though foreign interest receipts from

4. Furthermore, income is broken into different functional "baskets" in the calculation of applicable credits and limits. In order to qualify for the foreign tax credit, firms must own at least 10 percent of a foreign affiliate, and only those taxes that qualify as income taxes are creditable.

5. The incentive to defer repatriation of lightly taxed subsidiary earnings is attenuated by the Subpart F provisions, introduced in U.S. law in 1962, which treat a subsidiary's passive income, and income invested in U.S. property, as if it were distributed to its American owners, thereby subjecting it to immediate U.S. taxation. The Subpart F rules apply to controlled foreign corporations, which are foreign corporations owned at least 50 percent by U.S. persons holding stakes of at least 10 percent each. Controlled foreign corporations that reinvest their foreign earnings in active businesses can continue to defer any U.S. tax liability on those earnings. See Hines and Rice (1994) and Scholes and Wolfson (1992) for the behavioral implications of these rules.

6. It is interesting to note that the size of the tax obligation triggered by repatriation does not itself create an incentive to delay paying dividends from foreign subsidiaries since the U.S. tax must be paid eventually. See Hartman (1985).

7. See the evidence presented in Hines and Hubbard (1990).

high-tax countries are assigned their own "basket" and therefore are not averaged with other income in calculating the foreign tax credit. Royalty income received from foreigners, including foreign affiliates of U.S. firms, is also foreign-source income. Foreign governments often impose moderate taxes on dividend, interest, and royalty payments from foreign affiliates to their American parent companies; these withholding taxes are fully creditable against an American taxpayer's U.S. tax liability on foreign income.

10.2.3 Interaction of Interest Expense and Foreign Income Rules

American firms with foreign income are generally not permitted to deduct all of their interest costs in the United States against their domestic taxable incomes. Instead, the law provides for various methods of allocating interest expenses between domestic and foreign income. The intention of the law is to retain the full deductibility of interest expense against taxable U.S. income, but only for that part of interest expense that generates income subject to U.S. taxation.

From the standpoint of taxpaying firms, the U.S. tax law's distinction between domestic and foreign interest deductions is potentially quite important. If interest expense is deemed to be domestic, then it is deductible against the taxpayer's U.S. taxable income. Alternatively, if it is deemed to be foreign, then the interest expense reduces foreign taxable income *for the purposes of U.S. income taxation only*. Foreign governments do not use U.S. methods of calculating interest deductions and generally do not permit U.S. firms to reduce their taxable incomes in foreign countries on the basis of interest expenses incurred in the United States. Consequently, interest expenses allocated against foreign income are valuable to a U.S. firm only if it has deficit foreign tax credits. If it has deficit credits, then some of the firm's foreign income is subject to U.S. tax, and any additional dollar of interest expense allocated against foreign income reduces the firm's U.S. taxable income by a dollar.[8] With deficit foreign tax credits, firms are indifferent between allocating interest expenses against foreign income and allocating them against domestic income.[9] If, on the other hand, firms have excess foreign tax credits, then any interest expenses allocated against foreign income are useless from the standpoint of reducing tax liabilities because foreign income generates no U.S. tax liability anyway.

The Tax Reform Act of 1986 significantly changed U.S. tax law governing the allocation of interest expenses. Prior to 1986, the interest expenses of U.S. taxpayers were determined separately for each company within a controlled

---

8. Curiously, the law is written so that the additional dollar of interest expense reduces taxable income without reducing the foreign tax credits available for foreign income taxes paid.

9. This statement, along with much of the analysis described in the paper, abstracts from the ability of firms to carry excess foreign tax credits backward two years and forward five years. Firms that carry excess credits forward or back may (depending on specific circumstances) face incentives that are intermediate between those of deficit credit and excess credit firms.

group.[10] In principle, each company was required to allocate interest deductions between domestic and foreign source in proportion to domestic and foreign assets.[11] In practice, however, this rule permitted taxpayers to structure their finances in order to obtain a full tax deduction in the United States for interest expenses associated with borrowing done in the United States.

Consider, for example, the situation of an American corporation that borrows $100 in the United States, paying interest of $10 annually. The corporation has $150 of U.S. assets and $50 of foreign assets and earns profits of $15, gross of interest costs, in the United States and profits of $5 abroad. The corporation does no foreign borrowing. Under pre-1986 law, this corporation would be entitled to deduct only $7.50 (75 percent of $10) of its interest charges against U.S. income because only 75 percent of its assets produce U.S.-source income; the remaining $2.50 of interest deductions would be allocated against foreign-source income. The same firm, with the same real business activities, could, however, reorganize its affairs in a manner that would permit all of the $10 interest cost to be deductible against U.S. income. To do so, the parent firm need only borrow the $100 in the U.S. market and then contribute the money as paid-in capital to a wholly owned domestic subsidiary that owns the firm's domestic and foreign operations. The domestic subsidiary pays all of its profits to its parent as dividends. The parent firm and the domestic subsidiary file a consolidated tax return and annual report. The domestic subsidiary has $15 of U.S.-source income and $5 of foreign-source income; it has no interest expenses. The parent firm has $20 of income on the basis of dividends received from its subsidiary and $10 of interest deductions. The parent firm is entitled to deduct all of its interest expense against U.S. income since the firm's assets (its wholly owned subsidiary) are all in the United States.[12]

10. Separate allocation of interest deductions for each company within a controlled group was firmly established by Treasury Regulation §1.861-8, issued in 1977. Prior to 1977, U.S. law was somewhat vague about whether all of the companies within a controlled group should be consolidated for purposes of interest allocation, though in an important case based on pre-1977 U.S. law (*ITT v. United States*) the courts held that interest should be allocated on a consolidated basis.

11. Taxpayers were given the alternative of allocating interest deductions on the basis of gross domestic income and gross foreign income, though it is hard to understand why a tax-minimizing corporation would do so, since tax-planning opportunities are so attractive using the asset method on a single-company basis. The regulation provides that, if the income method is chosen, interest deductions allocated against foreign-source income cannot be less than 50 percent of the amount that would have been allocated against foreign-source income by the asset method. Taxpayers allocating their interest deductions on the basis of domestic and foreign assets were required to do so based on the book values of those assets, unless the taxpayer elected to allocate on the basis of fair market values and could demonstrate fair market values to the satisfaction of the IRS. Once it was chosen, taxpayers were required to continue to use the fair market value method until granted permission by the IRS to discontinue its use. Book values of stock (such as a parent corporation's stock in its foreign subsidiaries) were not adjusted to include undistributed earnings and profits reinvested by the subsidiary corporations.

12. Prior to 1986, U.S. law did not use sophisticated "look-through" rules to determine the extent to which a U.S. corporation represents a U.S. asset. Instead, a U.S.-located subsidiary was considered to be a U.S. asset as long as 20 percent or more of its gross income for the prior three

The Tax Reform Act of 1986 significantly changed the method by which interest deductions are allocated, specifically by introducing a "one-taxpayer rule" in which the attributes of all members of a controlled group—whether owned directly by a parent firm or owned by the parent through one or more subsidiaries—determine the allocation of interest deductions between domestic and foreign income.[13] The motivation for the tax change was the insight that financial fungibility implies that borrowing by one part of a controlled group directly or indirectly influences the economic activities of all of the group. The 1986 act provides that the interest expenses of a U.S. taxpayer should be allocated between domestic-source and foreign-source income based on the relative assets of the domestic and foreign operations of the controlled group. Of course, several complications attend the implementation of such a rule.

Controlled groups represent chains of 80 percent or greater ownership. Consequently, an American parent corporation that owns 75 percent of the voting stock of a domestic subsidiary, the other 25 percent of which is owned by unrelated parties, separately allocates the interest deductions of the parent corporation and the domestic subsidiary. The 80 percent rule corresponds to the requirements for filing consolidated tax returns and annual reports. The interest expenses of foreign corporations are never included within the controlled group for purposes of interest expense allocation.[14]

Taxpayers are required to allocate interest deductions between domestic and foreign source on the basis of the book values of assets held domestically and abroad.[15] In the cases of subsidiaries that are 10 percent or more owned by members of the affiliated group, the book values of stock held in the subsidiaries are adjusted to reflect accumulated earnings and profits of the subsidiaries. Hence, in the case of an American firm that initially finances its wholly owned French subsidiary with $100 of equity, and in which the subsidiary subsequently earns and reinvests an additional $400, the parent's book value of the subsidiary is adjusted to $500 for purposes of interest expense allocation.

The 1986 act provides for a curious treatment of foreign assets and foreign interest deductions by members of a controlled group. For this purpose, the

---

years had U.S. source. In the example, 75 percent of the domestic subsidiary's gross income has U.S. source.

13. The changes in the interest allocation rules introduced by the Tax Reform Act of 1986 were phased in over three years. Various phase-in rules apply to the interest on debt issued between 1983 and 1985.

14. There is an exception for financial institutions whose business is primarily with unrelated parties and that are required by law to be operated separately from nonfinancial institutions. Such financial institutions are not included with the rest of an affiliated group for purposes of interest allocation; instead, the financial institutions are treated as a separate entity for purposes of interest allocation. Special rules also apply to corporations claiming the U.S. possessions tax credit (available under §936): these corporations are included in the consolidated group for purposes of interest expense allocation if they otherwise meet all of the requirements for inclusion.

15. Taxpayers have the alternative of using the fair market values of assets held domestically and abroad, but if taxpayers do so, they are not again able to use book values without permission of the IRS.

gross value of U.S. assets and the net value of foreign assets are used. This leads to something of an asymmetric treatment of foreign and domestic borrowing for purposes of interest expense allocation. Consider, for example, the case of a U.S. firm that has $200 of U.S. assets, of which $150 is equity and $50 is debt borrowed from an unrelated party; the firm also has $200 of foreign assets, of which $150 is parent equity and $50 is debt borrowed by the subsidiary from an unrelated foreign party. The firm has U.S.-source gross income of $40, U.S.-source interest cost of $5, foreign-source gross income of $40, and foreign-source interest expense of $5. This firm is required to allocate almost half of its $5 domestic interest deduction against foreign-source income,[16] and the firm is not permitted to allocate any of its foreign interest expense against domestic-source income, even though the leverage situation of the foreign subsidiary is the same as the leverage situation of its American parent.

One of the consequences of the asymmetric treatment of U.S. parent firms and their foreign subsidiaries is that the tax law can encourage firms to finance their subsidiaries with debt from the American parent instead of parent equity or unrelated-party debt. Parent equity in foreign subsidiaries reduces the amount of domestic interest payments allocated against U.S.-source income. If, in the previous example, the subsidiary borrowed $50 from its parent company instead of from an unrelated party, and the parent financed the loan to its subsidiary by borrowing an additional $50 from unrelated U.S. parties, then the subsidiary's tax position would not change (it still gets a $5 deduction against taxable income in the foreign country for interest paid to its U.S. parent),[17] but the parent firm receives a larger interest deduction against U.S.-source income.

The U.S. Treasury issued regulations designed to prevent U.S. firms from reacting to the passage of the 1986 act by financing their foreign subsidiaries with loans from U.S. parents financed by U.S. borrowing. The first set of regulations was proposed in 1987 but never took effect.[18] A second set of regula-

---

16. The firm has domestic assets of $200 and foreign book assets of $150, so it allocates four-sevenths ($200/$350) of its domestic interest expense against domestic-source income, and the remaining three-sevenths against foreign-source income.

17. This is subject to two qualifications. Certain countries (including the United States) impose "thin-capitalization" laws that limit the amount of related-party interest foreign firms can deduct from local taxable income. In addition, countries often impose withholding taxes on cross-border interest payments; U.S. firms with deficit foreign tax credits receive foreign tax credits for paying these taxes. Withholding taxes on interest are usually reduced, often to zero, by bilateral tax treaties.

18. The 1987 proposal was ultimately dropped because of its draconian impact on certain taxpayers with extensive foreign operations. The 1987 proposal would have first allocated domestic interest expense against foreign income to the extent of any related-party interest receipts from controlled foreign corporations of the American parent company. Remaining domestic interest expense would then be allocated between U.S. and foreign source on the basis of assets. Hence, a firm with $100 of interest expense from borrowing by the U.S. parent in the United States, and $20 of interest receipts from its foreign subsidiary, would first allocate $20 of its U.S. interest expense against foreign income and then allocate the remaining $80 of interest expense between foreign and domestic sources based on relative assets.

tions was proposed in 1988 and was temporarily in effect from that time until 1991. Under the 1988 regulations, related-party debt influences interest allocation only if the U.S. parent company's ratio of third-party borrowing to total assets differs significantly from its foreign subsidiaries' (aggregate) ratio of third-party borrowing to total assets. The idea is to flag situations in which foreign subsidiaries route their third-party borrowing through their American parent companies. The 1988 regulation requires domestic interest expense to be allocated to foreign source if foreign subsidiaries' aggregate ratio of third-party indebtedness to total assets is less than 80 percent of the third-party indebtedness of the U.S. parent company.[19] In such cases, domestic interest expenses are allocated against foreign-source income until the third-party indebtedness of foreign subsidiaries *plus* domestic interest expenses, allocated in this way, equal remaining domestic-source third-party interest expenses. Remaining domestic interest expenses are then allocated between U.S. and foreign source according to the §861-8 statute.

The interest allocation rule just described is likely to have some curious effects on the actions of those firms that are bound by the 80 percent requirement. The 1988 regulations were, however, supplanted by new regulations in 1991, and taxpayers have the option of recalculating their prior tax liabilities using the new regulations in place of the 1988 regulations for every year that the 1988 regulations applied. At the time that the 1987 and 1988 regulations were proposed, many observers anticipated that they would be replaced by somewhat more flexible rules that would be made retroactively applicable. Consequently, it is unlikely that the 1988 regulations had an important effect on firm behavior.

The 1991 regulations compare current-year behavior of U.S. parent companies to their behavior over five-year "base periods." Specifically, the regulations provide that domestic interest expense deductions are allocated against foreign-source income if *both* (1) third-party indebtedness of the U.S. parent and (2) lending by the U.S. parent to its foreign subsidiaries exceed base levels (adjusted for acquisitions, dispositions, and changes in amounts of assets). Various exceptions apply to firms for whom the adjustment would be a small matter, and to firms that experience large year-to-year changes in their borrowing behavior. Once this intrafirm interest expense allocation is complete, remaining domestic interest expenses are allocated to foreign source based on the §861-8 statute. Given the complexity of the 1991 regulation, and the important role it gives to a firm's past behavior, it appears that the incentives it creates can be very firm specific. In what follows, firms are assumed not to be bound by the base-period ratio tests.

There are exceptions to the allocation rules introduced in the 1986 act. One exception concerns interest on certain nonrecourse debt. Taxpayers are permit-

---

19. The temporary regulation phased in the 80 percent requirement: the criterion was 50 percent for 1988, 65 percent for 1989, and 80 percent for 1990 and subsequent years.

ted to allocate all of their interest expenses against income derived from property acquired using nonrecourse debt, subject to various restrictions. Consequently, an American multinational that finances a $100 domestic investment with $60 of equity and $40 of nonrecourse debt is entitled to deduct the interest expenses generated by the $40 debt from the income flow of the $100 investment in calculating its taxable income.[20] There is a second exception in which nonfinancial firms are permitted to deduct interest expenses on debt used to purchase interest-bearing securities against the interest income from those securities, again subject to certain restrictions.

10.2.4   Incentives Created by the Tax Rules

The upshot of the rules just described is that firms with excess foreign tax credits and substantial foreign assets (as a fraction of total assets) could no longer enjoy the benefits of full deductibility of interest expenses incurred in the United States after 1986. Firms with deficit foreign tax credits, or those with no foreign assets, retain full benefits of interest expense deductibility. As a consequence, firms in the first category can be expected to reduce their borrowing relative to firms in the second and can also be expected to reduce the volume of their debt-financed investment activity.[21]

In order to analyze more carefully the incentives created by changes in the U.S. tax treatment of interest deductions, it is helpful to examine firm behavior within a very stylized model. We assume that an American firm's domestic profits after depreciation and other expenses (but before interest charges) is $Q(A)$, in which A represents domestic assets. Foreign profits after depreciation and other expenses *including* interest charges on foreign borrowing are $Q^*(A^*)$, in which A^* represents foreign assets net of foreign borrowing. Domestic assets have two components: equity (E) and debt (D), so $A = E + D$. The interest rate on domestic borrowing is r, the domestic corporate tax rate is τ, and the foreign tax rate is τ^*. Firms are assumed to repatriate their foreign after-tax profits as earned, and the foreign withholding tax rate on dividend repatriations is assumed to be zero.

We use α as an indicator variable that takes the value one if the firm has excess foreign tax credits (in this model, $\alpha = 1$ if $\tau^* > \tau$), and zero if the firm

---

20. The use of nonrecourse debt in a situation like this one offers a tax advantage, but is costly in that lenders typically require higher interest rates to compensate for the additional risks they bear due to the nonrecourse nature of the debt.

21. Three other studies examine the impact of interest allocation rules on the behavior of affected firms. Collins and Shackelford (1992) find that firms with large ratios of foreign to domestic assets are more likely than other firms to issue preferred stock (as a substitute for debt) in the period after 1986. Collins and Shackelford do not, however, distinguish excess foreign tax credit firms from deficit foreign tax credit firms. Altshuler and Mintz (1994) analyze the borrowing patterns of a sample of eight multinational firms, finding that firms that are unable to claim full tax deductions for interest payments in the United States are more likely to borrow abroad than to borrow in the United States. Froot and Hines (1994) examine the effect of interest allocation rules on the financing patterns of firms as they grow, finding that the tax change discouraged some firms from adding new assets to their balance sheets.

has deficit foreign tax credits. A firm is required to allocate domestic interest deductions of $rD[A*/(A + A*)]$ against foreign-source income. Firms with deficit foreign tax credits are unaffected by this requirement, while the after-tax profits of firms with excess foreign tax credits are reduced by the product of this amount and the statutory U.S. tax rate. The foreign operations of firms with deficit foreign tax credits are effectively taxed at the U.S. tax rate, while the foreign operations of firms with excess foreign tax credits are effectively taxed at foreign tax rates.

Firms are assumed to maximize total after-tax profits, which equal

$$(1) \quad \text{Profits} = [Q(E + D) - rD](1 - \tau) - \alpha\tau rD[A*/(E + D + A*)]$$
$$+Q*(A*)[1 - \alpha\tau* - (1 - \alpha)\tau] - \lambda A*,$$

in which λ is the shadow cost of resources devoted to foreign operations. Consider first the behavior of firms with excess foreign tax credits. Setting $\alpha = 1$, and solving for an interior maximum of equation (1) over the choice of D, yields

$$(2) \quad Q'(A) = r + r\tau A*(E + A*)/[(1 - \tau)(E + D + A*)^2].$$

Solving for an interior maximum of equation (1) over the choice of $A*$ yields

$$(3) \quad Q*'(A*) = \lambda + r\tau D(E + D)/[(1 - \tau)(E + D + A*)^2].$$

By contrast, the first-order conditions that characterize the behavior of firms with deficit foreign tax credits ($\alpha = 0$) are

$$(4) \quad Q'(A) = r,$$

$$(5) \quad Q*'(A*) = \lambda.$$

Examination of equations (2)–(5) indicates that the interest allocation rules raise the required marginal product of debt-financed domestic and foreign capital for firms with excess foreign tax credits. The degree to which required marginal products are raised depends, in part, on terms that include ratios of domestic indebtedness and domestic assets to the square of total assets. The squared terms appear due to the conflicting effects of interest allocation on the demand for domestic and foreign assets. Interest allocation raises the after-tax cost of marginal debt used to finance the domestic operations of firms with excess foreign tax credits. At the same time, interest allocation encourages firms with excess foreign tax credits to expand their domestic operations in order to allocate as much as possible of their inframarginal domestic interest expense against U.S.-source income. The combination of these two effects attenuates, but does not eliminate, the direct effect of interest allocation on the demand for domestic assets. Interest allocation raises the required marginal product of foreign capital through its effect on the allocation of inframarginal interest expenses for firms with excess foreign tax credits.

One complication that arises in using equations (2)–(5) to estimate the effect of interest allocation rules on firm behavior after 1986 is that foreign and domestic asset levels are themselves endogenous to the tax changes under consideration. We treat this problem by using 1986 levels of $A^*/(A + A^*)$ in the regressions as proxies for contemporaneous foreign asset fractions. Since foreign asset fractions did not influence the allocation of interest deductions in 1986, the 1986 level of this variable is arguably exogenous to the change in behavior induced by the tax change. Of course, more sophisticated treatments are possible, such as instrumenting for contemporaneous foreign asset fractions with the 1986 fraction, or parameterizing the model to include endogenously the tax-induced changes in the fraction of foreign and domestic assets. One of the difficulties that such investigations encounter is that available data are sketchy and, in particular, that asset and foreign tax credit information does not correspond exactly to definitions that apply for tax purposes. In addition, richer models that incorporate possible substitutability or complementarity of domestic and foreign assets are likely to suggest subtle variants of the procedure described above. Given the limitations inherent in using publicly available data, we proceed to analyze simple specifications of the relationships implied by equations (2)–(5).

10.3   Data and Preliminary Results

We use information reported by Compustat on the balance-sheet items of large publicly traded corporations. Compustat currently provides information on somewhat more than 7,500 companies. We select only multinational firms incorporated in the United States: firms are included if their reported foreign assets equal 1 percent or more of reported total assets for *each* year during 1986–90. This criterion is satisfied by 422 firms.

Foreign tax rate information is central to our analysis, because the hypothesis that firms maximize after-tax profits implies that deficit foreign tax credit firms will react quite differently to the Tax Reform Act of 1986 than will excess foreign tax credit firms. We construct foreign tax rates as the ratio of foreign income taxes paid to foreign pretax income as reported by Compustat. This variable is somewhat noisy, but is likely to capture the major differences between the foreign tax rates facing different firms.[22] In order to attenuate some of the difficulties that accompany annual measurements of the foreign tax rate variable, firms were classified into excess foreign tax credit status based on five years of data, 1986–90. Firms for which the average foreign tax rate over that period exceeds the contemporaneous average U.S. statutory corporate tax rate are classified as excess foreign tax credit firms; all other firms are classified

---

22. The introduction of the new interest allocation rules in 1986, along with other tax changes, gave some firms incentives to adjust the location and tax-avoiding behavior of their foreign affiliates. In the analysis that follows we take foreign tax rates to be exogenous to U.S. tax changes. Endogenizing foreign tax rates could change the interpretation of the magnitude of the estimated coefficients.

as deficit foreign tax credit firms.[23] From our initial sample of 422 firms, 6 additional firms were excluded, 5 due to insufficient tax rate information and 1 due to major ownership changes over the 1986–91 time period.[24] Thus the total sample is 416 firms. Hand checking of the Compustat data led to the correction of two errors.[25]

Mergers and other dramatic business events can complicate the interpretation of changes in the behavior of firms over the sample period. In the process of merging, firms can exhibit large changes in amounts of debt outstanding, ownership of property, plant, and equipment, and other variables that serve as indicators of reactions to changes in the interest allocation rules. One consequence is that an analyst might attribute some of these operational changes to tax incentives introduced by the 1986 act, when, in reality, the changes result from merger decisions that were uninfluenced by the 1986 act. Alternatively, the 1986 act might be responsible for important changes in capital structure or business operations, but these changes could be swamped by the effects of mergers.

These difficulties notwithstanding, it is important to bear in mind that merging firms face the same tax incentives as do firms that do not merge. One interpretation of the potential problem introduced by mergers is that firm-specific attributes captured by the constant term used in panel estimation may not remain constant for firms that merge. At the same time, merging firms may provide the clearest indication of the behavioral responses to the tax change, because firms undergoing mergers often simultaneously reexamine their capital structures, their needs for domestic and foreign assets, and other considerations that nonmerging firms may address only sporadically.

We address the problem of mergers by repeating our estimation on three data sets. The first is the universe of 416 firms described above. A second data set of 388 firms excludes any firms that record a 100 percent or greater change in assets in one year. The idea is that firms with greater than 100 percent changes in assets very likely experience substantial mergers that change the character of their business decisions. The third data set, consisting of 331 firms, uses a more restrictive threshold of 50 percent changes of assets. Because of space limitations, we do not report below all of the results using the

23. This classification of the foreign tax credit status of the firms in the sample is necessarily somewhat imprecise. The same firm may have excess foreign tax credits in one year and deficit foreign tax credits in another; furthermore, excess foreign tax credits may be carried forward five years or back two years. A firm's foreign tax credit status can be endogenous to discretionary decisions such as dividend repatriation choices. The regressions reported in the tables were all rerun replacing the zero-one foreign tax credit status variable with a continuous tax rate variable constructed as the average difference between foreign and U.S. tax rates. The results are similar to those reported in the tables.

24. Coltec Industries was taken private in 1988 and completed an IPO in early 1992.

25. Compustat reports that Alpnet's foreign-to-total asset ratio was 1.25 in 1988, while the firm's annual report implies that the ratio is 0.789; we use the latter figure. Compustat reports a jump in IBM's foreign-to-total asset ratio from 0.48 in 1990 to 0.98 in 1991. IBM's annual report indicates that the 1991 ratio was 0.469, which is the figure we use.

three data sets; instead, we report results for the largest available data set, while noting any important differences in the results that appear using the more restricted samples.

We use firm-level information available through Compustat to calculate changes over the 1984–91 time period in debt, capital in place, foreign assets, costs of goods sold, foreign sales net of intrafirm exports, taxes paid, and pretax income. Changes in debt are measured as the difference between the book values of total debt (long-term and current) in 1991 and total debt in 1986. Changes in capital are measured as the difference between net property, plant, and equipment (PPE) in 1991 and net PPE in 1986. Foreign assets are measured as total foreign assets in 1986, and the ratio of this variable to total assets in 1986 is used not only to control for firm characteristics (degree of multinationality) but as a component of the cost of debt finance after 1986. In some of the regressions, we use tax loss carryforwards (TLCF). Tax loss carryforwards are measured (for those firms reporting it) using 1986 data only.[26] We use 1986 levels of TLCF due to the potential endogeneity of TLCF over the 1986–91 period (since tax losses can be generated by rapid debt accumulation). Table 10.1 presents means and standard deviations of variables used in the regressions.

The empirical strategy is to use the identifying assumption that foreign tax credit status influences operational changes between 1986 and 1991 only through its effect, via interest allocation rules, on the cost of borrowing. Of course, differences in foreign tax credit status could reflect firm heterogeneity that is (for some reason) related in a nontax manner to operational changes over 1986–91. We attempt to control for firm heterogeneity in two ways. First, we use ratios of foreign assets to total assets, TLCF, and industry dummies to allow for industry- and firm-specific effects that may be correlated with foreign tax credit status. Second, we use firm behavior over the 1984–86 period as a control for behavior over 1986–91. If the results are driven by the 1986 tax change, foreign tax credit status should have no ability to explain changes in debt, assets, foreign operations, and other variables over the 1984–86 period. Alternatively, if the results are driven by omitted firm-specific factors that are constant over 1984–91 and correlated with the 1986 tax variables, then results for the prereform (1984–86) and postreform (1986–91) periods should look similar.

10.4   Regression Results

This section describes the results of regressions that estimate the effects of the changes in interest allocation rules on firm financing and operational patterns. The null hypothesis is that the changes in interest allocation rules had

---

26. Information on TLCF in 1986 is missing for 29 of the 416 firms in the sample; these 29 firms were dropped from the sample in specifications using TLCF as an explanatory variable.

Table 10.1   **Variable Means and Standard Deviation**

Variable	Mean	Standard Deviation	N
ΔDebt 1986–91/Assets 1986	0.2089	0.4566	416
ΔDebt 1984–86/Assets 1986	0.1341	0.5254	386
ΔPPE 1986–91/Assets 1986	0.2003	0.3903	414
ΔPPE 1984–86/Assets 1986	0.0874	0.2024	385
New leases 1986–91/Assets 1986	0.4315	0.8298	286
ΔForeign sales 1986–91/ Assets 1986	0.3114	0.7089	409
ΔCost 1986–91/Assets 1986	0.5051	0.9709	416
ΔCost 1984–86/Assets 1986	0.1750	0.8093	385
FTC dummy	0.4808	0.5002	416
$[A^*/(A + A^*)]^2$	0.0836	0.1104	416
FTC dummy $\cdot$ $[A^*/(A + A^*)]^2$	0.0400	0.0930	416
TLCF/Assets	0.0487	0.2432	387
Debt/Assets	0.2373	0.1887	416
FTC dummy $\cdot$ (Debt/Assets)	0.1132	0.1705	416

Note: Debt is the book value of total (domestic plus foreign) debt. Assets 1986 is the book value of total assets at year-end 1986. PPE is the book value of property, plant, and equipment. New leases is the difference between actual lease expenditures and long-term commitments at the start of the period. Foreign sales is foreign-produced foreign sales, i.e., the difference between total foreign sales and exports from the United States. Cost is the total (domestic plus foreign) cost of goods sold. The FTC dummy variable takes the value one if a firm has excess foreign tax credits, and zero otherwise. The term $A^*/(A + A^*)$ is the ratio of a firm's foreign assets to its total assets in 1986. The variable TLCF/Assets is the ratio of tax loss carryforwards to total assets at year-end 1986. Debt/Assets is the ratio of the book value of debt to the book value of total assets at year-end 1986.

no impact on firm behavior; this hypothesis implies that firms simply bear the tax cost of the 1986 act. We contrast this null hypothesis with two alternative hypotheses: (I) that firms respond to the tax changes by using nondebt financing and (II) that firms respond to the tax changes by reducing their foreign operations.[27]

27. The null and alternative hypotheses correspond to different theoretical specifications of the ease with which firms can adjust their financial and operating patterns. Stiglitz (1973) argues that the tax advantage to debt makes borrowing a firm's preferred method of financing marginal investments. If this argument is correct, and firms continue to prefer debt to other financing methods even after some of its tax advantages are lost due to the interest allocation rules, then firms will not react to the tax changes by substituting other financing methods for debt, but will react by reducing the size of foreign and total operations. Alternatively, the Miller (1977) model of financial equilibrium implies that firms affected by the interest allocation rules will change their capital structure to pure equity finance. As long as the capitalization of the affected firms does not exceed the initial amount of equity on the market, this type of financial arbitrage implies that the interest allocation rules will not affect the capital costs, or real operations, of any firms. Gordon and Malkiel (1981) examine a model in which debt is tax preferred but its use raises the probability that a firm will incur costs associated with bankruptcy; this model carries implications between those of the Stiglitz and Miller models.

We examine these alternatives by constructing independent variables that distinguish firms by their exposures to the tax change as of 1986. Firms with excess foreign tax credits and high ratios of foreign to domestic assets are the ones least able to take deductions against their U.S. tax liabilities for domestic interest payments. The foreign tax credit status dummy variable (described above) is a simple measure of firm exposure to the change in the interest allocation rules. It is possible to obtain more precision by measuring interaction effects. For example, we use the squared ratio of foreign assets to total assets, interacted with the foreign tax credit dummy variable, to detect differences in firm behavior based on foreign tax credit status, *given* the ratio of assets abroad. According to the model, excess foreign tax credit firms ought to show greater behavioral responses the higher are their ratios of foreign to total assets. We also control for other firm characteristics that might be correlated with firm responses, such as growth over the sample period, industry, and presence and amount of tax loss carryforwards.

We choose dependent variables to identify changes in (1) firm capital structure, (2) investment spending, (3) lease commitments, and (4) foreign operating levels. These variables are chosen because of their relationships with the alternative hypotheses. For example, alternative hypothesis I implies that firms can costlessly substitute away from higher-priced debt toward other financial vehicles; this behavioral response should appear as a change in capital structure. In addition, investment spending would tend to fall and leasing to increase in excess foreign tax credit firms, as they take assets off their balance sheets through leasing.[28] Finally, hypothesis I implies that foreign operating levels should not change in response to the 1986 act since managers finance costlessly around the tax change.

If alternative hypothesis II is correct, substitute financial vehicles are not perfect, and consequently, the tax change raises the cost of capital in certain businesses. This increase in costs may encourage firms to cut back on their operations. We also might expect some effect on financing methods, as firms substitute away from debt and toward leasing. However, we would also expect a decline in investment and foreign operations, measured by foreign-produced foreign sales or even by firmwide costs of goods sold.

If the null hypothesis is correct, then firms do little to change their financing *or* operating patterns; instead, they simply bear the additional burden created by the tax change. If this is the case, then changes in capital structure, leasing, investment, foreign operations, and firmwide operations need bear no relation to firms' exposures to the interest allocation provisions of the 1986 act. How-

---

28. Operating leases (to which we refer) are not included on the balance sheet, and the associated lease payments are fully deductible against U.S. taxable income. Capital leases, on the other hand, *are* included on the balance sheet, and their associated lease payments are (as is true of debt) allocated for tax purposes between domestic and foreign sources by §861-8. We use measures of investment that include changes in capital leases but not in operating leases, and it is operating leases that are preferred by firms unable to take full advantage of lease tax deductions. See, e.g., Smith and Wakeman (1985) and Edwards and Mayer (1991).

ever, one would expect to observe an increase in *total* costs (and a decline in after-tax profits) that reflects the additional tax burden.

10.4.1 A Nonparametric Look at the Sample

Table 10.2 describes some aspects of the behavior of the sample of firms after 1986.[29] Firms are classified into two groups on the basis of fraction of foreign assets (above median and below median); within each group, they are further classified by excess foreign tax credit and deficit foreign tax credit status. Roughly half of the firms in the sample (51.4 percent) are classified as having excess foreign tax credits.

Firms that differ in the fraction of their assets held abroad may differ in other important observable and unobservable ways. The model presented in section 10.2 implies that the 1986 act raised the cost of debt-financed investments for firms with excess foreign tax credits and significant foreign assets. The behavior described in table 10.2 is consistent with the predictions of the alternative hypotheses. Firms with excess foreign tax credits exhibit slower mean growth (over 1986–91) of outstanding debt relative to 1986 assets, and slower mean growth of property, plant, and equipment, than do deficit credit firms. This pattern appears for multinational firms with small fractions of foreign assets (except for a negligible difference in debt changes for excess and deficit foreign tax credit firms with small amounts of foreign assets), but is considerably more dramatic for firms with high fractions of foreign assets.

Figure 10.1 illustrates the mean growth of debt relative to 1986 asset levels for firms in each cell reported in table 10.2. The figure suggests that excess foreign tax credits affect only those firms with significant foreign assets, which is consistent with the theory sketched in section 10.2. Furthermore, there is a marked difference between the cumulative growth of debt in excess foreign tax credit firms and that in deficit foreign tax credit firms. A similar pattern appears in firms' accumulation of property, plant, and equipment, as illustrated by figure 10.2. This figure indicates that the impact of excess foreign tax credits on the accumulation of property, plant, and equipment is most dramatic for firms with significant foreign assets as a fraction of total assets.

Alternative hypothesis I indicates that firms react to higher after-tax costs of debt by replacing debt with alternative financing devices. Earlier work by Collins and Shackelford (1992) calls attention to the impact of changes in interest allocation rules on firms' proclivities to issue preferred stock. Only a small fraction of firms are financed with preferred stock, but Collins and Shackelford argue that the use of preferred stock expanded after 1986, in part because of the rising after-tax cost of debt.

Table 10.3 describes the responses of firms in our sample to the changing incentives to issue preferred stock after 1986. The mean behavior of firms as

---

29. Tables 10.2 and 10.3 describe the behavior of the sample of 388 firms that did not exhibit 100 percent or greater change in assets in a year. The larger sample of 416 firms has moments that are very similar to those reported in tables 10.2 and 10.3.

Table 10.2   **Debt and PPE Accumulation by Foreign Asset Concentration and FTC Status, 1986–91**

Variable	Foreign Assets/Total Assets Below Median		Foreign Assets/Total Assets Above Median	
	Excess FTC	Deficit FTC	Excess FTC	Deficit FTC
Number of firms	97	96	92	101
ΔDebt/Assets				
Mean	0.13678	0.13426	0.10556	0.15447
Median	0.11705	0.05519	0.06016	0.14446
Standard deviation	0.28151	0.22383	0.12348	0.24886
ΔPPE/Assets				
Mean	0.13847	0.15538	0.13395	0.18940
Median	0.11121	0.07145	0.13104	0.14902
Standard deviation	0.24350	0.29645	0.22000	0.29366

Note: Firms are classified into cells based on foreign asset/total asset ratios in 1986, and by foreign tax credit (FTC) status as calculated over 1986–91. ΔDebt/Assets represents the difference between total debt in 1991 and total debt in 1986, divided by total assets in 1986. ΔPPE/Assets represents the difference between net property, plant, and equipment in 1991 and net property, plant, and equipment in 1986, divided by total assets in 1986.

Table 10.3   **Changes in Preferred Stock by Foreign Asset Concentration and FTC Status, 1986–91**

Variable	Foreign Assets/Total Assets Below Median		Foreign Assets/Total Assets Above Median	
	Excess FTC	Deficit FTC	Excess FTC	Deficit FTC
Number of firms	97	96	92	101
ΔPreferred stock/assets				
Mean	0.00221	0.00584	0.00080	0.00275
Median	0	0	0	0
Standard deviation	0.01839	0.06027	0.03005	0.04661
Number of increases	9	10	17	10
Number of decreases	16	14	12	17

Note: Firms are classified into cells based on foreign asset/total asset ratios in 1986, and by foreign tax credit (FTC) status as calculated over 1986–91. ΔPreferred Stock/Assets represents the difference between preferred stock outstanding in 1991 and preferred stock outstanding in 1986, divided by total assets in 1986. Number of increases indicates the number of firms in each cell for whom the difference between preferred stock outstanding in 1991 and preferred stock outstanding in 1986 is positive. Number of decreases indicates the number of firms for which the difference is negative.

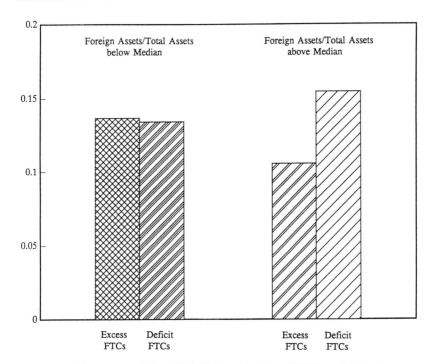

Fig. 10.1   Debt accumulation 1986–91 (as a fraction of 1986 assets), by tax status

Note: Bars measure the ratios of five-year changes (1986–91) in book values of debt to 1986 book assets. Entries depict this ratio for the firm with the median ratio in each cell: *left,* 193 firms had below-median ratios of foreign assets to total assets in 1986, of which 97 were classified as having excess foreign tax credits and 96 were classified as having deficit foreign tax credits; *right,* 193 firms had above-median ratios of foreign assets to total assets, of which 92 were classified as having excess foreign tax credits, and 101 as having deficit foreign tax credits.

reported in the table is not consistent with the hypothesis that tax considerations were responsible for a significant shift of financing away from debt and into preferred stock. The absence of an important effect in the means may reflect the omission of important variables that explain preferred stock issuances,[30] or may simply reflect the smallness of the fraction of the sample that ever issues preferred stock. One tidbit of evidence presented in table 10.3 is consistent with the theory of tax-motivated preferred stock issuances: excess foreign tax credit status is positively correlated with the fraction of high-foreign-asset firms that increase their outstanding preferred stock after 1986,

30. Collins and Shackelford (1992) include a number of additional explanatory variables in their regressions. Many of these additional variables, such as net operating loss status, are likely to influence preferred stock issuances, but most financial and operating variables are themselves endogenous to financing choices and may respond to unobservables that also influence financing decisions.

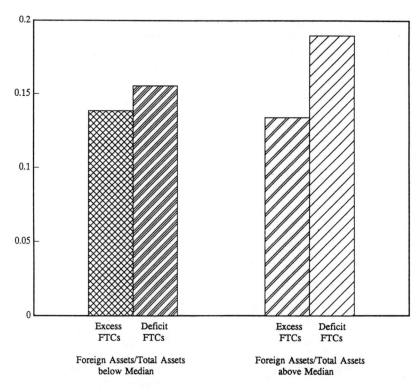

Fig. 10.2   PPE accumulation 1986–91 (as a fraction of 1986 assets), by tax status

Note: Bars measure the ratios of five-year changes (1986–91) in book values of property, plant, and equipment to 1986 book assets. Entries depict this ratio for the firm with the median ratio in each cell: *left,* 193 firms had below-median ratios of foreign assets to total assets in 1986, of which 97 were classified as having excess foreign tax credits and 96 were classified as having deficit foreign tax credits; *right,* 193 firms had above-median ratios of foreign assets to total assets, of which 92 were classified as having excess foreign tax credits, and 101 as having deficit foreign tax credits.

and negatively correlated with the fraction of high-foreign-asset firms that decrease their outstanding preferred stock after 1986. The reverse pattern appears for low-foreign-asset firms. Given the very small size of the sample of firms changing their preferred stock amounts, however, these correlations are no more than suggestive.

10.4.2   Capital Structure and Changes in Borrowing Patterns

Tables 10.4 and 10.5 report regressions of changes in capital structure, measured as the change in debt divided by beginning-of-period assets. The sample period used in the regressions reported in table 10.4 is the 1986–91 period, whereas the sample period used in the regressions reported in table 10.5 is 1984–86. All regressions are OLS.

Table 10.4   **Debt Accumulation, 1986–91**

Variable	(1)	(2)	(3)	(4)	(5)
Constant	0.2256	0.1907	0.1893		
	(0.0311)	(0.0281)	(0.0293)		
FTC dummy	−0.0348				
	(0.0448)				
$[A*/(A + A*)]^2$		0.5243	0.8858	0.5469	0.9237
		(0.2737)	(0.3309)	(0.2765)	(0.3354)
FTC dummy ·		−0.6410	−0.9253	−0.6724	−0.9698
$[A*/(A + A*)]^2$		(0.3247)	(0.3628)	(0.3288)	(0.3669)
TLCF/Assets			−0.2588		−0.2791
			(0.1005)		(0.1012)
Industry dummies	No	No	No	Yes	Yes
Adjusted R^2	−0.001	0.006	0.021	0.010	0.027
N	416	416	387	416	376

Note: Standard errors are in parentheses. The columns report coefficients from OLS regressions in which the dependent variable is the ratio of the change in the book value of a firm's debt over 1986–91 to its total assets in 1986 (ΔDebt 1986–91/Assets 1986). See note to table 10.1 for other variables.

Table 10.5   **Debt Accumulation, 1984–86**

Variable	(1)	(2)	(3)	(4)	(5)
Constant	0.1285	0.1819	0.1900		
	(0.0371)	(0.0340)	(0.0362)		
FTC dummy	0.0115				
	(0.0536)				
$[A*/(A + A*)]^2$		−0.7118	−0.6585	−0.7250	−0.6844
		(0.3228)	(0.4048)	(0.3297)	(0.4150)
FTC dummy ·		0.2911	0.2636	0.2793	0.2627
$[A*/(A + A*)]^2$		(0.3997)	(0.4540)	(0.4059)	(0.4609)
TLCF/Assets			−0.1215		−0.1178
			(0.1192)		(0.1215)
Industry dummies	No	No	No	Yes	Yes
Adjusted R^2	−0.002	0.009	0.008	−0.004	−0.006
N	386	386	362	386	362

Note: Standard errors are in parentheses. The columns report coefficients from OLS regressions in which the dependent variable is the ratio of the change in the book value of a firm's debt over 1984–86 to its total assets in 1986 (ΔDebt 1984–86/Assets 1986). See note to table 10.1 for other variables.

The first specification in table 10.4 regresses the change in debt from 1986 to 1991 (scaled by assets in 1986) on a constant and the foreign tax credit status dummy. The coefficient on the dummy term is negative as expected; however, it is not statistically significant. A more precise specification is that excess foreign tax credit firms should exhibit greater aversion to using debt the higher are their ratios of foreign to total assets. The second regression in table 10.4 tests this specification by including both the (squared) ratio of foreign to total assets and an interaction term between this ratio and the foreign tax credit status dummy. Here, the coefficient of -0.64 on the interaction term indicates that a firm with excess foreign tax credits and half of its assets abroad reduces its debt accumulation by 16 percent ($-0.64(1/2)^2$) of assets over five years, or about 3 percent per year.

This coefficient on the interaction term becomes larger and more significant when (as in the regressions reported in col. [3]) TLCF is included as an explanatory variable. The introduction of industry dummy variables, intended to capture differential pressure on debt accumulation across industries, also raises the magnitude of the estimated coefficient that reflects the impact of interest allocation rules. In the specification reported in column (5), one that includes both TLCF and industry dummies, the estimated coefficient on the interaction term is -0.96. This implies that the interest allocation rules encourage a firm with excess foreign tax credits and half of its assets abroad to reduce debt accumulation at an annual rate of 4.8 percent ($-0.96(1/2)^2/5$) of initial assets.

Table 10.5 reports estimated coefficients from regressions that repeat the same five specifications as those reported in table 10.4, except that the dependent variable is now the change in debt prior to the tax-law change (1984–86). If the results in table 10.4 are driven by unobserved, time-invariant, and firm-specific factors that are correlated with included tax variables, we would expect to find that the results reported in table 10.5 resemble those in table 10.4. Note, however, that this is not the case: the estimated coefficients on all of the explanatory variables (except TLCF) change sign and become insignificant. Thus, table 10.5 offers little support for the hypothesis that firm-specific unobservables are responsible for the results reported in table 10.4.[31] A better interpretation of the results of tables 10.4 and 10.5 is that excess foreign tax credit firms tend to substitute away from debt finance. As expected, this appears to be particularly true for firms with larger ratios of foreign to total assets.

Table 10.6 presents estimated coefficients from regressions that examine changes in PPE from 1986 to 1991, scaled by 1986 assets. Right-hand-side specifications are similar to those used in table 10.4. The first specification reported in table 10.6 shows that investment rates differ by foreign tax credit status. While the coefficient on the foreign tax credit dummy variable is statistically negative, it is relatively small: excess foreign tax credit firms invest at rates that are about 1.5 percent ($-0.074/5$) lower per year. Note that, as before, the effect becomes larger when interacted with the ratio of foreign to total assets. For example, the second specification reports an interaction coefficient of -0.56, implying that an excess foreign tax credit firm with half its assets

31. We ran the specifications presented in tables 10.4 and 10.5 for two smaller data samples that filter out those firms with year-on-year changes in assets of 100 and 50 percent, finding results that are similar to those above. However, in some cases the statistical significance of the parameter estimates was reduced.

Table 10.6   **PPE Accumulation, 1986–91**

Variable	(1)	(2)	(3)	(4)	(5)
Constant	0.2358	0.1844	0.1848		
	(0.0266)	(0.0241)	(0.0251)		
FTC dummy	−0.0739				
	(0.0383)				
$[A^*/(A + A^*)]^2$		0.4592	0.6469	0.4032	0.5888
		(0.2344)	(0.2837)	(0.2366)	(0.2869)
FTC dummy ·					
$[A^*/(A + A^*)]^2$		−0.5613	−0.6892	−0.5545	−0.6855
		(0.2781)	(0.3112)	(0.2814)	(0.3138)
TLCF/Assets			−0.2057		−0.2181
			(0.0861)		(0.0824)
Industry dummies	No	No	No	Yes	Yes
Adjusted R^2	0.007	0.007	0.016	0.013	0.027
N	414	414	386	414	386

Note: Standard errors are in parentheses. The columns report coefficients from OLS regressions in which the dependent variable is the ratio of the change in the book value of a firm's property, plant, and equipment over 1986–91 to its total assets in 1986 (ΔPPE 1986–91/Assets 1986). See note to table 10.1 for other variables.

abroad invests at an annual rate of 2.8 percent ($-0.56 (1/2)^2/5$) lower than a comparable deficit foreign tax credit firm.[32] When industry dummies and TLCF are added to the specification, the coefficient increases in magnitude, reaching -0.69 in the specification reported in column (5). The same regressions, when run using data on PPE accumulation over the 1984–86 time period, produce estimated interaction coefficients that are positive rather than negative (though not significantly different from zero). Table 10.7 presents estimated coefficients from these regressions.

There are two possible interpretations of the tendency for firms with excess foreign tax credits and high ratios of foreign to total assets to accumulate PPE more slowly than do other firms. The first is that the loss of debt tax shields experienced by these firms results in a higher overall cost of capital and, consequently, a lower level of investment. Of course, to the extent that firms substitute away from debt finance toward cheaper after-tax financing sources, these substitutions can mitigate the increased cost of capital. The second interpretation is that firms do not face *any* increase in the cost of *employing* capital, but that they reduce PPE expenditures by leasing rather than owning capital. Leases allow the lessor to use the debt tax shield from debt financing of PPE since the capital cost component of lease prices is not allocated between foreign and domestic source. Thus, leases may represent low-cost devices to preserve the tax shield for a given amount of PPE. This suggests that excess foreign tax credit firms—particularly those with higher foreign asset ratios—had

32. As above, percentage figures are expressed relative to beginning-of-period assets.

Table 10.7   **PPE Accumulation, 1984–86**

Variable	(1)	(2)	(3)	(4)	(5)
Constant	0.0825	0.0928	0.0967		
	(0.0143)	(0.0132)	(0.0138)		
FTC dummy	0.0104				
	(0.0207)				
$[A^*/(A + A^*)]^2$		−0.1512	−0.0765	−0.1418	−0.0765
		(0.1250)	(0.1536)	(0.1236)	(0.1524)
FTC dummy ·					
$[A^*/(A + A^*)]^2$		0.1888	0.1568	0.1183	0.0973
		(0.1547)	(0.1721)	(0.1520)	(0.1691)
TLCF/Assets			−0.1281		−0.1343
			(0.0452)		(0.0446)
Industry dummies	No	No	No	Yes	Yes
Adjusted R^2	−0.002	0.000	0.021	0.051	0.070
N	385	385	361	385	361

Note: Standard errors are in parentheses. The columns report coefficients from OLS regressions in which the dependent variable is the ratio of the change in the book value of a firm's property, plant and equipment over 1984–86 to its total assets in 1986 (ΔPPE 1984–86/Assets 1986). See note to table 10.1 for other variables.

incentives to expand more rapidly the use of leases than did deficit foreign tax credit firms.

Table 10.8 reports our attempts to test this latter interpretation. We regress a measure of *unexpected* increases in lease commitments over the 1986–91 period on the same explanatory variables used in earlier regressions. The dependent variable is unexpected increases in leases because that variable measures the differential effect of the 1986 tax act. It is unlikely that the interest allocation rules enacted at the end of 1986 were understood in detail prior to that year. In any case, to the extent that such changes were anticipated, the power of our tests is reduced. In order to measure unexpected increases in lease commitments, the numerator of the dependent variable equals the difference between actual lease payments in each year from 1986 to 1990 and the five-year lease commitments as of December 1985. This difference is scaled by 1986 assets. Table 10.8 reports the results from regressing this measure on right-hand-side variables similar to those in previous tables.

The first specification uses only the foreign tax credit dummy variable, finding there to be a small difference between excess foreign tax credit and deficit foreign tax credit firms. Similarly, both the foreign asset ratio and interaction term are statistically insignificant when added to the regression (as reported in col. [3]). One possibility is that the collinearity between these two terms, particularly the collinearity introduced by errors in measurement of the ratio of foreign assets to total assets, is responsible for the insignificance of individual coefficients. Column (2) reports estimated coefficients from specifications that omit the foreign-to-total asset ratio term. Omitting this ratio imposes the re-

Table 10.8   **New Leases, 1986–91 (without industry dummies)**

Variable	(1)	(2)	(3)	(4)	(5)
Constant	0.4694	0.3871	0.3608	0.4710	0.3842
	(0.0690)	(0.0530)	(0.0611)	(0.0891)	(0.0561)
FTC dummy	−0.0768			−0.2071	
	(0.0982)			(0.1221)	
$[A*/(A + A*)]^2$			0.5597	−0.0205	
			(0.6473)	(0.7303)	
FTC dummy ·					
$[A*/(A + A*)]^2$		0.9994	0.5309	1.4469	1.0152
		(0.4681)	(0.7162)	(0.8952)	(0.4793)
TLCF/Assets					0.1789
					(0.1946)
Industry dummies	No	No	No	No	No
Adjusted R^2	−0.001	0.012	0.011	0.018	0.013
N	286	286	286	286	268

Note: Standard errors are in parentheses. The columns report coefficients from OLS regressions in which the dependent variable is a ratio: the numerator of the ratio is the difference between a firm's leases of property, plant, and equipment over 1986–91 and its preexisting lease commitments at year-end 1986; the denominator of the ratio is the firm's total assets at year-end 1986 (New leases 1986–91/Assets 1986). See note to table 10.1 for other variables.

striction that there is no relationship between foreign assets and leases among deficit foreign tax credit firms. This restriction cannot be rejected by the data since the estimated coefficient on the ratio of foreign assets in the specification reported in column (3) is statistically indistinguishable from zero.

The estimates presented in column (2) indicate that the interaction-term coefficient increases in magnitude and becomes statistically significant once the asset ratio restriction is imposed. The interaction coefficient reported in column (2) implies that, among excess foreign tax credit firms, a 50 percent difference in the fraction of total assets that are foreign held is associated with an average difference in unexpected leases over five years of 25 percent $(1.00(1/2)^2)$ of assets, or about 5 percent per year.

The estimated coefficient on the interaction term is also large and marginally significant when the simple foreign tax credit status dummy variable is added (as in the specification reported in col. [4]). These results therefore suggest that deficit foreign tax credit firms on average do more leasing than excess foreign tax credit firms (the reverse of what one might expect); however, excess foreign tax credit firms with larger ratios of assets held abroad show a stronger tendency to lease. Overall, table 10.8 provides some evidence that excess foreign tax credit firms with high ratios of assets abroad tend to engage in additional, unexpected leasing subsequent to 1986. Table 10.9 reports estimated coefficients from identical regressions that include industry dummy variables; the results are similar, though of lower statistical significance.

To the extent that firms increase their leasing to avoid higher debt costs for

Table 10.9   New Leases, 1986–91 (with industry dummies)

Variable	(1)	(2)	(3)	(4)	(5)
Constant					
FTC dummy	−0.0910			−0.2048	
	(0.0845)			(0.1049)	
$[A^*(A + A^*)]^2$			0.0972	−0.4883	
			(0.5589)	(0.6318)	
FTC dummy ·					
$[A^*/(A + A^*)]^2$		0.5654	0.4845	1.3867	0.6105
		(0.4157)	(0.6247)	(0.7744)	(0.4306)
TLCF/Assets					0.1114
					(0.1683)
Industry dummies	Yes	Yes	Yes	Yes	Yes
Adjusted R^2	0.281	0.283	0.281	0.288	0.268
N	286	286	286	286	268

Note: Standard errors are in parentheses. The columns report coefficients from OLS regressions in which the dependent variable is a ratio: the numerator of the ratio is the difference between a firm's leases of property, plant, and equipment over 1986–91 and its preexisting lease commitments at year-end 1986; the denominator of the ratio is the firm's total assets at year-end 1986 (New leases 1986–91/Assets 1986). See note to table 10.1 for other variables.

on-balance-sheet assets, they are able to mitigate tax-induced changes in financing costs. The results reported in table 10.8 therefore provide some support for alternative hypothesis I, although they by no means rule out hypothesis II. Indeed, the evidence presented in tables 10.4–10.9 suggests that financing responses did occur, but not that operating responses *did not* occur. Thus, there appears to be evidence against the null hypothesis, and some evidence in favor of hypothesis I, but one cannot rule out hypothesis II.

10.4.3   Changes in Operating Patterns

One way to obtain additional evidence on hypotheses I and II is to investigate the level of firms' foreign operations. For example, by examining changes in foreign sales, and foreign costs of production (with and without financing costs), one might gain a better sense for whether excess foreign tax credit firms changed their operations as a result of higher capital costs. Unfortunately, relatively few data on firms' foreign operations are available. In this section we use different measures of operations, although in some cases we are forced to employ data that combine foreign and domestic operating information.

The first variable that measures changes in foreign operations is foreign-produced foreign sales. This variable is the difference between sales by foreign affiliates and intrafirm exports from the United States. This variable identifies firms that avoid higher capital costs by substituting away from foreign assets toward domestic assets, as reflected by a proclivity to service foreign markets by exporting rather than using local production.

Tables 10.10 and 10.11 report estimated coefficients from regressions that

Table 10.10   Foreign-Produced Foreign Sales, 1986–91

Variable	(1)	(2)	(3)	(4)	(5)
Constant	0.3389	0.3579	0.4169		
	(0.0486)	(0.0419)	(0.0562)		
FTC dummy	−0.0572				
	(0.0702)				
Debt/Assets			−0.3319		−0.2864
			(0.2110)		(0.2095)
FTC dummy ·					
(Debt/Assets)		−0.4151	−0.2442	−0.3043	−0.1583
		(0.2069)	(0.2334)	(0.1927)	(0.2201)
TLCF/Assets				−0.0979	−0.0766
				(0.1340)	(0.1347)
Industry dummies	No	No	No	Yes	Yes
Adjusted R^2	−0.001	0.007	0.011	0.003	0.013
N	409	409	409	381	381

Note: Standard errors are in parentheses. The columns report coefficients from OLS regressions in which the dependent variable is the ratio of the change over 1986–91 in a firm's foreign-produced foreign sales (the difference between total foreign sales and exports from the United States) to total assets at year-end 1986 (ΔForeign sales 1986–91/Assets 1986). See note to table 10.1 for other variables.

Table 10.11   Foreign-Produced Foreign Sales, 1986–91 (with additional variable)

Variable	(1)	(2)	(3)	(4)	(5)
Constant	0.2033	0.2623			
	(0.0697)	(0.0789)			
Debt/Assets		−0.3302			−0.2321
		(0.2093)			(0.2085)
FTC dummy ·					
(Debt/Assets)	−0.4045	−0.2344	−0.3747	−0.2936	−0.1760
	(0.2053)	(0.2315)	(0.2076)	(0.1908)	(0.2182)
TLCF/Assets				−0.1890	−0.1685
				(0.1362)	(0.1374)
Foreign assets/					
Total assets	0.6231	0.6220	0.5911	0.6502	0.6273
	(0.2254)	(0.2249)	(0.2272)	(0.2215)	(0.2224)
Industry dummies	No	No	Yes	Yes	Yes
Adjusted R^2	0.023	0.027	0.033	0.023	0.013
N	409	409	409	381	381

Note: Standard errors are in parentheses. The columns report coefficients from OLS regressions in which the dependent variable is the ratio of the change over 1986–91 in a firm's foreign-produced foreign sales (the difference between total foreign sales and exports from the United States) to total assets at year-end 1986 (ΔForeign sales 1986–91/Assets 1986). Foreign Assets/Total Assets is the ratio of book values of foreign assets and total assets in 1986. See note to table 10.1 for other variables.

use foreign-produced foreign sales as the dependent variable. In the regressions reported in table 10.10, the independent variables are similar to those presented in tables 10.4–10.9, with the difference that debt/assets is used as a regressor in table 10.10 in place of foreign assets/total assets. The reason for this substitution is that the margin of substitution tested in these regressions is one in which greater indebtedness raises the cost of each dollar of foreign assets, and not one in which the foreign asset ratio is appropriately held constant. If the tax change induces operating effects, the reason must be that firms find it costly to substitute away from debt financing. Thus, excess foreign tax credit firms with high levels of debt in 1986 will not, in these instances, be able inexpensively to reconstitute their capital structures, and thus are more likely to reduce their foreign-produced foreign sales.

The first specification reported in table 10.10 indicates that excess foreign tax credit firms on average reduce foreign-produced sales by about 5.7 percent over five years relative to deficit firms; this effect is not, however, statistically different from zero. Column (2) reports estimated coefficients from a more precise specification in which the foreign tax credit dummy variable is interacted with the ratio of debt to total assets. The estimated coefficient on this interaction term is significant and indicates that firms with excess foreign tax credits and 25 percent debt-to-asset ratios reduced their foreign sales by 2 percent per year (relative to assets) after 1986. Columns (3)–(5) of table 10.10 report the results of alternative specifications in which the estimated interaction effect remains negative while exhibiting reduced statistical significance.

Table 10.11 presents similar regressions that include an additional variable conditioning on the amount of debt in the capital structure as of 1986. The results are similar to those presented in table 10.10. Together, the results reported in tables 10.10 and 10.11 provide mild support for hypothesis II above, i.e., that firms responded to the tax change by cutting back on their foreign operations instead of fully absorbing the increase in capital costs.

One logical implication of the preceding analysis is that the interest allocation rules, by raising the cost of domestic operations and raising the cost of foreign operations, depress the level of total business operations by affected firms. Since the magnitude of total business operations is influenced by many important nontax factors, and, as a practical matter, can be measured in more than one way, this is a challenging hypothesis to test.

Table 10.12 presents estimated coefficients from regressions in which the dependent variables are changes in costs of goods sold between 1986 and 1991 (scaled by assets in 1986). The cost of goods sold variable includes foreign and domestic costs. In order to simplify matters, the independent variables are the same as those used in the regressions reported in table 10.4. Table 10.12 indicates that the tax effects take the expected negative sign—firms affected by the interest allocation rules reduced the scales of their operations—but the estimated coefficients are insignificant in every case. The statistical insignificance of the coefficients no doubt reflects, at least in part, the impossibility of

Table 10.12 Change in Scale of Operations, 1986–91

Variable	(1)	(2)	(3)	(4)	(5)
Constant	0.5560	0.4561	0.4485		
	(0.0660)	(0.0599)	(0.0632)		
FTC dummy	−0.1267				
	(0.0952)				
$[A*/(A + A*)]^2$		1.0492	1.7204	0.9010	1.5615
		(0.5829)	(0.7145)	(0.5840)	(0.7186)
FTC dummy · $[A*/(A + A*)]^2$		−0.9659	−1.4156	−0.9265	−1.3650
		(0.6914)	(0.7835)	(0.6945)	(0.7861)
TLCF/Assets			−0.4890		−0.4981
			(0.2170)		(0.2167)
Industry dummies	No	No	No	Yes	Yes
Adjusted R^2	0.002	0.003	0.014	0.024	0.035
N	416	416	387	416	387

Note: Standard errors are in parentheses. The columns report coefficients from OLS regressions in which the dependent variable is the ratio of the change in a firm's total (domestic plus foreign) cost of goods sold over 1986–91 to its total assets in 1986 (ΔCost 1986–91/Assets 1986). See note to table 10.1 for other variables.

controlling for many important factors that influence changes in costs of goods sold over this period. The evidence is certainly consistent with a sizable impact of interest allocation rules on scales of operation (the point estimate in the regression reported in col. [3] of table 10.12 implies that costs of goods sold were reduced by 2 percent per year, relative to assets, for affected firms with 25 percent foreign assets), but it is not possible to reject the hypothesis that there was no impact on operations.

Table 10.13 presents the results of specifications that repeat this estimation, taking as the dependent variable changes in costs of goods sold over 1984–86. Again, the tax terms are insignificant, thought they are of opposite sign to those reported in table 10.12. Taken together, the regressions reported in tables 10.12 and 10.13 provide suggestive but inconclusive (from a statistical standpoint) evidence that interest allocation rules may influence the overall magnitude of firm operations.

10.5 Conclusion

This paper examines the impact of interest allocation rules introduced by the Tax Reform Act of 1986. The incomplete tax deductibility of parent-company interest expenses appears to reduce significantly borrowing and investing by excess foreign tax credit firms. In addition, excess foreign tax credit firms affected by the interest allocation rules are the most likely to undertake new operating leases, presumably in lieu of acquiring new capital. These results are consistent with the hypothesis that firms substitute away from debt when it

Table 10.13   **Change in Scale of Operations, 1984–86**

Variable	(1)	(2)	(3)	(4)	(5)
Constant	0.2058	0.4561	0.4485		
	(0.0571)	(0.0599)	(0.0632)		
FTC dummy	−0.0645				
	(0.0826)				
$[A*/(A + A*)]^2$		−0.5799	−0.3883	−0.6469	−0.4708
		(0.5001)	(0.6263)	(0.5059)	(0.6348)
FTC dummy ·					
$[A*/(A + A*)]^2$		0.2256	0.1216	0.2388	0.1419
		(0.6189)	(0.7020)	(0.6224)	(0.7044)
TLCF/Assets			−0.3072		−0.3199
			(0.1844)		(0.1856)
Industry dummies	No	No	No	Yes	Yes
Adjusted R^2	0.002	−0.001	0.004	0.005	0.013
N	385	385	361	385	361

Note: Standard errors are in parentheses. The columns report coefficients from OLS regressions in which the dependent variable is the ratio of the change in a firm's total (domestic plus foreign) cost of goods sold over 1984–86 to its total assets in 1986 (ΔCost 1984–86/Assets 1986). See note to table 10.1 for other variables.

becomes more expensive, as well as the hypothesis that loss of interest tax deductibility can increase a firm's cost of capital.

Note, however, that the size and significance of the effects on borrowing, investment spending, and leasing do not imply that interest allocation rules necessarily impose large *costs* on excess foreign tax credit firms. All of the results just mentioned might appear even though nondebt financing substitutes are available at essentially the same cost as debt finance. If, for example, leasing can be done at the same after-tax cost as buying, then the tax law change may just encourage low-cost substitution.

Of course, many of the results are also consistent with the proposition that excess foreign tax credit firms face relatively greater costs of capital. Firms may choose to fund property, plant, and equipment off the balance sheet as a way of capturing *part* of the otherwise lost tax shields. The portion that cannot be captured is a real cost. This may lead excess foreign tax credit firms to underinvest, to grow more slowly, and to restrict the scope of foreign operations; this behavior, in turn, reduces their needs for debt financing. Some of the results reported in the paper suggest that firms affected by the change in interest allocation rules reduced their foreign and total operations in response. The tax law change may also skew investments by affected firms away from businesses in which the tax deductions are critical to competitiveness. In this way, the loss of U.S. multinational tax shields could represent substantial firm-specific costs.

References

Altshuler, Rosanne, and Jack Mintz. 1994. U.S. interest allocation rules: Effects and policy. NBER Working Paper no. 4712. Cambridge, Mass.: National Bureau of Economic Research, April.

Collins, Julie H., and Douglas A. Shackelford. 1992. Foreign tax credit limitations and preferred stock issuances. *Journal of Accounting Research,* 30:103–23.

Edwards, J. S. S., and C. P. Mayer. 1991. Leasing, taxes, and the cost of capital. *Journal of Public Economics* 44:173–97.

Froot, Kenneth A., and James R. Hines Jr. 1994. Losing interest: Interest allocation rules and the cost of debt finance. Harvard University. Mimeograph.

Gordon, Robert H., and Burton G. Malkiel. 1981. Corporation finance. In *How taxes affect economic behavior,* ed. Henry J. Aaron and Joseph A. Pechman. Washington, D.C.: Brookings Institution.

Hartman, David G. 1985. Tax policy and foreign direct investment. *Journal of Public Economics* 26:107–21.

Hines, James R., Jr. 1991. The flight paths of migratory corporations. *Journal of Accounting, Auditing, and Finance* 6:447–79.

Hines, James R., Jr., and R. Glenn Hubbard. 1990. Coming home to America: Dividend repatriations by U.S. multinationals. In *Taxation in the global economy,* ed. Assaf Razin and Joel Slemrod, 161–200. Chicago: University of Chicago Press.

Hines, James R., Jr., and Eric M. Rice. 1994. Fiscal paradise: Foreign tax havens and American business. *Quarterly Journal of Economics* 109:149–82.

Miller, Merton H. 1977. Debt and taxes. *Journal of Finance* 32:261–75.

Scholes, Myron S., and Mark A. Wolfson. 1992. *Taxes and business strategy: A planning approach.* Englewood Cliffs, N.J.: Prentice Hall.

Smith, Clifford W., Jr., and L. MacDonald Wakeman. 1985. Determinants of corporate leasing policy. *Journal of Finance* 40:895–908.

Stiglitz, Joseph E. 1973. Taxation, corporate financial policy, and the cost of capital. *Journal of Public Economics* 2:1–34.

Comment   Julie H. Collins

I applaud Froot and Hines for successfully embarking on a project that many in the international research community, including myself, have contemplated for some time. Froot and Hines investigate whether the more stringent interest allocation rules enacted in the Tax Reform Act of 1986 resulted in decreased domestic debt growth for U.S. multinationals. The most surprising aspect of their study is that their findings support such a conclusion despite the limitations of their data (gathered from publicly available financial statement information), which bias against such a finding.

As Froot and Hines illustrate, the interest allocation rules raise the cost of

Julie H. Collins is associate professor of business and accounting at the Kenan-Flagler Business School, University of North Carolina, Chapel Hill.

domestic debt only. However, Froot and Hines are able only to measure changes in total debt (*domestic plus foreign*) of the worldwide consolidated entity.[1] Their primary dependent variable thus is measured as (Worldwide debt$_{91}$ − Worldwide debt$_{86}$) / Assets$_{86}$. Examining changes in worldwide rather than domestic debt is particularly problematic because, first, as Froot and Hines acknowledge, the asymmetric treatment of domestic and foreign interest expense can encourage firms to finance their foreign subsidiaries with unrelated-party debt issued by the foreign subsidiary or with debt from the U.S. parent (often referred to as debt pushdowns) rather than parent equity. Such behavior would leave unchanged the total debt of the consolidated entity. Altshuler and Mintz (1994) suggest that U.S. multinationals in excess credit positions increased their foreign borrowings in response to the more stringent interest allocation rules. Thus, one would not necessarily expect a dampened growth in domestic debt to translate into a dampened growth in worldwide debt.[2]

Second, to the extent that excess credit firms have a greater proportion of their worldwide debt denominated in a foreign currency, exchange rate movements alone could give the appearance of faster debt growth. Since the dollar tended to weaken during this time period, debt denominated in a foreign currency and translated to U.S. dollars for financial reporting purposes likely appears larger in 1991 than 1986.[3]

Third, in 1986 U.S. multinationals were not required to consolidate their financing subsidiaries in their worldwide financial statements. However, beginning in 1988, U.S. accounting principles required the assets and liabilities of these subsidiaries be reflected in financial statements. Thus, finance subsidiary debt could be included in 1991 data, and both finance subsidiary assets and debt could be excluded from 1986 data. If firms with unconsolidated financing subsidiaries in 1986 are more likely excess credit firms, their debt likely appears to grow faster from 1986 to 1991 solely as a result of the consolidation.[4]

Nevertheless, despite these three potential serious biases against the predicted findings, Froot and Hines document a negative relation between

1. Foreign debt is defined here as debt with the associated interest deductible in a foreign country. It does not necessarily correspond to the currency the debt is denominated in, and it cannot be separately determined from publicly available financial statements.

2. Although Collins and Shackelford (1992) focus on the issuance of preferred stock in response to domestic interest allocation, we do not find a relation between the 1986–89 change in worldwide debt and the ratio of foreign assets to worldwide assets (our proxy for potential excess foreign tax credits) in a sensitivity test examining 1989 Fortune 100 firms. In our discussion (1992, 117), we not that the excess foreign tax credit proxy is expected to be negatively related to domestic debt but positively related to foreign debt and hence that we have no clear ex ante expectation with regard to the relation to worldwide debt.

3. E.g., one billion of debt denominated in deutsche marks would translate to approximately $520 million at the end of 1986 and $659 million at the end of 1991.

4. E.g., Aluminum Company of America, Amoco, Coca-Cola, Dow Chemical, Ford, General Electric, Philip Morris, and Xerox had unconsolidated finance subsidiaries in 1986. This is a nonrandom, incomplete list of companies and is provided only for illustrative purposes.

1986–91 debt growth and excess credit position. Thus, in many respects, Froot and Hines's results tell a more powerful story than is apparent at first blush.

Correlated omitted variables are a menace to any cross-sectional study. This is particularly the case here, where we are examining cross-sectional changes in capital structure or more specifically debt growth. Froot and Hines attenuate this concern by controlling for two firm-specific characteristics: industry and tax loss carryforward. Both are crucial, because debt-to-equity ratios and debt growth to assets are expected to vary by industry and U.S. taxpaying status.

In addition, Froot and Hines repeat the 1986–89 tests (see table 10.4) for 1984–86 changes in debt (see table 10.5). It is interesting to note that the only measure that changes between these two tables is the numerator of the dependent variable. The denominator of the dependent variable and all independent variables retain their 1986–91 observation period values. However, in table 10.5 the FTC dummy, the foreign assets to worldwide assets squared term, and the interaction of the two all reverse signs from those shown in table 10.4, and the asset squared term, rather than the interaction term, generally is significant in table 10.5. Given this rather peculiar pattern, which reemerges in subsequent analyses, it would be interesting to determine sensitivity to other specifications. For instance, what, if any, alteration in the results occurs if pre-1986 debt growth simply is added as a control variable in table 10.4 or if the average annual debt growth rates are computed for pre- and post-1986 periods and the dependent variable in table 10.4 is the difference between the two? Also, are the table 10.5 results sensitive to respecifying the dependent variable denominator and the independent variables to correspond to the 1984–86 time period?

Other potentially important correlated omitted variables that Froot and Hines do not control for in this study include firm growth and maturity and mergers and acquisitions. Demand for capital obviously is a function of investment opportunities. In a related paper, Froot and Hines (1994) interact 1986–91 asset growth and an excess foreign tax credit dummy and determine that excess foreign tax credit firms accumulate less debt for a given rate of asset growth. However, it also would be interesting to investigate the propensity of excess foreign tax credit firms to finance new investment through retained earnings. Firms operating in high-tax countries ($t_f > t_{US}$) and with a greater proportion of their worldwide assets located overseas could be more mature and hence have greater sources of internal capital than less mature firms.

Twenty (seven) percent of Froot and Hines's sample of 416 firms experience a greater than 50 (100) percent year-to-year change in assets in at least one year during the 1986–91 period. Thus, the 1991 debt numbers of these firms reflect substantially different operating entities than the 1986 debt and asset amounts. Froot and Hines elect to include these observations in the reported tests and note in footnote 31 that the statistical significance of the parameter estimates reported in tables 10.4 and 10.5 are reduced in some cases when these observations are excluded. Perhaps, it would be more informative to continue to use the full sample and add a mergers-and-acquisition control variable to the model specifications. The reader is left questioning what, if any, negative correlation exists between the 1986–91 debt growth rates of firms involved in substantial mergers and acquisitions and firms with excess foreign tax credits.

Two additional minor sensitivity tests may be warranted. Froot and Hines indicate in the paper and elaborate in footnote 2 that firms paying the alternative minimum tax (AMT) face idiosyncratic tax incentives with regard to debt and interest deductibility. However, it does not appear that AMT firms are excluded from the empirical analyses. Perhaps a control variable could be added to the model specification indicating firms paying AMT for some threshold number of years during the 1986–91 observation period. In addition, it may be of interest to separately examine current and long-term debt growth in the dependent variable.

Although my prior comments focus exclusively on what I perceive as the primary tests in the paper (tables 10.4 and 10.5), Froot and Hines commendably extend their analyses to examine the impact of changes in the interest allocation rules on preferred stock financing, investment spending, lease commitments, and foreign operating levels. These tests expand upon the notion that firms experiencing a meaningful increase in the cost of debt capital not only reduce debt but also substitute other forms of financing (preferred stock or operating leases) and/or make operational adjustments, such as reducing foreign activities.

Unlike Collins and Shackelford (1992), Froot and Hines do not find an increased proclivity to issue preferred stock among firms most likely affected by the interest allocation rule changes. This discrepancy likely occurs because of differences in sample firms and observation windows. Shackelford and I focus on the 1989 Fortune 100 companies. Short-term redeemable preferred stock (commonly issued for 49 days and often referred to as dutch-auction-rate preferred stock) is analogous to and a very attractive substitute for short-term debt or commercial paper. However, access to the dutch-auction preferred stock market generally is restricted to major U.S. multinationals ("blue-chip" companies). Froot and Hines's sample, which likely includes our sample of approximately 100 companies, as well as approximately 300 other companies, may be too diffuse around the handful of blue-chip companies for which it is economically viable to substitute preferred stock for debt to replicate our results.[5] In addition, Froot and Hines compare 1991 and 1986 preferred stock outstanding, and we compare 1989 and 1986 preferred stock outstanding. It is possible that some U.S. multinationals responded to the changes in the interest alloca-

5. Recall that since dividends paid on preferred stock are not deductible, preferred stock only becomes an attractive substitute for debt, which offers a diminished but still positive tax shield for excess credit firms, if the preferred stock issuer can capture a sufficient portion of the preferred stock implicit tax subsidy. This subsidy is generated by the dividends-received deduction available to corporate investors. See Collins and Shackelford (1992, 111–13) for further elaboration.

tion rules by issuing preferred stock, but the stock is no longer outstanding at the end of 1991. I am aware of at least one such case: Coca-Cola issued $300 million of auction-rate preferred stock in 1988 and redeemed it in late 1990, stating that the preferred stock was no longer needed to minimize excess foreign tax credits (Collins and Shackelford 1992, 112–13).

I found the property, plant, and equipment (PPE) and lease commitment investigations particularly interesting. Froot and Hines note two possible interpretations of their PPE results. Excess credit firms with high foreign-to-total asset ratios may engage in lower levels of investment or may reduce PPE expenditures by leasing rather than owning capital assets. Froot and Hines then follow through for the reader by investigating whether excess credit firms engaged in significantly more *unexpected* leasing after 1986. The dependent variable is measured cleverly by subtracting the five-year lease commitments as of December 1985 from the actual lease payments in each year from 1986 to 1990. Ideally, we would control for ex ante anticipated behavior (absent our treatment effect) in all our research designs. However, this information is rarely available, as it is in this case.

I was somewhat perplexed by the investigation of changes in firms' operating behavior or level of foreign activities. Froot and Hines indicate that firms may respond to higher capital costs induced by the interest allocation rule changes by servicing foreign markets with U.S. exports rather than foreign production. The tax incentives are somewhat more detailed than those alluded to in the paper. The foreign tax credit rules generally allow U.S. multinationals to treat 50 percent of their export earnings as foreign-source income, thus allowing excess foreign tax credit multinationals to effectively exempt 50 percent of their export earnings from tax.[6] Kemsley (1995) examines ratios of U.S. exports to unaffiliated customers to foreign-produced sales and provides convincing evidence that excess foreign tax credit firms respond to this incentive by substituting exports for foreign production. Thus, Froot and Hines may capture a somewhat incomplete glimpse of whether exports are being substituted for foreign production by simply examining 1986–91 changes in foreign-produced sales.

In conclusion, this paper meaningfully contributes to the international tax literature and genre of research examining the impact of taxes on capital structure and operating decisions. Although I suggest that the research community continue to explore the effect of additional correlated omitted variables on the robustness of these findings, I must reiterate that, given the data hurdles encountered in this study, Froot and Hines provide more powerful evidence of a decline in U.S. multinational domestic debt as a result of the interest allocation rule changes than may be apparent at first blush.

---

6. See *Internal Revenue Code* §863(b) and the related Treasury regulations.

References

Altshuler, R., and J. Mintz. 1994. U.S. interest allocation rules: Effects and policy. NBER Working Paper no. 4712. Cambridge, Mass.: National Bureau of Economic Research, April.

Collins, J., and D. Shackelford. 1992. Foreign tax credit limitations and preferred stock issuances. *Journal of Accounting Research* 30:103–24.

Froot, K., and J. Hines. 1994. Losing interest: Interest allocation rules and the cost of debt finance. Harvard University. Mimeograph.

Kemsley, D. 1995. The effect of taxes on the choice between exports and foreign production. Working Paper. University of North Carolina—Chapel Hill.

Contributors

Rosanne Altshuler
Department of Economics
New Jersey Hall
Rutgers University
New Brunswick, NJ 08903

Alan A. Auerbach
Department of Economics
549 Evans Hall
University of California, Berkeley
Berkeley, CA 94720

S. Lael Brainard
Council of Economic Advisers
National Economic Council
Executive Office of the President
Washington, DC 20500

Julie H. Collins
Kenan-Flagler Business School
CB# 3490, Carroll Hall
University of North Carolina
Chapel Hill, NC 27514

Jason G. Cummins
Department of Economics
New York University
269 Mercer Street, Seventh Floor
New York, NY 10003

Martin Feldstein
NBER
1050 Massachusetts Avenue
Cambridge, MA 02138

Kenneth A. Froot
Graduate School of Business Adminis-
tration
Soldiers Field
Harvard University
Boston, MA 02163

William M. Gentry
Department of Economics
Duke University
Box 90097
Durham, NC 27708

Roger H. Gordon
Department of Economics
University of Michigan
Ann Arbor, MI 48109

Trevor S. Harris
Graduate School of Business
Columbia University
Uris Hall 610
New York, NY 10027

David G. Hartman
ISF Kaiser International Inc.
9300 Lee Highway
Fairfax, NJ 22031

Kevin A. Hassett
Division of Research and Statistics
Board of Governors of the Federal
Reserve System
Washington, DC 20551

James R. Hines, Jr.
NBER
1050 Massachusetts Avenue
Cambridge, MA 02138

R. Glenn Hubbard
Graduate School of Business
Columbia University
Uris Hall 609
New York, NY 10027

Adam B. Jaffe
Department of Economics
Brandeis University
Waltham, MA 02254

Joosung Jun
Department of Economics
Ewha University
Daihyun-dong, Seodaimun-ku
Seoul, Korea

Robert E. Lipsey
NBER
269 Mercer Street, Eighth Floor
New York, NY 10003

Andrew B. Lyon
Department of Economics
University of Maryland
College Park, MD 20742

Jeffrey K. MacKie-Mason
Department of Economics
University of Michigan
Ann Arbor, MI 48109

T. Scott Newlon
Office of Tax Analysis
Department of the Treasury
Main Treasury Building, Room 5117
1500 Pennsylvania Avenue NW
Washington, DC 20220

William C. Randolph
Congressional Budget Office
Second and D Street SW, Room 422
Washington, DC 20515

Gerald Silverstein
Office of Tax Analysis
Department of the Treasury
Main Treasury Building, Room 5117
1500 Pennsylvania Avenue NW
Washington, DC 20220

Joel Slemrod
School of Business Administration and
    Department of Economics
University of Michigan
Ann Arbor, MI 48109

G. Peter Wilson
Sloan School of Management
Room E52-325B
MIT
50 Memorial Drive
Cambridge, MA 02142

Author Index

Subject Index